A History of East Central Europe

Volume I

Editors

Peter F. Sugar
University of Washington

Donald W. Treadgold
University of Washington

A History of East Central Europe

Volumes in the series

* Forthcoming.

Historical Atlas of
East Central Europe

Paul Robert Magocsi

Cartographic design by Geoffrey J. Matthews

University of Washington Press · Seattle & London

To my brother

Alexander Magocsi

for his wise counsel

throughout many years

Copyright © 1993 by the University of Washington Press
Maps copyright © 1993 by Paul Robert Magocsi
Printed in Hong Kong

Published in Canada by University of Toronto Press

Library of Congress Cataloging-in-Publication Data
Magocsi, Paul R.
    Historical atlas of East Central Europe/Paul Robert Magocsi;
cartographic design by Geoffrey J. Matthews.
        p. cm. —(A History of East Central Europe; v. 1)
    Covers "the lands between the linguistic frontier of German-
and Italian-speaking peoples on the west and the political
boundaries of the former Soviet Union on the east . . . roughly
the territory between 10°E and 35°E longitude . . . from about
400 c.e. (common era) to the present"—CIP introd.
    "Treated in depth are the Poles, Czechs, Slovaks, Hungarians,
Romanians, Yugoslav peoples, Albanians, Bulgarians, and
Greeks"—CIP foreword.
    Includes bibliographical references and index.
    ISBN 0–295–97248–3
    1. Europe, Eastern—Historical geography—Maps. 2. Europe,
Eastern—History. I. Matthews, Geoffrey J. II. Title.
III. Series.
DJK4.S93
[G2081.S1]
911.47—dc20   93–13783
                                             CIP
                                          MAP

Contents

Maps

Tables

Foreword

The systematic study of the history of East Central Europe outside the region itself began only in the last generation or two. For the most part historians in the region have preferred to write about the past of only their own countries. Hitherto no comprehensive history of the area as a whole has appeared in any language.

This series was conceived as a means of providing the scholar who does not specialize in East Central European history and the student who is considering such specialization with an introduction to the subject and a survey of knowledge deriving from previous publications. In some cases it has been necessary to carry out new research simply to be able to survey certain topics and periods. Common objectives and the procedures appropriate to attain them have been discussed by the authors of the individual volumes and by the coeditors. It is hoped that a certain commensurability will be the result, so that the ten volumes will constitute a unit and not merely an assemblage of writings. However, matters of interpretation and point of view have remained entirely the responsibility of the individual authors.

No volume deals with a single country. The aim has been to identify geographical or political units that were significant during the period in question, rather than to interpret the past in accordance with latter-day sentiments or aspirations.

The limits of "East Central Europe," for the purposes of this series, are the eastern linguistic frontier of German- and Italian-speaking peoples on the west, and the political borders of Russia/the former USSR on the east. Those limits are not precise, even within the period covered by any given volume of the series. The appropriateness of including the Finns, Estonians, Latvians, Lithuanians, Belorussians, and Ukrainians was considered, and it was decided not to attempt to cover them systematically, though they appear repeatedly in these books. Treated in depth are the Poles, Czechs, Slovaks, Hungarians, Romanians, Yugoslav peoples, Albanians, Bulgarians, and Greeks.

There has been an effort to apportion attention equitably among regions and periods. Three volumes deal with the area north of the Danube-Sava line, three with the area south of it, and three with both areas. Three treat premodern history, six modern times. Volume I consists of an historical atlas. Each volume is supplied with a bibliographical essay of its own, but we all have attempted to keep the scholarly apparatus at a minimum in order to make the text of the volumes more readable and accessible to the broader audience sought.

The coeditors wish to express their thanks to the Ford Foundation for the financial support it gave this venture, and to the Henry M. Jackson School of International Studies (formerly Far Eastern and Russian Institute) and its five successive directors, George E. Taylor, George M. Beckmann, Herbert J. Ellison, Kenneth Pyle, and Nicholas Lardy, under whose encouragement the project has moved close to being realized.

The whole undertaking has been longer in the making than originally planned. Two of the original list of projected authors died before they could finish their volumes and have been replaced. Volumes of the series are being published as the manuscripts are received. We hope that the usefulness of the series justifies the long agony of its conception and birth, that it will increase knowledge of and interest in the rich past and the many-sided present of East Central Europe among those everywhere who read English, and that it will serve to stimulate further study and research on the numerous aspects of this area's history that still await scholarly investigators.

Peter F. Sugar
Donald W. Treadgold

Introduction

This atlas is part of the multivolume History of East Central Europe published by the University of Washington Press, and for that reason it follows the basic guidelines of that series. The first of those guidelines concerns the geographical extent of what is called here East Central Europe. The series editors have defined East Central Europe as the lands between the linguistic frontier of the German- and Italian-speaking peoples on the west and the political boundaries of the former Soviet Union on the east. The north-south parameters are the Baltic and Mediterranean seas. Whereas the geographic parameters have not changed, the political structure of the area defined by the series as East Central Europe has been altered substantially since work on the atlas began in 1987. At present, this area comprises the countries of Poland, the Czech Republic, Slovakia, Hungary, Romania, Slovenia, Croatia, Bosnia-Herzegovina, Yugoslavia, Macedonia, Albania, Bulgaria, and Greece. However, this atlas, like some of the other volumes in the series, has expanded the geographic scope to include, toward the west, the eastern part of Germany (historic Mecklenburg, Brandenburg, Prussia, Saxony, and Lusatia), Bavaria, Austria, and northeastern Italy (historic Venetia), and toward the east, the lands of historic Poland-Lithuania (present-day Lithuania, Belarus, and Ukraine up to the Dnieper River), Moldova, and western Anatolia in Turkey.

In strict geographic terms, this "expanded" version of East Central Europe encompasses roughly territory between 10°E and 35°E longitude. Since Europe is traditionally considered to lie within the longitudinal boundaries of 10°W (the western costs of Ireland and Portugal) and 60°E (Ural Mountains), the territory covered in this atlas (10°E–35°E) is literally the central third of the European continent. Thus, while it would be more precise to call this territory Central Europe, the political divisions for most of the twentieth century have encouraged the popular rise of the term Eastern Europe, or the slightly more correct East Central Europe. The second of the series guidelines, concerning chronology, is easier to define. Coverage in this atlas, as well as the series in general, is roughly from about 400 C.E. (common era) to the present.

The contents of the *Historical Atlas of East Central Europe* reflect both the geographical and chronological guidelines discussed above and the practical restraints imposed by the enormous cost of producing full-color maps. With those factors in mind, I was allowed to conceptualize the historical development of East Central Europe as one consisting of fifty problems or aspects. Those fifty problems developed into chapters, each having one full-page map or two half-page maps, as well as in some cases inset maps and/or facing-page maps. Each chapter also includes an explanatory text related primarily if not exclusively to the map(s) in the given chapter. The result is a total of eighty-nine maps: thirty-five full-page, twenty-eight half-page, nine inset, and seventeen facing-page maps.

The order of maps is basically chronological. One goal is to show in a systematic fashion the political and administrative changes that have occurred in East Central Europe since 400 C.E. Hence there are several full-page maps showing the changing boundaries at certain key historical dates (Maps 5, 6, 10, 14, 18, 21, 24, 36, 38, 44, 50) interspersed with half- or full-page maps that focus on similar changes within individual countries or specific areas (Maps 7, 8, 9, 19, 20, 22, 25, 26, 27, 39, 40, 41, 42, 43). There are, of course, aspects other than political-administrative ones that warrant attention. These are addressed by thematic maps that deal with issues such as the economy (Maps 11, 12, 28, 49); ecclesiastical structures (Maps 13, 15, 16, 34, 35); education and culture (Maps 4a, 17, 31); demography and ethnicity (Maps 20d, 27a, 29a, 29b, 30, 32, 33, 48); and military affairs (Maps 6a, 23, 37, 45, 46).

In virtually every serious study of the countries that encompass East Central Europe there is an explanatory disclaimer regarding place names. More often than not, each town, city, and region has had more than one name in the course of its history. The variations may simply be a function of language or they may reflect a decision by ruling powers to have an entirely new name. An example of the first category is Warszawa (Polish), Warschau (German), Varshava (Russian), and Warsaw (English); an example of the second category is the city called Königsberg until 1945 and Kaliningrad since then. The problem is to avoid confusion by choosing a form that will respond to historical criteria as well as to the need for consistency.

It should be stressed that the choice about names used in this atlas in no way reflects any sympathy for a particular political or national orientation, even though I am well aware that the decision to use a particular form might be viewed by certain readers as reflecting some kind of bias. It should also be stressed that early in the preparatory stages of this atlas I became painfully aware that it was impossible to make a choice about names that would fulfill both historical criteria and consistency. Given this unenviable choice, I chose consistency.

This means that the main entry for the name of a town or city is the same on every map in this atlas, regardless of the historical period covered. As for the question of which form to use consistently, the criterion of present-day political boundaries is the determining factor. Thus the official language used within the boundaries of a present-day East Central European country is what determines the main entry of a town or city: Polish names within Poland, Slovak names within Slovakia, Romanian names within Romania, and so forth. This, moreover, is the principle adopted by the standard reference work, *Webster's New Geographical*

Dictionary (Springfield, Mass., 1980), which serves as the guide for place names used in this atlas.

Wherever *Webster's* provides an either/or choice (and there are several of these for East Central European place names), the first name indicated is the main entry used here. The only divergence from *Webster's* guidelines are the following. On Maps 2 through 6, the names of towns and cities located within territory of the Roman and Byzantine empires are given in their classical Latin or Greek forms. Also, throughout the atlas, names of towns and cities within the boundaries of the former Soviet Union are given in the language of the successor states, whether it is Lithuanian, Belorussian, Ukrainian, or Romanian (for Moldova). (*Webster's,* in contrast, uses Russian names for all places in what was then the Soviet Union.)

Since the *Historical Atlas of East Central Europe* is intended primarily for the English-language reader, the few English-language forms that exist for places in East Central Europe are the ones used here. Some are well known: Prague instead of Praha (Czech); Cracow instead of Kraków (Polish). Others are less evident: Herzegovina for Herce-govina (Serbo-Croatian); Cerigo for the Greek form, Kithíra (known, perhaps, even better in its Latin form, Cythera). Again, *Webster's* is the guide followed in determining whether or not there is an English form (or more precisely a "Websterian English" standard, which may often be based on German, Latin, or the language of a country that formerly ruled a given area).

Admittedly, I found it difficult to use as the main entry Kaliningrad for Königsberg, or Gdańsk for Danzig prior to 1945, and certainly there will be users who will bristle at seeing Wrocław for Breslau, Bratislava for Pressburg or Pozsony, and Cluj for Kolozsvár—to mention only a few of the numerous possible examples. In order to avoid confusion, however, it seemed preferable to use one name for the same town or city (and this applies to bodies of water as well) throughout the atlas and the text. On the other hand, on most maps I have provided, in parentheses below the main entry, as many alternate historic names as space would allow. Finally, the extensive index includes linguistic variants (with appropriate cross-references) in twenty-six languages.

A guide such as *Webster's* is particularly helpful regarding bodies of water. Rivers may flow through several countries and therefore have several different "official" names, not to mention local names designated by ethnolinguistic groups whose languages are different from the state language. Thus, to resolve the problem of choice between, let us say, the Elbe (German) or Labe (Czech), or between Tisza (Hungarian), Tisa (Serbo-Croatian), and Theiss (German), the first entry given in *Webster's* is what is used in this atlas.

In one category, however, the historical principle has been used instead of names in the official languages of present-day countries. This pertains to administrative subdivisions with clearly defined boundaries (in contrast to undefined historic regions, such as Slovakia or Thrace), whose names are given in the language of the country that created those subdivisions. Thus palatinate names in the Polish-Lithuanian Commonwealth are in Polish; counties in the Hungarian Kingdom in Magyar; provinces

in the Russian Empire in Russian; vilayets in the Ottoman Empire in Turkish. But here, too, English usage (following *Webster's*) has priority wherever possible; for example, Mazovia instead of Mazowsze (Polish), or Bohemia instead of Böhmen (German) or Čechy (Czech).

The principle of using historic names for clearly defined administrative subdivisions on the one hand, and names of towns and cities according to the official language used in present-day countries on the other, may seem strange on some maps because, in effect, two linguistic forms of the same name might be juxtaposed, such as Poznań (in Polish) for the city and Posen (in German) for the province of historic Prussia in which the city was located; Vilnius (in Lithuania) for the city and Vilna (in Russian) for the surrounding province of imperial Russia; or Ioannina (in Greek) for the city and Yanya (in Turkish) for the surrounding Ottoman vilayet. Despite appearances, this is not inconsistency, although it does reveal the problem of trying to reconcile historical and present-day criteria for place names.

The extensive chronological and geographic scope of the *Historical Atlas of East Central Europe* imposed a wide range of conceptual, factual, and technical concerns that would have been difficult if not impossible to resolve alone. In this regard, I was very fortunate to have as active consultants and reviewers a distinguished group of historians, geographers, and cartographers. Among the earliest of these who helped in both the conceptual stage and factual review was Ivo Banac (Yale University). Also, Henry Abramson (University of Toronto), Ľubica Babotová (Šafárik University, Prešov), Bohdan Budurowycz (University of Toronto), Charles Jelavich (Indiana University), Ljubomir Medješi (Novi Sad), Dean S. Rugg (University of Nebraska), Aurel Sasu (University of Cluj), Piotr Wandycz (Yale University), and Andrzej Zięba were unfailingly sympathetic in their critical reviews of the entire text and maps. A few specific chapters benefited from the review and emendations of Jerzy Kłoczowski and his staff at the Institute for the Historical Geography of the Church in Poland (Catholic University of Lublin) and of Michael K. Silber (Hebrew University of Jerusalem), while Zachary M. Baker (YIVO Institute for Jewish Research) was an indispensable source for Yiddish names that appear in the text and index. No less was the input from the editors of the series, Donald W. Treadgold (University of Washington) and most especially Peter F. Sugar (University of Washington), who encouraged this project from beginning to end with invaluable factual and editorial advice.

The actual creation of the atlas began with large-scale color drawings that I created for each map. These draft maps were given to the Office of Cartography at the University of Toronto where Chris Grounds made publication-size compilation maps from which, after editing, the final scribing was done by him and his fellow cartographers Brigid McQuaid, Jane R. Ejima, and Ada Cheung. Throughout this process the work was overseen by Geoffrey J. Matthews, whose cartographic design determined the beauty of the final maps.

A word of special thanks to Joan Winearls and her staff members, Patricia Bellamy and Sherry Smugler, at the Map Collection of the University of Toronto's John P. Robarts

Library. They not only provided me with a home away from home for nearly two years, they also protected the project's working space and nurtured its contents by bringing to my attention otherwise little-known maps and atlases from their rich collection. Finally, the painstaking task of transforming handwritten text into readable typescript and setting all the type for eighty-nine maps was done with consistent accuracy by the exceptionally resourceful Sally Leilani Jones (University of Toronto), who also forced a grudging technophobe to appreciate the advantages of the world of microcomputers and word processors.

As important as is human support, projects such as the *Historical Atlas of East Central Europe* would have been impossible without significant financial commitments. The project was initially made possible through two grants from the Social Sciences and Humanities Research Council of Canada and smaller grants from the Centre for Russian and East European Studies at the University of Toronto and the Stephen B. Roman Foundation in Toronto. The support from these institutions provided for professional leave and for the preparation of the manuscript and draft maps. The penultimate stage of the project, which required expensive cartographic scribing and preparation of camera-ready plates, was made possible by a generous grant from the National Endowment for the Humanities, an independent federal agency in Washington, D.C. When we were ready for publication, the final stage of the project was made possible by the professionalism of the directorate and staff at the University of Washington Press. I am especially grateful to the copyeditor, Leila Charbonneau.

I am greatly indebted to all of the above individuals and institutions, whose wise counsel has contributed to making this work better than it otherwise would have been. Nonetheless, whatever shortcomings remain are my sole responsibility. This project has, since the beginning, been both demanding and exciting. Hopefully, the result in the form of this *Historical Atlas of East Central Europe* will be a useful tool to help students and the public at large understand better this still relatively unknown but important area of the world.

PRM
Toronto, Ontario
January 1993

Historical Atlas of East Central Europe

1 East Central Europe: geographic zones

Just as there is no consensus regarding the name and extent of territory for what is described in this volume as East Central Europe, there is also no agreement on how to subdivide this area into geographic zones. For instance, geographers reject the notion that rivers can serve as borders of geographical units, because by their very nature rivers are bodies of water that unify rather than divide surrounding areas. This may be true in purely geographical terms, but it is equally true that rivers have been used as boundaries of political units, thus often deliberately restricting or even eliminating their otherwise "natural" unifying characteristics. The Elbe, Oder-Neisse, Zbruch, Sava, and Danube are among the better known examples of rivers that have served as definitive borders in East Central Europe.

Because of the historical emphasis of this atlas, the broad zones described here have been determined as much by historical as by geographic factors. Taking this into consideration, East Central Europe can be said to be subdivided into three geographic zones: (1) the northern zone; (2) the Alpine-Carpathian zone; and (3) the Balkan zone.

The northern zone is bounded by the Baltic Sea in the north and the crests of the Ore, Sudeten, and Carpathian mountains and the Prut River in the south. This area coincides with the medieval Slavic marchlands east of the Elbe River and the historic political entities of Prussia, Saxony, and Poland-Lithuania, which for several centuries reached as far east as the Dnieper River valley and beyond. Today this zone encompasses former East Germany, Poland, Lithuania, Belarus, Ukraine (west of the Dnieper River), and Moldavia. The predominant geographic feature of this northern zone is the broad sweep of an unbroken plain, which is part of the North European Lowlands that stretch in a west-east band across virtually the entire European continent. Along the southern fringe of this zone are plateaus (the Silesian and Volhynian-Podolian) and increasingly higher elevations (the Carpathian Forelands) that culminate in an east-west range of mountains: the Thuringian Forest, Ore Mountains, Sudeten Mountains, and the northwestern and forested (central) ranges of the Carpathian Mountains.

The Alpine-Carpathian zone is bounded in the north by the northwestern boundary of Austria, the mountain ranges (Bohemian, Ore, Sudeten) that surround the Bohemian Basin, the crests of the northwestern and forested Carpathians, and the Prut River. In the south, the Alpine-Carpathian zone ends at the Sava-Danube river line—from the Sava's tributary, the Kupa River, in the west, to the Black Sea mouths of the Danube in the east. This area roughly coincides with the lands of the historic Habsburg Empire (minus Galicia) before the mid-nineteenth century and the Danubian principalities of Moldavia and Walachia. Today this zone encompasses the Czech Republic, Slovakia, Austria, Hungary, Romania, Slovenia, Croatia (north of

the Kupa-Sava rivers), and northeast Italy. Geographically, this middle zone is dominated in the west by the Austrian Alps and the Bohemian Basin, and in the east by the Carpathian Mountains. The Carpathians are, in turn, divided into five subdivisions: the northwestern Carpathians (including Slovakia's Tatra and Ore ranges); the central, or forested, Carpathians; the eastern Carpathians; the southern Carpathians (or Transylvanian Alps); and the western Carpathians (including the Apuseni Mountains). The broad arc formed by these ranges surrounds what is known as the Carpathian Basin, itself divided into the Hungarian (or Pannonian) Plain and the Transylvanian Basin. Despite their often formidable heights, the Carpathians have never been an insuperable barrier because there are several passes, especially through the central (forested) and southern (Transylvanian Alps) ranges. South and east of the Carpathians are the Walachian Plain and Moldavian Tablelands bounded respectively by the Danube and Prut rivers.

The Balkan zone begins south of the Sava-Danube river boundary and extends as far south as the Mediterranean and Aegean seas. This area has generally been referred to as the Balkan Peninsula. Since "balkan" is a corrupted derivation of the Turkish word *balak,* meaning mountain, all the mountains in the peninsula are often called the Balkans, even though the Balkan Mountains (Stara Planina) are in fact found only in north-central Bulgaria. The Sava and Danube rivers have been chosen as the northern boundary of this zone, because it is south of that line that for most of early modern history (sixteenth to the early nineteenth centuries) the core provinces of the Ottoman Empire were found. Today, this formerly Ottoman sphere of East Central Europe includes the contemporary states of Croatia (south of the Kupa-Sava rivers), Bosnia-Herzegovina, Yugoslavia, Macedonia, Bulgaria, Albania, Greece, and European Turkey. Most of the Balkan zone is dominated by mountains, with only a few relatively small lowland areas, such as the Rumelian Basin in Bulgaria, the coastal areas of northern and central Albania, and the Thessaly Basin and

Mountain passes

1. Arlberg	
2. Brenner/Brennero	15. Rodna
3. Plöcken/Monte Croce	16. Tihutu
4. Loibl/Ljubelj	17. Oituz
5. Schober	18. Predeal
6. Semmering	19. Red Gate/Turnu Roşu
7. Jablunkov	20. Transylvanian Iron Gate/Poarta
8. Tylicz/Tylič	de Fier a Transilvaniei
9. Dukla/Duklia	21. Porata Orientală/Domaşnea
10. Łupków/Lupkov	22. Petrohanski
11. Uzhok	23. Vitinya
12. Torun/Vyshkiv	24. Zlatishki
13. Iablonytsia/Delatyn/Tatar	25. Shipka
14. Prislop	26. Iron Gate/Vratnik

NORTH
SEA

BALTIC
SEA

Store Bælt

*Kiel
Bay*

*Mecklenburg
Bay*

*Pomeranian
Bay*

*Oder
Haff*

*Courland
Lagoon*

*Gulf of
Danzig*

Neman

Venta

Western *Dvina*

Neris

Pregola

Elbe

Weser

Leine

Saale

Havel

Spree

Neisse

Oder

Noteć

Warta

Vistula

Western

Bug

Pilica

Wieprz

Styr

Horyn

Pripet

Pripet

Ptich

Berezina

Iput'

Sozh

Dnieper

*Kiev
Reservoir*

Desna

HARZ
MTS.

THURINGIAN
BASIN

THURINGIAN
FOREST

ORE MTS.

BOHEMIAN
BASIN

SUDETEN MOUNTAINS

SILESIAN
PLATEAU

PRIPET MARSHES

VOLHYNIAN-PODOLIAN
PLATEAU

Fulda

Eder

Werra

Main

Vltava

Elbe

Vistula

San

Dniester

*Kaniv
Reservoir*

Ros'

Sula

*Southern
Bug*

Styrikha

Ingul

BAVARIAN FOREST

BOHEMIAN FOREST

JURA MOUNTAINS

BAVARIAN ALPS

NORTHWESTERN

TATRAS

ORE

7 ‖

8 ‖ 9 ‖ ‖ 10

‖ 11 ‖ 12

‖ 13

C A R P A T H I A N S

FORESTED

Morava

Váh

Hornad

Danube

Isar

Inn

Lech

Iller

*Lake
Constance*

RHAETIAN
ALPS

1 ‖

2 ‖

A L P S

5 ‖

‖ 6

3

KARAWANKEN

DOLOMITES

JULIAN ALPS

4

*Neusiedler
Lake*

Enns

Mur

Rába

Vrbas

Drava

HUNGARIAN

PLAIN

*Lake
Balaton*

Tisza

Körös

Mureş

APUSENI
MTS.

TRANSYLVANIAN
BASIN

MOLDAVIAN
TABLELAND

EASTERN

14 ‖ ‖ 15

16 ‖

‖ 17

Somes

Prut

Dniester

Seret

COASTAL LOWLANDS

*Lake
Garda*

Adige

Po

Arno

Piave

*Gulf of
Venice*

DINARIC

D I N A R I C   R A N G E S

Kupa

Una

Sava

Bosna

Drina

SERBIAN
MTS.

20 ‖ 19 ‖ ‖ 18

21 ‖ TRANSYLVANIAN ALPS

*Iron
Gates*

Olt

Arges

Ialomita

WALACHIAN PLAIN

Danube

DOBRUJA TABLELAND

*Danube
River
Delta*

BLACK
SEA

A P P E N I N E S

Tevere

Ofanto

Basento

ADRIATIC

SEA

*Lake
Scutari*

Drin

Morava

Vardar

Iskur

Vit

22 ‖

23 ‖ 24 ‖ 25 ‖ ‖ 26

BALKAN MTS.

Timok

Tundzha

Kamchiya

*Gulf of
Burgas*

Struma

RUMELIAN BASIN

Maritsa

Bosporus

SAR
MTS.

RILA
MTS.

PIRIN MTS.

RHODOPE MTS.

*Lake
Ohrid*

*Lake
Prespa*

Mesta

Sakarya

SEA OF
MARMARA

*Iznik
Lake*

PINDUS MTS.

Shkumbin

Vijosa

Vistritsa

Acheloos

*Gulf of
Salonika*

THESSALY
BASIN

*Eğridir
Lake*

Simao

Gediz

Menderes

*Beyşehir
Lake*

Aksu

TYRRHENIAN

SEA

*Strait of
Messina*

*Gulf of
Taranto*

IONIAN

SEA

*Strait of
Otranto*

*Gulf of
Corinth*

AEGEAN

SEA

Dardanelles

MEDITERRANEAN

SEA

SEA OF
CRETE

Elevation in meters

2000
1000
500
200
Sea level

0   150 miles

0   150 kilometers

Scale 1:8 890 000

Copyright © by Paul Robert Magocsi

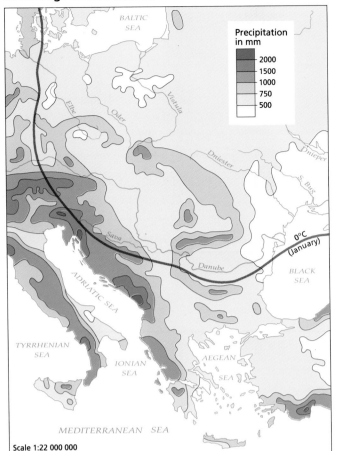

Precipitation
in mm

2000
1500
1000
750
500

0°C
(January)

Scale 1:22 000 000

Copyright © by Paul Robert Magocsi

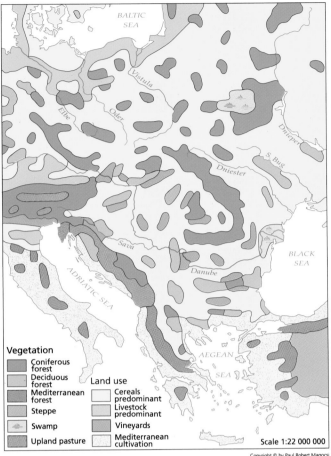

Vegetation

Coniferous
forest

Deciduous
forest

Mediterranean
forest

Steppe

Swamp

Upland pasture

Land use

Cereals
predominant

Livestock
predominant

Vineyards

Mediterranean
cultivation

Scale 1:22 000 000

Copyright © by Paul Robert Magocsi

the valleys of several rivers in northern Greece (Vardar, Struma, Mesta, Maritsa).

The rivers in East Central Europe form a widespread network with six drainage basins. Since many of these rivers—aided in modern times by canals—are navigable (see Maps 28 and 49), otherwise landlocked areas have historically had access for trade and commerce to the seas that surround the European continent. The six drainage basins with their major rivers that in part cover East Central Europe are: (1) the North Sea basin (Elbe); (2) the Baltic basin (Oder, Vistula, Neman); (3) the Black Sea basin (Dnieper, Southern Bug, Dniester); (4) the Danubian basin (Danube with its many tributaries, including the Morava, Váh, Drava, Tisza, Sava, Olt, Siret, and Prut); (5) the Adriatic basin (Po, Adige, Piave, Neretva, Vijosë, Achelous); and (6) the Aegean basin (Vardar, Vistritsa, Struma, Mesta, Maritsa).

In terms of climate, two-thirds of East Central Europe (basically north of the January 0° isotherm indicated on the Average Annual Rainfall map) is continental; that is, the average temperature in the coldest month is below 0°C (32°F) and in the warmest month below 22°C (72°F). The southern third, or Balkan zone, of East Central Europe has a truly Mediterranean climate, with mild winters and hot, dry summers except at higher elevations, where temperatures are colder. The annual precipitation varies greatly with elevation and tends to diminish from west to east. The highest levels of 1,000 to 1,500 millimeters (40 to 60 inches) annual rainfall are in the Austrian and Dinaric alpine ranges and in the Carpathians (see Map 12). The driest regions are in the rain shadow of the Carpathians: the Hungarian Plain and the Ukrainian coastal lowlands north of the Black Sea. Nor is the rainfall evenly distributed throughout the year, with most of it falling during the summer, especially in June and July. In the northern zone much of the winter precipitation is snow, and the colder temperatures leave the rivers in the Baltic drainage basin frozen and closed to navigation for up to two months each year.

2 East Central Europe, ca. 400

For the first four centuries of the common era, East Central Europe was divided into two spheres: the civilized world of the Roman Empire, and the uncivilized expanse of sparsely settled lands inhabited by sedentary peoples such as the Slavs and nomadic peoples such as the Germanic Goths, Vandals, and Sueves, and the Asiatic Alans and Huns. The basic dividing line between these two spheres was in large measure formed by the Rhine and Danube rivers, along which the Roman Empire established its northern frontier known as the limes.

In order to protect the Roman limes, a series of legionary camps and fortresses were established along the southern bank of the Danube, some of which are still the sites of important cities (indicated in parentheses): Troesmis, Durostorum (Silistra), Novae (Svishtov), Oescus, Viminacium (Kostolac), Singidunum (Belgrade), Mursa (Osijek), Aquincum (Budapest), Carnuntum, Vindobona (Vienna), Lauriacum (Lorch), and Regina Castra (Regensburg).

The only exception to the Danubian divide was the Roman province of Dacia, which reached into the heart of what is now Romania (Transylvania and western Walachia) and existed from 106 and 271 c.e. Also during the initial decades of Dacia's existence, the region just to the east (later inhabited by Visigoths) was incorporated into the Roman province of Moesia II (Inferior), which lay along the southern bank of the lower Danube. Although the Roman legions withdrew from Dacia before the end of the third century, they retained the name by creating two provinces on the southern shore of the Danube: Dacia Ripensis and Dacia Mediterranea. More important for subsequent developments is the fact that despite its short-lived existence, the province north of the Danube provided latter-day Romanian historians with the basis for what has come to be known as the Daco-Romanian continuity theory.

According to this theory, the present-day inhabitants of Romania are considered either (1) descendants of the Romans who before 271 c.e. inhabited Dacia north of the Danube or (2) descendants of local Geto-Dacian peoples living in Dacia who intermarried with the Roman colonists and assimilated their language and culture. In either case, the Romanians, or Vlachs as they were known at the time by their neighbors, took refuge in the Carpathian Mountains after the Roman legions evacuated Dacia in 271 c.e. The Daco-Roman continuity theory forms the basis of the Romanian understanding of their early history and, in particular, provides them with "historical precedence" that ostensibly justifies their rule of Transylvania (modern Dacia), which was only much later conquered by the invading Magyars and then ruled for centuries by the Hungarian Kingdom until it was finally "reunited" with the rest of Romania in 1918.

The Roman Empire was administratively divided into provinces, the number and extent of which varied. The greatest number existed during the reign of Emperor Diocletian (r. 284–305), who grouped them into large administrative units called dioceses. Under Emperor Constantine (r. 306–337), the dioceses were grouped, in turn, into still larger units called prefectures, which after 395 (as indicated on the accompanying map) included in East Central Europe the Orient, Illyricum, and Italy.

It was also under Diocletian that the principle was instituted of having two emperors, one ruling the eastern part of the empire and the other ruling in the west. This approach culminated during the reign of Constantine, who created on the west coast of the Bosporus a new capital—the New Rome—inaugurated in 330 (see Map 2b—inset). The New Rome, named Constantinople after its founder, was built on the site of the city of Byzantium, which had been in existence since the seventh century b.c.e. Constantinople was to become the most important city in postclassical Europe and to remain the capital of the East Roman (Byzantine) Empire. The idea of two Roman empires was fixed with the establishment of an east-west boundary in 395 that became permanent after 410.

In order to administer their far-flung empire and to encourage communication and trade, the Romans built a wide network of roads, many of which crossed East Central Europe. The most famous of these in the eastern part of the empire were: (1) the Via Egnatia, which connected Constantinople westward to the Adriatic coast, where it divided into a route north toward Dyrrhachium (and from there across the sea to Barium) and one south toward Apollonia (and from there across the sea to Brundusium); on the Italian side, the Via Appia from Brundusium with a connector road from Barium led directly to Rome; (2) the Via Militaris, which connected Constantinople northwestward via Adrianopolis, Serdica, and Viminacium to Singidunum (present-day Belgrade) at the juncture of the Danube and Tisza; and (3) the Via Viminacium-Constantinopolis, connecting Constantinople directly north along the Black Sea coast through Tomis to Ad Storna at the mouth of the southern Danubian channel (near present-day Sulina) and from there up the southern bank of the Danube to Viminacium. These and many other roads in the Roman system were to a large extent used long after the empire ceased to exist, while the sites of many Roman settlements still form the basis for many cities in East Central Europe: Juvavum (Salzburg); Savaria (Szombathely); Emona (Ljubljana); Napoca (Cluj); Scodra (Shkodër); Dyrrhachium (Durrës); Naissus (Niš); Serdica (Sofia); Philippopolis (Plovdiv); Tomis (Constanța); and Adrianopolis (Edirne).

The turn of the fifth century was a period of transition for East Central Europe. The Roman Empire's internal problems were aggravated by the incursion of Germanic tribes during the late fourth and early fifth centuries. These tribes sought refuge in the Roman Empire after 370, when they

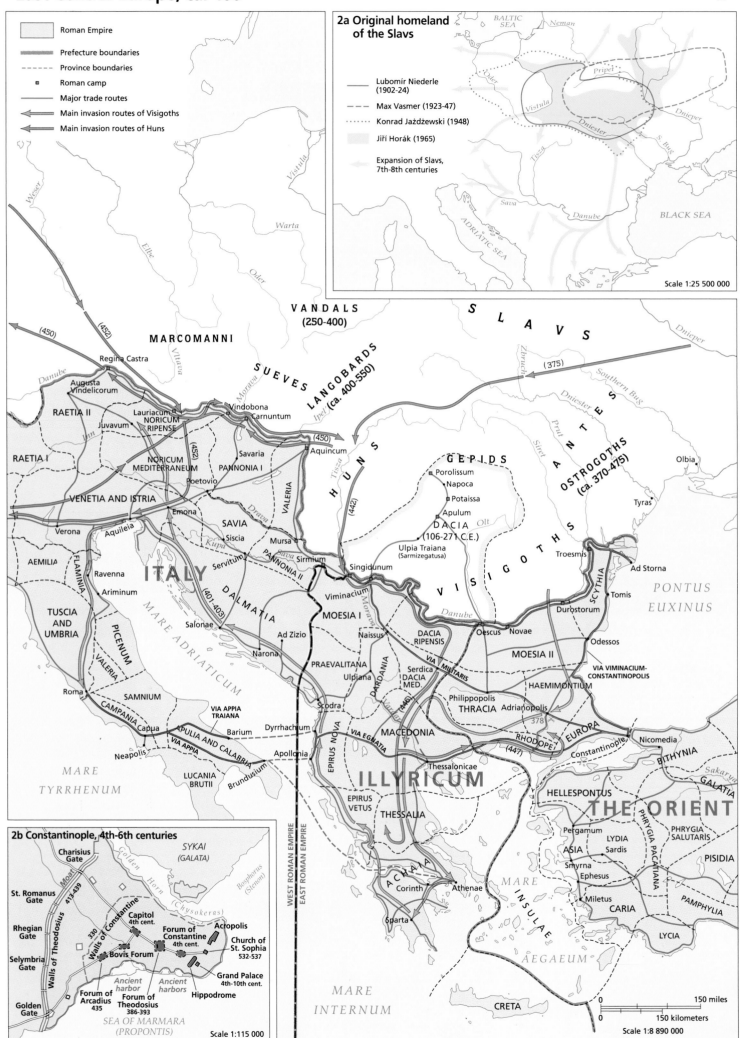

2a Original homeland of the Slavs

Lubomír Niederle (1902-24)

Max Vasmer (1923-47)

Konrad Jażdżewski (1948)

Jiří Horák (1965)

Expansion of Slavs, 7th-8th centuries

Scale 1:25 500 000

Legend:
- Roman Empire
- Prefecture boundaries
- Province boundaries
- Roman camp
- Major trade routes
- Main invasion routes of Visigoths
- Main invasion routes of Huns

BALTIC SEA

Neman

Oder

Vistula

Pripet

Dniester

Dnieper

S. Bug

Sava

Danube

Tisza

ADRIATIC SEA

BLACK SEA

VANDALS (250-400)

MARCOMANNI

SUEVES

LANGOBARDS

Ipel (ca. 400-550)

SLAVS

ANTES

HUNS

Dnieper

Zbruch

(375)

Southern Bug

Dniester

Prut

Siret

Olt

Weser

Werra

Vltava

Elbe

Warta

Oder

Vistula

(450)

(452)

Regina Castra

Augusta Vindelicorum

RAETIA II

Juvavum

Lauriacum

NORICUM RIPENSE

Vindobona

Carnuntum

(450)

Aquincum

Savaria

PANNONIA I

VALERIA

GEPIDS

Porolissum

Napoca

Potaissa

Apulum

OSTROGOTHS (ca. 370-475)

Olbia

Tyras

RAETIA I

Inn

NORICUM MEDITERRANEUM

Poetovio

(452)

Emona

SAVIA

Drava

(442)

DACIA (106-271 C.E.)

Ulpia Traiana (Sarmizegatusa)

VISIGOTHS

Troesmis

Ad Storna

SCYTHIA

VENETIA AND ISTRIA

Verona

Aquileia

Siscia

Kupa

Sava

Mursa

Sirmium

Singidunum

Danube

Viminacium

Tomis

PONTUS EUXINUS

AEMILIA

FLAMINIA

Ravenna

Ariminum

ITALY

DALMATIA

(401-403)

Servitium

MOESIA I

DACIA RIPENSIS

Oescus

Novae

Durostorum

MOESIA II

Odessos

MARE ADRIATICUM

Salonae

Ad Zizio

Narona

Naissus

VIA MILITARIS

VIA VIMINACIUM-CONSTANTINOPOLIS

TUSCIA AND UMBRIA

PICENUM

VALERIA

PRAEVALITANA

Ulpiana

DARDANIA

Serdica

DACIA MED.

Philippopolis

HAEMIMONTIUM

Roma

SAMNIUM

Scodra

Vardar

MACEDONIA

Adrianopolis

378

THRACIA

EUROPA

RHODOPE

(447)

Nicomedia

BITHYNIA

CAMPANIA

Capua

VIA APPIA TRAIANA

Barium

APULIA AND CALABRIA

Dyrrhachium

VIA EGNATIA

EPIRUS NOVA

Constantinople

Sakarya

GALATIA

Neapolis

VIA APPIA

Apollonia

ILLYRICUM

Thessalonicae

HELLESPONTUS

THE ORIENT

MARE TYRRHENUM

LUCANIA BRUTII

Brundisium

EPIRUS VETUS

THESSALIA

MARE INSULAE

Pergamum

ASIA

LYDIA

Sardis

PHRYGIA PACATIANA

PHRYGIA SALUTARIS

PISIDIA

ACHAIA

Corinth

Athenae

Smyrna

Ephesus

Miletus

CARIA

PAMPHYLIA

Sparta

AEGAEUM

LYCIA

MARE INTERNUM

WEST ROMAN EMPIRE

EAST ROMAN EMPIRE

CRETA

0 150 miles

0 150 kilometers

Scale 1:8 890 000

2b Constantinople, 4th-6th centuries

SYKAI (GALATA)

Golden Horn

Bosphorus (Stenon)

Charisius Gate

St. Romanus Gate

413-439

Moat

330

Walls of Constantine

Capitol 4th cent.

Forum of Constantine 4th cent.

Acropolis

Church of St. Sophia 532-537

Rhegian Gate

Selymbria Gate

Walls of Theodosius

Bovis Forum

Grand Palace 4th-10th cent.

Golden Gate

Forum of Arcadius 435

Forum of Theodosius 386-393

Hippodrome

Ancient harbor

Ancient harbors

SEA OF MARMARA (PROPONTIS)

Scale 1:115 000

Historical Atlas of East Central Europe

Copyright © by Paul Robert Magocsi

were driven out of the lands north of the Black Sea by the invasion of Huns from Central Asia. One Germanic tribe, the Visigoths, had already settled near the Roman limes north of the lower Danube before the end of the third century. In 375 they were allowed to enter Thrace (Thracia). Conflict broke out with the local authorities, however, leading to a Visigoth victory over a Roman army near Adrianopolis (378). This was followed by a long march of pillage throughout the Balkan Peninsula that was to last for a quarter of a century until under their leader Alaric the Visigoths reached Italy and sacked Rome in 410.

The Visigoths were followed in their flight before the Huns by the Langobards (Lombards) and Alans, who by the outset of the fifth century had also arrived on the borders of the Roman Empire seeking refuge. Then in the 420s, the Huns themselves were to transfer the center of their vast Euro-Asiatic empire to the plain between the Danube and Tisza rivers. From their center along the middle Tisza they had easy access to the Roman Empire, controlling before long much of Pannonia II (Inferior) and Moesia I (Superior) and ravaging large parts of East Central and western Europe under their leader Attila (d. 453). After the death of Attila, the Huns returned to the steppes north of the Black Sea and were replaced by the Ostrogoths, who by 454 controlled the Roman provinces of Pannonia, Savia, and Valeria.

Meanwhile, the various Slavic tribes, who were soon to become an integral part of the entire East Central European landscape, continued to lead a sedentary existence well beyond the Roman Empire but under the domination of Germanic, Hunnic, or other Asiatic nomads. In the absence of reliable written evidence, scholars have for long disagreed as to the original homeland (*prarodina/Urheimat*) of the Slavs. Early writers spoke of the Danube and then the Don river valleys, but by the nineteenth century the Carpathian Mountains and then the marshes of the Pripet River valley were all suggested as the location of the original Slavic homeland. During the twentieth century, scholars have relied largely on archaeological and reconstructed linguistic evidence. While they differ regarding the territorial extent of the original Slavic homeland, all do agree that it was centered in lands that today are located in present-day northwestern Ukraine, southwestern Belarus, and eastern Poland (see Map 2a—inset).

One group of Slavs, known as the Antes, were the first to have extensive contacts with the East Roman Empire. By the fourth century, the Antes were organized into a powerful tribal league by Alanic military leaders (from whom the name Antes derives). First settled in the basin between the Prut and lower Dniester rivers, they moved their base gradually northeastward toward the Southern Bug and Dnieper valleys. In the wake of the Hunnic invasions and breakup of Ostrogoth influence in the region, the Antes filled a power vacuum allowing them frequent raids of the East Roman Empire. The Antes are considered by some scholars to have formed the first Slavic state.

3 East Central Europe, 7th–8th centuries

The seventh and eighth centuries were marked in East Central Europe by three developments: (1) the survival of the Roman world south of the Danube in the form of the Byzantine Empire; (2) the arrival of new Asiatic warrior peoples—the Avars and the Bulgars; and (3) the dispersal of the Slavs throughout most of the region.

With the deposition in 476 of the last Roman emperor in the west, it was only in the east that the empire survived. There, New Rome underwent a revival during the reign of Emperor Justinian (r. 527–565), who was able to regain the Italian peninsula from the Germanic Ostrogoths. Most of these gains, however, were soon lost to a new Germanic tribe, the Lombards, although at the death of Emperor Heraclius I (r. 610–641), the empire was still able to retain certain lands in the west known as the Exarchate of Ravenna. It was also under Heraclius that the empire became a Greek monarchy, henceforth referred to in historic literature as the Byzantine Empire.

North of the Danube, the most significant political event happened in 578 with the arrival from Central Asia of the Avars, a nomadic people of Mongolian or Turco-Tatar origin. The Avars set up their fortified camp (hring) on the Pannonian Plain between the Danube and lower Tisza rivers, and by the end of the sixth century they dominated a vast territory north of the Danube stretching from the Frankish Kingdom in the west to the Black Sea in the east. Not only did the Avars force out of Pannonia the Germanic Lombards—who in turn crossed into the Italian peninsula to set up the Kingdom of Lombardy—they also brought with them Slavic tribes who settled large tracts within the Avar sphere. In that sphere developed a kind of Avar-Slavic symbiotic relationship, in which the Slavs were either vassals or allies who fought with the Avars in their military campaigns against the Byzantine Empire. The main difference was that during those campaigns the Avars returned to the Pannonian Plain after the battles and looting were over, while the sedentary-minded Slavs remained, resulting in a Slavic expansion into large parts of the Balkans (see Map 2a—inset). In some instances, as during the reign of Heraclius, the Slavs were invited to settle in the empire and to serve as allies of the Byzantines against the Avars. It was also during this period that Vlachs appeared throughout much of the mountainous areas south of the Danube.

On the western, eastern, and southern fringes of the Avar Khanate, new political entities were established. In the west, the Slavic tribes were caught between the Germanic Frankish Kingdom and the Avars. In 623, western Slavic tribes who were discontented with Avar domination called on a Frankish warrior merchant named Samo, who helped them in their revolt. Following their victory, Samo was proclaimed the leader of a Slavic state. From its center, perhaps in southern Moravia (near Mikulčice or Devín), Samo united several tribes into an independent political force until his death in 658. To the northeast, among the East Slavs, the remnants of the Antes "state" continued in the form of a tribal federation among the Dulebians in Volhynia.

In the Adriatic region, the Croats, Serbs, and other South Slavic tribes liberated themselves from Avar domination and entered the service of Byzantium. Settling in the former Roman province of Dalmatia, these groups were organized into six tribal federations—"Sclavinias" according to the tenth-century Byzantine emperor Constantine VII Porphyrogenitus (r. 905–959)—which became the nuclei of the future South Slavic states.

On the southeastern fringe of the Avar realm, a powerful new state was formed with the arrival in 679 along the lower Danube of the Bulgars, who represented several Turkic tribes that came from the basin of the lower Volga River in the East. Under the leadership of Khan Asparuch/Isperikh (r. 680–701), the Bulgars were able to bring under their control seven Slavic tribes already living along the banks of the Danube and, following military victories against the Byzantine Empire and the Avars, to establish in 681 the First Bulgarian Khanate (Empire). The Turkic Bulgars gradually amalgamated with the more numerous Slavs in their midst, so that by the ninth century the Bulgarian Empire became a Slavic state.

BALTIC SEA

ZEMGALIANS
LATVIANS
SELONIANS
POLOCHANIANS
KRIVICHIANS
KURS
LITHUANIANS
Western Deina

RANIANS
OBODRITES
VELETIANS
POMERANIANS
PRUSSIANS
SUDAVIANS
DREGOVICHIANS
RADIMICHIANS
Neman
Dnieper
Desna

SAXONS
Weser
Warta
KUYAVIANS
MAZOVIANS
Vistula
Western Bug
Pripet
DEREVLIANIANS
SEVERIANS

POLANIANS
LENDIZI
DULEBIANS/VOLHYNIANS
POLIANIANS

LUSATIAN SORBS
Oder
SILESIANS
VISTULANS
WHITE CROATS
Zbruch
ULICHIANS
Dniester
Southern Bug
TIVERTSIANS

THURINGIANS
FRANKISH
CZECHS
Vltava
MORAVIANS
Morava
SLOVAKS
Siret
Prut

ALAMANNI KINGDOM
Regensburg
Mikulčice □
Danube
Ipel'
AVAR KHANATE
Olt

Augsburg
BAVARIANS
Devin □
CARINTHIAN SLAVS
PANNONIAN SLAVS
Tisza
Inn
Salzburg
Drava

Verona
Aquileia
CROATIA/HRVATSKA
CROATS
Kupa
Avar hring □
BULGARIAN
BLACK SEA

LOMBARD
Ravenna
Sava
Sirmium
Danube
KHANATE
Pliska

EXARCHATE OF RAVENNA
BYZANTINE
PAGANIA/PAGANIJA
SERBIA/SRBIJA
Morava
SERBS
V L A C H S
Serdica

Roma
ZACHLUMIA/ZAHUMLJE
TERBOUNIA/TRAVUNIJA
Philippopolis
Maritsa
Adrianopolis

Capua
DIOCLEA/DUKLJA
Dyrrhachium
Constantinople
Nicomedia

Neapolis
Brundusium
Vardar
Thessalonicae
Sakarya

EXARCHATE OF RAVENNA
ADRIATIC SEA
KINGDOM
E M P I R E

Po
A E G E A N
Smyrna

IONIAN SEA
Athenae
S E A
Ephesus

Corinth

MEDITERRANEAN SEA

Legend:

Lombard Kingdom

Byzantine Empire under Heraclius (610-641)

Frankish Kingdom, ca. 741

Core lands of the Avar Khanate

–·–·– Bulgarian Khanate at the death of Asparuch, 701

– – – Independent Grand Duchy of Bavaria after 650

——— Farthest extent of Samo's state, 623-658

——— Slavic tribal unions and other union boundaries

CROATS Slavic peoples

KURS Baltic peoples

SAXONS Germanic peoples

VLACHS Romance peoples

0   150 miles
0   150 kilometers

Scale 1:8 890 000

Copyright © by Paul Robert Magocsi

4 East Central Europe, 9th century

The ninth century is most notable for the rivalry between three powers for control of much of East Central Europe: the Frankish Kingdom, the Byzantine Empire, and the Bulgarian Empire. In the midst of that rivalry a new state, the Greater Moravian Empire, arose among the West Slavs living north of the middle Danube, while in the northeast the East Slavic tribes under Varangian (Scandinavian) merchant warriors began to form a political entity known as Kievan Rus'.

The ninth century also witnessed the arrival of new invaders. Besides the Varangians, who in the 860s descended the Dnieper River from the north, the Arabic Muslims from the south were beginning in the 820s to raid Byzantine seaports. The Arabic domination of the Mediterranean was strengthened with the conquest of Sicily (827–878) and the control of Crete by Muslim freebooters after 826. Finally, from the east, the Magyars arrived in the Danubian basin in 895–896, changing the political and ethnographic composition of East Central Europe for centuries to come.

The outset of the ninth century saw the marked growth of the Frankish Kingdom in the west and the First Bulgarian Empire in the east. Under Charlemagne (r. 771–814) the Franks destroyed the Avar Khanate (see Map 3), thereby eliminating entirely that power from the Danubian basin and extending their eastern border along a line that ran roughly down the Elbe River, Bohemian Forest, and Pannonian Plain. Along their eastern border, which for the most part faced Slavic tribes, Charlemagne set up marches, or marks, which were to serve as springboards for further eastern conquest. Among these borderland entities were the Saxon Mark, facing the Obodrites and Polabians; the Thuringian or Sorbian Mark, facing the Lusatian Sorbs; the Ost Mark (the precursor of the Duchy of Austria), facing the Czechs and Moravians; and the Friulian Mark, facing the Croats. The attempt of Charlemagne and his successors to extend Frankish influence along the eastern Adriatic was undermined during the first half of the ninth century by Croat princes (Vojnomir, Ljudevit) in southern Pannonia and Dalmatia. As a result of resistance by the Croats and other South Slavs, the lands they inhabited were to remain under the control of local rulers. These rulers were at various times either independent or in vassal status to one or the other of the Frankish, Bulgarian, and Byzantine empires, which continued to challenge each other for control of the area.

The First Bulgarian Empire expanded significantly during the rule of Khan Krum (r. 803–814), following his victories over the Avars and Byzantines. In the north, the Bulgarian sphere under Krum included all of Transylvania and the plain as far west as the Danube River, stretching to the upper Tisza River and Carpathian foothills. In the south, Bulgarian expansion into Byzantine territory was accomplished under Khan Boris I (852–889), under whom the First Bulgarian Empire reached its farthest territorial extent. It was also under Boris that the capital was moved from Pliska to Preslav and that the Bulgars accepted Christianity from Byzantium (865). With arrival of the Magyars at the end of the ninth century, Bulgaria lost all of its lands north of the Danube, although under Symeon (r. 893–927), the first Bulgarian ruler to be called tsar, the empire expanded southwestward toward the Adriatic Sea. It was also in the south that Bulgaria encouraged the flowering of Christian culture at the monastery complex in Lychnidus (Ohrid).

While the collapse of Avar supremacy at the outset of the ninth century allowed for Bulgarian expansion into the eastern part of the Danubian basin, north and west of the middle Danube a power vacuum was created along the eastern fringes of the Frankish Empire. Responding to the increase of Frankish political and cultural (western Christian) influence in the area, a West Slav leader named Mojmír (r. 833–836) founded the Moravian state. Under his successor Rastislav (r. 846–869), the state expanded eastward from its base on the Morava River, reaching as far as the Tisza River and the Bulgarian Empire. It was also during the reign of Rastislav, whose expansion was opposed by both the Bulgarians and the Frankish Kingdom, that the Moravians sought an alliance with Byzantium. This resulted in the acceptance of the mission (863) led by Constantine/Cyril (d. 869) and Methodius (d. 885) and the conversion to Christianity of the Moravians and other Slavic peoples living within the sphere of Greater Moravia (see Map 4a).

The two brothers, Cyril and Methodius, were Byzantine missionaries who had learned the South Slavic dialects in the region of their native Thessalonika (Salonika). They formulated an alphabet for the Slavs and succeeded in having their Slavonic language recognized by the pope for liturgical purposes. Although the Cyril-Methodian cultural heritage eventually ended in Greater Moravia with the fall of that state, their achievements were disseminated by their students (especially Kliment and Naum) among those Slavic peoples who came under the influence of the Bulgarian Empire and of Kievan Rus'.

The flowering of the Greater Moravian Empire—as the state came to be known—reached its height under Svatopluk (r. 870–894), whose political influence stretched northward well beyond the Carpathians and southward into Pannonia. However, with the arrival of the Magyars and their attack against the West Slavic state at the outset of the tenth century, Greater Moravia ceased to exist.

While the West Slavic Moravian state was experiencing its last decades of existence at the end of the ninth century, the East Slavic tribes were being molded into what was to become the extensive realm of Kievan Rus'. During the 860s, Varangian (Scandinavian) military leaders and merchants first set up outposts in northern Russia (Novgorod)

Spheres of influence

- Bulgarian Empire, 814
- Papal States after 814
- Moravian Empire, 836
- Frankish Kingdom and the Duchy of Benevento, 843
- Byzantine Empire, 870
- Kievan Rus', 912

Farthest extent of Greater Moravia, ca. 894

Bulgarian Empire, 927

Arrival of the Magyars

Magyar raids

Arab raids

SERBS — Slavic peoples

VLACHS — Romance peoples

KURS — Baltic peoples

MAGYARS — Finno-Ugric peoples

Major concentrations of Magyar tribes, 10th century

0   150 miles

0   150 kilometers

Scale 1:8 890 000

Copyright © by Paul Robert Magocsi

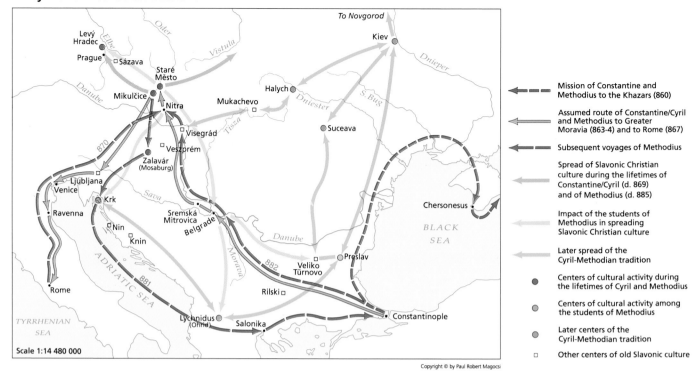

Map legend:

- Mission of Constantine and Methodius to the Khazars (860)
- Assumed route of Constantine/Cyril and Methodius to Greater Moravia (863-4) and to Rome (867)
- Subsequent voyages of Methodius
- Spread of Slavonic Christian culture during the lifetimes of Constantine/Cyril (d. 869) and of Methodius (d. 885)
- Impact of the students of Methodius in spreading Slavonic Christian culture
- Later spread of the Cyril-Methodian tradition
- Centers of cultural activity during the lifetimes of Cyril and Methodius
- Centers of cultural activity among the students of Methodius
- Later centers of the Cyril-Methodian tradition
- Other centers of old Slavonic culture

Scale 1:14 480 000

Copyright © by Paul Robert Magocsi

and Ukraine (Kiev). It was during the reign of Prince Oleg (880–912) that the limited control of territory along the Dnieper River was expanded, joining Novgorod in the far north via Smolensk with Kiev in the south, which henceforth served as the cultural and political center of Kievan Rus'.

It was the strong presence of the Varangian Rus' in Kiev that blocked the northward advance of the Magyars. This group of Finno-Ugric nomadic tribes was being forced westward from its homeland (Etelköz) in the Ukrainian steppes north of the Black Sea by the Turkic Pechenegs. Blocked in the north by the Rus', and with nowhere to turn, the Magyar tribes under their leader Árpád (d. 907) moved west, crossing the Carpathian passes in two groups into Transylvania (895) and Carpathian Rus' (896), with a third following the lower Danubian valley. They settled in the flat basin of the Tisza River, which reminded them of the steppe they had left north of the Black Sea, and also in the more wooded area west of the Danube and farther east in Transylvania. From their new home in the Danubian basin, the Magyars set out on numerous raids that were to ravage large parts of east central and western Europe. These destructive raids lasted over half a century until the Magyars suffered a decisive defeat by the Holy Roman Emperor Otto I (r. 936–973) at the battle of Lechfeld in 955. Subsequently, the Magyars remained permanently in the Danubian basin, where they established a political entity that in many ways replaced the Avar state (see Map 3) that had been destroyed at the outset of the ninth century.

5 Early medieval kingdoms, ca. 1050

By the eleventh century, the loosely organized tribal unions and embryonic state structures that had characterized much of East Central Europe had been transformed into kingdoms. Some would survive in one form or another for several centuries, and almost all would later be used politically as the basis for claims of historical continuity by modern national movements and by new or renewed states.

In the southern portion of East Central Europe, the most significant development was the revival of the Byzantine Empire under the successful Macedonian dynasty, which was to rule for nearly two centuries (867–1058). The empire reached its greatest territorial extent during the reign of Emperor Basil II (963–1025). The neighboring First Bulgarian Empire reached the height of its political influence during the reign of Samuel (976–1014), who expanded the country's boundaries from the Black Sea to the Adriatic Sea and transferred the capital southwestward to the religious and cultural center at Lychnidus (Ohrid) in the western Macedonia. Because of this transfer, later-day Macedonian writers have called Samuel the founder of the first Slavic Macedonian state.

The rise of Bulgarian power clashed with Byzantine interests in the area, and after nearly two decades of fierce military conflict (996–1014) the First Bulgarian Empire was destroyed and fully incorporated into the Byzantine Empire. The Byzantine campaigns were led by Emperor Basil II, who came to be known as the Slayer of the Bulgarians (Bulgaroktonos). Under Basil II, Byzantium was administratively divided into themes, or military recruitment areas. However, already at the outset of the eleventh century, Byzantine rule was being challenged, especially along the Adriatic coast. Venice, founded in 812, became independent of Byzantium in 1000 and began to extend its influence into Dalmatia. Dalmatia was to remain for the rest of the century an area of conflict between Venice, Croatia, and the kingdom of Doclea.

In contrast to the decline of the First Bulgarian Empire, the other South Slavs—Croats and Serbs—succeeded in establishing kingdoms, which were to survive even during the height of Byzantine influence. In the tenth century the Croat tribes in Dalmatia and Pannonia were united under Tomislav (r. 923–928), the local ruler (župan) of Nin, who was recognized by the pope (925) as the first king of Croatia. Tomislav's political authority, which found its base in the coastal cities of Nin and later Biograd, was enhanced by the activity of his contemporary, Bishop Grgur/Gregory of Nin, who fought a vigorous and temporarily successful battle for the independence of the Catholic diocese of Nin from the older archdiocese of Split as well as for the right of the Croat church to use the Slavonic liturgy and the Glagolitic alphabet (the script thought to have been invented by the Slavic missionary Cyril). Tomislav and his successors were recognized by both the pope and the Byzantine emperor, although it was the jurisdictional authority of Split and its Latin-rite influences that prevailed in Croatia. In the north, Croatia's influence was to be challenged by Hungary, with Pannonia changing hands several times between those two states, while in the southwest Venice was able to control most of the ports and offshore islands along the Dalmatian coast.

As for the Serbian tribes, they were united in the late eighth century by local župans, whose sphere of influence included at times Bosnia and Serbia as far north as the Sava River. However, internal quarrels and invasions by the powerful rivals for the area, Bulgaria and Byzantium, reduced Serbian influence. When a Serbian kingdom was revived in the mid-eleventh century, it was limited to a small territory near the Adriatic coast (excluding Dubrovnik and its offshore islands) known as Doclea (from the Roman name for its capital Duklja) or as Zeta (from the river on which Duklja was located).

North and west of the Danube, the Magyar tribes who had ravaged much of Europe in the first half of the tenth century were first consolidated under the Árpád dynasty's Géza (r. 972–997) and then transformed into a state by his son Stephen (r. 997–1038). Stephen administered his realm through counts (ispáns) placed over counties (comitatus, megye). He also suppressed Eastern Christianity—until then popular among the Magyar tribes and Slavs living among them—and invited Roman churchmen to his realm. In 1001, he was recognized as the first king of Hungary by the pope, who sent him a crown. At Stephen's death, Hungarian political influence reached the foothills of the Carpathians.

Following the destruction of the Greater Moravian Empire by the Magyars in 906, the West Slavic Slovaks were eventually to come under the control of Hungary, while the Czechs (of Bohemia) and Moravians were to be dominated by the Germanic Holy Roman Empire. From time to time, a prince like Břetislav I (the Restorer, r. 1034–55) might succeed in regaining political independence for Bohemia-Moravia and even expand its borders beyond the Carpathians into Silesia and as far as Cracow, but internal dynastic conflicts between members of the ruling Přemysl family resulted in the gradual integration of Bohemia and Moravia into the Holy Roman Empire.

Somewhat more successful in resisting the Germanic advance eastward during this period were the Slavic tribes farther north between the lower Elbe and Oder rivers. During the tenth and first half of the eleventh centuries, the Veletians succeeded in uniting several local Slavic peoples and in dominating the area north of Lusatia to the Baltic Sea. Farther west and facing directly Denmark and Saxony was another union of Slavic peoples headed by the Obodrites. From Starigard (modern Oldenburg) and from their active trading port of Reric/Veligrad (modern

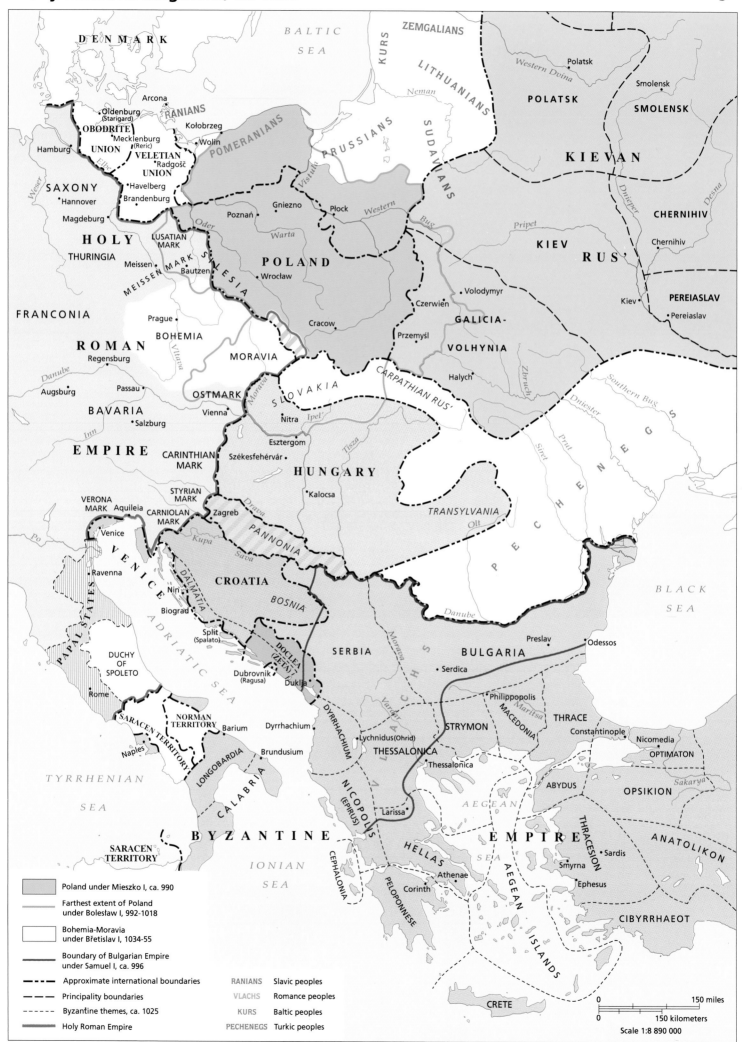

Early medieval kingdoms, ca. 1050

Legend:

- Poland under Mieszko I, ca. 990
- Farthest extent of Poland under Bolesław I, 992-1018
- Bohemia-Moravia under Břetislav I, 1034-55
- Boundary of Bulgarian Empire under Samuel I, ca. 996
- Approximate international boundaries
- Principality boundaries
- Byzantine themes, ca. 1025
- Holy Roman Empire

RANIANS	Slavic peoples
VLACHS	Romance peoples
KURS	Baltic peoples
PECHENEGS	Turkic peoples

150 miles

150 kilometers

Scale 1:8 890 000

Copyright © by Paul Robert Magocsi

Mecklenburg), the Obodrites reached their apogee during the reign of their western Christian duke Gotterschalk (r. 1043–66). Lastly, there was the tiny pagan Slav state of the Ranians, who, from their center of Arcona on the island of Rügen, dominated the Baltic Sea trade during the late eleventh and early twelfth centuries.

East of the Obodrites, Veletians, and the Germanic marks (borderlands) of Lusatia and Meissen, the first historic ruler of the house of Piast, Mieszko (r. 960–992), brought under his control territory that under his successor, Bolesław I (the Brave, r. 992–1025), would become the Kingdom of Poland. Bolesław laid groundwork for an administrative system (comites-castellani, with civil and military powers); he promoted an organizational structure for the Catholic Church; and he expanded the boundaries of the realm, incorporating at various times lands inhabited by the Pomeranians along the Baltic Sea (992–994), Silesia and Cracow (from 999), Slovakia (1001–18), the Lusatian Mark and part of the Meissen Mark (1002–5), Moravia (1003–4), and the Czerwien fortress borderland (1018–31) with Kievan Rus'. Just before his death in 1025, Bolesław became the first king of Poland. Most of his territorial gains were lost during or after his lifetime, so that by the second half of the eleventh century the focal point of the Polish kingdom was north of the Carpathians between the Oder and Vistula rivers.

On Poland's eastern borders, Kievan Rus' had by the outset of the eleventh century increased its control over all the East Slavs, while continuing its traditional interest in the Byzantine and Bulgarian lands farther south. (In fact, it was Kievan Rus's raids on Bulgaria in the 960s and 970s that contributed to the weakening of that empire and its eventual decline in the face of subsequent Byzantine attacks.) Kievan Rus' reached the height of its political and Eastern Christian cultural influence under Iaroslav (the Wise, r. 1019–54), after whose death the realm was divided into principalities, which soon evolved into practically independent entities. Of particular importance for East Central Europe was the Rus' principality of Galicia-Volhynia.

6   The period of feudal subdivisions, ca. 1250

The period of initial political consolidation experienced by the new states in East Central Europe during the tenth and early eleventh centuries was followed in the late eleventh and twelfth centuries by internal divisiveness within several states and by political consolidation and territorial expansion in a few others.

The most profound changes occurred in the Byzantine Empire, whose own status vis-à-vis the rest of Europe was altered significantly after 1054. In that year, the long-standing friction between the papacy and the eastern patriarch over the question of ultimate authority in the Christian world had come to a head. The immediate cause for the break was the papacy's recognition of the conquest by the Normans of Byzantine territories in southern Italy, which under their rule came to be known as the Kingdom of Two Sicilies. The long-term result was a schism between Rome and Constantinople—that is, between the Latin-rite Roman and the Byzantine or Greek-rite Orthodox branches of Christianity. This schism was to have a direct impact on East Central Europe, where the Roman Catholic–Orthodox division was institutionalized by states that eventually favored either the western Catholic or eastern Orthodox cultural and political spheres.

As for the profound political and territorial changes in the Byzantine Empire, the stage for these was already set in the eleventh century. Following the battle of Manzikert (1071) along the eastern frontier of the realm, the victorious Seljuk Turks took over most of Anatolia from the Byzantine Empire. It was the Seljuk capture of Palestine, however, which prompted western European rulers to undertake seven crusades between 1096 and 1254 with the ostensible purpose of liberating the Christian Holy Land. The subsequent Byzantine preoccupation with the Seljuks on its eastern frontier and the Norman encroachments (from their Kingdom of Two Sicilies) on the coast of the Adriatic (especially in Epirus) along its western frontier weakened the empire. The resulting conditions also allowed for the restoration of Bulgarian statehood following a successful revolt against the Byzantines in 1185–86. That revolt was led by two brothers of Vlach origin, Ivan and Peter Asen, and the state they established—ruled by the new Asenid dynasty from its capital at Veliko Tŭrnovo—came to be known as the "empire of Vlachs and Bulgars," or the Second Bulgarian Empire.

Even more ominous was the organization of the Fourth Crusade under the leadership of the pope, the Norman Kingdom of Two Sicilies, and Venice—all enemies of Byzantium. Originally intended to approach the Holy Land via Egypt, the expedition was diverted instead to Constantinople, which in 1204 fell to the Crusaders. The westerners set up a Latin Empire, also known as Romania, which in turn was divided into feudal entities in the western European style—the Kingdom of Thessaly, the Lordship of

Athens, and the Principality of Achaia. The Venetians administered the islands in the Aegean Sea, a strip of land south of Adrianopolis, and a part of Constantinople itself, while they ruled directly the major ports along the Adriatic and Mediterranean (Zadar, Dubrovnik, Methoní) and Crete. Meanwhile, the Byzantine Greeks under Theodorus Lascaris (r. 1206–22) retreated across the Bosporus to northwestern Anatolia, where they established the Nicaean Empire. Finally, to the west of the Latin Empire, self-styled Greek despots set up their own state in Epirus.

During the next half century until the restoration of the Byzantine Empire in 1261, the feudal divisions and internal power rivalries progressively weakened the Latin Empire. By 1250 it was limited to a small strip of land surrounding Constantinople on each side of the Bosporus. During that same time, the Greek Nicaean Empire expanded from its original base on the southern shores of the Sea of Marmara to control most of northwestern Anatolia, stabilizing its frontier with the Seljuk Turks in the east. The struggle to regain the Byzantine patrimony in Europe was more complicated. Athens and Achaia were to remain in the hands of Latin rulers, while the Aegean islands and Crete continued to be held by Venice. As for the rest of the peninsula, Macedonia and Thrace along with the former Latin kingdom of Thessaly were dominated first by Epirus (to 1230), then by Bulgaria (until 1246), and finally were restored to the Byzantine sphere of the Nicaean Empire.

North of the Byzantine sphere, the most important developments were the expansion of Hungary and the creation of Serbia as an independent kingdom. By the end of the eleventh century, the successors of Hungary's first king, Stephen I (r. 997–1038, canonized by Rome in 1083), had continued his strong Roman Catholic orientation and expanded the realm to the crests of the Carpathian Mountains in the north and east, thereby fully incorporating Slovakia, Carpathian Rus' (Marchia Ruthenorum), and Transylvania. The defense of these frontier areas was strengthened in the twelfth century by settling Saxons (Germans from the Rhineland and Luxembourg), who were given a wide degree of self-government. All these territories —inhabited by Slavs, Germans, Székelys, and Vlachs/ Romanians (who by the thirteenth century had "returned" from south of the Danube)—were, together with the largely Magyar-inhabited Danubian plain, considered by Hungary's rulers to be an indivisible part of the lands belonging to the crown of Saint Stephen.

Seemingly secure in the Danubian-Carpathian basin, Hungary then turned its attention southwestward, toward the Adriatic. In this region, the coveted ports and access to the sea were to be fought over and change hands several times between the Hungarians and the increasingly strong Venetian Republic, which gained the most important coastal ports (Zadar and Dubrovnik) by the outset of the thirteenth

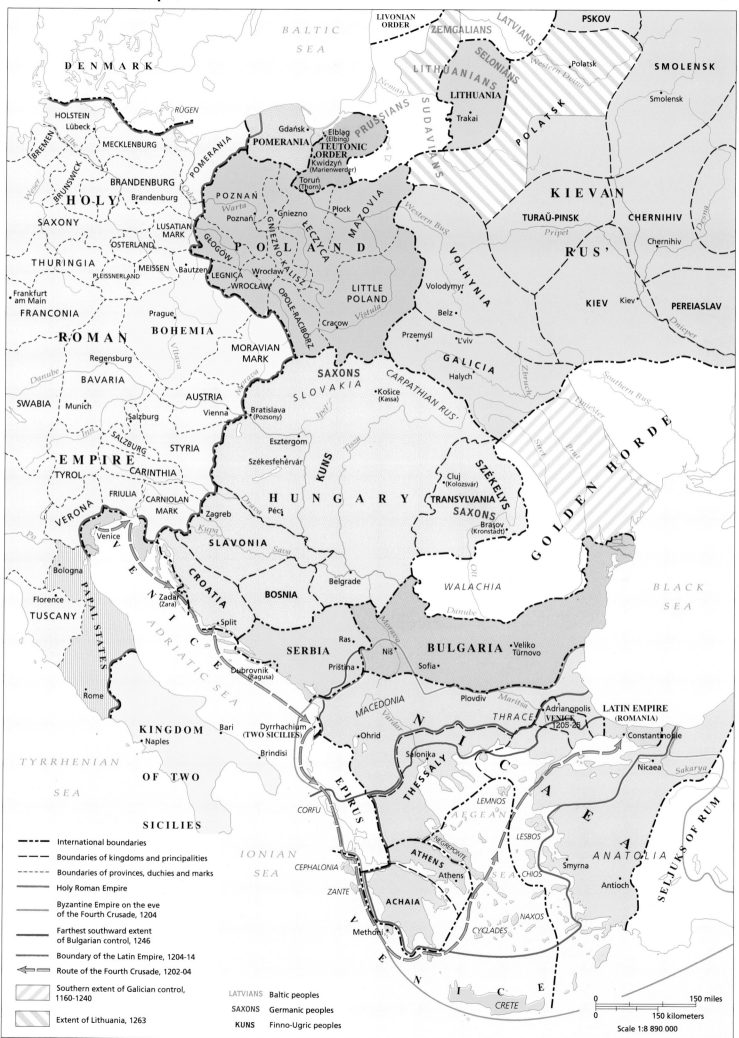

Historical Atlas of East Central Europe

Copyright © by Paul Robert Magocsi

century. As for the hinterland, the Kingdom of Croatia-Slavonia entered into a dynastic union with Hungary in the year 1102. This was the origin of the controversy over the so-called Pacta Conventa (recently proved to be a forgery). According to Croatian writers, Croatia-Slavonia voluntarily entered into union with the king of Hungary, Koloman (r. 1102–16), who allowed the Croatians to retain their own laws, diet, and local rulers (bans). The name Hungary-Croatia implies the duality of the kingdom. On the other hand, Hungarian writers have since the late nineteenth century argued that Koloman conquered and simply incorporated Croatia-Slavonia into his realm. Less permanent was what now might be called Hungary-Croatia's annexation of Bosnia (sometime before 1138), which nonetheless was permitted to retain its own rulers.

Hungary-Croatia's advance further southward was blocked by the rise of Serbia, which was no longer based along the coast in the former independent state of Doclea (taken over by Byzantium in 1094) but in the mountainous hinterland around the town of Ras, from which Serbia derives the name it was known by in the medieval period—Rascia (Raška). The new Serbian state was founded by Stefan Nemanja (r. 1168–96), whose son and successor, Stefan II (r. 1196–1228), was crowned king first by a papal legate (1217) and then with a crown from the Nicaean Empire (1222), thereby reaffirming Serbia's eastern Orthodox religious and cultural orientation.

In the northern half of East Central Europe, the Holy Roman Empire came under the leadership of the House of Hohenstaufen (1138–1268), a name derived from the family castle Staufen, in Swabia. The Hohenstaufens were the first German dynasty to be conscious of the full historical implications of imperial tradition based on Roman law. Their consequent efforts at centralization had a particular impact on the Slavic unions in the north (Obodrites, Veletians, Ranians; see Map 5), which by the late twelfth century ceased to exist. In their place, German marks and duchies like Holstein, Mecklenburg, Brandenburg, and Pomerania were created, and the Slavic populace was Christianized and eventually Germanized.

Although part of the Holy Roman Empire, Bohemia-Moravia came to have a special status. Following chronic dynastic conflicts during the eleventh and twelfth centuries between various members of the native ruling Přemyslide dynasty, Přemysl Otakar I (r. 1198–1230) took advantage of the succession struggle in the Holy Roman Empire to transform his own Kingdom of Bohemia (with its hereditary crown since 1156) into one of the leading powers in Central Europe. Though it remained (and was a dominant force) within the Holy Roman Empire, the Kingdom of Bohemia functioned as an independent state, and after 1212 elected its own rulers.

In contrast to Hungary-Croatia and Bohemia, the Kingdom of Poland was experiencing a period of internal political weakness, with a marked decline in the power of the king in favor of the great landlords (magnates) and military gentry (szlachta). By the thirteenth century, political fragmentation had deepened, with nine provinces and duchies (indicated on the accompanying map) headed by members of the ruling Piast family but fighting among themselves

and being less able to defend the realm against the aggressive Germanic advances from the west (Brandenburg, Pomerania) and north (the Teutonic Order), including Gdańsk Pomerania, which became an independent duchy in 1227.

Politically similar to Roman Catholic Poland was Orthodox Kievan Rus', where the process of division into virtually independent principalities that had begun after the death of Iaroslav the Wise in 1054 was completed by the thirteenth century. Among the most powerful of these principalities throughout all of Kievan Rus' was Galicia-Volhynia (united at the outset of the thirteenth century). Under the Romanovych dynasty, especially during the reign of Danylo (1238–64), who was crowned king by the pope's legate in 1253, Galicia-Volhynia extended its sphere of influence down the Prut and Dniester rivers to the Black Sea (1160–1240) as well as over the traditional center of the realm, the principality of Kiev (1238–40) and Turaŭ-Pinsk (1252–54).

The newest presence in the northern part of East Central Europe was along the Baltic Sea. Returning German knights and other adventurers from the Crusades accepted an invitation from the ruler of the Polish Duchy of Mazovia to help him defeat the pagan Prussians. In return, they could retain any lands they conquered. The knights arrived in 1229, defeated the Prussians, and created a state that was known as the Teutonic Order. Together with the Livonian Knights, a similar military order farther north, the Teutonic Order put pressure on the remaining Baltic tribes farther east.

By the last decades of the thirteenth century, the Sudavians/Iatvigians were defeated by the Teutonic Order. The Zemgalians and Latvians/Latgalians met the same fate at the hands of the Livonian Order and the Selonians ceased to exist by the middle of the fourteenth century. The remnants of these Baltic peoples were absorbed by either the Latvians or the Lithuanians. While the Latvians survived as a people, they fell under the domination of the Livonian Order. On the other hand, the Lithuanians were united under the leadership of their own Prince Mindaugas (r. ca. 1240–63), who by the 1240s had succeeded in creating the basis for a Lithuanian state with its center in Trakai. His personal conversion to Christianity and the acceptance of a crown from the pope in 1254 also helped to contain temporarily the threat from the Germanic knights. Mindaugas's immediate successor and the Lithuanian population as a whole remained pagan, however, and this provided an excuse for the Teutonic and Livonian orders to continue their aggressive military campaigns ostensibly to spread the Christian faith among northern Europe's "last heathens."

The 1240s were also marked by several destructive campaigns by the Mongols. Together with the Tatar soldiers under their leadership, the Mongols were responsible for the last invasions by nomadic peoples from inner Asia —invasions that had occurred periodically since the fifth century and that more often than not had ended by ravaging large parts of East Central Europe (see Map 6a). Under Khan Batu (r. 1227–55), the Mongols swept first through the northern principalities of Kievan Rus' (1237–38). They then moved south, settling for about a year in the steppe near the bend in the Don River. From there they displaced the frightened Polovtsians (Kipchaks, Cumans), about

40,000 of whose families fled westward to Hungary, where they were settled by Hungary's rulers between the Tisza and Danube rivers (henceforth known locally as Kuns). In late 1239 the Mongols set out on a new campaign into the heart of Europe, crossing rapidly through the southern principalities of Kievan Rus' (Kiev, Galicia-Volhynia). The main force of Batu crossed Carpathian Rus' into the Hungarian Plain, while secondary Mongol forces fanned out northward into Poland and Moravia and southward into Transylvania, all eventually converging in Hungary. In 1242 Batu was suddenly recalled to the Mongol homeland, and with an expeditionary force that joined him after passing through Croatia and Serbia, he descended the Danube and headed east. The following year, the Mongols established along the lower Volga the center of a state known as the Kipchak Khanate, or Golden Horde, which came to control the lucrative trade routes that crossed the steppe north of the Black Sea and that connected Central Asia with the Crimean ports and eventually with Byzantium and the Mediterranean.

6a The Mongol invasions

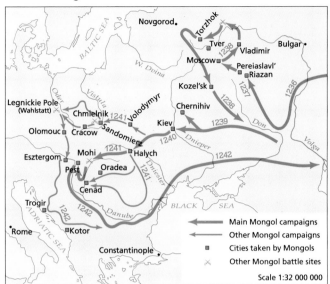

⟵	Main Mongol campaigns
←	Other Mongol campaigns
▪	Cities taken by Mongols
×	Other Mongol battle sites

Scale 1:32 000 000

Copyright © by Paul Robert Magocsi

7 Poland, Lithuania, and Bohemia-Moravia, 13th-15th centuries

Poland and Lithuania, 13th-14th centuries

The process of political fragmentation that had marked the history of Poland before 1250 continued, so that by the outset of the fourteenth century the country was reduced to its smallest territorial extent. For a while (1300–1306), Poland had even come under the rule of the Bohemian dynasty. While the country did regain its independence under Władysław I (Łokietek, r. 1305–33) and was able temporarily to recover Kuyavia and the nearby region north of Dobrzyń on the Vistula River (lost to the Teutonic Order in 1308), several other formerly Polish-ruled territories remained outside the kingdom. The northwest corner of Great Poland became the New Mark (Neumark) of Brandenburg; Pomerania (recovered briefly in the late thirteenth century) was lost first to Brandenburg and in 1309 transferred to the Teutonic Order, effectively cutting off Poland's access to the sea. Mazovia, which together with its county of Płock had by the outset of the fourteenth century regained its status as an independent Piast duchy, in 1329 came under Bohemian rule; while Silesia was divided into independent Piast duchies (Wrocław, Jawor, Świdnica, Ziębice) or duchies under the hegemony of the Kingdom of Bohemia.

Poland began to recover during the reign of Kazimierz/Casimir III (the Great, r. 1333–70), who reorganized the administration of the country (at his death there were ten palatinates, called województwa) and expanded the defense system through the construction of castles and new fortified towns. In foreign affairs he avoided conflict with the Teutonic Order in the north and the Bohemian Kingdom in the south, both of which were at their height of power. Instead, he recognized Bohemian rule over Silesia (with the exception of two small border areas) and Teutonic rule over eastern Pomerania, in return for which a peace was signed (1343) leading to Poland's recovery of Kuyavia and the Dobrzyń area, which after 1320 had been reconquered by the Teutonic Order. In 1351, he also succeeded in reincorporating into Poland Bohemian-controlled Mazovia with its county of Płock.

Essentially blocked from further expansion northward by the Teutonic Order and southwestward by Bohemia, Kazimierz turned his attention eastward, especially to the Rus' kingdom of Galicia-Volhynia (see also Map 6), whose own native ruling dynasty died out in the early fourteenth century. Reaching an accord with Hungary (which had its own claims on Galicia-Volhynia), Kazimierz acquired first the region near Przemyśl (1344), followed by the rest of Galicia (1349). Further conquests in this area included the Lithuanian-controlled Rus' lands of western Volhynia (including the Duchy of Chełm-Belz west of the Western Bug River) and western Podolia, all acquired in 1366. After Kazimierz's death in 1370, most of the lands he acquired were kept by his successors, with the exception of western Volhynia, western Podolia, and central Mazovia.

East of Poland was the Grand Duchy of Lithuania. Within a century of the death of its founder Mindaugas in 1263, Lithuania was transformed into the largest state in East Central Europe. Like Poland, Lithuania was unable to challenge seriously the Teutonic Order, which in 1237 had united with the Livonian Order, thereby surrounding Lithuania and virtually blocking its access to the Baltic Sea. Consequently, Lithuania turned eastward to the independent principalities that had formerly been part of Kievan Rus'. The only real challenge came from the Golden Horde, which since the mid-thirteenth century had extracted tribute from most of the Rus' principalities.

Into the Rus' power vacuum stepped the Grand Duchy of Lithuania, which under Gediminas (r. 1316–41) took control of the rest of the Polatsk principality, as well as Turaŭ-Pinsk, Podlachia, the Chełm-Belz regions, and Volhynia. Then, during the joint reign of Algirdas (1345–77) and Kestutis (1345–82), the Lithuanians completed their conquest of the southern lands of Kievan Rus', adding Chernihiv (1355), Novhorod-Sivers'kyi (1363), Briansk (1359), and Kiev, Pereiaslav, and Podolia (1362–63). These last conquests brought them into direct conflict with the heretofore universally feared Golden Horde, which the Lithuanians pushed back, so that by 1392 they had reached as far as the Black Sea along the shoreline west of the mouth of the Dnieper River.

The rapid Lithuanian advances also led to frequent wars with the Teutonic Order (which held Samogitia from 1398 to 1409), with Muscovy, and with Poland, which alternately ruled the Chełm-Belz lands and western Podolia in the course of the fourteenth and fifteenth centuries. Nonetheless, common concerns, especially the continual threat of the Teutonic Order, worked toward bringing Poland and Lithuania together. During the 1380s, which were marked by civil war in Lithuania and a succession crisis in Poland, a treaty was signed at Krewo between the two states (1385). According to this treaty, the Lithuanian grand duke Jogaila would become Władysław II Jagiełło, king of Poland (r. 1386–1434), in return for the conversion of the still pagan Lithuanians to Roman Catholicism and the eventual union of the two states. Lithuania's rulers and the ethnic Lithuanian population living in non-Rus' territories did become Catholic; the grand duchy, however, continued to function as an independent state.

Bohemia-Moravia, 13th-15th centuries

The Kingdom of Bohemia-Moravia continued its independent status within the Holy Roman Empire, and its

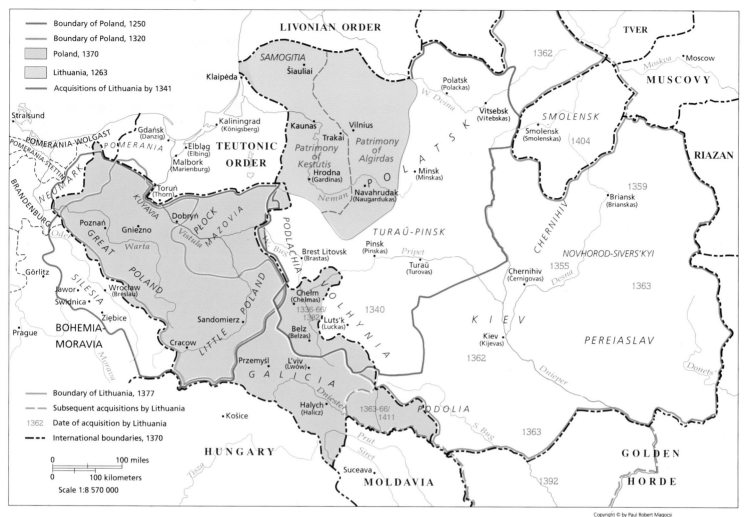

territory further expanded so that by the end of the fourteenth century it had become the leading power in central Europe. Initially, the expansive interests of Bohemia's rulers were directed southward, when in 1251, even before he became king in his own right, Přemysl Otakar II (r. 1253–78) was elected duke of Upper and Lower Austria. After becoming king he exploited the recently opened silver mines in Bohemia (Kutná Hora) and Moravia (Jihlava), which brought in significant wealth. Although in 1255 Upper Lusatia was lost to Brandenburg, Přemysl Otakar II continued the southward expansion of his realm, acquiring Styria (1260) and, during an interregnum that effectively ended the tenuous unity of the Holy Roman Empire, also Carinthia and Carniola (1269).

The changing status of the Holy Roman Empire was in part related to the policy of the new emperor, Rudolf of Habsburg (1273–91), who was primarily interested in increasing the political power of his own family beyond its original holdings in Swabia. Rudolf challenged Přemysl Otakar II's rule in Austria, Styria, Carinthia, and Carniola, and after driving him out of those areas in 1276, they became permanent Habsburg holdings and the new basis of that dynasty's growing power in the region. Consequently, by the time of his death in 1278, Přemysl Otakar II's territory was reduced to Bohemia and Moravia.

Driven from the southern "Austrian" sphere by the Habsburgs, Přemysl Otakar II's successors redirected

Bohemia's interests northward and eastward. In fact, of the last two Přemyslide rulers, Václav/Wenceslaus II (r. 1278–1305) was elected king of Poland (1300) and his son Václav/Wenceslaus III (r. 1305–6) was elected king of Hungary (1301).

Following the end of the Přemyslide dynasty (1306), the Bohemians were driven out of Poland and Hungary. The resultant interregnum ended in 1310 when Jan/Johann of Luxembourg (r. 1310–46) was elected king of Bohemia. Under the new house of Luxembourg, Bohemia was to reach its height of power and influence. The dynamic and aggressive Jan tried to regain the Polish crown for Bohemia. While he failed in this, he did manage to control for a while the duchy of Mazovia and its county of Płock (1329–51) as well as most of the Silesian duchies (between 1327 and 1355). Closer to home he also regained Upper Lusatia (1319), the region around Cheb (1322), and for a while the distant county of Tyrol (1335–42).

Under Jan's son, Karl or Charles I/IV (r. 1346–78), Bohemia entered its "golden age," with Prague becoming simultaneously the capital of the Kingdom of Bohemia and the Holy Roman Empire, of which Karl (as IV) was emperor. By the Golden Bull signed in Nürnberg in 1356, the king of Bohemia was given first place among the empire's electors. Besides the larger sphere of the Holy Roman Empire, Karl made Moravia, Silesia, and Upper Lusatia an indissoluble part of the Bohemian crownlands and he added to the

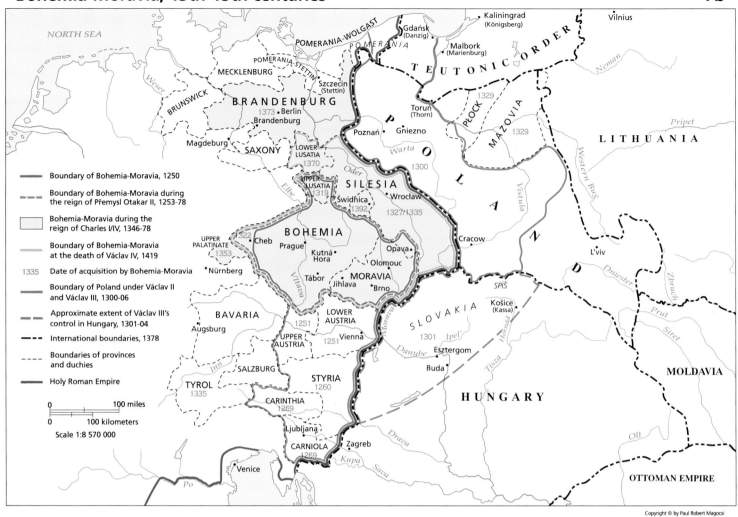

Legend (map):
- Boundary of Bohemia-Moravia, 1250
- Boundary of Bohemia-Moravia during the reign of Přemysl Otakar II, 1253-78
- Bohemia-Moravia during the reign of Charles I/IV, 1346-78
- Boundary of Bohemia-Moravia at the death of Václav IV, 1419
- 1335 Date of acquisition by Bohemia-Moravia
- Boundary of Poland under Václav II and Václav III, 1300-06
- Approximate extent of Václav III's control in Hungary, 1301-04
- International boundaries, 1378
- Boundaries of provinces and duchies
- Holy Roman Empire

0   100 miles
0   100 kilometers
Scale 1:8 570 000

Copyright © by Paul Robert Magocsi

kingdom several towns in the Upper Palatinate (1353). The era of Luxembourg rule also brought an increase in Germanic influence when, beginning in the mid-thirteenth century, large numbers of Germans were invited to settle in Bohemia-Moravia, in particular in its cities and in the mountainous borderland areas which later came to be known as the Sudetenland. It was during the last years of Karl's reign that Bohemia-Moravia also extended its influence northward into the heart of the Germanic world with the annexation of Lower Lusatia (1370) and Brandenburg (1373).

After Karl's death, the Germanic orientation began to decline. During the reign of his successor, Václav/Wenceslaus IV (r. 1378–1419), Brandenburg was lost (1411). Even more significant was the religious reform movement led by Jan Hus (1369–1415). What soon became known as the Hussite movement was characterized by a Czech nativist and anti-German orientation. With the execution of Hus (1415) and death of the king (1419), religious reform came to be fully identified with Czech national sentiment and a rejection of Germanic and Catholic influence in the country. The result

was more than a decade of conflict known as the Hussite wars (1420–33), during which four crusades led by the Holy Roman Emperor Sigismund (r. 1410–37) were sent against the Hussites. From their center at Tábor in southern Bohemia, the Hussites not only defeated the invaders but also organized six "countercrusades" that took place both within the lands of Bohemia-Moravia and well beyond—in Poland (as far as the Baltic Sea), Brandenburg, Saxony, Austria, and Hungary.

Although a compromise was finally reached, leaving the moderate wing of the Hussites to function legally in Bohemia-Moravia, the kingdom's political influence was to decline rapidly. During the reign of the last independent Bohemian ruler, the moderate Hussite Jiří Poděbrady (r. 1458–71), the kingdom was reduced to the territory of Bohemia. Its other territories—Moravia, Silesia, Upper and Lower Lusatia—by 1474 had been annexed by Mátyás Corvinus of Hungary-Croatia, who was recognized by the Catholic nobles in 1468 as king of Bohemia.

8 Hungary-Croatia and Venice, 14th-15th centuries

Hungary-Croatia

Hungary-Croatia entered the fourteenth century with the dying out of its native Árpád dynasty (1301). By that time, the nobility had already increased its political and social influence at the expense of the court. This was particularly the case after the king signed the Golden Bull (1222), which exempted the nobles from taxes and granted them freedom to dispose of their domains as they saw fit. The result was the increasing diffusion of political power during the second half of the thirteenth century, even during the reign of the otherwise able king Béla IV (1235–70). As part of his policy of reconstructing the country's defenses following the devastation caused by the Mongol invasions (1241–42), Béla IV encouraged the nobility to build castles, but these fortifications soon became bases for feudal warfare among the nobles as well as for campaigns against the king.

By the outset of the fourteenth century, the king's authority was limited for the most part to the lowland plain along the middle Danube and lower Tisza rivers. The rest of the country was divided among great magnates, or oligarchs, who ruled their holdings as virtually independent entities. During what is known as the oligarchal period in Hungarian history, the most powerful of these "little kings" were Mátyás Csák in northwestern Slovakia and László Kán in Transylvania.

The interregnum after the extinction of the Árpád dynasty lasted for nearly a decade, until 1308–10, when Charles I/ Károly (Charles Robert of Anjou, r. 1308–42) was elected king. His ascendency marked the beginning of the Angevin dynasty in Hungary. At his accession, the country not only included the lands of the Danubian basin up to the crests of the Carpathian Mountains as they enclose Slovakia, Carpathian Rus', and Transylvania, it also included the principality of Walachia (which included Severin), northern Serbia, Bosnia, and the Dalmatian coast, which it had regained from Venice.

Many of these lands were lost, however, during the approximately fifteen years it took Charles Robert to subdue the great magnates and, from his new capital at Visegrád, to consolidate royal authority throughout the whole country. The king also reformed the economy, which was enriched through the opening of new gold and silver mines in Slovakia (Kremnica, Banská Štiavnica, and others). Like his predecessors, Charles Robert invited German settlers to develop the new mines and settle the towns, where they were given self-governing privileges. It was also during the thirteenth century that organized efforts were undertaken to settle Carpathian Rus' (the old Rus' Mark/Marchia Ruthenorum) with East Slavic farmers and shepherds from neighboring Galicia.

While Charles Robert was restoring administrative and economic order within the country, Hungary-Croatia suffered some territorial losses, most especially in the south. The local ruler (voivode) of Walachia, named Basarab, set up an independent state after 1330, while Serbia extended its control northward to the Sava and Danube rivers. Meanwhile, the Dalmatian coastal region, only recently regained from Venice, was lost once again to that maritime power. In fact, the Dalmatian coast from Istria to Dubrovnik was to change hands between Venice and Hungary several times during the fourteenth and fifteenth centuries.

Hungary was able, however, to retain Croatia-Slavonia, which since 1102 had accepted the Hungarian king as its ruler. Croatia had a special status and was never considered among Hungary's "conquered lands," but rather its "annexed lands." Hungarian rulers were also crowned king of "Croatia and Dalmatia," and were represented there by an officer known as the ban or by their own relatives (sons or brothers), who were called dukes. The dukes in particular often acted as independent rulers, appointing bans and bishops, minting their own money, and convoking diets.

From the second half of the thirteenth century, Croatia had two bans, one for Croatia proper, the other for Slavonia. Under Charles Robert, Croatian judicial independence was reduced and Hungarian influence became stronger, especially in Slavonia. On the other hand, Croatia proper, in particular the cities along the Dalmatian coast (Rijeka/Fiume, Zadar/Zara, Šibenik/Sebenico, Split/ Spalato, Dubrovnik/Ragusa), continued to retain their self-governing status whether they were ruled by Hungary-Croatia or its chief rival in the area—Venice.

Under the next Angevin king, Louis/Lajos (the Great, r. 1342–82), Hungary-Croatia is said to have reached the apogee of its development. The royal capital was transferred from Visegrád to Buda, and Hungary's policy of expanding southward and eastward was revived. Before the end of Louis's reign, Hungarian sovereignty was again acknowledged by Walachia and Severin (ca. 1368), as well as for a while by Serbia and parts of northern Bulgaria. Along the Adriatic coast, the Republic of Dubrovnik (Ragusa) accepted Hungarian sovereignty in 1358, and after a long and costly war with Venice that ended in 1381, Louis was able to regain the rest of the Dalmatian coast. Yet Hungary's expansion was even more impressive in the north and east. In the late thirteenth century, Hungary had created a series of fortifications beyond the Carpathians in Moldavia more or less along the Siret River and even beyond, including what later became the cities of Kiliia near the Danubian delta and Bilhorod (Magyar: Nyeszter- fehérvár) at the mouth of the Dniester River. During Louis's reign, Moldavia recognized Hungary's suzerainty. Hungary's influence in the north was based on a dynastic arrangement (1354). Upon the death in 1370 of the Polish monarch, Kazimierz (Casimir the Great), Louis became king of

Poland. Hungary-Croatia's influence had become as large as it ever was to be.

After the death of Louis in 1382, the enormous territorial expanse of Hungary-Croatia was reduced. The Poles refused to recognize his successor, Sigismund/Zsigmond of Luxembourg (r. 1387–1437), as their king. Sigismund was also Holy Roman Emperor and, in any case, paid little attention to Hungarian affairs. In the southeast, Hungary-Croatia lost Dalmatia to Venice (1420–28). Dubrovnik, while continuing to recognize the sovereignty of Hungary-Croatia, accepted protection from the Ottoman Empire after 1440. It was also in the early fifteenth century that sixteen towns in the northern Spiš region (Spisz/Szepesség/ Zips) region of central Slovakia—near to but not including the royal Saxon towns of Kežmarok/Käsmark and Levoča/ Leutschau—were sold to Poland, under whose rule they remained from 1412 to 1772 (see Map 8a—inset).

The greatest danger to Hungary, however, came from a new source, the Ottoman Turks. Walachia (together with Severin) submitted to the Ottomans in 1417, while Bosnia, which by the outset of the fifteenth century had accepted Hungarian sovereignty, fell to the Turks in the 1460s. Although Hungarian armies under János Hunyadi—renowned throughout Europe for his defense of Belgrade in 1456—were able to stop the Turkish advance, it was clear that the country's traditional domination of large parts of the Balkans was coming to an end.

In such a situation, Hunyadi's son and Hungary's last outstanding ruler of the period, Mátyás Corvinus (r. 1458–90), turned instead his attention to the west. He was the first Hungarian ruler to create a standing army, and he hoped with its help to gain the crown of Bohemia and eventually become Holy Roman Emperor. Taking advantage of the religious conflicts in the Kingdom of Bohemia, in 1468 Mátyás undertook with papal blessing a crusade against its "heretical" Hussite king, Jiří Poděbrady. When peace was finally confirmed a decade later, the Bohemian Kingdom was divided. Mátyás acquired Moravia, Opava, Silesia, and the two Lusatias, and although he received the title "king of Bohemia," that territory itself did not become part of Hungary-Croatia. As for his ongoing quarrel with the Habsburg and Holy Roman Emperor Frederick III (elected king of Hungary-Croatia in 1439 by a faction of nobles), Mátyás was able to acquire Lower Austria and much of Styria (1478) and to transfer the capital of his expanded realm to Vienna (1485).

Venice

The remarkable growth of Venetian maritime power along the islands and coastal lands of the Adriatic, eastern Mediterranean, Aegean, and northern Black Sea was in large part the result of the crises in the Byzantine Empire at the outset of the thirteenth century. From then until the late eighteenth century, Venetian holdings on the Aegean, eastern Mediterranean, and southern Adriatic coasts were alternately to expand and contract. Venice was at first challenged by a revival of Byzantine power (after 1261), then by incursions from Angevin Naples and Aragon Sicily

(after 1267), and finally by the advance of the Ottoman Turks (beginning from the 1420s—see Map 9). Throughout this whole period Venice was to be continually challenged by its longtime rival for control of the lucrative trade with the east—Genoa.

Following a war with Genoa (1378–81) over Chioggia (a city just south of Venice), Venice was able to regain that city and thereby definitively drive its Genoese rival out of the northern Adriatic. Secure in its base along the coastal regions of the northern Adriatic coast, Venice turned to the Italian hinterland, where it systematically brought large segments of the region under its rule during the first three decades of the fifteenth century. To its previous acquisition of nearby Treviso (1339), Venice added several other city-states: Belluno, Padua, Vicenza, and Verona (1404–5); Aquileia (1421); and Brescia (1426). Subsequent acquisitions in this area included Ravenna (1441) and Rovigo just north of the Po (1482).

Along the eastern coast of the Adriatic, Venice had already held the port of Pula, the adjacent coastal region of Istria, and several Dalmatian islands. Then as a result of events connected with the Fourth Crusade (1202–4), Venice acquired several important Adriatic ports—Zadar/Zara (1202–1358), Dubrovnik/Ragusa (1204–1358), Durrës/ Durazzo (1202–68)—and the island of Corfu (1206–14), not to mention Crete and several Aegean islands (see Map 6). During the next century and a half, Venice lost many of these early Adriatic acquisitions, but by the end of the fourteenth century it was to regain Durrës/Durazzo (1392) and Corfu (1386) and add to its holdings several new ports —Butrint/Butrinto (1386), Shkodër/Scutari (1396), Párga (1401), and Kotor/Cattaro (1420)—as well as central Dalmatia.

Farther south, Venetian holdings were to change substantially in response to the revival of the Byzantine Empire in the fourteenth century and then to its final decline and the appearance of the Ottomans in the fifteenth century. Political developments in the western Balkans and Greece were particularly complex between the late thirteenth and early fifteenth centuries.

Among the early contenders for control of the region was the House of Anjou, which from its new base in the Kingdom of Sicily (Naples and Sicily) hoped to create a Mediterranean empire to succeed Byzantium. Its first advances were in the western Balkans: Corfu and the Latin kingdom of Achaia (1267), then the Greek despotate of Epirus (1272). With the conquest of Epirus, Charles I of Naples and Sicily (r. 1268–82) was crowned king of what was called Albania. Angevin rule in Albania was to last only until the return of a Byzantine despot in 1318, although the dynasty did manage to hold on to Achaia until the late fourteenth century. Nonetheless, the imperial hopes of the House of Anjou effectively ended in 1282, when Sicily seceded from the joint kingdom and placed itself under Aragon in Spain. While it is true that one descendant of the Angevins (Charles Robert) founded a powerful dynasty in Hungary-Croatia, it was the Aragonese from their new base in Sicily who were to play the more important role on the Greek mainland.

In 1303, the Byzantine emperor had engaged a company of Catalan soldiers (from Aragon) to help in the

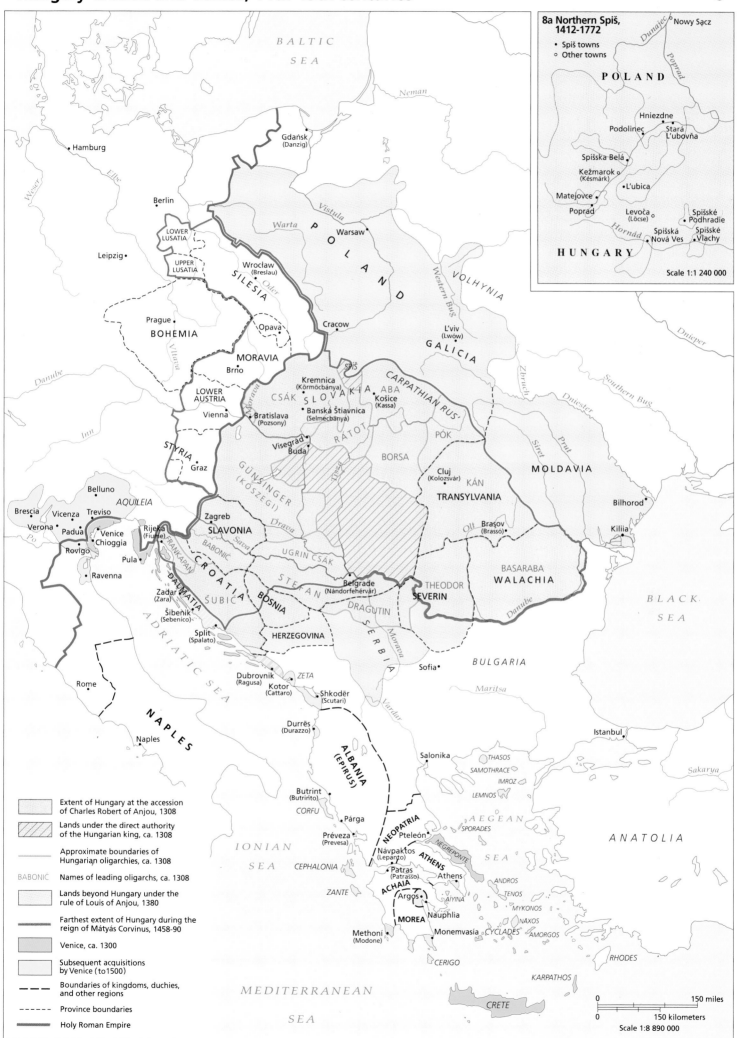

8a Northern Spiš, 1412-1772
- Spiš towns
- Other towns

Scale 1:1 240 000

Extent of Hungary at the accession of Charles Robert of Anjou, 1308

Lands under the direct authority of the Hungarian king, ca. 1308

Approximate boundaries of Hungarian oligarchies, ca. 1308

BABONIĆ Names of leading oligarchs, ca. 1308

Lands beyond Hungary under the rule of Louis of Anjou, 1380

Farthest extent of Hungary during the reign of Mátyás Corvinus, 1458-90

Venice, ca. 1300

Subsequent acquisitions by Venice (to 1500)

Boundaries of kingdoms, duchies, and other regions

Province boundaries

Holy Roman Empire

0   150 miles
0   150 kilometers
Scale 1:8 890 000

Copyright © by Paul Robert Magocsi

struggle against the Ottomans. After leading military expeditions throughout western Anatolia and the Aegean islands, the Catalan company settled in the former Latin duchy of Athens, which together with neighboring Neopatria remained until 1388 under either the direct rule of Aragon or that of its kingdom in Sicily.

With Angevin and Aragon rule entrenched in the southern Balkan mainland, the Venetian presence remained limited to the Aegean and Mediterranean islands and coastal cities. After the revival of the Byzantine Empire in the late thirteenth century, Venice lost most of the territory it had acquired after the fall of Constantinople to the Latin Crusaders in 1204 (see Map 6). Venice was, however, able to hold on to Crete, Negreponte, the southern Cyclades, and Methoní. By the second half of the fourteenth century several powerful families that were in vassalage to Venice began to recover some of their former possessions—Cerigo (1363), Amorgos (1370), and Corfu (1386). By the fifteenth century, the Byzantine threat to Venetian expansion was replaced by the challenge of the Ottoman Empire, with whom Venice fought several wars. By the time of its great war with the Ottomans (1463–79), Venice had reached the height of its territorial extent, ruling most of the islands in the northern and western Aegean as well as the coastal cities of Epirus and Morea.

Venetian acquisitions before 1500 along the eastern Adriatic and Aegean seas (Italian names stand alone or follow the slash)

Location	Duration	Location	Duration
Aíyina/Aegina	1451–1537	Monemvasía/	
Amorgos/Amorgo	1370–1446	Malvasia	1464–1540
Andros/Andro	1437–1440	Mykonos/Myconos	1390–1537
Argos/Argo	1388–1463	Nauplia	1388–1540
Athens/Atene	1394–1402	Návpaktos/Lepanto	1407–1499
Butrint/Butrinto	1386–1797	Naxos/Nasso	1437–1500
Cephalonia/		Negropont	
Cefalonia	1483–1485	(Euboea)/	
Cerigo	1363–1797	Negreponte	1209–1470
Corfu	1206–1214,	Párga	1401–1797
	1386–1797	Patras/Patrasso	1408–1419
Crete/Candia	1204–1669	Préveza/Prevesa	1499–1530
Cyclades/Cicladi	1207–1566	Pteleón/Pteleon	1323–1470
Dubrovnik/Ragusa	1204–1358	Salonika/Salonicco	1423–1430
Durrës/Durazzo	1202–1268,	Samothrace/	
	1392–1501	Samotracia	1464–1479
İmroz/Imbros	1466–1479	Shkodër/Scutari	1396–1479
Karpathos/		Šibenik/Sebenico	1412–1797
Scarpanto	1306–1538	Split/Spalato	1327–1358
Kotor/Cattaro	1420–1797	Tenos/Tino	1390–1715
Lemnos/Lemno	1464–1479	Thasos/Tasso	1464–1479
Mani/Maina	1467–1479	Zadar/Zara	1202–1358
Methoní/Modone	1206–1500	Zante	1481–1797

9 Bulgaria, Serbia, Bosnia, and the Ottoman Empire, 14th-15th centuries

With the recapture of Constantinople by the rulers of Nicaea in 1261, the Byzantine Empire was restored. In the area where Latin kingdoms and principalities had been established, Byzantine influence was gradually reinstituted (see Map 6). Among the first areas to witness a revival of Greek rule was Morea (1262), which from its center in Mistra was to become one of the great seats of late Byzantine culture. This was followed by the return of Byzantine rule, usually in the form of Greek vassals or despots, in Epirus (1318) and finally in Achaia and Athens (1430). In the Aegean Sea, most of the islands (with the exception of Crete) were by the late thirteenth century back under Byzantine control, although in Anatolia the Byzantines were unable to expand beyond the western part of the peninsula that had been held by Nicaea, because farther east they were blocked by the Turks. The reassertion of Byzantine authority coincided with a marked revival of the empire in the fourteenth century (especially during the reigns of Emperor Alexius II, 1297–1330, and John Alexius III, 1350–90), but by the outset of the fifteenth century Byzantium was in a period of irreversible decline until it ceased to exist in 1453.

The decline and fall of the Byzantine Empire was the result of internal dynastic and factional struggles as well as of a new external threat from the east—the rise in Anatolia of the Ottoman Turks. A decisive change in the political status of Anatolia came in 1243, when the Mongols defeated the Seljuk Turks, causing their once powerful Empire of Rum to disintegrate. In its stead, individual Turkic tribes established principalities in western Anatolia along the boundary with Byzantium (1260–1300). One of these was a principality that Europeans later called the Ottoman state. It was founded by Osman I (r. 1281/1300–1324) in northwestern Anatolia not far from the city of Bursa, which in the last year of his reign became the capital of the new state. From this base, the Muslim Ottomans began a program of conquests that within a century and a half saw them masters of most of Anatolia and the Balkans. In fact, by 1481 the Ottoman Empire more or less coincided with the boundaries of the Byzantine Empire as they were before its collapse in 1204.

This process of territorial acquisition began with Osman's two immediate successors. Orhan (r. 1324–60), who was the first to adopt the title sultan of the Ghazis (warriors of the faith), not only annexed the northwest corner of Anatolia but gained a foothold in Europe, across the Dardanelles in Gallipoli (1352–54). His successor, Murad I (r. 1360–89), added Thrace, Macedonia, and southern Bulgaria, while Serbia became an Ottoman vassal state following the Turkish victory at Kosovo (1389). During the next decade the rest of Bulgaria was annexed, so that it ceased to exist as an independent entity (1396); while across the Danube, Walachia had already become a Turkish vassal state in

1390. In recognition of the now firm Ottoman presence in Europe, the old Romano-Byzantine city of Adrianopolis became the new Ottoman capital of Edirne in 1402.

Byzantium's capital of Constantinople was now completely surrounded by Ottoman territory, although it continued to hold out during the reign of Sultan Murad II (r. 1421–44, 1446–51). He did, however, bring under Ottoman rule Epirus and Thessaly (minus the coastal strongholds that remained under Venice), as well as most of Serbia. It was Mehmed/Mohammed II (the Conqueror, 1451–81) who completed the final destruction of the Byzantine Empire. In 1453 he captured Constantinople. In the decades that followed he added Byzantium's only other remaining territories, the province of Morea (1458–60) and the Aegean islands of İmroz/Imbros (1470) and Lemnos (1479). The Ottomans also successfully challenged their Italian rivals in the Aegean, gaining from Genoa the islands of Thasos (1479), Samothrace (1479), Lesbos (1462), and Samos (1475). From the Venetians they took Negreponte (1470), the nearby city of Pteleón (1470), and the coastal region of southwestern Thessaly (1461–62). In the northwest, Mehmed II added the rest of Serbia (1459) and Bosnia-Herzegovina (1463–82) to his realm. Constantinople soon became the new Ottoman capital renamed Istanbul; and with the establishment of a centralist administration and elimination of local dynasties, Mehmed II came to be considered the real founder of the Ottoman Empire.

As the Ottoman state expanded into the Balkans during the fourteenth and fifteenth centuries, the alternative centers of power in the region rose and fell in a more or less chronological and geographic order that progressively moved from the southeast to the northwest. The first to feel the brunt of the Ottoman advance was Bulgaria. The Second Bulgarian Empire had reached its apogee (see Map 6) under Tsar Ivan Asen II (r. 1218–41). Bulgarian power was forever weakened, however, by the Mongol invasion of 1242. Neighboring Walachia and Moldavia came under the direct control of the Mongol Golden Horde, and the Bulgarians were forced to pay tribute to the Mongols and be subject to their destructive raids until about 1300. Bulgarian life was also marked by two other factors during the second half of the thirteenth century: (1) internal political disintegration and diffusion of power among several landlords (boyars), each of which competed for the royal crown; and (2) invasions by Byzantium from the south and by Hungary-Croatia from the north. The situation was stabilized during the reign of Todor Svetoslav (1300–1321), but soon thereafter Bulgaria lost most of its western lands, including Macedonia, to Serbia. With the decline of Serbia after 1355, those lands that had been under Serbian control came into the hands of petty rulers who set up for a time principalities based in Prilep and Velbuzhd, while in the far northeast the despotate of Dobruja became a separate entity in 1357. The rest of Bulgaria was divided into two kingdoms based in the imperial capital of Veliko Tŭrnovo and in Vidin along the Danube in the far northwest.

Beginning in the 1360s, the Ottoman Turks systematically conquered these outlying territories. By the last decade of the century, only the Veliko Tŭrnovo and Vidin kingdoms remained. When they fell respectively in 1393 and 1396, Bulgaria ceased to exist as an independent state. Bulgaria was the first Balkan state to fall to the Ottomans, who ruled it until the nineteenth century.

At the same time that Bulgaria began its decline, just to the west Serbia was becoming the new dominant power in the Balkans. Still ruled by the Nemanja dynasty, the Serbian Kingdom overcame the power of the strong secular and clerical aristocracy that had diffused central authority and caused conflicts regarding succession and inheritance.

A new period in Serbian history, which witnessed the restoration of royal authority and territorial expansion, was initiated by Stefan Uroš II (Milutin, r. 1282–1321), who acquired much of Macedonia and lands along the Adriatic. This trend was continued by Stefan Uroš III (Dečanski, r. 1321–31), who lost the Adriatic lands to the Bosnians but gained from the Bulgarians and the Byzantines control over most of the Vardar valley. The culmination of this process came under Stefan Dušan, whose reign (1331–55) is still considered the most glorious period in Serbian history. By 1344, Dušan had already doubled the size of the country he inherited, incorporating the rest of Macedonia, Albania, Epirus, and Thessaly. As part of this southward thrust, which he had hoped would eventually take him to Constantinople, Dušan made Skopje his capital and proclaimed himself emperor of the Serbs, Greeks, Bulgarians, and Albanians (1346). He enhanced further the prestige of the Serbian state by establishing at the same time a self-governing Serbian Orthodox Church ruled by its own patriarch in Peć/Ipek, a move that was first opposed but eventually accepted (1376) by the ecumenical patriarch of Constantinople. It is interesting to note that subsequent generations of Serbian patriots continued to look back to the reign of Stefan Dušan as the most glorious epoch in their history, since his conquests ostensibly established Serbia's right to all territories that formerly belonged to his empire.

Serbia's dominance over the western Balkans ended with the death of Dušan in 1355. His successor, who became the last of the Nemanja dynasty, set off to attack the heartland of the Ottomans, but in 1371 his army was routed in Thrace at a battle along the Maritsa River near Edirne. Military defeat and internal political divisiveness left Serbia open to Ottoman invasions, which culminated in 1389 with the defeat of Serbian (and Bosnian) forces and the death of the country's ruler, Lazar I (r. 1371–89), at Kosovo Polje—on the so-called field of the black birds. While Kosovo marked the end of Serbian independence, through epic folk poetry (the famous Kosovo Epic) it also became the symbol of Serbia's centuries-long struggle against foreign rule.

For over a half century following Kosovo, Serbia was ruled by local despots who became vassals of the Ottomans (see Map 9a—inset). The sphere of the Serbian despotate was progressively reduced, however, so that by the 1450s all

that remained was a small region south of the Danube with its capital at Smederevo. Then, in 1459, the Ottomans incorporated into their realm what remained of the despotate. Like Bulgaria, Serbia was not to be revived as an independent state until the nineteenth century.

With the breakup of Dušan's empire after his death in 1355, a new power center was established along the Adriatic near Lake Scutari (see Map 9a). There, the Balšić family revived the eleventh-century kingdom of Doclea, now called Zeta, and declared it an independent principality (1371). Under the Balšićes, Zeta was alternately allied or in conflict with the Serbian despotate in the north and the Venetians along the Adriatic coast. By the second half of the fourteenth century, Zeta had extended its boundaries along all four shores of Lake Scutari. In 1422, the Balšićes died out and were replaced by a new dynasty founded by Stefan Crnojević (r. 1422–65), who established the country's capital at Žabljak. His successor, Ivan Crnojević (the Black, r. 1465–90), was forced by the Ottoman advance to abandon the capital, as well as all of Zeta's territory around Lake Scutari, and move to Upper Zeta—the less accessible mountainous region around Cetinje. It was also at this time that Zeta came to be known as Montenegro (Crna Gora—the Black Mountain). From this smaller territorial base, Ivan Crnojević succeeded in resisting the Ottomans. He also established an important Orthodox monastery at his capital of Cetinje and a Cyrillic printing press at nearby Obod (1493). Finally, in 1499, the Ottomans annexed Montenegro, although their actual control of the country lasted at most a decade. While Montenegro subsequently paid tribute to the Ottomans, it was one of the few territories in the area to resist complete subordination to the Turks.

Chronologically, the last of the major Balkan power centers to come under Ottoman domination was Bosnia, a small country based originally along the upper Bosna River. Since the twelfth century, Bosnia had been a vassal state of Hungary-Croatia, which appointed local leaders, known as bans, as its representatives. It was not long before the Kotromanić family became the hereditary bans of Bosnia. For the most part, the Kotromanićes were left to rule the country by themselves and to defend it from neighboring Serbia as well as from Hungary-Croatia's own rulers (especially during the latter's efforts to stamp out Bosnia's Bogomil "heresy," which dominated Bosnian society from the late twelfth through thirteenth centuries).

Bosnia reached its apogee in the fourteenth century. Ban Stjepan II Kotromanić, who ruled from 1314 to 1353, expanded the country as far north as the Sava River, and he annexed that part of Herzegovina/Hum (together with the adjacent Adriatic coastal region) that was west of Stefan Dušan's Serbian state. Stjepan II's successor, Tvrtko I (r. 1353–91), went even further. He claimed descent from Serbia's powerful Nemanja dynasty and, in 1377, proclaimed himself king of Serbia, Bosnia, and the coastal lands. He eventually added to his title Dalmatia and Croatia as well. The energetic Tvrtko was able to follow up on some of his claims, since Bosnia's traditional rivals were each undergoing internal crises: Serbia had weak rulers after the death of Stefan Dušan (1355) and Hungary was going through an uncertain interregnum following the death of Louis of Anjou

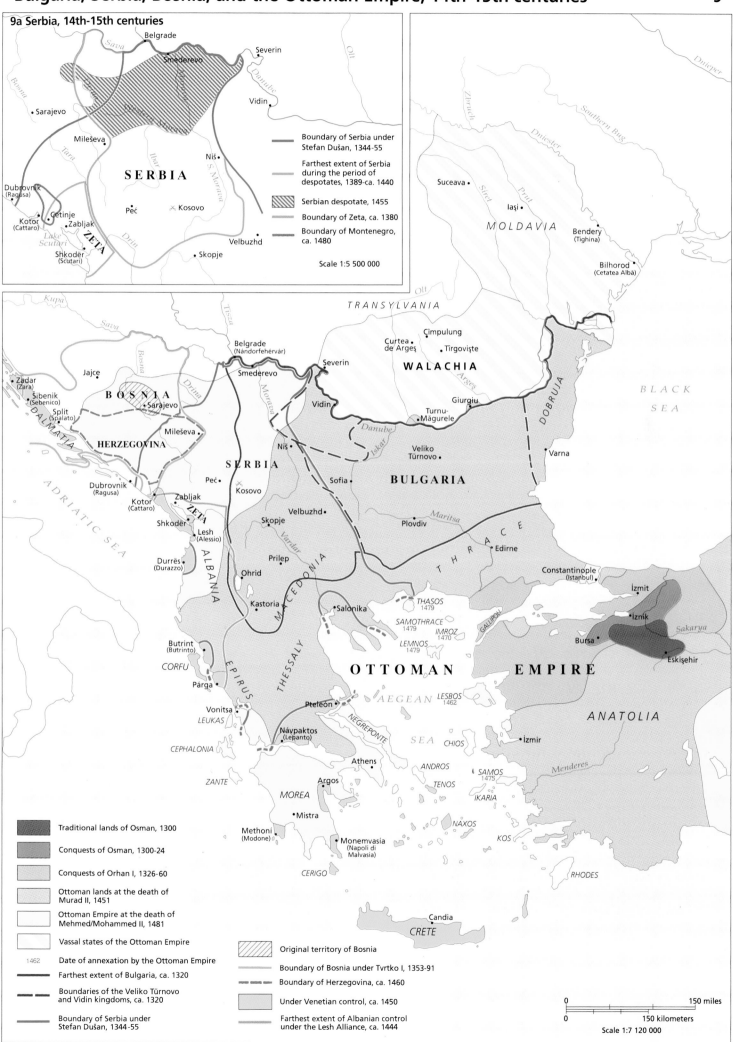

9a Serbia, 14th-15th centuries

Boundary of Serbia under
Stefan Dušan, 1344-55

Farthest extent of Serbia
during the period of
despotates, 1389-ca. 1440

Serbian despotate, 1455

Boundary of Zeta, ca. 1380

Boundary of Montenegro,
ca. 1480

Scale 1:5 500 000

Traditional lands of Osman, 1300

Conquests of Osman, 1300-24

Conquests of Orhan I, 1326-60

Ottoman lands at the death of
Murad II, 1451

Ottoman Empire at the death of
Mehmed/Mohammed II, 1481

Vassal states of the Ottoman Empire

1462 Date of annexation by the Ottoman Empire

Farthest extent of Bulgaria, ca. 1320

Boundaries of the Veliko Tŭrnovo
and Vidin kingdoms, ca. 1320

Boundary of Serbia under
Stefan Dušan, 1344-55

Original territory of Bosnia

Boundary of Bosnia under Tvrtko I, 1353-91

Boundary of Herzegovina, ca. 1460

Under Venetian control, ca. 1450

Farthest extent of Albanian control
under the Lesh Alliance, ca. 1444

0   150 miles

0   150 kilometers
Scale 1:7 120 000

Copyright © by Paul Robert Magocsi

(1382). As a result, Tvrtko annexed eastern Herzegovina, part of Serbia/Raška (as far as the monastery at Mileševa), and Dalmatia almost as far as Venice's port of Zadar. By the last decade of Tvrtko's life, Bosnia had become the major Slavic state in the Balkans.

After Tvrtko's death in 1391, most of Bosnia returned to vassal status under Hungary-Croatia. But local leaders resented their reduced status, and by the mid-fifteenth century many had allied with the advancing Ottomans against their Hungarian overlords. Consequently, it was farther south in Herzegovina/Hum that Bosnian independence was to be maintained, if only for a short while longer. There the Vukčić family, led by Stjepan Vukčić (r. 1440–66), assumed the title Duke (*Herceg*) of Saint Sava and proclaimed Herzegovina/Hum an independent state.

By the 1460s, however, the Ottomans were about to change profoundly the future of the region. In 1463 most of Bosnia along the upper Bosna and Drina rivers was annexed by the Ottoman Empire, and three years later, after the death of Stjepan Vukčić (1466), the same fate befell most of Herzegovina, although it was not until 1482 that its last stronghold was taken by the Turks. The northwestern part of Bosnia remained a vassal of Hungary-Croatia from 1464 to 1527, by which time the Ottomans annexed the region, capturing the last Bosnian-held fortress of Jajce in 1528.

In neighboring Albania, the sequence of events that led to eventual Ottoman rule was somewhat similar to Serbia and Bosnia. Albania had been part of Stefan Dušan's empire, but after the decline of Serbia during the second half of the fourteenth century, the country was divided among local Albanian warlords, none of whom was able to create a unified political entity. The Ottomans first invaded Albania between 1385 and 1395. Although they did not stay, their invasion weakened the Balšić family in neighboring Zeta/Montenegro, which gave up control of its southern lands around Shkodër. Into the resulting power vacuum along the coast stepped Venice, which through purchase and force acquired between 1392 and 1447 the ports of Durrës (Durazzo), Lesh (Alessio), Shkodër/Scutari, Kotor/Cattaro, and the coastal lands in between.

The Ottomans invaded Albania again in 1415, and by the 1430s controlled most of the hinterland south of Durrës. It was this second Ottoman presence that led to a revolt by an Albanian warlord, George Castriota (known as Iskender Bey to the Turks), who was to be known in subsequent history as Skanderbeg (1404–68). In 1444, Skanderbeg formed an alliance of Albanian leaders at Lesh, which for a few years held most of the country and which is considered by subsequent writers to represent the first Albanian state. After the Lesh Alliance broke down, Skanderbeg was able from his stronghold in northern Albania and his alliance with Montenegro to repel repeated Ottoman attacks until his death in 1468. From then until the end of the fifteenth century, all of Albania, with the exception of the coastal possessions of Venice, gradually came under Ottoman control.

Farther south, Venice continued its rule over the island of Corfu and the nearby coastal region of Epirus. The situa-tion on the islands of Leukas/Santa Maura, Cephalonia, and Zante was more complex. Since 1347, these islands had belonged to the Tocchi family, and together they formed the independent county of Cephalonia. During a prolonged struggle (1463–79 and 1499–1503) between the Ottomans and Venice for the coastal regions of Morea and Thessaly, the offshore islands changed hands several times and the Tocchi family was driven out. Venice was able to hold on to Zante (acquired in 1481) and to most of its coastal possessions in Epirus, Thessaly, and Morea; as well as to Crete and several Aegean islands. It also regained Cephalonia (1500). On the other hand, Dubrovnik, which had been a Venetian possession until 1358, remained under the nominal sovereignty of Hungary-Croatia, although it accepted Ottoman protection after 1382 and then paid annual tribute to the Turks beginning in the 1440s. With the fall of Hungary-Croatia in 1526, Dubrovnik continued to pay tribute to the Ottoman Empire, although in reality it functioned as an independent city-state.

On the other side of the Balkans, in the far northeast beyond the Danube River, Ottoman influence during this period was limited to maintaining a vassal relationship over local rulers in Walachia and Moldavia. By the late thirteenth century, Vlach/Romanian settlers from Hungarian-ruled Transylvania moved down from the mountains into the plain north of the Danube. This new land of the Vlachs —from which the name Walachia derives—was organized in 1290 as a province of Hungary, which appointed here, as elsewhere in the Balkans, its representatives known as bans. For the next century, Walachia wavered between being either fully subordinate to Hungary or virtually an independent state under powerful bans (voivodes, as they were called locally) such as Basarab I (r. 1330–40) and Mircea (the Old, r. 1386–1418). During the fifteenth century, Walachia's status continued to fluctuate: at times it was a vassal of Hungary, or a vassal of the Ottomans (for the first time in 1390), or a semi-independent state, as during the rule of the voivode Vlad II Dracul (1436–46) and his son Vlad III Ţepeş (1456–62 and 1476). Beginning in 1417, the Ottomans attached directly to their empire two parts of Walachia that gave them permanent fortifications north of the Danube—Turnu-Măgurele and Giurgiu. Finally, in 1476, following the death of Vlad III Ţepeş, Walachia became a permanent vassal state of the Ottoman Empire.

Ottoman influence over neighboring Moldavia came even later. Like Walachia, Moldavia was settled in the thirteenth century by Vlachs/Romanians from Transylvania and was governed either as a vassal—first of Poland (beginning 1387) and much later (for the first time in 1455) of the Ottomans—or by local leaders (voivodes) who were strong enough to become independent rulers. The most outstanding of these was Stefan (the Great, r. 1457–1504), who not only rejected Polish and Ottoman suzerainty but, from his capital at Suceava (1466), expanded Moldavia's sphere of influence to the mouths of the Danube and into Walachia. It was not until 1512 that Moldavia became definitively a vassal state of the Ottoman Empire.

10   East Central Europe, ca. 1480

By the end of the fifteenth century, East Central Europe had come to be dominated by five major states: Poland and Lithuania in the region north of the Carpathians; and Hungary, Venice, and the Ottoman Empire in the Danubian basin and the Balkans.

In Poland, the accession of Władysław II Jagiełło (r. 1386–1434) and his successors of the Jagiellonian dynasty ushered in a new period of growth and prosperity for the country. Allied with Lithuania through the person of the Polish king, both countries joined in the struggle against their common enemy, the Teutonic Order. The first stage in Poland's campaign to regain access to the Baltic Sea came with its victory over the Teutonic Knights at the battle of Grunwald, which took place in 1410 near the East Prussian villages of Grunwald and Tannenberg/Stębark. Despite the Polish-Lithuanian military victory, the borders did not change until another war began in 1454. When a new peace was signed in 1466, Poland gained its coveted access to the sea, regaining eastern Pomerania, which came to be called Royal Prussia, and a strip of land called Warmia right in the heart of the Order's Prussian territory. As for the Teutonic Order, it had lost Neumark to Brandenburg in 1455; then as a result of the peace treaty in 1466, its remaining lands in Prussia became a vassal state of the Polish crown.

Even though Poland and Lithuania had a dynastic alliance and the founder of the Jagiellonian dynasty and some of his successors were former Lithuanian grand dukes, the two countries continued to quarrel over their respective frontiers. Podlachia remained in Lithuania, but it increasingly came under Polish influence. As for the Chełm region and Podolia, they changed hands several times until respectively, in 1387 and 1430, they were finally incorporated into Poland (see Map 7a). Farther south, Polish influence extended even to Moldavia, which from 1387 to the mid-fifteenth century was a vassal state of Poland. In the west, Poland made smaller gains, including the duchies of Siewierz (1443), Oświęcim (1454–56), and Zator (1494) in far-eastern Silesia. Poland also acquired from Mazovia the areas around Gostynin and Rawa (1462); however, from its capital at Warsaw, the Duchy of Mazovia was to remain independent until 1526.

South of Poland, the formerly powerful Bohemian Kingdom, which had reached its apogee in the fourteenth century, was reduced by the 1470s to the territory of Bohemia (see Map 7b). It was Hungary that filled the power vacuum. The Hungarians had in the fourteenth century become the dominant force in the Balkans, controlling directly or in a vassal relationship parts or all of Bosnia, Serbia, and Walachia. But by the end of the fifteenth century the Ottomans were a formidable challenge in the area, and although the Hungarians were able to hold back the Turkish advance

at the Danube and along a line south of the Sava River, their own expansionist desires had to be directed elsewhere.

Therefore, under Mátyás Corvinus, Hungarian interests turned especially toward the west, to former Bohemian lands and the Habsburg holdings. In fact, by the time of Mátyás's death in 1490, Hungary had acquired (in 1469) the former Bohemian lands of Moravia, Silesia, and Upper and Lower Lusatia and (in 1478) Habsburg Lower Austria (with Vienna) and most of Styria.

As for the Hungarian heartland in the Danubian basin, surrounded as it was by the crescent of the Carpathian Mountains, two areas had particular territorial status —Croatia and Transylvania. Croatia (together with Slavonia) was a distinct kingdom, each of whose two parts maintained separate diets. Croatia continued its separate status, but after 1442 Slavonia started sending its deputies to the Hungarian diet, and this began a process that was to reduce its particular status. On the other hand, Transylvania continued and even enhanced its autonomous status. As a result of a major peasant rebellion in 1437, Transylvania's three legally recognized estates or "nations"—the Magyars, the Saxons, and the Székelys—decided to unite to preserve their leading position in society. The result was the Union of Three Nations, which was successful in maintaining special privileges and social status in its own community while also enjoying guarantees of local self-rule within Hungary as a whole, in the form of the Transylvanian diet.

By the close of the fifteenth century, the most notable change in the territorial status of East Central Europe was to be found in the southern Balkans that had once belonged to the Byzantine Empire, the Bulgarian Empire, and more ephemeral states like the Latin kingdoms, Serbia, and Bosnia. The change in this area was the result of a remarkable expansion by the Ottoman Turks. Beginning in the early fourteenth century as a tiny territory in northwestern Anatolia (between Eskişehir and Nicaea), this empire by the end of the fifteenth century had reached the Danube River and beyond (see Map 9).

The first major power to fall to the Ottomans was Bulgaria, followed by what remained of Byzantium (mainly Constantinople and Morea, 1453 and 1460), Serbia (1459), Bosnia (1463), and Herzegovina (1466–82). Ottoman influence also extended to the Republic of Dubrovnik, from which (beginning in the 1440s) it received an annual tribute, and to Walachia, which was an Ottoman vassal state periodically from the late fourteenth century until it came under definitive Turkish control in 1476. Moldavia began a similar relationship with the Ottomans as of the mid-fifteenth century, although it did not come under direct Turkish control until 1512. The Montenegrins in their tiny principality of Zeta managed to remain free of direct Turkish

International boundaries
Boundaries of duchies and vassal states
Provincial boundaries
Holy Roman Empire
Ecclesiastical states

0   150 miles
0   150 kilometers
Scale 1:8 890 000

Copyright © by Paul Robert Magocsi

control, even though they had vassal status after 1499.

The only major power to challenge the Ottoman advance successfully was Venice. Ever since the first fall of Byzantium in 1204 and the final fall in 1453, Venice had been able to hold or reacquire most of the islands in the southern Aegean —either through its leading families or in a vassal status as the Duchy of Naxos—as well as the coastal strongholds in Morea, Epirus, and Albania. Farther north, Venice continued to maintain its control of the Dalmatian coast and to expand into the north Italian hinterland.

11 Economic patterns, ca. 1450

The development of East Central Europe during the later medieval period can be viewed as the history of individual cities as well as the changing fate of the empires, kingdoms, and duchies in which those cities were located. In a real sense, the period from the thirteenth to fifteenth centuries witnessed the evolution of cities into distinct entities, set off somewhat like islands from the surrounding countryside. Not only did these urban islands acquire various degrees of political autonomy and become centers of economic wealth through trade and manufacture, but their inhabitants were usually different in origin from the people living in the surrounding countryside. Most often, East Central European cities were developed by Jews, Greeks, and Armenians, who were invited to settle there. But by far the most important of these "immigrant developers" were the Germans, whose appearance marked the foundation of numerous cities in East Central Europe (see Map 12f).

For the most part, East Central Europe's cities had smaller populations than their counterparts either farther west (Germany, Italy, France, etc.) or east (Muscovy). While the region did include one of the two cities in Europe that could boast over 200,000 inhabitants—Constantinople/Istanbul (the other being Paris)—the region's other five largest cities were much smaller: Wrocław/Breslau and Prague had less than 100,000 inhabitants each; Gdańsk/Danzig, Vienna, and Salonika less than 50,000 inhabitants each.

The small size of East Central Europe's cities was demographically paralleled in the rural countryside. Of the areas in Europe that had the highest concentrations of rural settlement, only a few areas were in East Central Europe: the Elbe and Spree valleys in Brandenburg; the Oder valley in Silesia; parts of the Warta and Pilica valleys in central Poland; the Baltic coast near the lower Vistula in East Prussia; the upper Dniester valley in Galicia; the Váh and lower Morava valleys in Slovakia; the Hungarian Plain west of the Danube; and the upper valley of the Olt River in south-central Transylvania.

East Central Europe had a wide variety of mineral resources and agricultural products. Some of the materials produced or extracted were processed and consumed domestically, but increasing amounts were exported to central and western Europe. Among the most valuable of the minerals were the gold and silver of Bohemia, Moravia, Slovakia, Transylvania, and Serbia, and the salt of southeastern Poland and Transylvania. By the fifteenth century, grain was becoming increasingly important in Polish lands, not only as a staple to support a growing population but as a source of revenue from trade with central and western Europe. Poland's grain trade was to become of particular importance in the sixteenth century.

Looking at the Continent as a whole, it could be said that by the fifteenth century East Central Europe, with its smaller number of cities and population, had already become primarily a source of raw materials for the more economically developed and heavily populated centers in Germany, northern Italy, and farther west. It is not surprising, therefore, that the main trade routes across the region ran for the most part in an east-west direction, such as from Smolensk and Vilnius to the Baltic Sea; from Kiev through central Poland to central Germany; or from the Black Sea coast and Transylvania to Cracow, Vienna, and beyond. It was along these east-west trade routes north of the Carpathians that three of Europe's major trade fairs were held at least once each year—at Poznań, Wrocław, and Lublin.

South of the Carpathians, international trade with the rest of the Continent was worse off. Whereas the north-south land route from Vienna and Buda to Salonika and Constantinople/Istanbul had long been important, the advance of the Ottoman Turks during the fourteenth and fifteenth centuries had disrupted and altered the traditional pattern of land trade in East Central Europe south of the Danube. For instance, access to the Hungarian Plain for goods from Constantinople was more likely to be via Black Sea ports and across Walachia, Moldavia, and Transylvania than via the north-south Salonika-Buda-Vienna route.

Maritime trade was dominated in the north by the Hanseatic League and in the south by Venice and to a lesser degree by Dubrovnik and Genoa. The Hanseatic League, or Hansa (from the medieval German word *Hanse*, meaning guild or association), was an organization founded in the 1280s by north German and Rhineland towns and commercial groups to defend their trading interests. They protected those interests by eliminating pirates and brigands along their Baltic trade routes, by promoting safe navigation practices and building lighthouses, and by establishing commercial enclaves and depots in foreign towns. The high point of Hanseatic activity was from the late thirteenth to fifteenth centuries, when the league included over one hundred cities and towns. Two of the five major Hanseatic cities were in the east: Gdańsk/Danzig and Riga (just to the north of the accompanying map). The other three were Lübeck, Hamburg, and Brunswick. By the fourteenth century, the Hansa had come to dominate international trade in East Central Europe north of the Carpathians, with cities like Kaliningrad/Königsberg, Elbląg/Elbing, Toruń/Thorn, Szczecin/Stettin, Frankfurt an der Oder, Wrocław/Breslau, and Cracow belonging to the League, and others farther east having Hanseatic commercial offices (*Kontore*) and counting houses (*Faktoreien*) —Warsaw, Volodymyr, and L'viv/Lwów in southeast Poland and Kaunas, Vilnius, Polatsk, Vitsebsk, and Smolensk in northeastern Lithuania.

In the Adriatic, Aegean, and eastern Mediterranean, Venice continued to be the dominant trading power, whose sea routes were connected by Venetian-held ports along the eastern Adriatic, the Greek peninsula, many Aegean

Map legend:

More than 200 000 people
100 000–200 000
50 000–99 999
20 000–49 999
10 000–19 999
• Fewer than 10 000 people

Areas of heaviest rural settlement
Major trade routes
Other important trade routes
Navigable rivers
Major sea routes
Sea routes of the Hanseatic League
GDANSK Main centers of the Hanseatic League
Rostock Other centers of the Hanseatic League
Venice Foreign commercial offices and other foreign depots of the Hanseatic League
Trade fair cities

A	Alum
Am	Amber
C	Copper
G	Gold
I	Iron
L	Lead
Q	Quicksilver
S	Salt
Si	Silver
T	Tin

Scale 1:8 890 000

0   150 miles
0   150 kilometers

islands, and Crete. In particular, Venice was interested in trade connecting the hinterlands of its coastal holdings with Constantinople/Istanbul and beyond to the northern shores of the Black Sea and the Crimea, or southward past Crete and Rhodes to Cyprus, the Near East, and Egypt. In turn, Venice acted as an emporium from which goods from the East were sent to central and East Central Europe, in particular along the so-called Venice land route (Venezian-erstrasse) that led north across the Alps through the Tarvisio, Zirbitz, and Semmering passes to Vienna. Dubrovnik/Ragusa was to become a rival to Venice in the sea trade. But Dubrovnik also had other commercial interests and dominated trade in the western Balkans, where several mining centers, such as Novo Brdo, became virtual colonies of the Adriatic seaport.

12 The city in medieval times

Wrocław/Breslau, Cracow, Vienna, Prague, and Dubrovnik/Ragusa

Since the largest number of inhabitants lived in the northern half of East Central Europe, it is not surprising that by the fifteenth century that is where the largest number of the region's cities were to be found. It is also the area in which the largest number of German immigrants settled, whose presence is directly related to the growth of cities.

The eastward colonization of Germans (see Map 32b) was encouraged by rulers in Poland, Bohemia, and Hungary. At various times between the thirteenth and fifteenth centuries, Polish, Bohemian, and Hungarian kings invited Germans, known for their more advanced economic and technical skills, to settle in cities, to develop mines, and to work the land. As an incentive, the Germans were given various economic and political privileges. Among these was the right to urban self-rule.

In fact, even though cities in the northern part of East Central Europe had been centers of habitation and commerce going back in some cases to the ninth and tenth centuries, it is the granting of privileges known as the German law that is considered to represent the time when these cities were founded. Therefore, the "birth" of most cities in the northern half of East Central Europe took place during the thirteenth and fourteenth centuries.

In central and western Europe, cities had become entities in which three elements coexisted: the rulers and their administration (secular or religious); the merchants and tradesmen; and the townsmen. This particular type of city was brought to the northern half of East Central Europe with the German colonization. Places like Wrocław/Breslau, Cracow, Prague, and Vienna graphically reveal in their layout the basic elements that made up these "new" cities.

One part contained the oldest seat of the local rulers (the *Burg*), which was often set off geographically on a hill or separated by a river. This area was dominated by the ruler's residence (secular or religious) and the cathedral church. Another part was the city proper, built around a central market square (*Marktplatz*), or ring (*Ring/rynek/náměstí*), where the wealthiest merchants resided, where tradesmen conducted their business, and where a church was either built or restored to serve specifically this element of the city's population. Around the ring, streets fanned out in a grid or in concentric circles (semicircles if the city was on a river), and along these and other cross streets were built the residences of artisans and other townsmen. The city was surrounded by a wall and/or moat with gates that may have been entirely new or a continuation or enlargement of an earlier defense system.

This "German" pattern was in stark contrast to cities in the southern half of East Central Europe, which more often than not had continued uninterruptedly their urban existence since the Roman Empire or even classical Greece.

By the medieval period, it was cities along the Adriatic and Aegean coasts that were most important, and like Dubrovnik/Ragusa (Ragusium in classic times) they frequently followed the Italianate, specifically Venetian, model. Whereas Dubrovnik nearly tripled its size by expansion in the second half of the twelfth century, the ruling structure of the "new" as well as "old" city remained the same. It consisted of a small group of wealthy patrician families (seventy-eight by the end of the fourteenth century), who for centuries dominated both the economic and political life of the city. The very land of the city belonged either to the patricians or to the church.

The development of German law cities

In the northern half of East Central Europe, German colonists brought not only models of urban layout but also legal models that formed the basis of their privileged status. This meant that alongside the older rulers still resident in the city (secular dukes or Catholic bishops), the Germans could within their "new" cities direct their economic activity and govern themselves through an elected city council (Magistrat) without interference from the local temporal or secular ruler. They also had their own courts which dealt with criminal and some civil matters, and sometimes their own military forces. Whereas these privileges were initially limited to Germans, they were gradually extended to all inhabitants of the "new" city.

These privileges came to be known popularly as the German city law (Deutsches Stadtrecht) or German municipal concerns (Deutsches Städtewesen). German law consisted of three basic types derived from earlier twelfth-century models in Lübeck, Magdeburg, and Nürnberg-Vienna. Several variants of these three models developed in East Central Europe, as depicted on the accompanying map.

Lübeck Law in the far north was adopted by several Baltic seaports (Lübeck, Rostock, Kołobrzeg/Kolberg, Gdańsk/Danzig) and by cities in the immediate hinterland (Koszalin/Köslin, Elbląg/Elbing, Braniewo/Braunsberg) whose urban inhabitants were concerned primarily with maritime trade. Magdeburg Law (No. 7 on the accompanying map) covered a broad expanse in the middle region and included several variants: the most widespread was the Neumarkt-Magdeburg Law in Poland, Silesia, Lithuania, Ukraine, and northern Slovakia; the Kulm/Chełmno Law (No. 6) in the lands of the Teutonic Order and Mazovia; the Leitmeritz/Litoměřice Law (No. 12) in northern Bohemia; and the Olmütz/Olomouc Law (No. 15) in northern Moravia. Finally, there was the South German Law, based largely on the models of either Nürnberg or Vienna. Nürnberg Law formed the basis for the Eger Law (No. 10) and the Old Prague Law (No. 11). It should be noted that

12a Wrocław/Breslau, ca. 1300

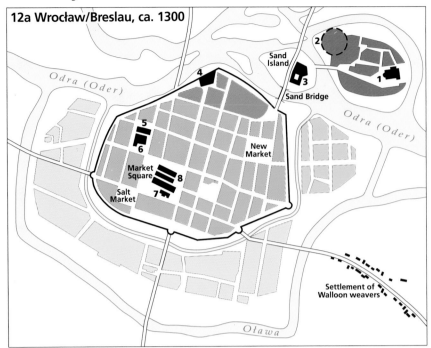

Odra (Oder)

Sand Island

Sand Bridge

4

2

3

1

5

6

New Market

Market Square

8

7

Salt Market

Settlement of Walloon weavers

Ołava

Copyright © by Paul Robert Magocsi

Wrocław/Breslau

- The oldest settlement
- Ducal sector (Burg)
- The City, 1241
- The New City, 1263
- Expansion of the city during the 2nd half of the 13th century
- Walls and gates of the city, 1241

1 Cathedral

2 Site of the oldest ducal castle

3 Monastery of the Blessed Virgin

4 Ducal castle

5 Butchers' stalls

6 Church of St. Elizabeth

7 City hall (Rathaus)

8 Cloth hall and merchants' stalls

12b Cracow, ca. 1350

Market Square

5 6 7

Small Market

3 4

2 1

Old Vistula

Market Square

Vistula

Copyright © by Paul Robert Magocsi

Cracow

- Royal palace (Wawel)
- Cracow (Biskupi) before 1241
- The City, 1257
- Okół, annexed in the late 13th century
- Stradom, originally the castle's town, annexed in the early 14th century
- Kazimierz, royal town founded by Casimir the Great, 1335
- Kleparz, suburb founded 1366
- Walls and gates of the city, ca. 1300

1 Royal palace

2 Cathedral

3 Franciscan church and monastery

4 Dominican church and monastery

5 City hall (Rathaus/Ratusz)

6 Cloth hall and merchants' stalls

7 Church of the Virgin Mary

All the maps are at the same scale

0   1000 feet

0   250 meters

Scale 1:14 000

12c Vienna, ca. 1300

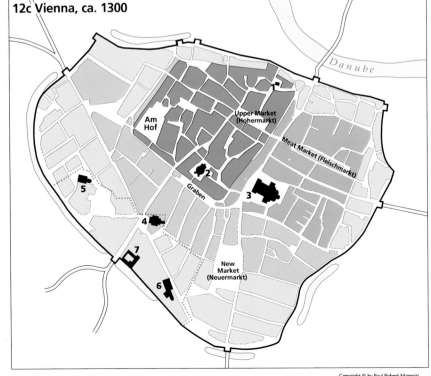

Danube

Am Hof

Upper Market (Hohermarkt)

Meat Market (Fleischmarkt)

5

2

Graben

4

3

7

New Market (Neuermarkt)

6

Copyright © by Paul Robert Magocsi

Vienna

- The oldest settlement, ca. 1000
- Expansion of the city by 1150
- Expansion of the city by 1175
- Expansion of the city by 1200
- City walls and gates, ca. 1200
- Castle district (Hofburg) after 1270s

1 Church of St. Rupert

2 Church of St. Peter

3 Church of St. Stephen

4 Church of St. Michael

5 Church of the Minorite Friars

6 Church of St. Augustine

7 Castle (Hofburg)

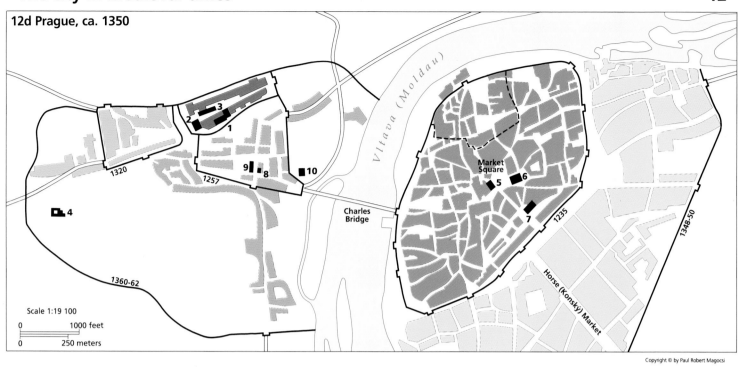

12d Prague, ca. 1350

Scale 1:19 100

0 — 1000 feet

0 — 250 meters

Copyright © by Paul Robert Magocsi

12e Dubrovnik/Ragusa, ca. 1475

Scale 1:4 800

0 — 250 feet

0 — 100 meters

Copyright © by Paul Robert Magocsi

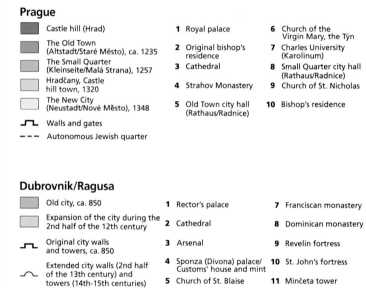

Prague

■	Castle hill (Hrad)
■	The Old Town (Altstadt/Staré Město), ca. 1235
■	The Small Quarter (Kleinseite/Malá Strana), 1257
■	Hradčany, Castle hill town, 1320
■	The New City (Neustadt/Nové Město), 1348
⊓	Walls and gates
- - -	Autonomous Jewish quarter

1 Royal palace
2 Original bishop's residence
3 Cathedral
4 Strahov Monastery
5 Old Town city hall (Rathaus/Radnice)

6 Church of the Virgin Mary, the Týn
7 Charles University (Karolinum)
8 Small Quarter city hall (Rathaus/Radnice)
9 Church of St. Nicholas
10 Bishop's residence

Dubrovnik/Ragusa

■	Old city, ca. 850
■	Expansion of the city during the 2nd half of the 12th century
⊓	Original city walls and towers, ca. 850
⌒	Extended city walls (2nd half of the 13th century) and towers (14th-15th centuries)
- - -	Shoreline before 1250

1 Rector's palace
2 Cathedral
3 Arsenal
4 Sponza (Divona) palace/ Customs' house and mint
5 Church of St. Blaise
6 St. Claire's convent

7 Franciscan monastery
8 Dominican monastery
9 Revelin fortress
10 St. John's fortress
11 Minčeta tower

Prague's newer city, the Malá Strana (Small Quarter) on the left bank of the Vltava River, followed the Leitmeritz Law. Vienna Law formed the basis of the Brünn/Brno Law (No. 14) as well as for cities throughout Austria and most of Hungary-Croatia, where it was known simply as the South German Law.

Sandwiched in between the Lübeck, Magdeburg, and South German models were a few local systems (Görlitz Law, Löwenberg/Lwówek-Śląski Law, Neisse/Nysa Law, Leobschütz/Głubczyce Law), which were limited to small areas or were developed for specific concerns. Among the latter was the Iglau/Jihlava Law (No. 13), which served as a model for mining towns not only in Bohemia (Kutná Hora/Kuttenberg) and Moravia (Jihlava/Iglau) but also in northern Slovakia (Kremnica/Kremnitz) and Transylvania (Sebeş/Mühlbach, Sibiu/Hermannstadt).

The spread of German law throughout the northern half of East Central Europe generally moved in a west-east direction, beginning in lands closest to Germany and then following the gradual eastward expansion of Poland, Lithuania, and Hungary. Thus the first appearance of German law in East Central Europe came during the early thirteenth century in three areas: (1) along the lower Vistula River in lands then under the control of the Teutonic Order; (2) along the upper Oder valley in Silesia, where the German inhabitants were able to obtain self-rule from a weakened Polish state; and (3) in Bohemia (Prague/Prag, Litoměřice/Leitmeritz) and Moravia (Brno/Brünn, Olomouc/Olmütz) under Václav/Wenceslaus I (r. 1230–53) and in western Hungary-Croatia (Sopron/Ödenburg, Buda, Pest, Székesfehérvár, Pécs/Fünfkirchen, Vukovar, Varaždin/Warasdin, Zagreb/Agram) under Béla IV (r. 1235–70). The rulers in both those kingdoms had initiated large-scale German immigration into their respective realms.

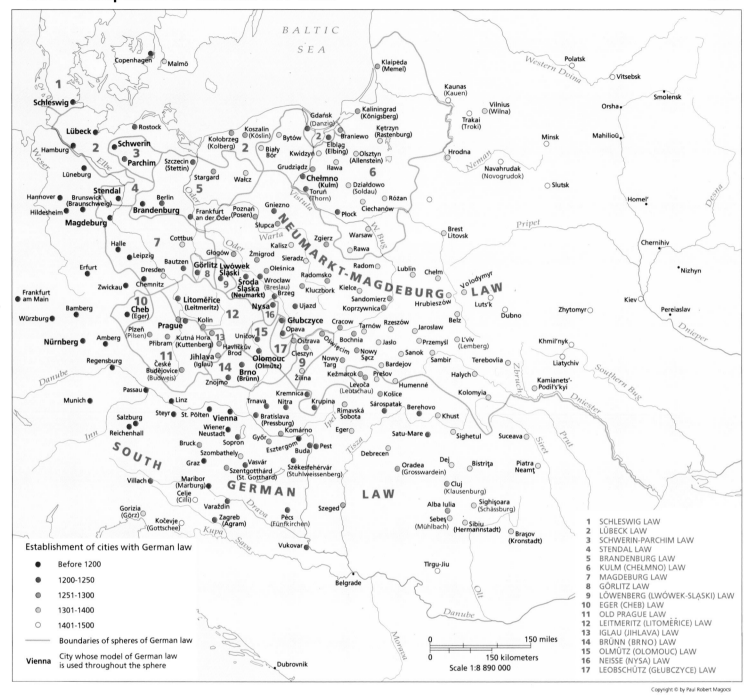

Establishment of cities with German law

- ● Before 1200
- ● 1200–1250
- ● 1251–1300
- ○ 1301–1400
- ○ 1401–1500
- — Boundaries of spheres of German law
- *Vienna* City whose model of German law is used throughout the sphere

1 SCHLESWIG LAW
2 LÜBECK LAW
3 SCHWERIN-PARCHIM LAW
4 STENDAL LAW
5 BRANDENBURG LAW
6 KULM (CHEŁMNO) LAW
7 MAGDEBURG LAW
8 GÖRLITZ LAW
9 LÖWENBERG (LWÓWEK-ŚLĄSKI) LAW
10 EGER (CHEB) LAW
11 OLD PRAGUE LAW
12 LEITMERITZ (LITOMĚŘICE) LAW
13 IGLAU (JIHLAVA) LAW
14 BRÜNN (BRNO) LAW
15 OLMÜTZ (OLOMOUC) LAW
16 NEISSE (NYSA) LAW
17 LEOBSCHÜTZ (GŁUBCZYCE) LAW

Scale 1:8 890 000

The advance of German law was especially evident in fourteenth-century Poland. This was connected with the acquisitions of Kazimierz/Casimir III (the Great, r. 1333–70), most especially in Mazovia (Warsaw/Warschau, Dział-dowo/Soldau), Galicia (Jarosław/Jaroslau, Sanok, Przemyśl, L'viv/Lemberg), and Volhynia (Belz, Volodymyr/Włodzimierz Wołyński). It was also during the fourteenth century that Transylvania's leading cities (Braşov/Kronstadt, Sighişoara/Schässburg, Bistriţa/Bistritz) began functioning under German law, even though self-governing privileges had been awarded by Hungary's rulers to the "Saxons" of Transylvania as early as 1224.

The fifteenth century witnessed the further spread of German law eastward into Lithuania (Kaunas/Kauen, Navahrudak/Novogrudok, Polatsk, Vitsebsk/Witebsk, Minsk, Kiev/Kiew), although in that country, which included present-day Belarus and Ukraine, it was not the presence

of German colonists that made such privileges possible. Rather, Lithuania was at the time adopting Polish models in its administration, and this included the Neumarkt/Środa Śląska variant of the Magdeburg Law that had already been instituted throughout most of Poland. Lithuania continued in the sixteenth century to grant German law to cities on the far-eastern borderlands of its realm. When, during the following century, Poland-Lithuania lost some of its eastern territory in the Dnieper River valley to Muscovy, the tsarist government reaffirmed—or granted for the first time—the privileges of Magdeburg Law to its newly acquired cities (Kiev, Smolensk, Orsha, Mahilioŭ, Homel', Chernihiv, Nizhyn, Pereiaslav, and others). Magdeburg Law was to remain in force throughout Muscovite and later Russian-controlled territory (that is, eventually Lithuania, Belarus, Ukraine, and Poland minus Galicia) until the 1830s.

Variants of German law (names after slash are in German; dates indicate year when law was introduced)

1. SCHLESWIG LAW
   Schleswig

2. LÜBECK LAW
   Braniewo/Braunsberg (1254)
   Elbląg/Elbing (1217)
   Gdańsk/Danzig
   Hamburg
   Kołobrzeg/Kolberg (1255)
   Koszalin/Köslin (1266)
   Lübeck (1143)
   Rostock (1218)

3. SCHWERIN-PARCHIM LAW
   Parchim (1225)
   Schwerin (1160)

4. STENDAL LAW
   Stendal

5. BRANDENBURG LAW
   Berlin
   Brandenburg (1170)
   Frankfurt an der Oder (1253)
   Stargard/Stargard in
     Pommern (1253)
   Szczecin/Stettin (1243)
   Wałcz/Deutsch-Krone (1303)

6. KULM (CHEŁMNO) LAW
   Biały Bór/Baldenburg
     (1382)
   Bytów/Bütow (1346)
   Chełmno/Kulm (1231)
   Ciechanów/Ciechanow
     (1400)
   Działdowo/Soldau (1344)
   Grudziądz/Graudenz (1291)
   Iława/Deutsch-Eylau (1305)
   Kaliningrad/Königsberg
     (1286)
   Klaipėda/Memel (1258)
   Kwidzyń/Marienwerder
     (1233)
   Olsztyn/Allenstein (1348)
   Płock/Plozk (1237)
   Rawa
   Różan/Rozan (1378)
   Toruń/Thorn (1231)
   Warsaw/Warschau (1334)

7. MAGDEBURG LAW
   Bautzen
   Chemnitz
   Cottbus
   Dresden (1216)
   Halle
   Leipzig (ca. 1160)
   Magdeburg

8. GÖRLITZ LAW
   Görlitz/Zgorzelec

9. LÖWENBERG (LWÓWEK-ŚLĄSKI)
     LAW
   Cieszyn/Teschen (1374)
   Lwówek Śląski/Löwenberg
   Oświęcim/Auschwitz
   Žilina/Sillein (ca. 1312)

10. EGER (CHEB) LAW
    Cheb/Eger (1266)

11. OLD PRAGUE LAW
    České Budějovice/Budweis
      (1251)
    Plzeň/Pilsen (1298)
    Prague/Prag (ca. 1230)
    Příbram/Przibram

12. LEITMERITZ (LITOMĚŘICE) LAW
    Kolín/Kolin (1261)
    Litoměřice/Leitmeritz (1230)

13. IGLAU (JIHLAVA) LAW
    Havlíčkův Brod/Deutsch-Brod
    Jihlava/Iglau (1249)
    Kremnica/Kremnitz (1328)
    Kutná Hora/Kuttenberg
    Prague/Prag-Malá Strana (1267)
    Sebeş/Mühlbach
    Sibiu/Hermannstadt (1224)

14. BRÜNN (BRNO) LAW
    Brno/Brünn (1243)
    Znojmo/Znaim

15. OLMÜTZ (OLOMOUC) LAW
    Olomouc/Olmütz (1261)
    Ostrava/Ostrau
    Uničov/Mährisch-Neustadt
      (1223)

16. NEISSE (NYSA) LAW
    Nysa/Neisse

17. LEOBSCHÜTZ (GŁUBCZYCE)
    Głubczyce/Leobschütz

18. NEUMARKT (ŚRODA ŚLĄSKA)-
      MAGDEBURG LAW
    Bardejov/Bartfeld (1320)
    Belz (1377)
    Bochnia (1253)
    Brest Litovsk/Brest Litowsk
      (1390)
    Brzeg/Brieg (1248)
    Chełm/Cholm (1392)
    Cracow/Krakau (1257)
    Dubno (1507)
    Głogów/Glogau (1253)
    Gniezno/Gnesen
    Halych/Halicz
    Hrodna/Grodno (1391)
    Hrubieszów/Hrubieszow
      (1400)
    Humenné/Hommenau
    Jarosław/Jaroslau (1351)
    Jasło/Jaslo (1366)
    Kalisz/Kalisch (1282)
    Kamianets'-Podil's'kyi/
      Kamenez Podolsk (1374)
    Kaunas/Kauen (1408)
    Khmil'nyk/Chmelnik (1448)
    Kielce
    Kiev/Kiew (1494)
    Kluczbork/Kreuzburg in
      Oberschlesien (1253)
    Kolomyia/Kolomea (1405)
    Koprzywnica/Kopreinitz
      (1268)
    Krupina/Karpfen (1238)
    L'viv/Lemberg (1356)
    Lublin (1317)
    Luts'k/Luzk (1432)
    Minsk (1496)
    Navahrudak/Novogrúdok
    Nowy Sącz/Neu Sandez
    Nowy Targ/Neumarkt (1346)
    Oleśnica/Oels (1255)
    Opava/Troppau (1273)
    Polatsk/Polozk
    Poznań/Posen (1253)
    Przemyśl/Przemysl (1353)
    Radom
    Radomsko/Radomsk
    Rzeszów/Rzeszow (1354)
    Sambir/Sambor (1390)
    Sandomierz/Sandomir
    Sanok (1339)
    Sieradz/Schieratz
    Słupca/Slupca (1296)
    Slutsk/Sluzk (1441)
    Środa Śląska/Neumarkt
      (1211)
    Tarnów/Tarnow (1328)
    Terebovlia/Trembowla (1389)
    Trakai/Troki
    Ujazd/Ujest (1223)
    Vilnius/Wilna (1387)
    Vitsebsk/Witebsk (1547)
    Volodymyr/Wladimir Wolynsk
      (before 1324)
    Wrocław/Breslau (1261)
    Zhytomyr/Shitomir (1444)
    Zgierz
    Żmigród/Trachenberg (1253)

19. SOUTH GERMAN LAW
    Alba Iulia/Karlsburg
    Amberg
    Berehovo/Beregszász (1342)
    Bistriţa/Bistritz
    Braşov/Kronstadt
    Bratislava/Pressburg (1291)
    Bruck
    Buda/Ofen (ca. 1350)
    Celje/Cilli
    Cluj/Klausenberg
    Dej/Desch
    Eger/Erlau
    Esztergom/Gran
    Gorizia/Görz (1307)
    Graz (1281)
    Győr/Raab
    Kežmarok/Käsmark
      (1269)
    Khust/Hust
    Kočevje/Gottschee
    Komárno/Komorn
    Košice/Kaschau (ca. 1249)
    Levoča/Leutschau
    Linz (1241)
    Maribor/Marburg
    Munich
    Nitra/Neutra (1248)
    Nürnberg
    Oradea/Grosswardein
    Passau
    Pécs/Fünfkirchen
    Pest
    Piatra Neamţ
    Prešov/Preschau (1299)
    Regensburg
    Reichenhall
    Rimavská Sobota/Gross-
      Steffelsdorf
    St. Pölten
    Salzburg
    Sárospatak
    Satu-Mare/Sathmar
    Sighetul/Marmarosch
      Sziget
    Sighişoara/Schässburg
    Sopron/Ödenburg
    Steyr
    Suceava/Sutschawa
    Szeged/Szegedin
    Székesfehérvár/
      Stuhlweissenburg
    Szentgotthárd/
      St. Gotthard
    Szombathely/
      Steinamanger
    Tîrgu-Jiu
    Trnava/Tyrnau (1238)
    Varaždin/Warasdin
    Vasvár/Eisenburg
    Vienna
    Villach
    Vukovar
    Wiener Neustadt (1192)
    Zagreb/Agram (1242)

13   Ecclesiastical jurisdictions, ca. 1450

East Central Europe was the meeting place of the two Christian worlds—Roman-rite Catholicism and Byzantine-rite Orthodoxy. In the centuries following the 1054 schism between Rome and Constantinople, the two branches of Christendom grew progressively apart until they were struggling as fierce enemies for control of their respective and each other's flocks. That struggle, which became intimately involved with secular politics, was played out throughout much of East Central Europe from the Baltic to the Adriatic and Aegean seas.

The Roman-rite Catholic world was headed by the pope and his administration at the Vatican in Rome. The church was administratively divided into archdioceses (indicated by the boundaries on the accompanying map), which in turn were divided into dioceses. In general, the archdioceses were self-governing and responsible to their archbishop resident at the archepiscopal see. There were a few exceptions to this structure: three ecclesiastical territories (Kamień/Kołobrzeg, Fulda, Bamberg) were governed by bishops responsible directly to the pope, as were the bishops in the Papal States (with the exception of the archbishopric of Ravenna and bishopric of Bologna, raised to the status of an independent archbishopric in 1582). Also an exception in the Catholic ecclesiastical structure were the patriarchates of Aquileia and of Grado (in 1451 transferred to Venice). The Roman-rite patriarchal office is basically an honorary title, and in this regard it is in sharp contrast to the Eastern churches, where patriarchs serve as the highest ecclesiastical authority within a given territory.

Like secular political boundaries, although by no means as often, the boundaries of Catholic archdioceses changed. Those changes were frequently related to the evolution in the status of secular political entities. For instance, as the Slavic states north of the Carpathians increased their political power, their archdioceses made gains at the expense of Germanic archdioceses. In 1344 an independent archdiocese was created for Bohemia and Moravia (with a see in Prague), whose bishoprics had previously been part of the archdiocese of Mainz.

Similarly, the growing power of Poland led to the acquisition by the archdiocese of Gniezno at the end of the twelfth century of the dioceses of Poznań and Lebus (which had previously been part of the archdiocese of Magdeburg), and in the late thirteenth century of the diocese of Chełmża/Kulmsee (previously from the lands of the Teutonic Order that were part of one large archbishopric with its see in Riga in northern Livonia). The outset of the fifteenth century saw even greater territorial gains for Gniezno. With the conversion of the Lithuanian grand prince Jogaila/Jagiełło to Christianity, new dioceses came into being immediately at Vilnius (1388) and later at Varniai (1417), both of which respectively in 1409 and 1440 were joined to the Gniezno archdiocese. Farther south in Polish-annexed Galicia, a

separate Catholic archdiocese was established at Halych (1365), whose seat was moved in 1415 to Ľviv (which had had a Catholic bishopric going back to 1390). This eastward expansion of Poland brought the Catholic Church into direct territorial competition with the Orthodox Church in the Rus' lands of Galicia, Volhynia, Ukraine, Podolia, and neighboring Moldavia, where beginning in 1358 several new Catholic dioceses were set up, often alongside older Orthodox eparchies as in Volodymyr, Halych, Przemyśl, Kamianets'-Podil's'kyi, Ľviv, Luts'k, and Kiev.

The second area of Catholic-Orthodox territorial conflict was the eastern Adriatic. There a high concentration of Catholic archdiocesan and diocesan sees had been established as early as the sixth century (in Istria), and from that time until the twelfth century they expanded southward as far as Albania. This strong ecclesiastical network helped to keep Croatia, Slavonia, and Dalmatia within the Catholic fold as well as to attract from time to time the inhabitants of Orthodox Serbia, Zeta (Montenegro), and Albania, territories for which the Catholic archbishopric of Bar/Antivari was set up in 1062.

The Catholic archbishoprics along the coast were frequently in competition with each other and with archdioceses in Hungary for control of the Slavic hinterland. For instance, the diocese of Zagreb, established at the end of the eleventh century, was subordinated to the Hungarian archdiocese of Kalocsa. The fate of the diocese of Bosnia was particularly complex. The Bosnian diocese of Brdo based at Vrhbosna was, during the eleventh century, a source of conflicting claims between the coastal archdioceses of Split, Bar, and Dubrovnik, to whom it finally was jurisdictionally subordinated. By the 1230s the Bosnian Catholic diocese of Brdo had been transferred to the jurisdiction of the archdiocese of Kalocsa in Hungary, and by about 1300 its bishops had left Vrhbosna, transferring their seat to Đakovo, which at the time was under Hungary's direct political control.

As for Bosnia proper, the Catholic-Orthodox rivalry was challenged by a third force. As early as the tenth century, neo-Manichean ideas of dualism—a belief in the conflict between good and evil or between two deities (the God of Light and the God of Darkness)—had taken hold in the country. The followers of the movement were known as Bogomils ("lovers of God"), who favored an ascetic lifestyle and who rejected both the Catholic and Orthodox churches for their teachings and material opulence. In turn, both churches branded the Bogomils as heretics. Nonetheless, by the late twelfth century, Bogomilism had been adopted by Bosnia's rulers, and the movement's adherents, who called themselves simply Christians (*kristijani*), set up their own Church of Bosnia, which dominated the life of the country until the second half of the fourteenth century. As the state expanded, the Catholics (under Tvrtko's

Copyright © by Paul Robert Magocsi

Bosnian kingdom) and then the Orthodox (under Stjepan Vukčić's Herzegovina) reasserted their influence.

It was in the third area—the Aegean region—that the Catholic incursion was, at least initially, the most successful. In the wake of the Fourth Crusade of 1204, which resulted in the capture of Constantinople and the establishment of Latin kingdoms throughout the southern Balkans (see Map 6), an intense network of Catholic archdioceses and dioceses was established alongside already existing Orthodox archeparchies and eparchies, and also in new places. Their survival, however, depended on the existence of the Latin states. Following their decline and the restoration of the Byzantine Empire, the only remaining Catholic hierarchs were on the isle of Rhodes (the last of the islands held by the Knights of Saint John, who left after the Turkish conquest of 1522) and at Durrës (under Venetian rule until 1501).

As for the Orthodox sphere in East Central Europe, it should be noted that the role of the church in the enhancement of secular rule was even more important than in Catholic countries. This is because secular rulers made use of the symbolic value of Orthodoxy in their struggle for political independence from the Byzantine Empire. In short, with independence came the need for a separate church ruled by autocephalous metropolitans or preferably by a patriarch who theoretically would be equal to the ecumenical patriarch in the imperial capital of Byzantium. The presence of a patriarch or an autocephalous metropolitan lent enormous prestige to secular states.

The first of these new patriarchates was established in 917 in Bulgaria. A decade later it was recognized by the ecumenical patriarchate, and its subsequent evolution was directly related to the fate of the Bulgarian state. During the First Bulgarian Empire, the patriarch of the independent (autocephalous) Bulgarian Orthodox Church resided in Preslav (917–971) and then Ohrid (971–1018), which after the fall of Bulgaria (1018) became an autocephalous archeparchy that was to survive until 1767. During the Second Bulgarian Empire, the Bulgarian patriarchate was restored with a new see in the country's capital of Veliko Tŭrnovo (1235–1393). However, after the fall of the second empire (1393–96), much of the Bulgarian patriarchate reverted to the jurisdiction of Constantinople, although Ohrid retained its status as an autocephalous archeparchy.

Just to the west in Serbia, the rulers of the new dominant power in the Balkans sought as well to create an independent Orthodox church. This occurred in the wake of the crowning in 1217 of Stefan Nemanja II as king of Serbia. Instrumental in the creation of the new church was the king's brother, the monk Sava (1175–1236), who was recognized by Constantinople as the hierarch of an autocephalous archeparchy based at the monastery of Žiča. Aside from the already existing eparchies of Ras and Prizren, Sava founded at least nine (some say twelve) new eparchies. For his work on behalf of the church, Sava was later canonized and has been the patron saint of Serbia ever since.

A century after Sava's death, the Serbian church once again was directly influenced by political developments. At that time, the powerful ruler Stefan Dušan (r. 1331–55) decided to proclaim himself emperor. According to the rules of the day, such a ceremony required the presence of a patriarch. Thus, in 1346, a week before his own coronation, he convened a church council (*sabor*) at Skopje, which created a Serbian patriarchate. Because this act was initiated by a secular ruler, it was rejected by the ecumenical patriarch in Constantinople, and thus the Serbian patriarchate was not recognized until half a century later (1395). The town of Peć/Ipek was made the seat of the new patriarchate, whose boundaries—more or less those of the older archeparchy of Ohrid—were to coincide with the lands claimed by Dušan as "emperor of the Serbs, Greeks, Bulgarians, and Albanians" (see Map 9). Also, the eparchies of Ras and Prizren were raised in status to metropolitan sees.

In fact, it was only in Serbia itself that the patriarchate was able to function effectively. Even there, with the end of that country's independence in 1459, the Serbian patriarchate declined as well. Under the country's new Ottoman rulers, however, the patriarchate was restored in 1557, again with its see at Peć but with jurisdiction toward the north over Orthodox communities in Turkish-controlled Hungary, Croatia, and Dalmatia as well as Serbia.

With the development of state structures in Romanian-inhabited Walachia and Moldavia, the local secular rulers (voivodes) felt that the church could help them enhance their political prestige and independence from Hungarian Catholic influence. In 1359, the ecumenical patriarch in Constantinople approved the request of voivode Nicolae Alexandru (r. 1352–64) for the creation of the metropolitan see of Ugrowalachia at his capital of Curtea de Argeş. A decade later, a second see was created farther west at Severin (1370).

Moldavia's Orthodox population had been under the jurisdiction of either the archeparchy of Halych in Galicia or the autocephalous archeparchy of Ohrid in the south. Hungarian influence was also strong, as evidenced by the renewal in the 1370s of activity of the older Catholic diocese of Milcovia near the border with Walachia and the creation of two new dioceses at Siret and Baia. In response, Moldavia's ruler, in the 1370s, requested recognition of the appointment of a metropolitan for his country. The ecumenical patriarch at first did not accept the initiative of Moldavia's secular ruler, but finally in 1401, during the long and prosperous reign of Alexandru I (the Good, 1400–1432), Constantinople recognized the metropolitanate of Moldovalachia with its see in Suceava and two eparchies in Roman and Rădăuţi.

The last major Orthodox church jurisdictions were on lands that had formerly been under the rule of Kievan Rus'. The Rus' church had since the eleventh century been headed by its own metropolitans in Kiev under the jurisdiction of Constantinople. But after the Mongol invasion of the 1240s, Kiev's metropolitans began to reside temporarily in the northern Rus' lands, eventually establishing their residence permanently in Vladimir (1299) and then Moscow (1326), where their presence lent prestige to the yet politically unimportant but growing Duchy of Muscovy. The hierarchs resident in Moscow continued to hold the title "Metropolitan of Kiev and all Rus'," although their authority was effectively limited to territories under the rule of Muscovy and the neighboring Rus' principalities in the north.

The vast majority of western Rus' lands (present-day Belarus and Ukraine) had by the fourteenth century come under Lithuanian or Polish rule. The rulers of those countries wanted, too, the prestige that went with having separate church jurisdictions with their own metropolitans. Thus, in 1303, during the period of the independent Galician Rus' kingdom, a separate metropolitan see was established at Halych for jurisdiction over those eparchies within the political sphere of Galicia (Halych, Chełm, Przemyśl, Luts'k, Volodymyr, Pinsk-Turaŭ). Farther north, another metropolitanate had already been established in 1299–1300 for Lithuania, with its seat at Navahrudak/Naugardukas.

Although the Galician and Lithuanian metropolitanates were approved by the ecumenical patriarch of Constantinople, the metropolitans of Kiev resident in Moscow opposed the new ecclesiastical structures, which they felt impinged on Kiev's jurisdiction. As a result of protests from Muscovy, the Galician and Lithuanian metropolitanates were abolished respectively in 1328 and 1330. The ecumenical patriarch restored and then abolished Halych twice more (1337, 1371–1401) and Lithuania once more (1354–64). Subsequently, the grand duke of Lithuania unilaterally made a short-lived attempt to recreate a metropolitanate (1415–19) for his country.

By taking such action, the ecumenical patriarch reiterated the principle of the unity of the Kievan metropolitanate, while Lithuania and Muscovy continued to compete with each other for the residence of the metropolitan to be placed on its respective territory (at Navahrudak or Moscow). This struggle came to a head in 1448, after which a synod in Moscow elected without approval of the ecumenical patriarch its own metropolitans (who assumed the title Metropolitan of Kiev and all Rus'), thus effectively becoming an independent church. Muscovy's ecclesiastical alienation from Constantinople lasted until 1589, when the ecumenical patriarch finally recognized the independence of what by then was the Russian Orthodox Church headed by its own patriarch resident in Moscow. Moscow's new patriarch continued to claim the Kievan inheritance, which it was gradually to recover as Muscovy's and later Russia's boundaries expanded southward and westward.

Even after the Muscovite church with its own Kievan metropolitan began to function independently, from 1458 until the end of the sixteenth century the ecumenical patriarch continued to appoint metropolitans of "Kiev, Galicia, and all Rus'," who resided at Navahrudak in Lithuania. The Kievan metropolitan in Navahrudak had by the late fifteenth century under his jurisdiction eparchies in three countries: Lithuania (Navahrudak, Vilnius, Polatsk, Pinsk-Turaŭ, Minsk, Hrodna, Slutsk, Volodymyr-Brest, Luts'k-Ostrih, and—until its conquest by Muscovy in 1503—Chernihiv-Briansk); Poland (Chełm, Przemyśl, and after 1539 Halych-L'viv); and Hungary (Mukachevo).

While the jurisdictional framework of the various Orthodox churches was frequently influenced by political factors, the spiritual direction of the church was determined for the

13a Mount Athos

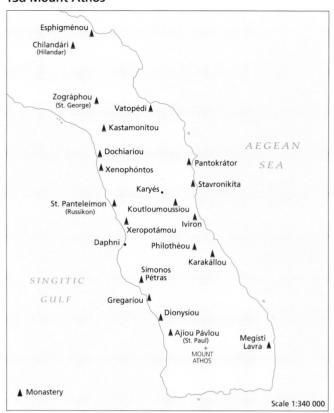

Esphigménou ▲
Chilandári ▲
(Hilandar)
Zográphou ▲
(St. George)
Vatopédi ▲
▲ Kastamonítou
▲ Dochiaríou
▲ Xenophóntos
▲ Pantokrátor
Karyés ●
▲ Stavronikíta
St. Panteleímon ▲
(Russikon)
Koutloumoussíou ▲
▲ Iviron
Xeropotámou ▲
Daphni ●
Philothéou ▲
Karakállou ▲
Símonos ▲
Pétras
Gregaríou ▲
Dionysíou ▲
▲ Ajíou Pávlou
(St. Paul)
+
MOUNT
ATHOS
Megísti
Lavra ▲

AEGEAN SEA

SINGITIC GULF

▲ Monastery

Scale 1:340 000

Copyright © by Paul Robert Magocsi

most part by monasteries. Monasteries not only served as centers of spiritual renewal, they also were often the cultural centers where the historical inheritance of the secular states was preserved and enhanced. Foremost among these were the monasteries at Ohrid founded by Saint Kliment, at Rila founded by Ivan of Rila, at Kiev in the Caves (Pechers'ka Lavra) founded by Antony of Liubech, at Studenica founded by Stepan Nemanja, and at Mileševa founded by Saint Sava.

Besides these and other local monasteries, the Orthodox world had its own "monastic state," the republic of Mount Athos—the Holy Mountain (Map 13a). This was actually a peninsula of land jutting into the Aegean Sea that from the ninth century became the home of an increasing number of monks from the Orthodox world. From the tenth century, Athos had its own form of self-government, based at Karyés, which was for the most part respected by first the Byzantine and then the Ottoman Empire.

Although initially monks from different Orthodox lands were integrated within the various types of monasteries, by the twelfth century they had largely become differentiated according to "national" background. These included the Megísti Lavra (Studios), Vatopedi, and Philothéou for the Greeks; Ivíron for the Georgians; Zográphou (Saint George) for the Bulgarians; Saint Panteleímon (Russicon) for the Rus'; and Chilandári (Hilandar) for the Serbs.

The monasteries on Mount Athos provided a setting for continual interaction between churchmen from all the Orthodox lands. They were also frequently endowed with rich libraries and promoted scholarly and artistic activity of great significance for the enhancement of the varying cultures they represented.

14 East Central Europe, ca. 1570

The major change in the status of East Central Europe during the sixteenth century was the growth and consolidation of three major states: the Ottoman Empire, the Habsburg Empire, and Poland, or the Polish-Lithuanian Commonwealth. By about 1570 these three entities alone accounted for virtually the entire territory throughout the region.

The further expansion of the Ottoman Empire into the heart of the Danubian basin occurred during the reign of Sultan Suleiman I (the Magnificent, 1520–66), under whose rule the empire reached its greatest extent. The Ottomans captured from Venice all of its Aegean islands (with the exception of Crete) and its coastal possessions in Morea (Ottoman Mora) and Epirus (Ottoman Yanya and Tirhala), incorporated Zeta-Montenegro (made part of Ottoman Iskenderye, 1499), and placed the independent city-state of Dubrovnik under the empire's protection (1526). The Ottomans then turned farther north (for details, see Map 20a).

The main turning point in the Ottoman advance came in 1526 with the defeat of Hungary's army at Mohács and the death of its king. During the following two decades, most of Hungary-Croatia as far as the Carpathian foothills became part of the Ottoman Empire. What remained of this formerly dominant power in the Danubian basin were two separate regions: (1) Transylvania, which as a vassal state of the Ottomans from 1541 became a stronghold of anti-Habsburg Hungarian political traditions; and (2) Royal Hungary, a small strip of land in the north and west (including Croatia) which came under Austrian Habsburg control. The Ottomans also acquired several neighboring territories north of the Danube: Walachia (1476) and Moldavia (1512) had already become permanent vassal states, while the Black Sea coastal lands, Jedisan (1526) and Budzhak (1538), were annexed outright.

The year 1526 also proved to be a crucial turning point for the Habsburgs, whose fortunes in the previous three decades had become closely linked to those of their Bohemian and Hungarian neighbors. After the death of Mátyás Corvinus in 1490, the Hungarians chose as their king Úlászló II /Władysław (r. 1490–1516) of the Polish Jagiellonian dynasty. He had in 1471 already been elected (as Ladislav II) king of Bohemia. Úlászló not only reunited Moravia, Silesia, and Lusatia with the Bohemian Kingdom, he also restored Lower Austria and Styria to the Habsburgs. The era of Jagiellonian rule in Hungary and Bohemia continued under Lajos/Louis II (r. 1516–26; Ludvík I in Bohemia). He also agreed to a family compact that had been signed with the Habsburgs in 1515.

When the twenty-year-old Lajos perished on the battlefield of Mohács in 1526 and left no successor, the Habsburg ruler, Ferdinand I (r. 1526–64), put forth a claim to the crowns of Bohemia and Hungary-Croatia on the basis of the Habsburg-Jagiellonian agreement of 1515. While the Bohemian estates refused to recognize the hereditary right of the Habsburgs, they nonetheless, in 1526, did elect Ferdinand I as their king. The situation in Hungary was even more complex, since most nobles chose the Transylvanian prince, János Zápolyai, to be their king. However, in December 1526, another group of Hungarian nobles elected the Habsburg Ferdinand as king of Hungary, and one month later the diet of Croatia followed suit.

The status of the Habsburgs was further enhanced when, to prevent conflicts over succession, Ferdinand arranged for his heirs to be recognized as future kings in Bohemia (after 1549) and Hungary-Croatia (after 1563). In practice, this meant that these two kingdoms now became hereditary Habsburg possessions. Whereas Habsburg rule over the various lands of the Kingdom of Bohemia (Bohemia, Moravia, Silesia, Lusatia) seemed secure, their hold over Hungary-Croatia was limited to the northern and western parts of the kingdom, so-called Royal Hungary. But even these areas were to be constantly threatened by the Ottomans and by their vassal state of Transylvania (for details, see Map 19b).

North of the Carpathians, clearly the dominant power was Poland. The centuries-long domination by the Teutonic and Livonian orders on the Baltic Sea came definitively to an end. In 1525, Teutonic Prussia became a Polish vassal state known as Ducal Prussia. In 1561, Courland also became a vassal state, while in the same year Livonia was annexed to Poland. As part of its ongoing struggle with Muscovy, Lithuania's eastern border was to advance and recede several times in the course of the sixteenth century, especially in the region of Smolensk (for details, see Map 19a). In response to this external threat, Lithuania (linked in a personal union since 1385) drew closer to Poland. The result was the creation in 1569 of the Polish-Lithuanian Commonwealth, whereby the country was henceforth ruled by a common diet. At the same time, Poland annexed outright from Lithuania its southern regions of Volhynia and Ukraine. What remained of Lithuania was divided into the same administrative subdivisions—known as palatinates (województwa)—that existed in the Polish part of the commonwealth (see Map 18).

Historical Atlas of East Central Europe

Copyright © by Paul Robert Magocsi

Map labels

DENMARK

BALTIC SEA

COURLAND
LIVONIA

Western Dvina

MUSCOVY

Hamburg
Bremen
MECKLENBURG
POMERANIA-WOLGAST
POMERANIA
STETTIN

Gdańsk
ROYAL PRUSSIA

Kaliningrad (Königsberg)
DUCHY OF PRUSSIA

Neman

Vilnius (Wilno)
Minsk
LITHUANIA

Smolensk

BRANDENBURG
•Berlin
Magdeburg

GREAT POLAND
Poznań

Hrodna (Grodno)

MAZOVIA
Warsaw
POLAND

Warta

Vistula

Pripet

Chernihiv

LUSATIA

Leipzig
SAXONY (Elect.)
Dresden

SILESIA
Wrocław (Breslau)

LITTLE POLAND

Western Bug

VOLHYNIA

Kiev (Kijów)

Fulda
SAXONY (Duchy)

Oder

UKRAINE

Bamberg
BAYREUTH
Prague

Würzburg
UPPER PALATINATE

BOHEMIA

Morava

Cracow

L'viv (Lwów)

GALICIA

Zbruch

Dniester

Southern Bug

Danube

Brno (Brünn)
MORAVIA

HABSBURG

BAVARIA
Augsburg
Munich

Vienna
Bratislava (Pozsony)

ROYAL HUNGARY

Košice (Kassa)

Ipel

Eger

Tisza

Iaşi
Prut
Siret

JEDISAN

Bendery

AUSTRIA
Salzburg
SALZBURG

EMPIRE

Buda

Debrecen

Cluj (Kolozsvár)

MOLDAVIA

Bilhorod (Akkerman)

SWITZ.
TYROL
VORARLBERG

Inn

STYRIA
CARINTHIA

Drava

HUNGARY

TRANSYLVANIA

BUDZHAK

CARNIOLA

Zagreb

Mohács

Braşov (Brassó)

VENICE

CROATIA

Kupa

Sava

WALACHIA

SILISTRE

BLACK SEA

Venice

PARMA
MODENA

Po

Ravenna

Zadar (Zara)

Belgrade

IZVORNIK

SEMENDIRE

Morava

VIDIN

Olt

Danube

LUCCA
Florence
FLORENCE

Šibenik (Sebenico)
Split (Spalato)

BOSNA

ALACAHISAR

O T T O M A N

NIĞBOLU

PAPAL STATES

ADRIATIC SEA

HERSEK

Niš

VULÇITRIN

BIRZERIN

SOFYA

Sofia (Sofija)

Maritsa

ÇIRMEN

Rome

Dubrovnik (Ragusa)
Kotor (Cattaro)
Budva

ISKENDERYE

KUSTENDIL

Plovdiv (Filibe)

Edirne

VIZE

Istanbul

Durrës (Diraç)
OHRI

Vardar

D I R N E

GELIBOLU

İznik

NAPLES (Spain)
Naples

ELBASAN

Salonika (Selänik)

İzmir

Sakarya

Vlorë (Avlonya)

FILORINA

TYRRHENIAN SEA

AVLONYA

E M P I R E

IONIAN ISLANDS (Venice)

YANYA

TIRHALA

AEGEAN SEA

MIDILLI

Palermo

YANINA
EĞRIBOZ
Athens (Ateni)

İzmir

IONIAN SEA

KARLI-ELI

MORA

SICILY (Spain)

CRETE (Venice)
Candia

Legend

—··—·· International boundaries

— — — Boundaries of principalities, duchies and vassal states

– – – – Provincial boundaries

········· Sanjak boundaries, ca. 1525

━━━━ Holy Roman Empire

▦ Ecclesiastical states

▨ Habsburg lands

0   150 miles

0   150 kilometers

Scale 1:8 890 000

15 Protestant Reformation, 16th century

East Central Europe was always characterized by its religious diversity. It was at the center of the dividing line between the Catholic and Orthodox worlds (see Map 13); it experienced the first serious challenges to the unity within those two Christian worlds (Bogomilism in religiously mixed Bosnia during the thirteenth and fourteenth centuries and Hussitism in Catholic Bohemia-Moravia in the fifteenth century); and virtually its entire southern half had by the sixteenth century come under the rule of the Ottomans, who implanted the Muslim faith throughout their expanded domain. With such a tradition of religious pluralism, it is not surprising that the lands of East Central Europe, in particular its northern "non-Ottoman" half, proved to be fertile ground for the spread of the Protestant Reformation.

That Reformation is traditionally dated from 1517, when a reform-minded Catholic monk and professor, Martin Luther (1483–1546), posted on the doors of the University of Wittenberg in the Electorate of Saxony a list of ninety-five propositions critical of Roman Catholic Church practices, especially regarding indulgences, which by then had become monetary payments for dispensation from sins. Within four years of the Wittenberg posting, Luther was condemned by the pope, and when he refused to recant, the followers of his reform movement broke with the Catholic Church. From these protests, Protestantism was born.

The spread of Luther's ideas was helped enormously by the technological advance of the printing press, which made it possible for easy-to-obtain religious tracts (often written in the vernacular, not Latin) to be widely available throughout Germanic and neighboring lands (see Map 17). As a result, during the 1520s and 1530s, other reformers came on the scene. Following Luther's lead, they set up churches that were even farther from the Roman Catholic norm. These reformers included Huldreich Zwingli (1484–1531) and later John Calvin (1509–1564) in Switzerland as well as the more radical Anabaptists and Anti-Trinitarians, whose divergent sects became active in various parts of Europe.

Luther's doctrine of "justification through grace by faith alone" formed the basis of what came to be known as Lutheranism. The Lutherans basically preserved the Roman Mass, although it was said in the vernacular instead of Latin and was now enhanced by congregational singing and preaching. The sacraments of the Lord's Supper (Communion) and baptism were retained as well. Lutheranism spread from the Electorate of Saxony and took hold especially in the north German lands, becoming the official religion in certain states there (Duchy of Saxony, Brandenburg, Pomerania-Stettin) and throughout Scandinavia. Luther's earliest supporters called themselves Evangelicals, a term still used to describe adherents of Lutheranism in East Central Europe, where their churches are also referred to as "churches of the Augsburg Confession" in reference to the 1530 statement that still forms the guidelines of Lutheran dogma.

The Reformed Church grew out of the religious movement based in the Swiss Confederation, or Switzerland. That movement had accepted many of the changes proposed by Luther but then went farther in distinguishing its practices from those of the Catholic Church. The changes were initiated by Zwingli and further elaborated and eventually disseminated beyond the borders of the Swiss Confederation by his successor, Calvin. With regard to church practices, Zwingli abolished the use of Latin and eliminated all music from services. But his greatest theological difference from Luther had to do with his assertion that the bread and wine of Communion were simply symbolic representations of Christ, and not transformed into his actual body and blood as both the Catholics and Lutherans continued to believe.

Under Calvin's leadership, the organization of the Reformed Church was given a firm base. The elaborate hierarchy of the Roman Catholic Church (preserved in part by the Lutherans) was replaced by a corporate body in which pastors were elected by the congregation instead of consecrated by bishops. In terms of theology, Calvin was best known for the view that all things are governed by God's providence. The corollary, a lack of personal human freedom outside of God's will, led Calvin to believe in the precept of predestination: that God determines what will become of each person ("eternal life is decreed for some [the elect], eternal damnation for others").

Based on Calvin's example in the far-western Swiss city of Geneva, the Reformed churches hoped, wherever possible, to establish a kind of theocracy in which society as a whole should be regulated by the precepts of the official church. From its base in Switzerland, the Reformed movement became particularly dynamic in the second half of the sixteenth century, spreading to Holland and Scotland as well as to several countries in East Central Europe.

Another Protestant orientation were the Anabaptists. They were less interested in reforming the Catholic Church than in returning to what they believed were the principles of early Christianity. The movement originated in the north-central Swiss city of Zürich, where young intellectuals rebelled against Zwingli's apparent subservience to local political authority. The Anabaptists were best known for rejecting infant baptism, and during the first generation of the movement, converts were rebaptized—an act that at the time was a crime punishable by death and for which many Anabaptists were martyred. The Anabaptists believed in the separation of church and state; they refused to swear civil oaths; and most rejected the use of arms—beliefs that were considered a violation of civil law and which led to the execution of thousands of followers. They also were convinced that the apocalypse was imminent, and thus often

Map legend:

- – – – International boundaries, ca. 1570
- – – Boundaries of vassal states
- – – Boundaries of duchies, electorates and bishoprics
- ▬ Holy Roman Empire
- Lutherans/Evangelicals
- Reformists (Calvinists, Zwinglians)
- Bohemian and Moravian Brethren, Utraquists (Hussites)
- Anabaptists, Anti-Trinitarians, Socinians
- ○ Lutheran university
- △ Reformed university
- ▽ Reformed academy
- □ Anti-Trinitarian schools
- ▭ Bohemian and Moravian Brethren *gymnasia*

Where two dates are given for universities, the second indicates when it became a Protestant institution.

0 ___ 150 miles
0 ___ 150 kilometers
Scale 1:8 890 000

Copyright © by Paul Robert Magocsi

welcomed martyrdom in a world they believed was soon to end anyway with the Second Coming of Christ. A related sect that accepted many of the tenets of the Anabaptists were the Anti-Trinitarians (Unitarians), who rejected the divine nature of Christ and the doctrine of the Trinity.

Turning to the impact of the Reformation in East Central Europe, it is not surprising that Bohemia and Moravia, given their own recent experience with Hussitism and their geographical proximity to the Electorate of Saxony and other north German states, would be well prepared to receive the new religious doctrines. As a result of the fifteenth-century "Czech Reformation," two churches had come into existence alongside the Roman Catholic Church: (1) the followers of Hus, also known as Utraquists, because they received communion in both kinds (*sub utraque specie*); and (2) the Unity of Brethren (Unitas Fratrum/ Jednota), who broke away from the Utraquists in 1467, rejected most liturgical traditions, elected their own hierarchs, and considered the Bible their sole source of faith.

Other orientations were soon to follow. When the Reformation from the Germanic lands began to reach Bohemia and Moravia, Lutheranism became especially popular among the German-speaking population. Calvin's Reformed version of Protestantism as well as Lutheranism also found adherents among the more radical or Neo-Utraquists. These various groups had enough similarities among them to adopt a common doctrinal statement formulated by the Utraquists in 1575 and known as the Bohemian Confession (Confessio Bohemica). This document eventually became the basis for a National Czech Evangelical Church. Outside that framework, however, was the Anabaptist movement, which developed roots in Moravia, especially in the town of Mikulov/Nikolsburg. One group of Anabaptists known as Hutterites sought refuge in 1528 on the estates of tolerant feudal nobles in Moravia. Led by their founder, the Tyrolian Jakob Hutter (d. 1536), the Hutterites were allowed to live in communal settlements and to abjure military service, in return for which they provided their protectors with the high quality products of their crafts and husbandry.

The Reformation first reached Hungary-Croatia in the 1530s, when most of the country was coming under Ottoman domination. The movement was to spread rapidly during the next two decades, so that by the end of the sixteenth century nearly 90 percent of Hungary's population followed some form of Protestantism. Lutheranism was the first to make its presence felt among German-speaking city dwellers and then among Magyar peasants and burghers. Even before the Lutherans became organized, Calvinism became the religion of many people, especially in the region east of the Tisza River. In 1562, the Calvinists organized a synod at their center in Debrecen, where they adopted the Hungarian Confession (Confessio Hungarica), which provided the theological basis for an independent Hungarian Calvinist Reformed Church.

As the Lutherans in Hungary were being challenged by the Calvinists, the latter were, in turn, being challenged by the Anti-Trinitarian movement. In the end, the Anti-Trinitarians (later Unitarians) were limited to Transylvania. In this semi-independent Ottoman vassal state, the religiously tolerant ruler, Prince István Báthory (r. 1571–86), passed a decree in 1572 which placed Unitarians alongside the Catholics, Lutherans, and Reformed Calvinists as one of the four "accepted" religions of the country. It was not long before the various religions in Transylvania followed ethnic divisions: the Magyars were either Calvinists or Catholics, the Saxons were Lutherans, and the Székelys were mainly Unitarian. Transylvania was also home to Jews, Armenians, and a large number of Orthodox (mostly Romanians), but these groups were only "tolerated." This meant that they could practice their religion but their clergy had no official positions, rights, or other privileges granted to the four accepted religions.

On the other side of the Danubian basin, Lutheran influence became especially strong in Slovenia (Austrian Carniola and southern Styria), having come from the neighboring Habsburg provinces as early as the 1520s. In eastern Slavonia, both Reformed Calvinism and Lutheranism became especially popular among German settlers. On the other hand, the Reformation was less successful in Croatia. That region's religious law of 1608 did not provide toleration for Protestantism, which therefore made only a few inroads into areas immediately adjacent to the border with Carniola and Styria.

In Poland-Lithuania as in Hungary-Croatia, the initial stage of the Reformation took the form of Lutheranism followed later by Reformed Calvinism, the Bohemian-Moravian Brethren, and Anti-Trinitarianism. Lutheranism first spread during the 1520s and 1530s among the German population in Poland's recently acquired vassal state, the Duchy of Prussia, and in neighboring Royal Prussia, as well as in cities with a German population throughout the kingdom. The intellectual center of Lutheranism in Poland was the newly founded university at Kaliningrad/Königsberg (1544).

The Reformed Church was especially attractive to the Polish nobility because Calvin's teachings did not invest the secular power with control over the church, a precept of particular interest to a nobility always concerned with limiting the influence of Poland's kings. During the second half of the sixteenth century, Calvinism took root among the nobility in Great Poland and from there it spread to Lithuania. Under the leadership of its most active proponent, the powerful magnate and chancellor of Lithuania Prince Mikołaj Radziwiłł/Radvilas (the Black, 1515–65), a synod at Vilnius in 1557 brought into being the Calvinist Lithuanian Evangelical Reformed Church. The second half of the century also saw a number of Polish nobles in Great Poland join the Unity of Brethren, many of whom had emigrated from Bohemia after 1548, making their centers of activity Poznań and Leszno in western Poland. It was at Leszno that the Brethren's famous last bishop, Jan Amos Komenský/Comenius (1592–1670), implemented his new teaching methods after his exile there in 1620.

The three Protestant churches in Poland—Lutheran, Reformed Calvinist, and Unity of Brethren—reached an agreement in 1570 (Consensus Poloniae) which, while not uniting them, did provide a basis for mutual coexistence. As for the Polish royal government, the restrictions that had existed during the first half of the sixteenth century were gradually removed during the period of extensive tolerance under King Sigismund August (r. 1548–72). Lutheran worship was permitted in Gdańsk/Danzig and Royal Prussia (1557) and in Livonia (1561). This trend culminated in 1573 with the Compact of Warsaw, called the Pax Dissidentium (the peace of those who differ), which granted toleration to Catholics, Lutherans, Calvinists, and the Brethren.

Outside the framework of the legal Protestant churches were the Anti-Trinitarians and Anabaptists, who were originally from Italy. They came to Poland via the Swiss Confederation, where they were persecuted. By the end of the sixteenth century, the Anti-Trinitarian movement, which had already become divided, was reinvigorated by the arrival of the Italian Fausto Sozzini/Socinius (1539–1604), from whom the movement subsequently came to be known as Socinianism, or Arianism. The main Socinian centers were in Lewartów and Raków, and the greatest strength of the group was found in Lithuania and the eastern part of the Kingdom of Poland, most especially in Volhynia.

16 Catholic Counter Reformation, 16th-17th centuries

The Protestants were not the only ones concerned with reform. By the 1570s, Catholic churchmen were formulating wide-ranging changes for their church, a reform movement that culminated in the papal-inspired Council of Trent, which met, with interludes, from 1545 to 1562. Unlike previous efforts at Catholic reform, the doctrinal work at the Council of Trent revealed that there was now an unbridgeable divide separating Catholic and Protestant. The Council provided a practical program for the reconstruction of a militant Catholic Church, and with this new approach the Counter Reformation had begun.

Among the basic elements in the Tridentine (Council of Trent's) reform program were: (1) a strictly organized hierarchical church structure from the pope, to archbishop, to bishop, and parish priest; (2) the requirement that bishops and priests must reside in their dioceses and parishes and that they must preach; and (3) the subordination of religious orders to local episcopal control. In order to enhance papal influence over the church—and to gather invaluable information on local religious and political conditions—a system of papal legates was strengthened in the form of nuncios who took up permanent residence in cities that were in countries on the front line of the Counter Reformation in East Central Europe (Vienna, 1524; Warsaw, 1570; Prague, 1576).

To ensure that the Tridentine reforms would function properly and oppose successfully the Protestant "heretics," great emphasis was placed on the creation of a wide network of printing presses and Catholic colleges and seminaries. In the process of achieving a restored militant church led by an educated clergy, one religious order was to play a particularly significant role. This was the Society of Jesus, or Jesuits, founded in 1540 by Ignatius Loyola (ca. 1491–1556). Led by figures like Peter Canisius (1521–97), the Jesuits implemented the precepts of the Council of Trent. Through their increasingly large number of high quality colleges and their role as teachers in seminaries and universities, the Jesuits became the vanguard of the Catholic Counter Reformation in its efforts to regain territory and influence lost to the Protestants.

In East Central Europe the Jesuits established their first colleges during the 1550s and 1560s, in Bohemia-Moravia and Silesia. By the 1570s they were active especially in the eastern lands of Poland-Lithuania. The Jesuits also had their own provinces for East Central Europe. Initially, the Austrian province was created in 1563 for the entire region. In 1574 a separate Polish province was set up, from which in turn was carved out a separate Lithuanian province (1608). Finally, a Bohemian province was created in 1622 for Bohemia, Moravia, Silesia, and Lusatia.

Until the end of the sixteenth century, the Catholic recovery was achieved largely through the ideological reclamation of individual Catholic rulers, who, influenced by the Jesuits, set out to implement the decisions of the Council of Trent. However, such Catholic-Protestant rivalry on an intellectual plane was replaced at the outset of the seventeenth century by intolerance and conflict, the most infamous example of which was the Thirty Years' War (1618–48).

The spark for that conflict was the policy of the new Habsburg king of Bohemia and Hungary-Croatia and Holy Roman Emperor, Ferdinand II (r. 1619–37). Educated by the Jesuits at the University of Ingolstadt in Bavaria, Ferdinand was determined to rid the Habsburg lands of Protestantism. Even before Ferdinand came to power, the Hutterites in Moravia had been subjected to three decades of persecution beginning in 1590 until they were finally driven out of the province. But widespread change came only after Ferdinand's defeat in 1620 of the Czech nobles, with whom the Protestants had allied. In 1627 an imperial edict outlawed Protestantism throughout the Habsburg realm, Protestant churches were destroyed, and their followers were forcibly Catholicized or, as in the case of many Czech and Moravian Brethren, forced into exile. To implement these changes, teams of Catholic priests flooded into Protestant centers in Bohemia, Moravia, Silesia, and other Austrian provinces. In the part of Hungary controlled by the Habsburgs, the Croatian diet after 1606 banned all but the Catholic faith, while farther north the Hungarian Jesuit Archbishop Péter Pázmány (1616–37) regained most of Slovakia for the Catholic Church. Only in Transylvania, which with the help of the Ottomans remained beyond Habsburg control, was Protestantism protected by law according to the decree of 1572.

North of the Carpathians in Poland-Lithuania, religious tolerance prevailed somewhat longer, despite the presence of devout Catholic kings. This was largely because the politically influential Polish and Lithuanian magnates and gentry considered religious diversity important to their jealously guarded independence from the crown. But when an increasing number of Protestant magnates and gentry sent their children to be educated at the excellent Jesuit colleges, there began a gradual drift of the new generation of gentry back to Catholicism. This trend, together with the king's power of patronage (including royal protection of the Jesuits beginning in 1565), changed the status of Poland-Lithuania's religious groups, so that by 1668 the Polish diet made conversions from Catholicism punishable by death and confiscation of property.

Thus, by the second half of the seventeenth century, the Catholic Church had regained a dominant role throughout most of the northern half of East Central Europe. Only in the Electorate of Saxony, Brandenburg, and Mecklenburg (as well as all of Scandinavia) did Protestantism remain preeminent. In fact, these areas remained outside the Roman Catholic hierarchical order (Terrae Sedis Apostolicae) and instead reverted to a field for Catholic missionaries,

Catholic Counter Reformation, 16th-17th centuries

SWEDEN

MUSCOVY

LIVONIA
(to Sweden)

BALTIC SEA

Riga

Lund

Daugavpils
(Dyneburg)

Polatsk
(Połock)

DENMARK

Vitsebsk
(Witebsk)

Varniai
(Medininkai)

Ilūkste

Smolensk

Orsha
(Orsza)

Kražiai
(Kroże)

W. Devina

Bremen

(to Sweden)

MECKLENBURG

Braniewo

Reszel

Kaunas
(Kowno)

Vilnius
(Wilno)

LITHUANIA

Hrodna
(Grodno)

Navahrudak
(Nowogródek)

Minsk

Mahiliou
(Mohylew)

Gdańsk

Malbork

DUCHY OF PRUSSIA

Chojnice

Heiligenstadt

Grudziądz

Chełmno

Niasvizh
(Nieśwież)

Slutsk
(Słuck)

Novhorod Sivers'kyi
(Nowogród Siewierski)

Hildesheim

BRANDENBURG

Wałcz

Bydgoszcz

Toruń

Łomża

Magdeburg

Gniezno

Płock

Pułtusk

Brest Litovsk
(Brześć Litewski)

Pinsk

Paderborn

Heiligenstadt

Poznań

Włocławek

W. Bug

Drohiczyn

Turaù
(Turów)

Pripet

Chernihiv
(Czernihów)

Desna

Erfurt

SAXONY
(Elect.)

Żagań

Głogów

Kalisz

Łowicz

WARSAW
ca 1570

Łuków

Lublin

Ovruch
(Owrucz)

Fulda

Piotrków

Rawa

Vistula

Chełm

Volodymyr

Luts'k
(Łuck)

Krasnystaw

Kiev
(Perejasław)

Würzburg

Bamberg

Litoměřice

Wrocław
(Breslau)

Cracow

Sandomierz

Zamość

Ostrih
(Ostróg)

Pereiaslav
(Perejasław)

Chomutov

Jičín

SILESIA

Kłodzko

L'viv
(Lwów)

Kremianets
(Krzemieniec)

VOLHYNIA

UKRAINE

Ingolstadt

PRAGUE
1576-1612

BOHEMIA

Opava

Jarosław

Przemyśl

Vinnytsia
(Winnica)

Eichstädt

Neuburg

Regensburg

Jindřichův
Hradec

Jihlava

Olomouc

MORAVIA

Žilina

GALICIA

Krosno

Sambir
(Sambor)

Bar

Dillingen

Straubing

Český
Krumlov

Brno

Uherské
Hradiště

Liptovský
Mikuláš

Prešov

Ivano-Frankivs'k
(Stanysławów)

Smotrych

Kamianets'-Podil's'kyi
(Kamieniec Podolski)

Mindelheim

Augsburg

Landshut

Telč

Znojmo

SLOVAKIA

Banská
Bystrica

Levoča

Humenné

Uzhhorod
(Ungvár)

Kamianets Podolski

Landsberg

BAVARIA

Passau

Linz

Danube

Skalica

Trenčín

Žnievom

Banská
Štiavnica

Košice
(Kassa)

CARPATHIAN RUS'

Southern Bug

MUNICH
1573-83

Burghausen

Inn

VIENNA
1524

Trnava

Klášter pod
Znievom

Sárospatak

Dniester

Hall

Salzburg

Sopron

Bratislava
(Pressburg)

Ipeľ

TRANSYLVANIA

Siret

Prut

Innsbruck

SALZBURG

HABSBURG

Esztergom
(Gran)

Tisza

OTTOMAN

MOLDAVIA

CRIMEAN
KHANATE

Trent

Gurk

EMPIRE

Klagenfurt

Varaždin

Kalocsa

Cluj
(Kolozsvár)

Aquileia

Gorizia

Ljubljana
(Laibach)

Lepoglava

Zagreb

Drava

Alba Iulia
(Gyulafehérvár)

Olt

VENICE
1500

Trieste

Rijeka
(Fiume)

Sava

BLACK
SEA

MANTUA

PARMA

MODENA

Po

CROATIA

EMPIRE

WALACHIA

Ravenna

SAN
MARINO

Zadar
(Zara)

Belgrade

Bucharest

LUCCA

FLORENCE

ADRIATIC
SEA

Split
(Spalato)

Morava

Danube

PAPAL
STATES

(to Spain)

Sofia

Rome

Dubrovnik
(Ragusa)

Maritsa

Bar
(Antivari)

Vardar

NAPLES
(to Spain)

Naples

TYRRHENIAN
SEA

Istanbul

AEGEAN
SEA

Sakarya

(to Venice)

IONIAN
SEA

Palermo

SICILY
(to Spain)

International boundaries, 1648

Catholic university or faculty

Boundaries of vassal states

Catholic seminary, academy,
or secondary school

Boundaries of duchies, electorates
and bishoprics

Jesuit colleges
(secondary schools) to 1700

Holy Roman Empire

Orthodox academies and colleges

Roman Catholic hierarchical order
(Terrae Sedis Apostolicae)

Orthodox and brotherhood schools

Churches in union with Rome

Foundation of institution

Patriarchal see

1550-79

1580-99

Archiepiscopal see

1600-29

Archiepiscopal see no longer existing

1630-89

VENICE Seat of a papal nuncio (with dates)

Not known

0 — 150 miles
0 — 150 kilometers

Scale 1:8 890 000

Copyright © by Paul Robert Magocsi

which after 1622 became the responsibility of the Vatican's Congregation for the Propagation of the Faith (Congregatio de Propaganda Fide).

Related to the renewal of the Catholic Church during the Counter Reformation was the change in status of the Orthodox population living in the eastern part of Poland (Lithuania, Ukraine, Volhynia, Galicia) and Hungary (Carpathian Rus', Transylvania). Located along the borderland between the Catholic and Orthodox worlds, these lands had in the past been the object of efforts at church union, the most recent attempt being the aborted Council of Florence (1439). By the second half of the sixteenth century, in the changed political circumstances of Polish rule in which the Orthodox found themselves to be politically, socially, and economically second-class citizens, an Orthodox religious and cultural revival took place. This early revival was led by wealthy magnates who organized Orthodox schools, academies, and printing presses in the 1570s and 1580s (especially in Lithuania and Volhynia). Even more influential were townsmen who founded the Orthodox brotherhood movement, whose express purpose was to preserve the Orthodox faith in the face of the Jesuit and Protestant advances. The first of the Orthodox brotherhoods was in L'viv (1586), and with its schools and printing presses the movement spread eastward to Volhynia, Lithuania, and Ukraine in the seventeenth century (see also Map 17).

The course of the Orthodox cultural revival was also marked by a renewed interest in the question of church union. The result was the Union of Brest (1596), at which one Orthodox faction led by several, but not all, the Rus' (Belorussian and Ukrainian) bishops pledged their loyalty to the pope in return for the maintenance of their Eastern (Orthodox) liturgy and traditions. The new Uniate Church created at Brest was for a time the only legal Eastern Christian religious body, although between 1607 and 1632 Orthodoxy was once again given legal status. This meant that now there was a Uniate Church and an Orthodox Church in Poland-Lithuania. Each had its own bishops and metropolitan of Kiev, with the Uniates under the jurisdiction of the pope in Rome and the Orthodox under the ecumenical patriarch of Constantinople (Istanbul). From the moment the union of Brest was proclaimed in 1596, there was constant friction between the Uniates and Orthodox. At the same time, the Catholics through their Jesuit education network were able to gain new converts especially among the Uniate and Orthodox gentry and magnates.

The Uniate example in Poland-Lithuania was repeated at the Union of Uzhhorod in 1646, which applied to the Rus' population of northeastern Hungary, a region that frequently changed hands between Habsburg Austria and Transylvania. In Transylvania proper, the Orthodox Romanians had by the end of the century realized that if they wished to improve their status they must become associated with one of the four recognized religions in the country (Catholic, Lutheran, Calvinist, Anti-Trinitarian). Following the example of the Orthodox in Poland-Lithuania and northeastern Hungary, between 1697 and 1700 the Romanian Orthodox hierarchy joined the Catholic fold in Transylvania and created a Romanian Uniate Church.

17 Education and culture through the 18th century

As in central and western Europe, the development in East Central Europe of education and culture was related to the intellectual interest in humanism of the fourteenth and fifteenth centuries and to the practical needs of ideological competition during the Reformation and Counter Reformation of the sixteenth and early seventeenth centuries. With a few exceptions, these developments did not occur in the southern third of East Central Europe—the area south of the Sava-Danube rivers that from the sixteenth century was under the firm control of the Ottoman Empire (see Maps 14 and 18). The Ottomans were not particularly supportive of cultural developments among their subject peoples; in fact, they actively opposed the ideological and technological changes taking place throughout most of the rest of Europe.

In contrast, as early as the fourteenth century some of the continent's first universities were established in the northern half of East Central Europe: Prague (1348), Cracow (1364), Vienna (1365), Pécs (1367), Erfurt (1379), and Buda (1389). Subsequently, there was a general lull in the establishment of new educational institutions until the sixteenth century Reformation and the founding of Lutheran and Reformed universities, Reformed academies, and Anti-Trinitarian schools, most especially in Saxony, Poland, and Transylvania (see Map 15). At the same time, however, the Turkish inroads into Hungary resulted in the closing of its two universities (Pécs and Buda) in 1526. In the late sixteenth and outset of the seventeenth centuries, the school network was advanced further by the Counter Reformation, marked in particular by the growth of Catholic seminaries and Jesuit colleges in Poland-Lithuania and the Habsburg-ruled lands (Silesia, Bohemia, Moravia, Slovakia, Croatia, and the Austrian provinces), and Orthodox schools and academies in eastern Poland (Ukraine and Lithuania) —see Map 16.

Another important indication of cultural development was the spread of the printing press. Following the invention of printing with movable metal type by Johann Gutenberg (ca. 1397–1468) at his first press in Mainz in 1454, printshops spread rapidly into East Central Europe. Often the presses were set up in centers that already had universities or colleges, or that became centers of Protestant sects. Also, quite often a printshop might be in operation only a few years before moving on to another place or becoming dormant until another printer came along (the dates on the accompanying map refer to the first presses in a given place—until 1700 in East Central Europe and until 1500 elsewhere).

The earliest printshops in East Central Europe date from the 1470s, and not surprisingly they were found in Mecklenburg-Schwerin (Rostock), Saxony (Merseburg and Erfurt), Silesia (Wrocław), and Bohemia (Plzeň and Prague);

that is, in those lands within the Germanic cultural sphere where printing began. That same decade also saw the birth of printing in Poland, where beginning with its first shop in 1473, Cracow was to become the center of Polish book production for at least the next two centuries. In Hungary, presses functioned at Buda as early as 1473 and at Bratislava/Pressburg perhaps by 1477, although these ceased operating during the next decade. Before the end of the fifteenth century, more printshops were established in Saxony and Bohemia, as well as in Prussia, Brandenburg, Moravia, Austria, Venetia, Croatia, and Montenegro.

The rapid incursion of the Ottoman Turks into the Balkans and the Danubian basin, which reached its height in the decades after 1526, made printing difficult in central Hungary and among the South Slavs. The Ottoman resistance to this new technological advance was partly due to religious scruples but perhaps even more to the entrenched opposition of the traditional scribes. In any case, there was no Ottoman Turkish press in the country's capital of Istanbul until 1727, although a Hebrew press printed books there as early as 1493 and the offices of the Orthodox ecumenical patriarch had a Greek press beginning in 1627.

Thus, for most of the southern third of East Central Europe (below the Sava-Danube rivers), there were hardly any printing presses before the eighteenth century. Among the few exceptions were Montenegro (Cetinje) and Croatia (Senj), which had presses as early as the last decade of the fifteenth century, and several short-lived presses at monasteries in Bosnia (Goražde), Serbia (Mileševa), and Albania (Shkodër) during the sixteenth century.

Because of the limited printing facilities, outlets were sought beyond the region. German (Tübingen, Regensburg) and Italian (Rome, Milan, Florence) cities, but most particularly those of the Venetian Republic (Padua, Verona, and most especially Venice), became important printing centers in the sixteenth and seventeenth centuries for Slovenian, Croatian, Serbian, Albanian, Bulgarian, and Hungarian books. The Hungarians also made use of presses in Habsburg-controlled Royal Hungary (at Pápa) and in semi-independent Transylvania (at Debrecen, Cluj, Brașov), where the first books in Romanian (at Sibiu, Brașov, and Cluj) and Bulgarian (at Brașov) were printed as well.

The appearance of printing presses in specific places was more often than not related to the presence of religious movements during the Reformation and Counter Reformation, so that the largest percentage of earliest book production included theological works and religious polemics. Part of this need to communicate religious truths influenced as well the printing of the first works in the local vernacular, such as Czech (1468–75 at Plzeň), Greek (1476 at Milan), Glagolitic Croatian (1483 at Venice), Polish (1513 at Cracow), Hungarian (1533 at Cracow), Lithuanian (1547

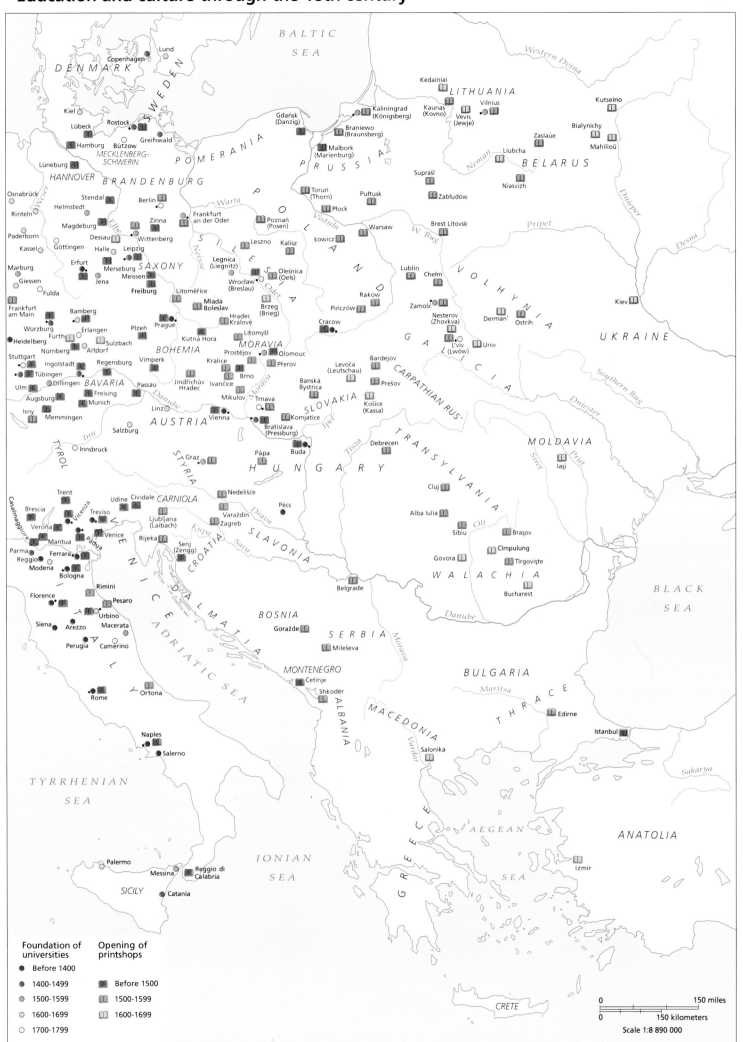

Foundation of universities

- Before 1400
- 1400-1499
- 1500-1599
- 1600-1699
- 1700-1799

Opening of printshops

- Before 1500
- 1500-1599
- 1600-1699

0   150 miles

0   150 kilometers

Scale 1:8 890 000

at Kaliningrad), Slovenian (1550 at Tübingen), Romanian (1559 at Braşov), Belorussian (1562 at Niasvish), Slovak (1581 at Bardejov), and Bulgarian (1651 at Rome).

Related to this was the appearance of the first printshops using Cyrillic fonts to publish works in Church Slavonic, a liturgical language that in its various forms was understood by all its Orthodox readers, although it varied linguistically from country to country in the regions where it was used (as influenced in particular by local speech). The earliest of these printers is considered to be Schweipoldt Fiol (d. 1526), whose first Cyrillic books appeared in Cracow (1483). The subsequent geographical sequence of the earliest Cyrillic imprints was Cetinje (1493). Tirgovişte (1508), Prague (1517–19), Venice (1519), Vilnius (1522), Sibiu (1546), and Niasvizh (1562). In the East Slavic lands, the work of Ivan Fedorov (ca. 1525–83) was of special importance. Following the appearance in Moscow of his *Apostol* (Acts and Epistles, 1564), Fedorov went to Poland-Lithuania, where he moved his press from Zabłudów (1569) to L'viv (1574), and finally to Ostrih. It was at Ostrih that he published the first complete Slavonic Bible (1580–81). The Fedorov tradition of printing in Cyrillic in eastern Poland-Lithuania was carried on in the seventeenth century by the Orthodox brotherhoods, the most important of which was at L'viv.

As with Cyrillic, printing in Hebrew required special fonts, which were acquired by existing printshops or by newly established special Hebrew-language ones. In fact, some of the earliest printshops anywhere were for Hebrew publications; all were in Italy and date from the 1470s (Rome, Ferrara, Reggio de Calabria, Mantua), followed by four more Hebrew shops (Bologna, Casalmaggiore, Naples, Brescia) before the end of the fifteenth century. It was also before the end of the fifteenth century that Hebrew printing made its appearance in Istanbul (1493), followed by Edirne in the sixteenth century and by Salonika and İzmir in the seventeenth century. These were the only printshops in the heartland of the Ottoman Empire, which at the time frowned on this new technology. Hebrew printshops continued to spread in East Central Europe and Italy during the sixteenth and seventeenth centuries, whether in places where there was already a well-established tradition of printing (Hamburg, Berlin, Leipzig, Cracow, Prostějov, Prague, Frankfurt am Main, Nürnberg, Augsburg, Venice) or where they represented the first printing establishments (Frankfurt an der Oder, Dessau, Fürth, Sulzbach, Isny, Oleśnica, Brzeg Dolny, Lublin, Nesterov, Rimini, Pesaro, and Ortona).

18 East Central Europe, 1648

The political landscape of East Central Europe during the sixteenth century, dominated as it was by Poland, the Habsburg Empire, and the Ottoman Empire (see Map 14), remained basically the same during the seventeenth century. The only changes were some territorial expansion on the part of Poland and the Ottoman Empire and the further internal administrative consolidation of those states as well as of the Habsburg Empire.

Among the newer developments was the eastward growth of the Germanic states. In 1648, Brandenburg acquired Pomerania-Stettin and some church lands along the Baltic Sea and its border with Poland. Between 1635 and 1648, the Electorate of Saxony acquired Lusatia from the Habsburg-ruled Bohemian crownland (see Map 14). And with its acquisition of Pomerania-Wolgast in 1648, Sweden appeared for the first time on the southern shores of the Baltic Sea.

Poland, or the Polish-Lithuanian Commonwealth, expanded its boundaries farther east as a result of victories over Muscovy, enabling it thereby to acquire the region around Smolensk. By the 1630s the commonwealth had reached its farthest territorial extent. Internally, Lithuania was integrated further into the Polish administrative and social system following the Union of Lublin in 1569. The commonwealth was divided into palatinates (województwa), each of which had at its administrative center a dietine (sejmik) made up of local nobles who elected representatives to the national diet (Sejm) in Warsaw. The Duchy of Prussia and the Duchy of Courland remained vassal entities (fiefs) outside the palatinate structure.

The position of the Habsburgs also changed during the first half of the seventeenth century. In terms of territory, they lost Lusatia to the Electorate of Saxony; a borderland strip of Royal Hungary to the Ottoman Empire; and Carpathian Rus' and a part of northeastern Hungary to the Ottoman vassal state of Transylvania. As for what remained, the Habsburgs were able to transform their previously loosely connected holdings into what could subsequently be called an empire.

This process of internal consolidation began in 1526, when to their Germanic alpine hereditary lands (Upper and Lower Austria, Styria, Carinthia, Carniola, and Tyrol), the Habsburgs added the crownlands of Bohemia (Bohemia, Moravia, Silesia, Lusatia) and of Hungary-Croatia.

The political integration was significantly strengthened between 1526 and 1648 largely because the Turkish advance, which coincided with the Habsburg succession in Hungary-Croatia, created the need for a common defense. In addition, the struggle between the Reformation and ultimately the victorious Counter Reformation in Habsburg lands during the first half of the seventeenth century helped to establish stronger political bonds between the empire's new and old hereditary lands. It is said as well that the new and old hereditary lands supplemented each other, and this was certainly true of Bohemia, Moravia, and western Hungary in relation to the imperial capital of Vienna.

As for the Ottoman Empire, it had by the outset of the seventeenth century reached its farthest extent in East Central Europe. In order to control their vast domains, the Ottomans experimented with various administrative entities. Initially, the empire was divided into administrative districts known as sanjaks/sançaks (see Map 14). These eventually came to be known as eyalets, which in turn were subdivided into sanjaks (later referred to as livas). In East Central Europe, the oldest eyalet was Rumeli, established as early as the 1360s. Subsequently, Cezayir (1533), Bosna (1580), and Silistre (1599) came into being. As the Ottomans consolidated their authority in the Danubian basin, eventually four eyalets (Budin, Timişvar, Eğri, Kanije) were carved out of what was formerly the heart of the Hungarian Kingdom.

The eyalets were under the direct control of the central Ottoman administration in Istanbul. There were, however, other so-called hereditary provinces (hükümet sançaks), which managed their own affairs under traditional local leaders, whether tribal leaders or vassal princes. Among the hereditary provinces were Moldavia, Walachia, and Transylvania. As semi-independent Ottoman vassal states, they were obliged to pay tribute, to pledge political loyalty, and to admit imperial garrisons in larger fortifications, but otherwise they governed their own affairs. Transylvania was the largest and by the seventeenth century the most powerful of these vassal states. Transylvanian princes conducted their own foreign policy, and because of their rival claim to the Hungarian crown, they were virtually in a continual state of war with the Habsburgs.

Legend:

- ▬·▬· International boundaries
- ▬ ▬ Boundaries of duchies and vassal states
- - - - Boundaries of provinces and palatinates
- ········· Ottoman eyalet boundaries, ca. 1610
- ▬▬ Holy Roman Empire
- ◉ Polish ducal and palatinate centers

VOLHYNIA Name of palatinate other than administrative center

Ecclesiastical states

Habsburg lands

Scale 1:8 890 000

0 ———— 150 miles
0 ———— 150 kilometers

Copyright © by Paul Robert Magocsi

19 Poland-Lithuania, the Habsburgs, Hungary-Croatia, and Transylvania, 16th-17th centuries

Poland-Lithuania, 16th-17th centuries

During the sixteenth and seventeenth centuries, Poland —known as the Polish-Lithuanian Commonwealth—was to reach its greatest territorial extent. The centuries-long process of drawing the Grand Duchy of Lithuania into the Polish sphere, a development that began with a personal union between the countries in 1386, reached another significant stage at the Union of Lublin in 1569. As a result of this union, the Grand Duchy of Lithuania and the Kingdom of Poland were henceforth ruled by a common diet as well as a common sovereign. Lithuania was to retain its own laws as well as a separate army and administration, but its territorial extent was reduced. The Union of Lublin recognized the incorporation into the "Polish half" of the commonwealth of the entire southern half of Lithuania—namely, Volhynia, Podolia, and Ukraine—as well as Podlachia along the grand duchy's western border.

It was in the east that the boundaries of the Polish-Lithuanian Commonwealth were to change most often. This was the result of a nearly constant state of war between Poland and Muscovy during the sixteenth century, which culminated in Polish advances as far as Moscow (1610–11 and 1618) during the latter's Time of Troubles at the outset of the seventeenth century. The lands that changed hands most often between Poland and Muscovy included the regions around Smolensk, Starodub, and Chernihiv. It was in 1619, following the truce of Deulino, that Poland's borders reached their farthest eastward extent.

In the north, Poland's expansion was challenged not only by Muscovy but also by Sweden and Denmark. In 1557, a succession crisis in the northern "Livonian" lands of the Teutonic Order resulted in the invasion of the Baltic region by Russia and a claim put forward by Denmark to Courland. Poland's presence in both territories dates from 1561, although it was not until 1569 that Livonia was brought definitively under joint Polish and Lithuanian rule. In the 1620s a new threat to the area came from Sweden, which after 1629 came to control most of Livonia (that is, north of the Polish-Muscovite-Swedish boundary of 1667/1686), leaving only the southeast corner under joint Polish and Lithuanian rule, and therefore known as Polish Livonia. Whereas the lands acquired from Muscovy along the eastern frontier were made part of Lithuania, Livonia was administered jointly by Poland and Lithuania while Courland remained a vassal state of the commonwealth.

The seventeenth century also witnessed the gradual loss of the Duchy of Prussia, which had been a vassal state of Poland since 1466. At the outset of the seventeenth century, Poland allowed neighboring Brandenburg to administer the Duchy of Prussia (1603). Although nominally still a vassal of Poland, the duchy had by 1657 ended its vassal status and in 1660 was annexed by Brandenburg. As for other border changes along Poland's western frontier, these were minor, with Brandenburg acquiring small pieces of territory near Bytów/Butow and Lębork/Lauenburg that had changed hands several times in the seventeenth century.

It was along the southeastern frontier, however, where Poland was to have the most difficulty. After it annexed Ukraine, Volhynia, and Podolia from Lithuania in 1569, Polish landlords moved in, developing large parts of the sparsely settled regions and transforming them into a center of grain production. As grain exports increased, by the second half of the seventeenth century, this commodity became the most important source of wealth in Poland's foreign trade.

The grain-producing southeast was also part of the open and difficult-to-defend steppe, where the Polish-Lithuanian Commonwealth was to clash with the still expanding Ottoman Empire. Sometimes the conflict took the form of large Polish and Ottoman armies invading each other's territory, especially in the region of Podolia, with its fortified stronghold of Kamianets', and in neighboring Ottoman-controlled Moldavia, where major battles of this kind took place at Cecora (1620) and Khotyn (1621). More often, however, the Polish-Turkish struggle was carried out through proxies: the Crimean Tatars for the Ottomans and the Zaporozhian Cossacks for the Poles. The steppe was crossed by a network of trails used by the Tatars in their annual foraging raids and sometimes major invasions, as in 1624 when a Tatar army moved up the Dniester River and reached as far west as Przemyśl in Galicia. Analogously, the Zaporozhian Cossacks, who were Polish subjects, made raids deep into Ottoman territory, in some cases as far as its capital, Istanbul. On the other hand, neither the Cossacks nor the Tatars (especially the Nogai branch) were obedient subjects of their nominal rulers, and it was not uncommon for them to act against the interests of the states in which they lived.

The most serious example of misunderstanding occurred in 1648, when a Cossack army under the newly elected Zaporozhian leader Bohdan Khmel'nyts'kyi (1595–1657) left the group's stronghold (Stara Sich) on the lower Dnieper River and defeated several Polish armies (battles of Zhovti Vody, Korsun', Pyliavtsi), reaching as far as Zamość in Little Poland. Following an armistice in August 1649, the Cossacks set up their own state. Poland's subsequent efforts to defeat the Cossack army (battles of Batih and Zhvanets') between 1651 and 1653 and to crush Ukrainian peasant revolts failed. Finally, in 1654, the Cossacks reached an agreement at Pereiaslav, in which they came under the rule of Muscovy. This immediately led to a new Polish-Muscovite war, which lasted with interruptions until the Treaty of Andrusovo/Andruszów (1667) and later "eternal peace" (1686). As a result, Muscovy acquired all of the previously disputed Smolensk, Starodub, and Chernihiv regions, and its rule was recognized over the Cossack state east of the

Copyright © by Paul Robert Magocsi

Dnieper River—that is, eastern Ukraine (including the city of Kiev and surrounding area on the west bank of the Dnieper) and Zaporozhia.

Khmel'nyts'kyi's revolt of 1648 permanently weakened Poland's control over its eastern Ukrainian-inhabited territories; it intensified the level of animosity between Poles and Ukrainians that was to last for centuries; and it resulted in the large-scale destruction of Jewish communities, which some writers suggest was second only to the Holocaust of World War II. On the other hand, the creation of a Cossack state provided subsequent generations of Ukrainians with memories of independent statehood—an independence they felt had been achieved in the mid-seventeenth century and should be recreated in their own time.

The year 1648 also initiated a series of events that within less than a century would see Muscovy replace Poland as the dominant power in eastern Europe. Allied with Khmel'nyts'kyi's Zaporozhian Cossacks, Muscovy was emboldened to invade Poland in 1654. In the north, the joint forces took over much of Lithuania and captured Vilnius; in the south, the campaign began with an indecisive battle at Dryzhypole (January–February 1655) and continued with military operations throughout Volhynia and Galicia.

Even more serious for Poland was the invasion by Sweden that began at the end of 1655. This ushered in a six-year period known in Polish history as the Deluge (*Potop*), during which most of the country's strongholds, including Warsaw, fell to Swedish armies from the north led by Marshal Wittenberg, Magnus de la Gardie, and two expeditions under King Charles X Gustavus (r. 1654–60). As a result of the military invasion (marked by decisive battles at Ujście and Warka) and the surrender of many Polish and Lithuanian magnates, all of Poland as far east as Zamość and Przemyśl as well as northwestern Lithuania and Courland came under Swedish domination. Even Transylvania's Prince György II Rákóczi (r. 1648–60), in alliance with the Swedes and Khmel'nyts'kyi, invaded the southern and central part of the country in the first half of 1657, besieging L'viv, Cracow, Brest Litovsk, and Warsaw until his defeat at the battle of Medzhybizh/Międzybóż (July 1657) in southern Volhynia.

It was during the Polish reaction to the Swedish and Transylvanian invasions, which turned into a war for national liberation, that the sieges of various fortresses came to play an important role. These included Daugavpils, Elbląg, Poznań, Warsaw, Cracow, and Brest Litovsk, which were captured by the Swedes, as well as others like Puck, Gdańsk, Toruń, Zamość, and L'viv, which successfully resisted—the most famous among the latter being the Monastery at Jasna Góra in Częstochowa (November–December 1655), which subsequently became a powerful patriotic symbol of Polish resistance to outside invasion.

In the end, the Swedes were unable to take advantage of their victories, and by the Treaty of Oliwa (1660) their presence in Poland, with the exception of Livonia, effectively came to an end. On the other hand, a new war with Ottomans resulted in the loss by Poland in 1672 of Podolia and the central Ukraine, which the Turks were to rule until the very end of the century.

Perhaps the only encouraging event for Poland during the second half of the seventeenth century was a military campaign under King Jan III Sobieski (r. 1674–96). In 1683 he led a Polish army that was instrumental in relieving the siege of Vienna. This was the second unsuccessful effort of the Ottomans to take the city, and the victory over the Turks that was achieved with Polish help marked an important turning point for the Habsburg Empire, which within two decades was able to remove permanently the Turkish presence from the Danubian basin.

The Habsburgs, Hungary-Croatia, and Transylvania, 16th-17th centuries

The sixteenth and seventeenth centuries witnessed the expansion of Habsburg power in East Central Europe and the transformation of Hungary-Croatia from a unified kingdom into three distinct territories. It is from this period that

Hungary-Croatia's long-standing and eventually intimate relationship with the Habsburgs began.

This process started in 1526, when an Ottoman Turkish army defeated the Hungarians at the Battle of Mohács. The king was killed in that battle, and to replace him Hungary-Croatia's lower nobility elected János Zápolyai (r. 1526–40) of Transylvania, while the magnates turned to the Habsburg ruler Ferdinand I, at the time regent of Austria's hereditary lands and then king of Bohemia and Hungary-Croatia (r. 1526–64). The result was civil war between supporters of the Transylvanian and Habsburg claimants to the throne and, in the presence of the all-powerful Ottomans, the division of Hungary-Croatia into three spheres.

The Habsburgs were able to control the northern and western parts of the kingdom (Slovakia, Carpathian Rus', far-western Transdanubia, and Croatia), which came to be known as Royal Hungary, although they were obliged to pay tribute for this territory to the Ottoman Empire until the beginning of the seventeenth century. The Ottomans, who originally supported the candidacy of Zápolyai, decided to rule directly over the central part of the country, eventually dividing it into Turkish administrative units called eyalets (see Map 18). Farther east, the successors of Zápolyai ruled the principality of Transylvania, which, although it was a vassal state of the Ottoman Empire, nonetheless had such a wide degree of autonomy that by the mid-seventeenth century it was virtually an independent state.

The border changes within the Kingdom of Hungary-Croatia shown on the accompanying map reflect the following developments: (1) a steady northward expansion of the

The Habsburgs, Hungary-Croatia, and Transylvania, 16th-17th centuries

Ottoman Empire, which culminated in the siege of Vienna in 1683 and the advance of the Habsburg-Ottoman boundary farther westward; and (2) the territorial growth of Transylvania, at first westward into a region known as the Partium (1606), and then northward into the upper basin of the Tisza River (eastern Slovakia and Carpathian Rus'), which was acquired in 1645 as part of the principality's ongoing conflict with the Habsburgs.

As for the Habsburgs, when the sixteenth century began, their domain was limited to the family's hereditary lands in the Alpine region (Upper and Lower Austria, Styria, Carinthia, Carniola, Gorizia, and Tyrol). But even in the Alpine regions, Habsburg rule was not complete, since the Catholic Church still held large territories, most especially the ecclesiastical states of Salzburg and Trent.

The events in Hungary-Croatia after 1526, however, and the invitation to the Habsburg ruler to become the Hungarian king immediately changed the territorial base of the country. Even if the Habsburgs were effectively limited by the Ottomans and Transylvania to only a small portion of historic Hungary-Croatia, their claim to the Hungarian crown brought with it the Kingdom of Bohemia, which included Bohemia as well as Moravia, Silesia, and Lusatia. By 1541 the Habsburgs were hereditary rulers of both the Bohemian and Hungarian crowns. It is from this period that writers began to refer to the country as the Habsburg Empire.

While periodic wars raged on the eastern frontier with the Ottoman Empire and Transylvania, the Habsburgs were able to consolidate further control over their new hereditary lands. The challenge of the Reformation, which in Bohemia and Moravia was linked to the discontent of Protestant nobles with further integration into the Habsburg realm, reached its culmination in 1618. A revolt in Prague against Habsburg rule initiated three decades of conflict that eventually involved much of Europe in what became known as the Thirty Years' War (1618–48). It was during the initial phase of that war that the last vestiges of independence for the Bohemian crownlands came to an end following the victory of imperial Habsburg forces at the battle of the White Mountain (on the outskirts of Prague) in November 1620. White Mountain (Bílá Hora) was later to become for Czechs the symbol of national defeat and their subjugation to Austrian rule, while the imperial victory helped to transform the Habsburg Empire into the bulwark of Catholicism in Danubian East Central Europe.

Regional particularities within the Habsburg Empire were also gradually ended. In Silesia, for instance, the descendants of the Silesian Piasts had continued to rule in several tiny principalities (sixteen by the late fifteenth century), even after the line of Piasts in Poland had died out in 1370. The Silesian Piasts, who had become vassals of the Bohemian crown in 1335, were still ruling in five principalities at the time Silesia came under Habsburg control. Gradually, each of the principalities lost its independence (usually after its ruling family produced no male heir) and became an integral part of Habsburg Silesia—Opole/Oppeln (1532), Cieszyn/Teschen (1653), and Brzeg/Brieg, Wołów/Wohlau, and Legnica/Liegnitz (all 1675). Outside of the Hungarian sphere, the only territorial loss suffered by the Habsburg Empire during these centuries was Lusatia, ceded to the Electorate of Saxony in 1635 and then confirmed by the Treaty of Westphalia that ended the Thirty Years' War in 1648.

20 The Ottoman Empire, the Habsburgs, Hungary-Croatia, and Transylvania, 16th-17th centuries

The Ottoman Empire, 16th-17th centuries

The expansion of the Ottoman Empire beyond the Danube into Hungary-Croatia began and was largely completed during the reign of Suleiman I (the Magnificent, r. 1520–66), generally considered the greatest of the sultans. The signal for the Ottoman advance came in 1521, when the sultan's armies captured Belgrade. Then, beginning in 1526 and lasting for the next four decades, Suleiman himself led six major invasions into the heart of Hungary-Croatia, as well as another in 1538 into Moldavia in order to defeat the growing power of a local ruler (Petru Rareş, r. 1527–46) and to reassert the Ottoman vassal status of that land. Of those military campaigns against Hungary-Croatia, all but two (1532 and 1566) followed the path of the first in 1526. It was during the 1526 campaign that Suleiman routed the Hungarian army at Mohács and then proceeded to capture that country's capital of Buda. Subsequent campaigns were directed at Habsburg territory, including the unsuccessful siege of Vienna in 1529, and a campaign

that in 1532 brought the Ottoman armies as far as Sopron and Graz.

Initially, Suleiman had hoped to rule Hungary-Croatia as a tributary state through the person János Zápolyai (r. 1526–40) of Transylvania. But when Zápolyai's successors proved incapable of winning the civil war with the Habsburgs, who also claimed Hungary-Croatia, Suleiman returned on another campaign in 1541, from which time the Ottomans decided to rule directly over the central part of the country. The rest of the century was marked by continual conflict with the Habsburgs until 1606, when the first treaty was signed (Zsitvatorok) fixing the boundary between the Ottomans and the Habsburgs, and absolving Vienna from having to pay further tribute for its rule over Royal Hungary and Croatia.

Beginning in 1585, the Ottoman state experienced an extended period of internal conflict that weakened its effectiveness, but by the second half of the seventeenth century the empire's internal stability and expansive designs were restored. In 1660, the Ottomans invaded Transylvania

The Ottoman Empire, 16th-17th centuries

20a

Legend:
- Ottoman territory, ca. 1500
- Ottoman expansion by 1547
- Ottoman expansion by 1606
- Ottoman expansion by 1683
- Transylvania, ca. 1500
- Boundary of Transylvania, 1606
- Boundary of Transylvania, 1645
- International boundaries, 1640
- Holy Roman Empire
- Boundaries of vassal states
- Provincial boundaries
- Ottoman eyalet boundaries
- Major Ottoman military campaigns

0   100 miles
0   100 kilometers
Scale 1:9 780 000

Copyright © by Paul Robert Magocsi

(which in 1645 had expanded its own borders northward at the expense of the Habsburgs), replaced its independent-minded ruler with a puppet prince, and incorporated the Partium under direct Ottoman rule. The following decade, the Ottomans moved beyond the Carpathians, acquiring in 1672 from Poland new territory in Podolia and Ukraine. This same acquisition also brought the Ottomans for the first time into direct territorial contact with Muscovy along the Dnieper River.

Finally, in 1682, the Ottomans began a new assault on the Habsburg Empire. Not only did they gain new territory in Croatia and Royal Hungary, but for two months in 1683 (July 17–September 12) they also laid siege to the Habsburg capital of Vienna. Their failure to capture Vienna, however, proved to be a significant turning point for the Ottomans. Before the century was over, they were to be driven out of most of the historic Kingdom of Hungary and back beyond the Danube-Sava line.

The Ottoman sphere in East Central Europe was basically divided into two categories: (1) core provinces ruled directly by the Ottoman central administration in the capital of Istanbul; and (2) vassal or tributary states that had varying degrees of self-rule and in some cases virtual independence. The system of administrative division in the core provinces developed gradually and took different forms, but by the end of the sixteenth century units know as eyalets formed the basic structure of the empire (see Map 18). Although the provincial administrations of the eyalets were under the direct control of officials appointed by the central government, there were a few areas that remained "self-governing" regions ruled by local potentates whom the Ottomans generally left on their own in return for the receipt of taxes and recognition of their suzerainty. Most of these regions were in the inaccessible mountainous areas, such as Montenegro, parts of Albania, the Pindus Mountains and area around Ioannina/Yanya in Epirus, and, farther south, the Mainalon Mountains north and east of Tripolis in the Morea (see Map 18).

The second category, vassal or tributary states, included Walachia, Moldavia, and Transylvania as well as the Crimean Khanate north of the Black Sea. The Danubian principalities of Walachia and Moldavia became, respectively in 1476 and 1512, permanent vassals of the Ottoman Empire. This meant that while they had the right to choose their own rulers, both principalities paid an annual tribute to the Ottomans, whose ultimate sovereignty was accepted. This did not preclude, however, the rise at times of certain princes who followed an independent foreign policy, such as Petru Rareş of Moldavia (r. 1527–46), whose designs were curtailed only after an Ottoman invasion in 1538, or Mihai of Walachia (the Brave, r. 1593–1601), who expanded his rule to include briefly (1600) neighboring Moldavia and Transylvania (according to its 1606 boundaries). Although Mihai's control over the three provinces was short-lived, he has been considered by latter-day Romanian historians the founder of the first "unified Romanian" state of Walachia, Moldavia, and Transylvania. The recreation of Mihai the Brave's state was to become a goal of Romanian nationalist ideology in the nineteenth and twentieth centuries.

Like Moldavia and Walachia, Transylvania had the right to elect its own princes, but because these princes were always Hungarians who felt that they had to safeguard Hungary's (i.e., the Hungarian nobility's) freedom, they repeatedly fought the Habsburgs. The height of Transylvanian power was reached during the first half of the seventeenth century under the leadership of Gábor Bethlen (r. 1613–29) and the Rákóczi family. From their capitals at Alba Iulia/Gyulafehérvár and later Cluj/Kolozsvár, they followed an independent foreign policy which allowed them to negotiate in 1645 the acquisition from the Habsburgs of seven counties in eastern Slovakia and Carpathian Rus'. It was this independent orientation, however, that prompted in 1660 an Ottoman invasion deposing Prince György II Rákóczi (r. 1648–60) and restoring Transylvania to the status of a vassal state subservient to Istanbul.

In contrast to the three Ottoman vassal states in East Central Europe was the Republic of Dubrovnik/Ragusa. Dubrovnik was the first of these territories to sign a treaty placing it under Ottoman protection (1458), but it was to function effectively throughout its history as an independent city-state. Aside from paying annual tribute to the Ottomans, Dubrovnik governed itself as a city-republic and even maintained consuls in foreign states with which it concluded treaties. Besides the city of Dubrovnik itself, the republic included the immediate coastal region to the north (Primorje) and south (Konavli) as well as several offshore islands (Lastovo, Pelješac, Mljet), a territorial expanse that was brought about between 1272 and 1427 (see Map 20c).

20c The Dubrovnik Republic

Copyright © by Paul Robert Magocsi

The Habsburgs, Hungary-Croatia, and Transylvania, 1683–1718

The defeat of the Ottoman forces on the plain below the Kahlenberg heights overlooking Vienna in 1683 and the success of the Habsburgs and their Polish and German allies in relieving the second Turkish siege of the city represent a turning point in the history of East Central Europe. By 1683, the Ottomans had attained their farthest territorial advance; less than two decades later, the Habsburgs pushed the Ottomans back and extended their own holdings as far as the Danube-Sava line.

In essence, what was at stake was the territorial inheritance of the Kingdom of Hungary-Croatia as it had been before the Ottoman victory at Mohács in 1526. In their

advance southward and eastward after 1683, the Habsburgs were faced with two problems: (1) the military defeat of the Ottomans, and (2) the establishment of their own rule over traditionally anti-Habsburg Hungarian leaders, most especially in Transylvania.

The anti-Ottoman military aspect occurred mainly in two phases, during which some of the Habsburg Empire's most famous generals were to make their mark—Duke Charles of Lorraine, Margrave Ludwig of Baden, and most especially Prince Eugene of Savoy (1663–1736). Besides such foreign generals in the service of the Habsburgs, the empire was part of the so-called Holy League that included the Papal States, Poland, and later Venice and Muscovy. All joined forces against the Ottomans on several fronts.

In the wake of the Ottoman retreat from Vienna, the Habsburgs pressed forward rapidly, taking Buda (1686) and reaching beyond the Sava River to Belgrade (1688) and deep into Serbia (Niš and Priština, 1689). When a peace was finally signed at Sremski Karlovci/Karlowitz in 1699, the Habsburgs were back north of the Sava, but had nonetheless acquired most of the old Hungarian kingdom, including Transylvania, the rest of Croatia, and most of Slavonia. The second phase of the military aspect began in 1716 after the Ottomans invaded Hungary-Croatia, but were annihilated by Eugene of Savoy at Petrovaradin/Pétervárad/Peterwardein (1716). Two years later at the peace of

Požarevac/Passarowitz (1718), the Habsburgs added to their previous conquests the Banat, western Walachia (Oltenia), the rest of Slavonia (southeastern Syrmia), and south of the Sava River a strip of northern Bosnia and northern Serbia.

The establishment of Habsburg rule over historic Hungary-Croatia took almost as long to achieve as their military campaigns against the Ottomans. It was in the northern and eastern parts of the kingdom (Slovakia, Carpathian Rus', Transylvania) that the Habsburgs had the most difficulty. In the 1670s, attempts in Transylvania to overthrow Habsburg rule led by a segment of the Hungarian nobility resulted in political and religious repression (especially against the Protestants), which in turn led to new anti-Habsburg revolts. The first of these that began in 1678 (the *kuruc* rebellion of Imre Thököly) was supported by the Ottomans, and it ended in the 1690s when the Habsburgs drove the Turks beyond the Danube. The second began in 1703 as a peasant uprising in Carpathian Rus' and eastern Slovakia, then was transformed into an anti-Habsburg Hungarian national rebellion led by the last independent prince of Transylvania, Ferenc II Rákóczi (r. 1704–11). When the uprising ended in 1711, Transylvania was reduced to the boundaries it had in Hungary before the sixteenth century. The Habsburgs did reiterate guarantees (1691) for the political and religious autonomy of the three "nations" of Transylvania (Magyar, Székelys, Saxons)—to whom were added those Orthodox

Romanians who in 1699–1700 joined the new Uniate (Greek) Catholic Church. However, Transylvania was no longer to have its own prince; it was separated from the rest of Hungary-Croatia, and it was henceforth administered by a Habsburg governor responsible to a chancellery set up in the imperial capital of Vienna.

In an attempt to seal off further Ottoman invasions, the Habsburgs established permanently policed military frontier zones along their new southern borders. These areas were settled by agricultural colonists who, in return for land grants, served in military units headed by their own members. Such frontiersmen (graničari/Grenzer) were made up primarily of Croats, Serbs, and German colonists. The zones they inhabited came under the direct control of the central government in Vienna, not the local authorities. The first of the military frontiers (Vojna Krajina) was established in 1538 in Croatia and was initially under the authority of the local diet (Sabor) and Croatian ruler (ban). The Habsburgs provided financial support from the outset, and in 1630 took over the frontier's administration. The territorial extent and internal organization of the Croatian Military Frontier changed often during the Habsburg-Ottoman wars and was restored to the extent shown on Map 20b during the first decades of the eighteenth century.

The Ottoman presence beginning in the early sixteenth century and the Habsburg conquest and reconstruction in the early eighteenth century had a profound effect on the ethnographic picture of the Danubian basin. At the beginning of the Ottoman era, the Hungarian Plain east of the Danube—including the Bačka, Banat, Syrmia, and part of Slavonia—was significantly depopulated as Magyars,

Romanians, and Slavs (Serbs and Croats) living there took refuge by fleeing to the north, west, and east. When, by the early eighteenth century, the Ottomans were driven out, the Magyars and Romanians were drawn back into the central plain and to the Danubian-Drava frontier areas. The Habsburg authorities encouraged peoples from other parts of their empire to settle as well, including German and Croat colonists from the west, and Slovak and Rusyn colonists from the north (see Map 20d).

Serbs from south of the Sava River, where their homeland was still largely under Ottoman rule, were also drawn into this area. In order to attract Serb immigrants to Hungary's southern borderland, Emperor Leopold I decreed that they would be allowed to elect their own ruler, or vojvoda, from which the territorial name Vojvodina derives (see Map 20a). In 1690, an estimated 60,000 to 70,000 Serbs crossed the Sava and Danube rivers into the Vojvodina (eastern Slavonia, Bačka, and Banat). In Serbian history, this became known as the Great Exodus. The Habsburgs did not allow the Serbs to elect their own vojvoda, however, and instead incorporated the region into the military frontiers of eastern Slavonia and the Banat. Nonetheless, the strong Serb presence in southern Hungary was to make the Vojvodina the cradle of the Serbian renaissance during the nineteenth century. The net result of these demographic changes was a decline of the Magyar and an increase of the non-Magyar populations in Hungary-Croatia, not to mention the resultant great ethnic diversity that now prevailed in the new Habsburg regions of the Bačka, the Banat, and Slavonia, as well as in Transylvania (see Map 20d).

20d Resettlement of the Danubian basin

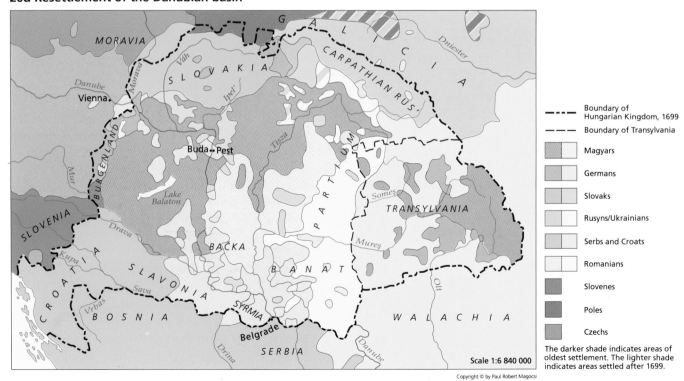

Boundary of Hungarian Kingdom, 1699

Boundary of Transylvania

Magyars

Germans

Slovaks

Rusyns/Ukrainians

Serbs and Croats

Romanians

Slovenes

Poles

Czechs

The darker shade indicates areas of oldest settlement. The lighter shade indicates areas settled after 1699.

Scale 1:6 840 000

Copyright © by Paul Robert Magocsi

21 East Central Europe, ca. 1721

During the first half of the eighteenth century, most territory in East Central Europe remained, as before, within the borders of three states: Poland, Austria, and the Ottoman Empire. The interrelationship of these three powers had changed, however, from the preceding two centuries. In particular, Habsburg Austria was to expand southward at the expense of the Ottoman Empire, while an increasingly weakened Poland was being pressed on the east by Muscovy/Russia and in the north and west by Brandenburg/Prussia. The only other contender was Venice, whose holdings especially on the Greek peninsula and offshore islands actually increased at the end of the seventeenth century, only to be reduced once again by Turkish reconquest on the eve of 1721.

Although Poland was to survive its period of "Deluge" during the second half of the seventeenth century and to regain the Right-Bank Ukraine (west of the Dnieper River) and also Podolia, which had been held by the Ottomans (1672–99), it was not to recover lands farther east ceded in wars with Muscovy (see Map 19a). In essence, Poland's eastern boundary established in 1667/1686, which gave Kiev, the Left-Bank Ukraine (east of the Dnieper), and Zaporozhia to Muscovy, was to remain in effect throughout most of the eighteenth century. The threat from Sweden was also turned back, although not before Poland and the Electorate of Saxony (with which Poland was in dynastic union, 1697–1763) had become the major battle zones during the first phase of the Great Northern War (1700–1721) between Sweden and Muscovy. That first phase ended after two major invasions by Sweden's Charles XII (r. 1697–1718), with his defeat by Muscovy at the battle of Poltava (in the eastern Ukraine) during the summer of 1709.

To the north and west of Poland, Brandenburg was steadily becoming transformed into the strongest Germanic state in the northern part of the Holy Roman Empire. Between 1648 and 1680, the former church lands of Magdeburg, Halle, and Minden were added to Brandenburg; then in 1720 western Pomerania (west of the Oder River) was acquired. But the most significant event occurred in 1701, when the elector of Brandenburg was crowned Frederick I (r. 1701–3), king of Prussia (i.e., "East" Prussia). That land, which had always been outside the Holy Roman Empire, now became the basis of a new powerful kingdom based on the territories of the old Duchy of Prussia in the east and electorate of Brandenburg in the west, still separated from each other by the Polish territory.

The expansion of Habsburg Austria was even more remarkable. Besides their reconquest of historic Hungary-Croatia in two stages (1699 and 1718), the Habsburgs added territory beyond the Danube and Sava rivers in northern Bosnia and Serbia as well as the western part of Walachia known as Little Walachia or Oltenia (see also Map 20b). On the Italian peninsula, the Habsburgs acquired Naples (1714–35) and Sicily (1720–35) for a few decades. More lasting was their acquisition of Mantua (1714) and two coastal regions of Tuscany (1714), from which they were to expand in the 1730s into neighboring Parma and the rest of Tuscany (see Map 22b).

As before, Venice remained the most important of the Italian states with regard to holdings in East Central Europe. Despite its own internal decline beginning in the second half of the seventeenth century, Venice did for a while hold its own in the long-standing rivalry with the Ottoman Empire for control of the Greek peninsula and most especially the islands and coastal cities of the Aegean, Mediterranean, and Adriatic seas. From 1468 to 1718, this rivalry was marked by as many as seven major wars between Venice and the Ottomans. Following one of these, the long Candian War (1645–69) for control of Crete, Venice was forced to cede the island (known as Candia in Venetian sources), which it had held since 1204. In 1684, Venice joined Austria and Poland in a Holy League aimed at the "Turkish infidel." Venetian forces conquered from the Ottomans the Morea/Peloponnese (1687); added Santa Maura/Leukas (1684) and Vónitsa (1699) to its previous holdings in the Ionian Islands; and briefly held Athens (1687, during which Ottoman ammunition stores exploded in the Parthenon), the islands of Chios (1694–95) and Icaria (1694–95) in the Aegean, and the city of Kotor/Cattaro (1699–1700) in Dalmatia. Territories continued to change hands, but when the Treaty of Požarevac/Passarowitz was signed in 1718, the Venetians were forced to give up the Morea and Tenos, the last of the islands they held in the Aegean. Thus, by 1721, all that Venice retained of its once large Graeco-Aegean holdings were the Ionian Islands, a few coastal cities nearby, and the island of Cerigo.

Between 1683 and 1718 the third of the major states in East Central Europe, the Ottoman Empire, was forced out of much of the Danubian basin by Habsburg Austria. As for its tributary states in this region, the Ottomans lost Transylvania permanently but held on to Moldavia and most of Walachia. The autonomous political status of both those provinces was actually reduced, since beginning in 1711 in Moldavia and 1715 in Walachia, the locally elected princes were henceforth replaced by Ottoman appointees drawn largely from Greek (Phanariot) families in Istanbul. As for Dubrovnik, it continued to pay an annual tribute to the Ottoman Empire, although as before it functioned practically as an independent city-republic.

Finally, nearby Montenegro remained one of those areas within the so-called core provinces of the Ottoman Empire, but because of its inaccessible location high in rugged mountain terrain, it led a rather independent existence. In 1516 the ruling Crnojević dynasty had come to an end and

East Central Europe, ca. 1721

SWEDEN

DENMARK
Copenhagen

BALTIC
SEA

COURLAND

POLISH
LIVONIA

Polatsk
(Połock)

Western Dvina

Smolensk

MUSCOVY

MECKLENBURG-
SCHWERIN

Hamburg

HANNOVER

POMERANIA

Szczecin

Gdańsk

Kaliningrad
(Königsberg)

PRUSSIA

Vilnius
(Wilno)

Halouchyn
(Hołowczyn)
14.VII.1708

Liasnaia
(Lesna)
9.X.1708

Minden

Magdeburg

Halle

Minden

PRUSSIA

BRANDENBURG

Berlin

ELECTORATE

Poznań

Warta

Oder

Cottbus

Wschowa 29.X.1706

1708

Vistula

1702

Hrodna
(Grodno)

Neman

1706

Minsk

LITHUANIA

Pinsk

Pripet

Chernihiv

Dnieper

(to Poltava 8.VII.1709)

Kiev

Desna

Leipzig

OF

Dresden

SAXONY

Wrocław
(Breslau)

Cottbus

P

O

L

Warsaw

W. Bug

Lublin

Luts'k
(Łuck)

VOLHYNIA

A

N

D

Desna

UKRAINE

Würzburg

Bamberg

Nürnberg

Regensburg

BOHEMIA

Prague

Vltava

MORAVIA

Brno
(Brünn)

Morava

SILESIA

Kliszów
19.VII.1702

Cracow

GALICIA

L'viv
(Lwów)

PODOLIA

Zbruch

Dniester

Southern Bug

ZAPOROZHIA

Danube

BAVARIA

Munich

Linz

UPPER
AUSTRIA

LOWER
AUSTRIA

Vienna

SLOVAKIA

Ipel'

Košice
(Kassa)

CARPATHIAN RUS'

Iaşi
(Jassy)

Prut

Siret

VORARLBERG

SWITZ.

Innsbruck

TYROL

SALZBURG

Salzburg

STYRIA

Graz

CARINTHIA

Bratislava
(Pozsony)

Buda
Pest

Tisza

Eger

HUNGARY

Debrecen

Szeged

Cluj
(Kolozsvár)

TRANSYLVANIA

MOLDAVIA

Bendery

Trent

GORIZIA

Ljubljana
(Laibach)

CARNIOLA

Zagreb

Drava

Timişoara
(Temesvár)

BANAT

Sibiu
(Nagyszeben)

Braşov
(Brassó)

Venice

ISTRIA

Rijeka
(Fiume)

CROATIA-SLAVONIA

Sava

Severin

WALACHIA

Bucharest
(Bükreş)

BLACK
SEA

PARMA

MODENA

Bologna

Lucca

Florence

TUSCANY

SAN
MARINO

V

E

N

I

C

E

DALMATIA

Zadar
(Zara)

Split
(Spalato)

NORTH BOSNIA

BOSNIA

Sarajevo
(Bosna-Saray)

Belgrade

Morava

Požarevac

SERBIA

Niš
(Niš)

OLTENIA

Olt

Giurgiu
(Yergöğü)

Varna

PAPAL
STATES

Rome

ADRIATIC SEA

Dubrovnik
(Ragusa)

Kotor
(Cattaro)

MONTENEGRO

Sofia
(Sofya)

Danube

Plovdiv
(Felibe)

Maritsa

Edirne

Istanbul

İzmit

Sakarya

NAPLES

Naples

Taranto

TYRRHENIAN
SEA

OTTOMAN

Salonika
(Selânik)

Vardar

EMPIRE

Bursa

SICILY
(to Savoy)

Palermo

IONIAN
SEA

CORFU

IONIAN ISLANDS

LEUKAS
(SANTA
MAURA)

CEPHALONIA

ZANTE

Vónitsa

PELOPONNESE
(MOREA)

Athens
(Atina)

LEMNOS

AEGEAN

SEA

LESBOS

CHIOS

İzmir

TENOS

IKARIA

Monemvasía
(Menavişa)

CERIGO

RHODES

MEDITERRANEAN
SEA

Candia
(Girid)

CRETE

International boundaries

Boundaries of principalities and duchies

Provincial boundaries

Holy Roman Empire

Campaigns of Charles XII of Sweden
during the Great Northern War

Ecclesiastical states

Habsburg lands.

0   150 miles

0   150 kilometers

Scale 1:8 890 000

Historical Atlas of East Central Europe

Copyright © by Paul Robert Magocsi

Montenegro was transformed into a theocratic state ruled by Orthodox bishops (vladikas) elected by local assemblies. The rule of the vladikas, or prince-bishops, was to last until the mid-nineteenth century; however, beginning in 1696 the elective principle was replaced by a hereditary one, whereby bishops of the Njegoš family (through uncles and nephews) retained their rule over the country. Although the fiercely anti-Muslim policy of this Orthodox theocratic state prompted several Ottoman invasions of Montenegro throughout the seventeenth century, the principality—often with the aid of Muscovy/Russia—continued to lead a separate existence that was only nominally under the authority of the Turks.

22 Poland, Austria, and the Ottoman Empire, 18th century

Partitions of Poland, 1772–1795

Poland was able to survive both the era of civil war and foreign wars in the second half of the seventeenth century and then the destructive foreign invasions during the first phase (1700–1709) of the Great Northern War. However, by the second decade of the eighteenth century, the country was severely weakened so that its political life was increasingly dominated by neighboring Russia. This trend became especially pronounced following the War of the Polish Succession (1733–35), after which Poland's kings—Augustus III (r. 1734–63) and Stanisław Poniatowski (r. 1764–95)—became rulers who could do little without the approval of their eastern neighbor. Attempts to remove Russian influence led to Polish movements such as the Confederation of Bar (1768) based in a small town in the southeastern part of the country, but this revolt was crushed by the direct intervention of tsarist troops.

Russian foreign policy interests were directly related to what was to become the first partition of Poland, in 1772. Following Russia's victory over the Ottoman Empire that year, Austria became so alarmed that it threatened to make war on Russia. In order to avoid the potential of a general European conflict, Frederick II (the Great, r. 1740–86) of Prussia proposed to annex parts of Poland, giving territory to Russia that would not be objectionable to Austria while at the same time allowing his own country and Austria to join in the spoils. As a result of the partition, Russia received 93,000 square kilometers (35,900 square miles) with 1,300,000 inhabitants living in Polish Livonia and parts of the palatinates of Połock, Witebsk, and Mścisław (see Map 18 for palatinate boundaries). Prussia acquired 36,300 square kilometers (14,000 square miles) with 580,000 inhabitants in several small palatinates in the northwestern part of the country (but not Gdańsk), which were designated by the new rulers as West Prussia, as well as the Netze District. Austria was awarded 81,900 square kilometers (31,600 square miles) with 2,650,000 inhabitants in the palatinate of Rus' (Galicia) and in parts of the Sandomierz and Cracow palatinates, but excluding the city of Cracow itself on the north bank of the Vistula River. This new Austrian acquisition was named the Kingdom of Galicia-Lodomeria, recalling the title in the Hungarian crown (held since 1526 by the Habsburgs), whose origins went back to a twelfth-century claim of Hungary's kings to the medieval Rus' principalities of Galicia and Volhynia (Lodomeria).

Austria's presence in Galicia had begun in 1769, when Habsburg troops occupied the sixteen Polish-held towns and villages in the Spiš region on the southern slopes of the Carpathians (see Map 8a—inset) as well as a small body of territory on the northern slopes near the town of Nowy Sącz. These acquisitions were then confirmed by the partition of 1772.

Within its reduced post-1772 boundaries, Poland's leaders responded by promulgating a new constitution (May 3, 1791) that altered the governing structure of the country, giving more power to what was to become a hereditary monarchy. At the same time, what remained of Lithuania ceased to exist as a distinct grand duchy. There were opponents of the new constitutional structure, however, and they formed another Polish military confederation. It was actually drawn up in the tsarist capital of St. Petersburg and based in the far southeastern part of Poland, at Torhovytsia/Targowica. The Confederation of Targowica, as it came to be known, cooperated with tsarist Russia in order to overthrow the supporters of the new 1791 constitution. The result was a Russian invasion in 1792 (with major battles at Borushkivtsi/Boruszkowce, June 15; Zelentsi/Zieleńce, June 18; and Dubienka, July 18) and a Prussian invasion that ended in a Polish defeat and the second partition of the country (1793) by the two victors. Russia acquired 250,200 square kilometers (96,600 square miles) with 3,000,000 inhabitants in a large tract of territory that included the eastern half of the former Grand Duchy of Lithuania and the Ukrainian-inhabited palatinates of Kiev, Podolia, and Bracław. Prussia acquired 57,100 square kilometers (22,100 square miles) with 1,000,000 inhabitants in the region around Gdańsk and in several more western palatinates in Great Poland (Poznań, Gniezno, Kalisz, Sieradz, Brześć Kujawski, Płock, Łęczyca, Rawa), which it designated as South Prussia. The second partition also resulted in a treaty of alliance whereby Russia was given a free hand to station its troops in what remained of the country and to control Poland's relations with other countries.

A last attempt to reverse Poland's fortunes began in March 1794 with the outbreak of a national uprising led by Tadeusz Kościuszko (1746–1817). After several major battles against Russia (Racławice, April 4; Szczekociny, June 6; Chełm, June 8; Warsaw, July 7–10; Krupczyce, September 17; Terespol, September 19; Maciejowice, October 10; Praga, December 4, 1794) and against Prussia (Bydgoszcz, October 2, 1794), the Polish revolutionaries were defeated. What remained of Poland was given to victorious Russia and Prussia, as well as to noncombatant Austria in order to maintain a balance between the three powers. According to the third partition, Russia again was given the largest share—a total of 120,000 square kilometers (46,400 square miles) with 1,200,000 inhabitants—that included the Duchy of Courland, most of the rest of the old Grand Duchy of Lithuania (i.e., parts of Żmudź, Troki, Wilno, Nowogródek, Brześć Litewski, and Chełm palatinates), and Volhynia in the south. Prussia received 48,000 square kilometers (18,500 square miles) with 1,020,000 inhabitants—that is, the rest

Copyright © by Paul Robert Magocsi

of western Lithuania (Troki palatinate) and most of Pod-lachia and Mazovia palatinates in the heart of Poland—an area renamed New East Prussia—as well as a small piece of territory northwest of Cracow that was added as "new" Silesia to its own region of that same name. Finally, Austria was able to extend its holdings beyond the Vistula, acquiring 47,000 square kilometers (18,200 square miles) with 1,500,000 inhabitants—an area that included the rest of the Cracow, Sandomierz, and Lublin palatinates as far as the Pilica and Western Bug rivers. This region was called West Galicia.

As a result of the third partition, Poland disappeared from the map of Europe. The total acquisitions on the part of Poland's neighbors during the three partitions (1772, 1793, 1795) were:

	Square kilometers (square miles)	Inhabitants
Russia	463,200 (178,900)	5,500,000
Prussia	141,400 (54,600)	2,600,000
Austria	128,900 (49,800)	4,150,000

Austria and the Ottoman Empire, 1718–1792

After the Habsburg acquisition of Hungary-Croatia from the Ottoman Empire in 1699 (see Map 20b), the eighteenth century was to witness several changes in the border

separating these two powers. The border changes followed several wars not only between the Ottomans and Habsburg Austria (1716–18) but also between the Ottomans and the Russian Empire (1710–11, 1736–39, 1768–74, 1789–92), in which at times the Austrians participated as well (1736–39, 1788–91). Despite the participation of Austria on the side of Russia, the Habsburgs were generally concerned about the advance of tsarist influence in the Danubian basin, and this suspicion between the two "allies" often permitted the Ottomans to be victorious on the battlefield or at the peace table.

Following the military successes of the Ottomans against Austria and Russia in the war of 1736–39, Austria lost northern Bosnia, northern Serbia, and western Walachia (Oltenia/Craiova), which it had held since 1718. From that year until the end of the century, the Austrian-Ottoman boundary was to remain the southern frontier of historic Hungary-Croatia, that is, the Sava-Danube rivers and the crest of the Carpathians between Transylvania and Moldavia-Walachia.

Along their side of the border, the Austrians continued to extend their military frontier districts. The Croatian frontier was reorganized and took its final form in 1752, by which time it was subdivided into Croatian and Slavonian districts with headquarters respectively in Zagreb and Petrovaradin. It was also at this time that Croatian political distinctiveness was curtailed with the abolition of the

Croatian Royal Council in Vienna (1779). The unilateral Habsburg action was eventually accepted by the Croatian diet (Sabor) in 1790. Although the latter continued to exist, it had only nominal authority, so that Croatia became effectively integrated into the rest of Hungary. Beyond Croatia to the east, new military frontiers were set up between the 1760s and 1780s in the Banat and Transylvania.

On the Ottoman side of the border, the Turks also increased their control over the borderland region. Their policy was to reduce the previously semi-independent status of the Ottomans' Danubian principalities of Moldavia and Walachia. Beginning in 1711 in Moldavia and 1715 in Walachia, these areas were no longer ruled by locally elected princes but by governors called hospodars appointed by the central Ottoman authorities in Istanbul. This new status marked the period of Phanariot rule in Moldavia and Walachia (lasting until 1821), so named because initially most of the hospodars were members of Greek families (from the Phanariot district in Istanbul) who were loyal to the Ottomans. Before long, however, many came from the local Romanian nobility who had adopted a Phanariot Greek life-style as well as subservience to the Ottomans.

During the frequent wars between the Ottomans and their northern neighbors, Moldavia and Walachia were occupied by Austrian and Russian armies, especially in 1769–74 and 1787–92. Although the provinces were returned to the Ottoman Empire, outside influence increased. This was particularly the case following the Treaty of Kuchuk Kainardzha/Küçük Kajnarca of 1774, whereby the Russian Empire gained the "right" to establish within the Ottoman Empire consulates in Iaşi and Bucharest, and to make representations on behalf of Moldavia and Walachia in the Ottoman capital.

That same year (1774), Austria occupied a part of northern Moldavia known as Bukovina. The following year the acquisition was recognized by the Ottomans, and in 1787 Austria attached Bukovina to its recently acquired province of Galicia. The last border changes came as a result of the Russian-Ottoman war of 1787–92, in which Austria participated. By the Treaty of Iaşi (1792), the Austrians returned Belgrade to the Ottomans. The city, which had been acquired by Austria only three years earlier, was exchanged for a small strip of land in northern Bosnia. The Ottomans, for their part, ceded the Jedisan to Russia.

23 The Napoleonic era, 1795–1814

The Napoleonic era inaugurated the direct presence in East Central Europe of an entirely new power—France. The era began in 1795 when General Napoleon Bonaparte (1769–1821) assumed the leadership of the military forces of the Directory, revolutionary France's new government. Less than one decade later, the French republic was transformed into an empire when, in May 1804, Bonaparte was proclaimed Napoleon I, emperor of the French. The era ended in 1814 after the final defeat of France's armies and the exile of its emperor by a coalition of most of Europe's states.

The Napoleonic era was marked by extensive French military campaigns that in the course of two decades changed the political map of Europe several times. Centuries-old states ceased to exist, others expanded or contracted their territorial extent, and still others were created anew, usually under French tutelage. East Central Europe, in particular its northern half, was also the scene of most of Napoleon's major military campaigns.

The boundaries on the accompanying map date from 1812, the height of French influence throughout Europe. North of the Carpathians, the border changes resulted mainly from France's war against Prussia and Russia, indicated on the map by Napoleon's campaign of 1806–7. As a result of the treaties signed at Tilsit/Sovetsk (July 7–9, 1807), Prussia lost the lands it had only recently gained in the second (1793) and third (1795) partitions of Poland (see Map 22a). A Polish state was in fact, if not in name, restored in the form of the Duchy of Warsaw, created initially from Prussia's territorial losses. Placed under the hereditary rule of the king of Saxony, the Polish Duchy of Warsaw became, like Saxony, a dependency of France. The Treaty of Tilsit also disposed of two other formerly Prussian-ruled territories: the district around Białystok was ceded to Russia; and Danzig became a free city-state nominally under joint Prussian-Saxon protection although really under French military control. The only subsequent territorial change in this area came in 1809, when after Austria's defeat by Napoleon, the Duchy of Warsaw nearly doubled its size with the acquisition of West Galicia.

In the Germanic lands west of Prussia, the greatest changes involved the elimination of the Holy Roman Empire between 1801 and 1806. At the same time the remaining ecclesiastical states (see Map 21) were secularized, which together with the many petty German states were added to larger units. In the south, Württemberg and in particular Bavaria expanded in size, while in the north a newly established Westphalia (1807) was carved out of Prussian holdings. In the end, all of these states became dependencies of France in the form of the Confederation of the Rhine, which first included Bavaria, Württemberg, and Frankfurt (1807), and to which were subsequently added Würzburg, Thuringia, Saxony, Westphalia, and Mecklenburg-Schwerin (1810).

The boundaries of Austria changed quite often during the Napoleonic era, expanding and contracting in the wake of each of its three losses to France. The first loss followed Napoleon's campaign in northern Italy in 1796–97. After several French victories on Venetian territory (Castiglione, August 5, 1796; Bassano, September 8; Arcole, November 15–17; Rivoli, January 14, 1797) that culminated in the fall of Austria's fortress at Mantua (besieged from May 1796 to February 1797), Napoleon crossed the Alps into Austria, reaching as far as Leoben, where a preliminary peace was signed in April 1797. According to the subsequent Treaty of Campo Formio (October 17, 1797), Austria ceded to France its holdings in Belgium and along the Rhine River in return for Venetia, Istria, and Dalmatia, which had all belonged to Venice (see the accompanying map for the Austrian boundary dated 1804). As a result, once-powerful Venice soon ceased to exist, most of its territory going to Austria and its Ionian Islands to France. Then, as the Holy Roman Empire was gradually being transformed and ecclesiastical states secularized, Austria received the bishopric of Trent in southern Tyrol and Salzburg (1803). Since Austria's Habsburg ruler was simultaneously the Holy Roman Emperor (as Francis II), the abolition of that entity left him without a proper dignity among European monarchs. Therefore, on August 11, 1804, he proclaimed himself Francis I (r. 1804–35) "emperor of Austria," a title that was to become hereditary among his successors. In practice, the Habsburgs loosened their ties to the Germanic lands of central Europe, but at the same time they gave their own possessions a new identity as the Austrian Empire. Finally, on August 6, 1806, Francis I (II) laid down the old imperial crown and the Holy Roman Empire ceased to exist.

Austria's territorial acquisitions along the northern Adriatic proved to be short-lived. Following Napoleon's victorious campaign of 1805 that culminated at the battle of Austerlitz/Slavkov, the subsequent French-Austrian Treaty of Pressburg/Pozsony/Bratislava (December 26, 1805) required Austria to surrender all the lands it had recently acquired from the Republic of Venice (Venetia, Istria, and Dalmatia) to a newly created French dependency called the Kingdom of Italy. Austria was forced as well to cede northern Tyrol to France's client state of Bavaria. Another victory by Napoleon following his campaign of 1809 forced Austria at the Treaty of Schönbrunn (October 14, 1809) to make further territorial concessions: (1) Salzburg to Bavaria; (2) part of Carinthia and Croatia south of the Sava River, which together with Istria and Dalmatia were formed into the so-called Illyrian Provinces attached directly to France; (3) West Galicia to France's Duchy of Warsaw; and (4) the district of Ternopil' in far-eastern Galicia to France's recent ally, Russia. It is useful to note that although the new territory of Illyria was directly under French rule, its brief existence (1809–13) subsequently provided Romantic

Campaigns of Napoleon

International boundaries, 1812

Boundaries of kingdoms, principalities and duchies, 1812

Boundaries of provinces and districts, 1812

French Empire

French dependencies

Austrian territory, 1804

Italian campaign, 1796-97

1805

1806-07

1809

Russian campaign of 1812

Napoleonic battles, 1805-13

Major battles in Russo-Turkish wars, 1806-12

Copyright © by Paul Robert Magocsi

nationalists in the 1830s and 1840s with one of the bases of the so-called Illyrian movement, which called for the unity of the southern Slavs (Yugoslavs) into an independent state.

The southern third of East Central Europe—the sphere of the Ottoman Empire—underwent less change during the Napoleonic era, although its peripheral areas in particular were affected by the political and military turmoil that rocked most of the rest of the continent. The initial changes came about along the Mediterranean and Adriatic coasts. They were directly related to the fact that the two centuries-old antagonists, the Russian and Ottoman empires, had for at least a brief period (1798–1805) become allies. With Ottoman acquiescence, a Russian fleet entered the Mediterranean and a joint Russo-Turkish force took over the Ionian Islands from the French (1798–99). It was also through Russian intervention that the Ottomans finally agreed to recognize formally the independence of Montenegro (1799), which in any case had virtually functioned as an independent state for at least a century.

The Greek-inhabited Ionian Islands were to experience the most frequent changes of rule during the Napoleonic era. With the fall of Venice in 1797, the islands were annexed by France. At the end of 1798, however, the Russians and Ottomans drove out the French, and in 1800 they set up the so-called Septinsular Republic. Then in 1807, a secret clause of the Treaty of Tilsit returned the islands to France, which incorporated them as part of Illyria directly into the empire. Under French rule, a constitutional government based on western patterns was established, making the Septinsular Republic the first Greek national government in modern times. French rule was again short-lived, because in 1809–10 the British occupied all the islands except Corfu and Paxos, which remained with France until the fall of Napoleon (1814).

On the eve of their departure from the area, the Russians also occupied Kotor (1806). In response, the French requested and were allowed by neighboring Dubrovnik to enter its territory. The French never left, and in early 1808 incorporated Dubrovnik along with Kotor (1807) into the Illyrian Provinces of the French Empire. Thus the city-republic of Dubrovnik, which for nearly three centuries had enjoyed virtual independence under Ottoman protection, ceased to exist.

Ottoman rule was also undermined in Serbia, when in 1804 a revolt against local authorities soon became a conflict against the imperial armies. By 1806 the insurgents, led by a former Robin Hood–like brigand known as Karadjordje (Djordje Petrović, 1768–1817), had driven the Ottomans out of Serbia. The Ottomans were unable to put down the Serbian revolt, because their erstwhile alliance with Russia had broken down and beginning in 1806 they were engaged in a new war with tsarist forces.

The newest Russo-Turkish war lasted from 1806 to 1812 and was marked by several battles in the lower Danube valley and naval engagements in the northern Aegean Sea. The Russians quickly occupied Moldavia and Walachia, and they provided some assistance to neighboring Serbia, which hoped to obtain independence under Russian protection. Concern over the impending invasion of its own country by Napoleon, however, forced Russia to cease its hostilities against the Ottomans. By the Treaty of Bucharest (May 28, 1812), Walachia and Moldavia were returned to Ottoman rule, with the exception of the eastern part of Moldavia known as Bessarabia, which was annexed by Russia. The Ottoman military was now free to turn to Serbia. The revolt was crushed in 1813 and the area restored to Ottoman rule.

The turning point in the Napoleonic era came at the end of 1812 with the failure of the French campaign in Russia. Setting out in May from east Prussia with 450,000 men—a force that subsequently grew to 600,000—Napoleon's Grande Armée captured Moscow in September. But the onset of an unusually cold winter and the scorched-earth and evasive tactics used by the Russian army combined to decimate French forces, which returned to Prussia in December with no more than 100,000 men.

The following year, Napoleon restored the French army, which was now confronted by the combined forces of Russia, Prussia, and Austria. Several battles took place in Saxony and Bohemia, culminating in a French defeat in the "battle of nations" at Leipzig (October 16–19, 1813). Before the end of the year, Napoleon's armies had retreated across the Rhine into France. In April 1814, the emperor abdicated, thereby effectively ending the French presence in East Central Europe.

24 East Central Europe, 1815

The boundaries of Europe in 1815 were set at the Congress of Vienna, which met from September 1814 to June 1815. At that lavish meeting, the representatives of the allied powers—Austria, Great Britain, Prussia, and Russia—redrew the map in order to allot the victors territories that had been conquered by Napoleon or that were dependencies of France. In East Central Europe, the greatest gains at the Congress of Vienna were made by Prussia, Russia, and Austria.

Prussia regained territories along its western frontier and added more territory, including Westphalia and the Province of Saxony, while along its southern frontier it annexed the northern part of the Kingdom of Saxony (compare with Map 23). In the north and east, Prussia acquired: (1) Pomerania west of the Oder River and the island of Rügen from Sweden; (2) the territory of Danzig with its main center of Gdańsk/Danzig, whose status as a free city-state ended; and (3) the district of Posen, which it had acquired during the second partition of Poland (1793) but then lost to Napoleon's Duchy of Warsaw in 1807.

The only other change in central Europe, which was nominal rather than territorial, was the creation of the Germanic Confederation. In a sense, this took the place of the Holy Roman Empire, which formally ceased to exist in 1806, and was a response to those patriots who preferred to see a unified German state. In actual fact, however, the new Germanic Confederation was no more than a mutual defensive alliance of thirty-nine princes of independent states (including twelve of Austria's mostly Germanic provinces) and four free cities.

Russia's main territorial gain came along its western frontier, where a Polish state was restored in the form the Kingdom of Poland. Also known as the Congress Kingdom, its territory represented only a small portion of what had been the pre-partition Polish-Lithuanian Commonwealth; and, without the district of Posen, it was even smaller than the Napoleonic Duchy of Warsaw. The Polish Congress Kingdom did have its own government and Polish administration, however, and its constitution underscored a permanent unification with the Russian Empire through the person of the tsar, now declared the hereditary king of Poland. As a distinct entity within Russia, Poland was not divided into the provincial administrative units (guberniias) which, since the reforms of 1802, were being implemented gradually throughout the rest of former Polish-Lithuanian lands that had become part of the empire.

Among other parts of the former Duchy of Warsaw was the city of Cracow, which together with surrounding territory north of the Vistula River became an independent city-state under the joint protection of neighboring Russia, Prussia, and Austria.

Austria's boundaries expanded considerably toward the southwest. The Habsburgs regained all those territories they had held prior to the Napoleonic era (western Upper Austria, Tyrol, Vorarlberg, Tuscany, an area south of Ternopil' in far-eastern Galicia), as well as those they had acquired in 1797 and then lost between 1805 and 1809 to the French Empire's Illyrian Provinces, and to Napoleon's client states of Bavaria (Salzburg, northern Tyrol) and the Kingdom of Italy (Venetia)—see the 1804 boundary on Map 23. Added to these reacquisitions were the former city-republic of Dubrovnik and formerly Venetian-held Kotor, which were joined to the Austrian province (crownland) of Dalmatia.

The only other change in the Mediterranean region came on the Ionian Islands. After Napoleon's first abdication in April 1814, the island of Corfu was ceded to Great Britain, which since 1809–10 had held the rest of the islands. Then, according to the second Treaty of Paris (November 9, 1815) that followed Napoleon's abortive attempt to restore his empire, the United States of the Ionian Islands was created as a dependency of Great Britain.

As for the Ottoman Empire, the close of the Napoleonic era and the Congress of Vienna in 1815 brought, with one minor exception, no boundary changes, although the empire's peripheral areas entered a period that was to lead gradually toward semi-autonomy, then full autonomy, and before the end of the century to independence. The one permanent border change was the city-republic of Dubrovnik, where nominal Ottoman suzerainty was replaced by French rule in 1808 and then incorporation into Austrian Dalmatia in 1815.

As for the other peripheral areas, the Danubian provinces of Moldavia (minus Bessarabia) and Walachia were restored to the Ottomans by the Russian Empire, which had occupied them from 1806 to 1812. Russian influence remained paramount, however, and the frequently changing Phanariot governors (hospodars) appointed by Istanbul were replaced by new governors, often of local Romanian background, who were chosen for a fixed period (seven years) and were not to be removed except with the express consent of Russia.

Neighboring Serbia was also able to obtain a new status within the Ottoman Empire. Following the defeat of the Serbian revolution led by Karadjordje (1768–1817), in 1813, a new uprising broke out in April 1815 under the direction of Miloš Obrenović (1780–1860). The result was an agreement with the Ottoman government whereby Obrenović was recognized as the supreme prince (knez) of Serbia, which in turn attained a semi-autonomous status with its own Serbian administration and favorable tariff and trading privileges.

International boundaries
Boundaries of semi-independent kingdoms
Provincial boundaries
Ottoman eyalet boundaries
Boundary of the Germanic Confederation
Austrian military frontier districts

0   150 miles
0   150 kilometers
Scale 1:8 890 000

Historical Atlas of East Central Europe

Copyright © by Paul Robert Magocsi

25 The Austrian and Austro-Hungarian Empire, 1815–1914

The Austrian Empire, 1815–1866

During the years 1815–66, the boundaries of the Austrian Empire, at least as they pertained to East Central Europe, remained for the most part unchanged. Those years did witness, however, three developments that were to affect the internal and external direction of the empire for the rest of the century. First the Revolution of 1848, in particular events in Hungary, seriously threatened the very existence of the empire, even though it was restored, with its territory intact, the following year. Second, the rise of Sardinia-Piedmont and the subsequent drive toward Italian unification successfully challenged Austrian rule in Italy. Third, the unexpectedly rapid defeat of Austria at the hands of Prussia in 1866 definitively eliminated Habsburg influence in the south Germanic lands, after which Vienna's foreign policy ventures would be directed away from central Europe and increasingly toward the Balkans.

The revolution in Austria broke out when news of the February Revolution in Paris reached Vienna and Buda-Pest during the first week of March 1848. The success of the demonstrations in Vienna prompted uprisings in Lombardy and Venetia (where a Venetian Republic was proclaimed on March 22), and in support of those protests Sardinia-Piedmont declared war on Austria. By the summer of 1848, however, a victory by Austrian forces under General Josef Radetzky (1766–1858) at the battle of Custozza (July 24, 1848) eliminated the Piedmontese presence and restored Austrian rule in northern Italy.

As for the revolutionaries in Vienna, they met in a constituent assembly (July 22), which by early October had retreated for safety to the Moravian town of Kroměříž/Kremsier a few weeks before the imperial capital was brought under the control of Habsburg armies led by General Alfred Windischgrätz (1787–1862).

But the most serious challenge to Austria came from the Hungarians. Their diet at Bratislava/Pozsony adopted a series of laws in early April 1848, which, accepted by Vienna, transformed Hungary into a constitutional hereditary monarchy linked to the Austrian Habsburg realm only through the person of the king. Yet what began as a lawful revolution attempting to secure self-governing status for Hungary as a whole soon degenerated into a conflict between the Magyars and the kingdom's several nationalities, who had their own ideas about the revolution and their future status within the empire.

The Croatian diet (Sabor) in Zagreb wanted for the Kingdom of Croatia-Slavonia the same rights that the Hungarians had won. In April and May, the other minorities all met in their own national councils—the Serbs at Sremski Karlovci, the Saxons at the Transylvanian diet at Cluj, the Slovaks at Liptovský Mikuláš, and the Romanians at Blaj—to express their own demands, which were frequently in conflict with the program of the new Hungarian government. The Hungarian program made no mention of specific rights for national minorities, and moreover it included the unification of Transylvania with Hungary proclaimed at Cluj in June over the protests of Romanian and some Saxon representatives. Faced with these realities, all national minorities were before the end of the year to take up arms against Hungary either in the name of the emperor or on the side of the imperial Habsburg forces.

The Serbs in the Banat (eastern Vojvodina) were the first to revolt, in June. But a more serious threat came from Croatia. As early as April, the newly appointed ban of the diet of Croatia-Slavonia, Josip Jelačić (1801–59), had ordered the Croatian authorities to break all contact with the Hungarian government. Proclaiming loyalty to the Habsburgs, Jelačić himself led an army that set off on September 13, 1848, toward Budapest with the aim of crushing the "rebellion in Hungary." The Hungarians were able to turn back Jelačić at Pákozd (September 29, 1848), and he retreated westward toward Vienna. There he helped General Windischgrätz retake the imperial capital from Austrian revolutionaries. In early October, the Habsburg authorities dismissed the Hungarian government, declared as rebels any who opposed the imperial government, and appointed Jelačić its military commander in Hungary. With the dispersal of their constitutional government, the Hungarians came under the leadership of a revolutionary National Defense Committee headed by Lajos Kossuth (1802–94), who, with General Arthur Görgey (1818-1916), organized the country's defense.

When in December 1848, a new emperor, Franz Joseph I (r. 1848–1916) ascended the throne, the Hungarians declared that they were not bound to him because he was not crowned king in Hungary. The Austrians responded with an invasion led by Windischgrätz. The imperial forces captured Buda (January 5, 1849) and continued eastward to win a victory at Kápolna (February 26–27, 1849). These successes were short-lived, however, because in April the Hungarians under Görgey drove back the Austrians from virtually the entire country. That same month the Hungarian diet meeting in Debrecen proclaimed Hungary an independent republic under the leadership of Kossuth.

In these critical circumstances, Franz Joseph accepted an offer from Tsar Nicholas I of Russia (r. 1825–55) to help him suppress the Hungarian revolution. During the second half of June 1849, tsarist armies descended from Galicia in the north and from Moldavia and Walachia in the east and south, where they had helped to put down revolutionary activity the year before in the Danubian principalities. Meanwhile, an Austrian army under General Julius Haynau (1786–1853) advanced from Vienna through Buda and

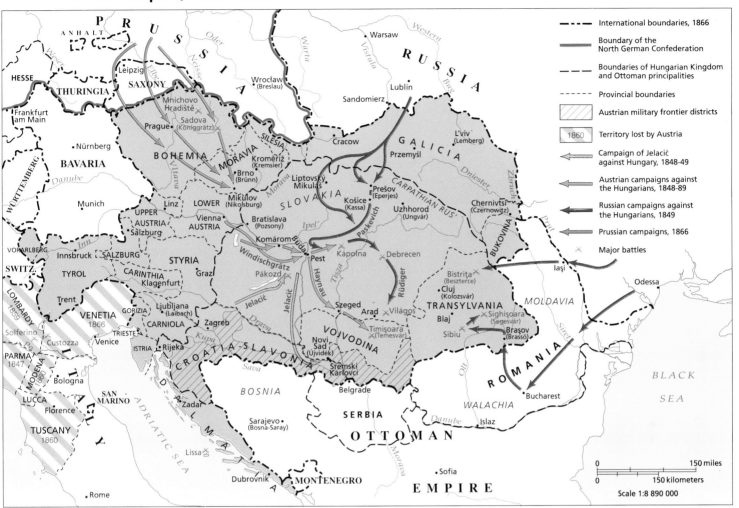

Szeged to defeat the Hungarians at Timişoara/Temesvár (August 9, 1849). Kossuth had already fled the country, leaving General Görgey to surrender to tsarist troops at Világos (August 13). The Hungarian revolution was over.

The only territorial change in the Austrian Empire from this period actually came on the eve of 1848. When a Polish revolution broke out in Galicia in 1846, in which Cracow was an important center for the conspirators, the Austrians suppressed the revolt and then annexed the free city-state that same year, incorporating it into the province of Galicia.

It was not until a decade later that Austria's borders changed, this time with losses in Italy. Backed by France, Sardinia-Piedmont declared war on Austria in 1859, and although the results of the Austro-Sardinian conflict (such as the battle of Solferino, June 24, 1859) were indecisive, international agreements and local plebiscites resulted in Austria's loss of Lombardy (1859), Modena (1860), and Tuscany (1860), followed by their unification with Piedmont-Sardinia, which one year later (March 17, 1861) was transformed into the Kingdom of Italy.

The last of Austria's territorial losses came during the Seven Weeks' War (June-August) of 1866. Although the Austrians defeated Italy in two major engagements (Custozza, June 24, and the Adriatic naval battle near the island of Vis/Lissa, July 20), they had previously agreed to cede Venetia to France in return for the latter's neutrality,

especially with regard to Austria's imminent conflict with Prussia. France did remain neutral, but promptly (July 3) ceded Venetia to Italy, though minus the territory of western and southern Istria (see Map 24), which became part of an Austrian province of the same name.

Austria's hopes for greater influence in the Germanic states were dashed following the lightning three-pronged attack into Bohemia led by Prussia's General Helmuth von Moltke (1800–1891). The turning point came with the Prussian victory at Sadova near Hradec Králové/Königgrätz (July 3, 1866) and their advance into Moravia, where a preliminary peace was signed at Mikulov/Nikolsburg (July 26). According to this agreement, several north German states were incorporated into Prussia, forming an alliance with Saxony, Thuringia, and others, known as the North German Confederation. It replaced the Germanic Confederation of 1815, which had also included the Germanic provinces of Austria (see Map 24).

With regard to the internal structure of the Austrian Empire, the division of the non-Hungarian part of the empire into provinces (crownlands) remained in place. Only slight alterations in provincial boundaries took place at the far ends of the empire. In the northeast, Bukovina, which was separated from Galicia in 1854, became after several changes a distinct province in 1861. In the southwest, the Littoral (Küstenland), which formed a province with part of Istria in Austrian Venetia (see Map 24), was reorganized in the 1860s. In 1861, Gorizia-Gradisca and Istria became separate provinces, while in 1867 the city of Trieste with its immediate hinterland became a province as well.

Greater administrative changes came in the Hungarian part of the empire, and these were related to the revolutionary events of 1848–49. From the outset of the revolution, discontented nationalities in the Hungarian Kingdom (Croats, Romanians, Serbs, Slovaks, Carpatho-Rusyns) opposed in varying degree the Magyar nationalist orientation of the revolution and instead demanded autonomy and/or separation from Hungary. When Austrian rule was restored in 1849, the imperial authorities used these demands as part of their own attempt to weaken Hungary. The Slovaks wanted an "autonomous Slovak territory in upper Hungary," the Serbs an autonomous Vojvodina, and the Romanians an autonomous Transylvania. Autonomy was not granted to individual nationalities, however, but rather to multinational regions which, in any case, were simply ruled directly from Vienna.

Transylvania, whose military districts were abolished in 1851, was—with its Magyar, Saxon, Székely, and Romanian minorities—administered directly by Vienna from 1849 until 1863, after which efforts were undertaken to reestablish its historic autonomy. The Vojvodina—with its Serb, German, and Romanian minorities—was in those areas located north of the military districts given autonomy between 1849 and 1860. The Slovaks were unsuccessful in gaining any autonomy, although their numerically smaller Carpatho-Rusyn neighbors did manage to transform one of Vienna's five military districts in Hungary (which were set up between 1849 and 1860) into a Rusyn district with its center in Uzhhorod/Ungvár for a brief period in 1849–50. On the other hand, the Croats, who under Jelačić had fought loyally on the side of the Habsburgs and who for their services were promised autonomy for Croatia-Slavonia together with Dalmatia (the so-called Triune Kingdom), were allowed no self rule and were simply administered directly by Vienna.

The Austro-Hungarian Empire, 1867–1914

The year 1867 was an important turning point in the history of the Austrian Empire. In 1860 the Habsburg imperial government had embarked on a series of experiments concerned with governing the empire as a whole and especially with attempting to resolve the problem of Hungary, which had been under martial law since the failure of its revolution in 1849. The constitutional experiments and the failures of Austrian foreign policy ventures (losses to Sardinia in 1859 and especially to Prussia in 1866) culminated in the need for a compromise with Hungary. The result was the agreement, or Ausgleich, of 1867, which brought into being the dual monarchy, known as Austria-Hungary or the Austro-Hungarian Empire.

According to the compromise of 1867, Hungary and the rest of Austria effectively became two states joined in personal union through a common monarch (the Habsburg emperor of Austria and king of Hungary); with common ministries of foreign affairs, war, and finance; and with annual delegations composed of delegates from the separate parliaments in Vienna and Budapest who decided matters of common interest to the two states.

The non-Hungarian half of the dual monarchy did not, in effect, have its own name, and was officially referred to as the "kingdoms and crownlands represented in the imperial parliament." In popular terms, this half of the empire came to be known as Austria, or more prosaically as Cis-Leithania —that is, the lands on "this side" (from the perspective of Vienna) of the tiny Leitha River, a tributary of the Danube that flowed through the town of Bruck and formed part of the boundary of Austria and Hungary. The seventeen Austrian provinces, or crownland (Kronländer), were varied in terms of their titular stature and included three kingdoms (Bohemia, Dalmatia, Galicia-Lodomeria); two archduchies (Lower Austria, Upper Austria); six duchies (Bukovina, Carinthia, Carniola, Salzburg, Silesia, Styria); two margraviates (Istria, Moravia); three counties (Gorizia-Gradisca, Tyrol, Vorarlberg); and one town (Trieste).

Despite the seeming differentiation in political status reflected in these divergent historic titles, and despite the efforts from time to time of certain provinces or groups within them (i.e., Czechs in Bohemia, Poles in Galicia) to acquire autonomy or enhanced privileges, each of Austria's seventeen provinces remained administratively equal. Each had its own diet, which was reconstituted or created according to a new law (the February Patent) of 1861, and each province was proportionally represented in the imperial parliament in Vienna that began to function that same year.

The 1860s also witnessed the gradual removal of direct Austrian rule in Hungary, and then, during the next two decades, unification with the rest of the kingdom of those regions that had been autonomous or ruled by Vienna. These included (with their dates of reincorporation into Hungary): the Vojvodina (1860), Transylvania (1865–68), Vojvodina military frontier (1872), and, into Croatia, the Croatia-Slavonia military frontier (1881). The only exception was Croatia-Slavonia, which according to a separate agreement (Nagodba) of 1868 was allowed a degree of self-government under its own diet (Sabor) in Zagreb. The promise to incorporate Dalmatia into a Triune Kingdom of Croatia, Slavonia, and Dalmatia never materialized, however, and Dalmatia remained an Austrian province.

Throughout Hungary, the basic unit of administrative division was the county (megye/comitatus). In the 1870s, this was made uniform throughout the kingdom, including Croatia-Slavonia, following the incorporation of formerly autonomous regions (the Saxon lands in Transylvania) and "privileged districts" (for Kuns, Jazyges, Haiduks) into the county administrative pattern. By 1876, there were in Hungary seventy-one counties, twenty-four boroughs with county status, and two cities with a separate status: the port of Rijeka/Fiume and the capital of Budapest (united in 1873 from former Buda and Óbuda on the right bank of the Danube and Pest on the left bank).

Austria-Hungary's boundaries expanded in 1878, when, as part of a general European settlement in the Balkans,

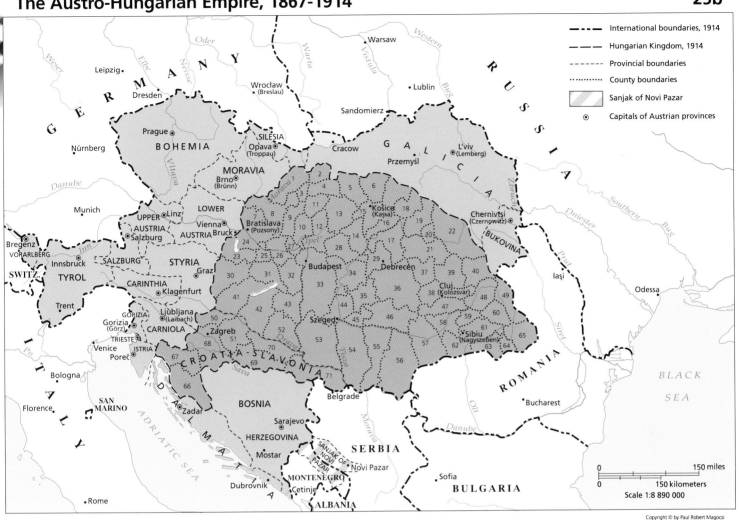

Hungarian counties (Seat indicated in parentheses if different from county name; second name is the Hungarian language form)

1. Trencsén (Trenčín)
2. Árva (Dolný Kubín/ Alsókubin)
3. Turóc (Martin/ Turócszentmárton)
4. Liptó (Liptovský Mikuláš/ Liptószentmiklós)
5. Szepes (Levoča/Lőcse)
6. Sáros (Prešov/Eperjes)
7. Pozsony (Bratislava)
8. Nyitra (Nitra)
9. Bars (Zlaté Moravce/ Aranyosmarot)
10. Hont (Šahy/Ipolyság)
11. Zólyom (Banská Bystrica/ Besztercebánya)
12. Nógrád (Balassagyarmat)
13. Gömör és Kishont (Rimavská Sobota/ Rimaszombat)
14. Borsod (Miskolc)
15. Abaúj-Torna (Košice/ Kassa)
16. Zemplén (Sátoraljaújhely)
17. Szabolcs (Nyíregyháza)
18. Ung (Uzhhorod/Ungvár)

19. Bereg (Berehovo/ Beregszász)
20. Ugocsa (Vynohradiv/ Nagyszőllős)
21. Szatmár (Carei/ Nagykároly)
22. Máramaros (Sighetul Marmaţiei/ Máramossziget)
23. Sopron
24. Moson (Magyaróvár)
25. Győr
26. Komárom
27. Esztergom
28. Heves (Eger)
29. Hajdú (Debrecen)
30. Vas (Szombathely)
31. Veszprém
32. Fejér (Székesfehérvár)
33. Pest-Pilis-Solt-Kiskun (Budapest)
34. Jász-Nagy-Kun-Szolnok (Szolnok)
35. Békés (Gyula)
36. Bihar (Oradea/Nagyvárad)
37. Szilágy (Zalău/Zilah)

38. Kolozs (Cluj/Kolozsvár)
39. Szolnok-Doboka (Dej/Dés)
40. Beszterce-Naszód (Bistriţa/Beszterce)
41. Zala (Zalaegerszeg)
42. Somogy (Kaposvár)
43. Tolna (Szekszárd)
44. Csongrád (Szentes)
45. Csanád (Makó)
46. Arad
47. Torda-Aranyos (Turda/ Torda)
48. Maros-Torda (Tîrgu-Mureş/ Marosvásárhely)
49. Csík (Miercurea-Ciuc/ Csíkszereda)
50. Varasd (Varaždin)
51. Belovár-Körös (Bjelovar/ Belovár)
52. Baranya (Pécs)
53. Bács-Bodrog (Sombor/ Zombor)
54. Torontál (Bečej/ Nagybecskerek)
55. Temes (Timişoara/Temesvár)

56. Krassó-Szörény (Lugoj/ Lugos)
57. Hunyad (Deva)
58. Alsó-Fehér (Aiud/ Nagyenyed)
59. Kis-Küküllő (Tîrnăveni/ Dicsőszentmárton)
60. Udvarhely (Odorhei/ Székelyudvarhely)
61. Nagy-Küküllő (Sighişoara/ Segesvár)
62. Szeben (Sibiu/Nagyszeben)
63. Fogaras (Făgăraş)
64. Brassó (Braşov)
65. Háromszék (Sfîntu-Gheorghe/ Sepsiszentgyörgy)
66. Lika-Krbava (Gospić)
67. Modrus-Fiume (Ogulin)
68. Zágráb (Zagreb)
69. Pozsega (Slavonska Požega)
70. Verőce (Osijek/Eszek)
71. Szerém (Vukovar)

the empire was given the right to occupy indefinitely the provinces of Bosnia (Bosna) and Herzegovina (Hersek), even though they in theory remained under the suzerainty of the Ottoman Empire. The Habsburgs were granted permission as well to station troops in a slice of territory known as the Sanjak (District) of Novi Pazar that separated Montenegro and Serbia. Bosnia and Herzegovina were administered jointly by the Austro-Hungarian ministry of common finance. In 1908, Austria annexed Bosnia-Herzegovina, and while that now single province remained under the joint jurisdiction of both Austria and Hungary, a diet was set up on the pattern of other provinces in the Austrian half of the empire. That same year, 1908, Austria-Hungary pulled its troops out of the Sanjak of Novi Pazar, whose territory was later divided between Serbia and Montenegro.

26 The Balkan peninsula, 1817–1912

The Balkan peninsula, 1817–1877

The six decades following the end of the Napoleonic era and the Congress of Vienna (1815) were marked in the Balkans by three developments: (1) the activity of several nationalist movements and the creation of autonomous or independent states; (2) the intervention in the region of Europe's major powers, especially Austria, Russia, Great Britain, and France, in what they considered the Eastern Question; and (3) the attempts at internal reform within the Ottoman Empire. Each of these developments was to have an effect on both the international and domestic boundaries within the Balkan peninsula.

Serbia was the first to experience political change. Two years after the defeat in 1813 of the revolution led by Karadjordje and the restoration of Ottoman rule, a new uprising broke out under Karadjordje's rival, Miloš Obrenović. By 1817, Obrenović was recognized prince of Serbia (pashalik of Belgrade, r. 1817–39), and the principality was given a measure of self-government under Ottoman suzerainty. In 1829, the Russo-Turkish Treaty of Adrianople (Edirne) reiterated Serbia's autonomous status and promised to restore its boundaries such as they were at the time of the first Serbian revolt (see Map 23). When the Ottomans demurred on that agreement, Obrenović organized uprisings in the disputed districts and annexed them in 1833.

Even more successful than the Serbs during this period were the Greeks. Among the many Greek revolutionary organizations at the outset of the nineteenth century was the Philike Hetairia (Society of Friends), founded in 1814 among Greek merchants in the Russian port of Odessa. This movement had as its goal a general uprising throughout the Balkans, and it found a Greek in Russian service, Alexander Ypsilantes (1792–1828), to serve as its leader. Eventually, the Phanariot-ruled Ottoman provinces of Moldavia and Walachia were chosen as the site of the first Balkan uprising. In February 1821 a revolt in Walachia against Ottoman-Phanariot rule broke out, and this induced Ypsilantes to act. But the expected intervention from Russia did not materialize (the tsar was fearful of revolutions), and the Ottoman forces were, with Russian acquiescence, able to enter Walachia and easily defeat the Greek revolutionaries at the battle of Drăgășani (June 26, 1821).

At the same time that the Ypsilantes venture failed, a more successful revolt broke out in Greek lands proper, in particular the Peloponnese (Morea). By early 1822, an assembly at Epidaurus declared Greek independence. In response, the Ottoman sultan, with the help of his powerful vassal in Egypt, led in 1825 a joint Ottoman-Egyptian force which overran the whole Greek peninsula and restored Ottoman rule. It was this invasion that aroused the sympathies of western Europe, which under the impact of the Romantic ideology of Philohellenism saw

the Greeks as descendants of the classical world who now were renewing the struggle against modern (Turkish-Egyptian) "barbarians."

After some initial hesitation, Britain, France, and Russia intervened, and in 1827 (Treaty of London) they agreed to the creation of an autonomous, though not sovereign, Greek state. Despite the military successes of the European powers (including their naval victory over the Egyptian fleet in the harbor of Navarino, October 20, 1827), the Ottomans refused to yield on Greek statehood. As a result, Russia declared war on the Ottoman Empire (April 1828). This prompted the great powers to sign a new agreement (the London protocol of March 1829), which reiterated the call for a Greek state and proposed specific boundaries. With the Ottoman defeat in the Russo-Turkish War, the resultant Treaty of Adrianople (September 1829) granted Russia control of all three mouths of the Danube River and at the same time included the provisions of the London protocol calling for a Greek state. The three powers secured autonomy for Greece, and then, in February 1830, complete independence under their protection. The only subsequent change in boundaries came in 1864, when the Ionian Islands (a British protectorate since 1814) were ceded to Greece. It was also in the course of the Greek revolutionary wars that the Ottoman ally, Egypt, occupied Crete and held it from 1822 to 1840.

The neighboring provinces of Walachia and Moldavia also gained full autonomy according to the Treaty of Adrianople (1829). That autonomy was protected by a Russian occupation that lasted until 1834. It was during this period as well that the Danube River became Walachia's definitive southern and eastern boundary, since in 1829 the Ottomans were forced to give up their beachheads on the northern bank of the river near Turnu-Măgurele, Giurgiu, and Brăila. Then, in 1856, following Russia's defeat in the Crimean War, Moldavia expanded its boundaries slightly to the east by acquiring a slice of southern Bessarabia from Russia.

Actually, it was in the wake of the Crimean War that the Romanian question was placed on the agenda of the great powers. In 1858 a compromise was reached whereby the two lands became the United Principalities of Moldavia and Walachia. They remained under the suzerainty of the Ottoman Empire but with international guarantees for their autonomy. Each principality retained its own assembly, both of which elected the same governor (hospodar). Subsequent negotiations with Istanbul resulted in the creation in February 1862 of a single state named Romania, with its capital at Bucharest. Although Romania remained a vassal state of the Ottomans, the agreement reached in 1861–62 prompted local leaders to proclaim that a modern Romanian state had finally come into being.

In the face of national revolts and invasion by European

powers (especially Russia), the Ottoman Empire, beginning in 1839, made several efforts to reform its government and administration along lines that would be more acceptable to the liberal concerns of western Europe (Britain, France), while at the same time making possible a modern centralized administration to control more effectively territories still under its rule. In the process, not only were the Ottomans able to retain their sovereignty over Serbia and Romania, they were also able to acquire territory from Russia in 1856 after the Crimean War (the Danubian delta for themselves and southern Bessarabia for Moldavia). The Ottomans even restored their authority in the remote mountainous land of Montenegro, which they invaded in 1852–53. The Montenegrins made some small territorial gains in 1860, but the following year the Ottomans invaded again, forcing them to accept subordination to Istanbul.

Among the Ottoman reforms was a law passed in 1864 that standardized the provincial administration throughout the empire, a process carried out initially between 1867 and 1871, but which continued gradually until 1893. Generally, the former administrative units known as eyalets were transformed into smaller vilayets (districts), which in turn were subdivided into sanjaks. The governors (valis) of each district (vilayet) were, as before, appointed by the central government, but now assemblies were also established in district capitals to participate in the local administration. The Ottoman vassal states—Serbia, Romania, and Montenegro—remained outside the provincial system. In the core lands of the Ottoman Europe, including Crete (Girit) and the eastern Aegean Islands (Cezayir-i Bahr-i Sefid), there were thirteen districts by 1877.

The Balkan peninsula, 1878–1912

The ability of the Ottomans to maintain or restore their rule in the Balkans was to be challenged successfully during the 1870s as a result of internal revolts and external intervention, most especially from the Russian Empire. During the 1860s several states followed the lead of Greece in reaching secret bilateral agreements that were intended to result in a united Balkan uprising against the Ottoman Empire. These efforts at Balkan unity failed, however, and instead the following decade witnessed uncoordinated revolts against Ottoman rule that broke out in several areas. The revolts attracted the immediate attention of the great European powers, who were drawn into Balkan affairs. The result was what came to be known as the Eastern Crisis (1875–78).

The first uprising began in 1875 in Ottoman-ruled Hersek (Herzegovina), followed soon after by another in Bosna (Bosnia) and the following year in central Bulgaria. Also in 1876, Serbia and Montenegro declared war on the Ottomans. The Serbians were defeated at Aleksinac (September 1), and this prompted the self-styled protector of these small Balkan states, the Russian Empire, to invade the Ottoman Empire. The result was the Russo-Turkish War of 1877–78, memorable for the stubborn six-month resistance of the Ottomans against a joint Russian-Romanian force at Pleven (July 19–December 10, 1877). Pleven did finally fall, and after another victory at Sheinovo south of the Shipka pass (January 8–9, 1878), the Russians were able to advance as far as the outskirts of Istanbul.

Just outside the Ottoman capital, in the little village of Yeşilköy/San Stefano, the sultan was forced to accept Russia's terms for redrawing Balkan borders. Known as the Treaty of San Stefano (March 3, 1878), the agreement's chief feature was the creation of a large independent state of Bulgaria, which, it was assumed, would be a Russian satellite and include not only Bulgarian territory north and south (East Rumelia) of the Balkan Mountains but also parts of Thrace and virtually all of Macedonia as far as the Aegean Sea. Russia's other Balkan allies—Montenegro, Serbia, and Romania—were to become fully independent, each expanding its territory, with Romania being given the Dobruja and the Danubian delta in return for surrendering a portion of Bessarabia (just north of the Danubian delta) to Russia. Finally, Bosnia-Herzegovina, where in 1875 the revolt that touched off the Eastern Crisis had begun (and which was promised to Austria in 1877 by Russia should the latter win its war with the Ottomans), was now to remain part of the Ottoman Empire connected via a small strip of land in the middle of the Sanjak of Novi Pazar.

The Treaty of San Stefano with its large Russian client state of Bulgaria alarmed other Balkan states (Romania, Serbia, Greece) as well as the great powers (especially Austria-Hungary and Britain). Consequently, an international congress was convened at Berlin, resulting in a new agreement reached on July 13, 1878, that abrogated the arrangements made at San Stefano. According to the Treaty of Berlin, Bulgaria, with substantially reduced boundaries, became an autonomous tributary state of the Ottoman Empire with its own prince (designated by the Congress of Berlin) and national assembly. The other Bulgarian territory, East Rumelia, became a separate semi-autonomous province with a Christian governor appointed by the Ottomans. Thrace and Macedonia were to remain under direct Ottoman rule.

On the other hand, Serbia, Montenegro, and Romania were, as at San Stefano, recognized as fully independent states, each acquiring territorial additions. Austria-Hungary was allowed to occupy Bosnia-Herzegovina indefinitely, under a European mandate, and was permitted to station troops in the neighboring Sanjak of Novi Pazar, even though both areas were still theoretically part of the Ottoman Empire.

In the decade following the Congress of Berlin, the only territorial changes in the Balkans came in Greece and Bulgaria. Despite a pro-Greek uprising in Thessaly in 1878, Greece was denied this area at the Congress of Berlin. Finally, three years later, Thessaly and part of southern Epirus were acquired by Greece through agreement with the Ottomans. Small parts of northern Thessaly were regained by the Ottoman Empire in 1897 following Greece's loss in a war with the Turks.

Greece also aspired to annex the island of Crete, but this goal took much longer to fulfill. The complicated history of the island, which was returned to Ottoman rule in 1840, was marked by a series of uprisings (1841, 1858, 1866–68) by the Greek population against its local Muslim and

The Balkan peninsula, 1817-1877

Map 26a legend:

- —·—·— International boundaries, 1877
- — — — Boundaries of kingdoms and principalities
- ············ Ottoman district boundaries
- ⊙ Capitals of Ottoman districts
- 1833 Dates of territorial acquisition
- ⤬ Battles of the Greek revolution

Scale 1:9 780 000

0 — 150 miles
0 — 150 kilometers

Copyright © by Paul Robert Magocsi

The Balkan peninsula, 1878-1912

Map 26b legend:

- ——— Proposed boundaries of Treaty of San Stefano, 1878
- —·—·— International boundaries, 1912
- — — — Boundary of Hungarian Kingdom
- ------ Boundaries of Austrian provinces
- 1881 Dates of territorial acquisition
- ⟵ Main Russian campaigns during Russo-Turkish War, 1877-78
- ⤬ Major battle sites

Scale 1:9 780 000

0 — 150 miles
0 — 150 kilometers

Copyright © by Paul Robert Magocsi

Historical Atlas of East Central Europe

converted-Muslim Greek rulers. Uprisings in 1896 and 1906 called for union with Greece, but this was blocked by the great powers, especially Great Britain, which did not want to see the Ottoman Empire weakened any further. The Ottomans withdrew their forces in 1898, and Crete functioned thereafter as an autonomous state governed by an assembly at Canea under the protection (and until 1909 under the occupation) of the great powers.

Bulgarian expansion occurred in 1885, when nationalist leaders in East Rumelia overthrew their semi-autonomous government and demanded union with Bulgaria. A year later, the signatories to the Treaty of Berlin, with the exception of Russia, recognized the rule of Bulgaria's prince over East Rumelia. This was to have been for only five years, but it became in fact permanent. Finally in 1908, Ferdinand I (r. 1887–1918) proclaimed himself tsar and declared Bulgaria to be an independent country. This unilateral Bulgarian move came at the same time as the international crisis over Bosnia-Herzegovina, which was annexed by Austria on October 6, the day after Bulgarian independence was declared. Overshadowed by the Bosnian crisis and in the throes of their own postrevolutionary reform era, the Ottomans eventually accepted Bulgaria's independence.

Despite the unification with East Rumelia (1885) and the attainment of independence (1908), Bulgarian nationalists regarded the boundaries set at the Treaty of San Stefano as the true borders of the country. Moreover, the boundaries of the Exarchate of the Bulgarian Orthodox Church, established in 1870 by the Ottoman government (see Map 35), largely coincided with the San Stefano borders of Bulgaria. This was to cause great friction with the Serbian Orthodox metropolitan in Belgrade and the Orthodox ecumenical patriarch in Istanbul, both of whom refused to recognize the Bulgarian exarchate's jurisdiction. It was this struggle to ''restore'' Bulgaria according to San Stefano that was to create a new Balkan crisis on the eve of World War I.

27 The Balkan peninsula on the eve of World War I

Ethnolinguistic distribution

The Balkan peninsula contained a wide variety of distinct ethnolinguistic groups. Some of these, like Greeks, Turks, Albanians, Italians, and Romanians, were distinguished primarily by the language they spoke. Others were linguistically related but differentiated by religion, such as Serbo-Croatian-speaking Catholic Croats from Orthodox Serbs, Serbo-Croatian-speaking Muslim Bosnians from Orthodox Serbs and Catholic Croats, or Bulgarian-speaking Muslim Pomaks from Orthodox Bulgarians. Still others, like the Jews, were distinguished solely by religion. Finally, some groups became distinct because of the region they inhabited (Montenegrins and Macedonian Slavs from linguistically related Serbs and Bulgarians) or because of their life-style (Gypsies and Vlachs).

Some of the region's groups lived in compact ethnolinguistic territories, while others were intermixed and no clear territorial boundaries separated them. The most complex ethnolinguistic areas were found in those lands left to the Ottoman Empire following the Treaty of Berlin of 1878. Particularly problematic were Thrace and Macedonia, located in the heart of Ottoman East Central Europe.

Macedonia covered about 65,000 square kilometers (25,000 square miles) from the Šar Mountains near Prizren in the north to the Pindus Mountains, Mount Olympus, and the Aegean Sea in the south; and from Lake Ohrid in the west to the Rhodope Mountains in the east. Within this area there were fewer than two million people, divided into as many as nine distinct groups: Turks, Bulgars, Greeks, Serbs, Macedonians, Albanians, Vlachs or Kutzo-Vlachs, Jews, and Gypsies. All of these except the Jews were represented in the countryside; the cities (Salonika, Kastoria, Florina, Serrai, Skopje, Ohrid, Bitola) contained significant percentages and sometimes a majority of Turks, Greeks, and Jews.

After the San Stefano boundaries of Bulgaria (which included most of Macedonia—see Map 26b) were rejected at the Congress of Berlin (1878), scholars and politicians from Bulgaria, Serbia, and Greece began to claim that

The Balkan peninsula: ethnolinguistic distribution, ca. 1910   27a

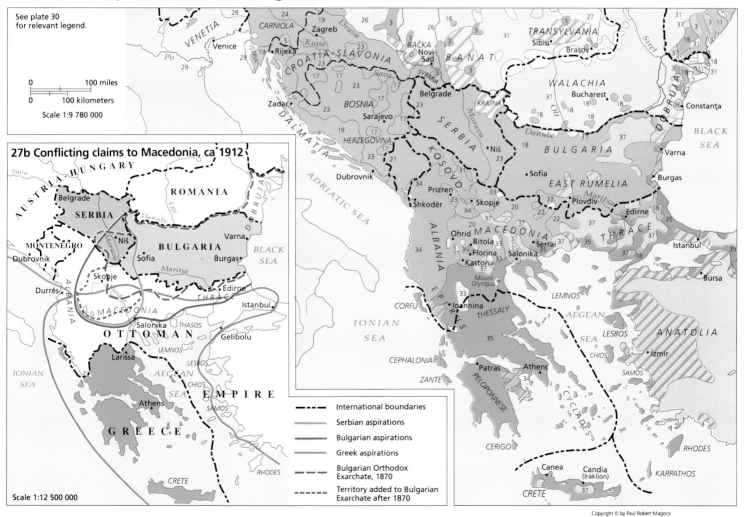

Macedonia rightfully belonged to their respective countries. By the 1880s, each orientation had its own organization—the Cyril and Methodius Society for the Bulgarians, the Society of Saint Sava for the Serbs, and the National Society (Ethnike Hetairia) for the Greeks. These competing organizations propagandized not only among their own respective groups within Macedonia but also among the Macedonian Slavs living there. Thus each of the three rival claimants for Macedonia denied that the Slavs living there were a distinct people, but rather were Bulgarians, Serbs, or "Slavophone" Greeks.

Of great importance to the Bulgarians in this struggle for the allegiance of Macedonia's Christian Slavs was the Bulgarian Exarchate, created in 1870 by the Ottoman government and expanded in the following decades. Not only did the exarchate challenge the jurisdiction of the Greek ecumenical patriarchate and Serbian patriarchate in Macedonia, it also promoted the Bulgarian national orientation there. The Ottomans allowed any district to join the Bulgarian exarchate if two-thirds of its inhabitants chose to do so, and by the first decade of the century most of the Christians (Macedonian Slavs and Bulgarians) in Macedonia and Thrace did just that.

Besides cultural and religious organizations, in 1893 the Internal Macedonian Revolutionary Organization (IMRO) was founded. It supported the idea of political autonomy for Macedonia. IMRO was soon challenged by a Macedonian Supreme Committee based in Sofia, which rejected "separatism" and wished to unite Macedonia with Bulgaria. As a result, Macedonia became a field for underground sabotage and terrorist activity carried out by these two groups as well as by Greek and Serbian infiltrators. Such revolutionary activities culminated in 1903 with the Ilinden Uprising organized by IMRO, which hoped to seize the district of Monastir (see Map 26a) as the first step to the liberation of all of Macedonia.

Why was this rivalry between Bulgaria, Serbia, and Greece so intense? They all had three main reasons for wanting control of Macedonia: (1) it would enlarge the respective state and incorporate more of its nationals; (2) it would also mean gaining control of the Vardar and Struma valleys and railroads, with their great economic advantages; and (3) it would transform whoever controlled the territory into the strongest power in the region. But the Ottomans were able to suppress the Ilinden Uprising, and especially following the Young Turk revolution of June-July 1908 and the establishment of a constitutional government, the Turks were more determined than ever to keep their European territories (Macedonia, Thrace, Albania). Therefore, the Balkan rivals became convinced that before their own claims to these areas could be secured, Ottoman rule first had to be eliminated.

The Balkan peninsula, 1912–1913

Despite the determination of the new Ottoman government to hold on to its Balkan lands, within a few months of the Young Turk revolution the empire suffered two major losses: in October 1908 Bulgaria unilaterally declared its independence, and Austria-Hungary annexed Bosnia-Herzegovina outright, agreeing only to remove its garrisons from the Sanjak of Novi Pazar, which was returned to full Ottoman rule (see Map 26b).

Russia viewed the events of 1908 as a setback to its Balkan policy, and to restore its influence in the area the tsarist government began to cooperate with Italy, which had its own agenda vis-à-vis Ottoman territory. It was, in fact, an Ottoman defeat at the hands of Italy in Libya (1911) and the Italian occupation of Rhodes and other Dodecanese Islands (1912) that encouraged the Balkan states to act.

During the first half of 1912, Bulgaria, Serbia, Montenegro, and Greece signed unilateral treaties of alliance (including a Bulgarian-Serbian agreement to divide Macedonia), which resulted in the creation of a Balkan League directed against the Ottoman Empire. Russia saw the Balkan League as a useful ally against further Austro-Hungarian advances in the area, but the Balkan states acted independently to achieve their own territorial interests. The result was the outbreak of the First Balkan War in October 1912.

In Macedonia, the Serbs and Bulgarians advanced separately from the north, defeating the Ottomans at Kumanovo (October 24, 1912), Štip (October 29), and Bitola/Monastir (November 18), while simultaneously the Greeks advanced from the south, defeating the Ottomans at Sérvia (October 23) and Yiannitsa (November 1–2). The Greeks also moved westward, securing the coastal regions near Préveza and then moving inland to force the capitulation of Ottoman forces at Ioannina (March 3, 1913). In Thrace, the Bulgarians not only won battles at Kŭrdzhali/Kircaali (October 10, 1912) and Lüleburgaz/Liule-Burgas (October 30), they laid siege to and eventually captured Kırklareli/Lozengrad (October 24–29) and Edirne (October 23–March 26, 1913), and they advanced as far as Istanbul, which they besieged for two months (November–December 1912) before being held to a stalemate along a line at the fortifications of Çatalca/ Chataldzha. After an abortive peace conference in London (December–January), the war continued until April 1913, by which time the Ottomans were driven entirely out of Europe except for small strips of land they retained on the peninsula of Gallipoli and behind the Çatalca line near Istanbul (see the demarcation line on Map 27c).

Peace negotiations were renewed in London, and on May 30 the great powers imposed a treaty. Bulgaria was permitted to retain the territories along its demarcation line with the exception of eastern Thrace, where territory beyond a line stretching from Enez/Enos to Kıyıköy/Midiia was returned to the Ottomans. The other Balkan states were also frustrated in their territorial designs because the great powers, especially Italy and Austria-Hungary, were determined to block Serbian access to the Adriatic and the Albanian town of Durrës, which the Serbs hoped to make their only seaport.

It was at this point that the Albanian question became a topic on the international agenda. The Albanians themselves had organized a league at Prizren as early as 1878 to press for autonomy within the Ottoman Empire. The Albanian (or Prizren) League failed to achieve its goals,

International boundaries, 1913

Boundary of Hungarian Kingdom

Boundaries of Austrian provinces

Demarcation line following the
First Balkan War, April 1913

Bulgarian-Ottoman boundary determined
by the Treaty of London, May 30 1913

1913   Date of territorial acquisition

Copyright © by Paul Robert Magocsi

however, and it was abolished in 1881. Nonetheless, the Albanians continued to press for autonomy. Always concerned with the territorial designs of their Montenegrin, Serb, and Greek neighbors, the Albanians sought security by remaining loyal to Ottoman rule. But when Albanian demands remained unfulfilled, an armed rebellion began at Priština in 1910. For the next two years, several new Albanian revolts broke out which, combined with pressure from neighboring Balkan states, forced the Ottoman government in August 1912 to grant an—albeit limited —autonomy to the Albanians. No sooner was Albanian autonomy achieved than the First Balkan War broke out. In the face of the invading armies of Serbia, Montenegro, and Greece, the Albanian leaders met at Vlorë (November 28, 1912), where, in light of these new circumstances, they decided to declare their independence.

The great powers recognized Albanian independence, and at the London conference (May 1913) they agreed to form an international commission to determine the new country's boundaries. Meanwhile, the three victors were forced to surrender their Albanian conquests—Serbia the center and Adriatic coast, Montenegro the north (including Shkodër), and Greece the south. Serbian territorial frustration was subsequently compensated in Macedonia, which was supposed to have been divided between Serbia and Bulgaria according to their treaty of alliance

on the eve of the war. Although the Greeks were denied southern Albania (which they call northern Epirus), they did acquire a large portion of southern Macedonia (including Salonika), Epirus, and international recognition of their rule in Crete, to which the Ottomans now abandoned all further claim. The eastern Aegean islands were left to the disposition of the great powers.

The Treaty of London proved unsatisfactory to all the Balkan states, but most especially to Bulgaria, which felt it had deserved Macedonia. As a result, one month later on June 29–30, 1913, Bulgaria attacked Serbian and Greek positions, precipitating the Second Balkan War, in which Montenegro, Romania, and the Ottomans joined Serbia and Greece in an anti-Bulgarian alliance. The war was over within a month. According to the Treaty of Bucharest (August 10), defeated Bulgaria was forced to give up Edirne and the rest of eastern Thrace to the Ottomans, southern Dobruja to Romania, and all of Macedonia except for Strumica to Serbia and Greece. Also, the Sanjak of Novi Pazar was divided between Montenegro and Serbia, and the eastern Aegean islands of Thasos, Lemnos, Lesbos, Chios, and Samos were joined to Greece. Finally, before the end of the year, an international commission settled the boundaries of independent Albania, which left the Albanians of Kosovo (the former Sanjak of Novi Pazar) outside the new state.

28 Canal and railway development before 1914

The nineteenth century, in particular its second half, was the era of the railroad. East Central Europe contained some of the continent's earliest railway systems, but parts of the region, especially the southern Balkans, had few if any railway lines even as late as the outset of the twentieth century.

Before the first railroads appeared in the 1840s, river transport and overland roads were the main means of communication. One of the earliest canals constructed in East Central Europe was the Plauen Canal (1745), which connected the Elbe River at Magdeburg with the Havel River near Brandenburg, and from there continued eastward past Berlin to the Finow Canal (1746), connecting with the lower Oder River near the Baltic port of Szczecin/Stettin. Other early waterways included the Bydgoszcz Canal (1774), linking the city of Bydgoszcz/Bromberg, by way of the Noteć, Warta, and Oder rivers, with the Frankfurt an der Oder region; and far to the south, the Bega Canal (ca. 1710), connecting the town of Timişoara/Temesvár with a tributary that reached the Danube River between Novi Sad and Belgrade.

Canal building continued in East Central Europe during the nineteenth century both before and after the coming of the railroad. Some canals were intended to connect river systems such as the Dnieper and Vistula system via the Pripet and Western Bug rivers near Brest (Dnieper-Bug Canal, 1841), and the Neman and Vistula system via the Narew and Neman rivers near Hrodna/Grodno (Augustów Canal, 1830). Others were built to link industrial and commercial centers with their hinterland, such as from Gdańsk/Danzig via the Vistula (1850) and Oberland (1860) canals, from Vienna via the Wiener Neustadt Canal (1804), and from the Danube River via several canals into the Hungarian Plain (Franz Canal, 1803; Sarvíz Canal, 1840; Franz Josef Canal, 1875).

The most significant achievement in water transport occurred when the Danube was finally made accessible to traffic that could travel from the Black Sea mouths of the river to Vienna and eventually as far as Ulm in far-eastern Württemberg. The possibility of such navigation was a long process that began in the 1830s with the widening of the riverbed in the Hungarian Plain, and it culminated with an extensive program of canal building and channel work at the river's mouths, especially along the middle mouth between Tulcea and Sulina. Nonetheless, the portion of the Danube known as the Iron Gates, between Orsova and Turnu Severin, remained problematic. Despite several canals and channel blasting completed in 1895, upstream traffic had to be towed through the Iron Gates by winch steamer and later (after World War I) by a locomotive running on an isolated section of track along the canal bank. This method was used until the completion of new locks as part of the Iron Gates hydroelectric project in 1971.

Much more important than canals for East Central Europe was the railroad. In fact, it was the lack of access to waterways, and therefore the potential for decline as a commercial center, that led developers in Leipzig to construct Europe's first long-distance steam railway in 1839. The initial line ran from Leipzig eastward to Dresden. Thus, East Central Europe, in particular Saxony, was in the forefront of railway development from its earliest stages. By the mid-nineteenth century, Berlin, Vienna, and Buda/Pest were focal points for a network of lines connecting the industrial areas of Saxony, Silesia, Bohemia, Moravia, and Lower Austria with ports on the Baltic (Kiel and Szczecin) and the Adriatic (Trieste and Rijeka).

The economic profitability of railroads was soon enhanced by their military value as a quick and efficient means of transporting weapons and soldiers. The economic and strategic complementarity of railroads was most evident in the so-called Three Emperors' Corner (Dreikaiserecke) where the German, Russian, and Austrian empires met in upper Silesia (near Katowice), southwestern Poland (Częstochowa), and western Galicia and northern Moravia (Cracow and Ostrava). Some of the earliest and subsequent lines connected this area with the three imperial capitals: Berlin (via Wrocław), Vienna (via Ostrava and Přerov), and St. Petersburg (via Warsaw and Vilnius).

The greatest growth of long-distance railways in East Central Europe was during the 1860s and 1870s in the German and Austro-Hungarian empires, and to a lesser degree in the western regions of the Russian Empire. In contrast, the Ottoman-controlled Balkans lagged behind, although some early lines were built in the 1870s in what was by then self-governing Romania. As for the Ottomans themselves, their earliest interest in railroad building was directly related to military concerns. Thus the line from Salonika to Titova Mitrovica built as early as 1873 was constructed specifically for easier control of potential disturbances in Macedonia. Similar concerns prompted the beginning of lines through Ottoman Thrace and Bulgaria, into which connecting lines were completed in 1873 from Istanbul to Alexandroúpolis and through Edirne to Plovdiv and beyond. This work was interrupted by the Eastern Crisis of 1878. In any case, the great powers were not anxious to see the development in the Ottoman Empire of better railroad communications that could be used for military purposes. By the 1890s, however, German and French companies were building railroad lines for the Ottomans that had strategic value, connecting Istanbul via Alexandroúpolis directly to Salonika and from there north to Bitola.

The ongoing commercial interests of western European developers, combined with the expansionist concerns of new state railway companies in Romania (1882), Bulgaria (1884), and Serbia (1887), eventually made it possible to

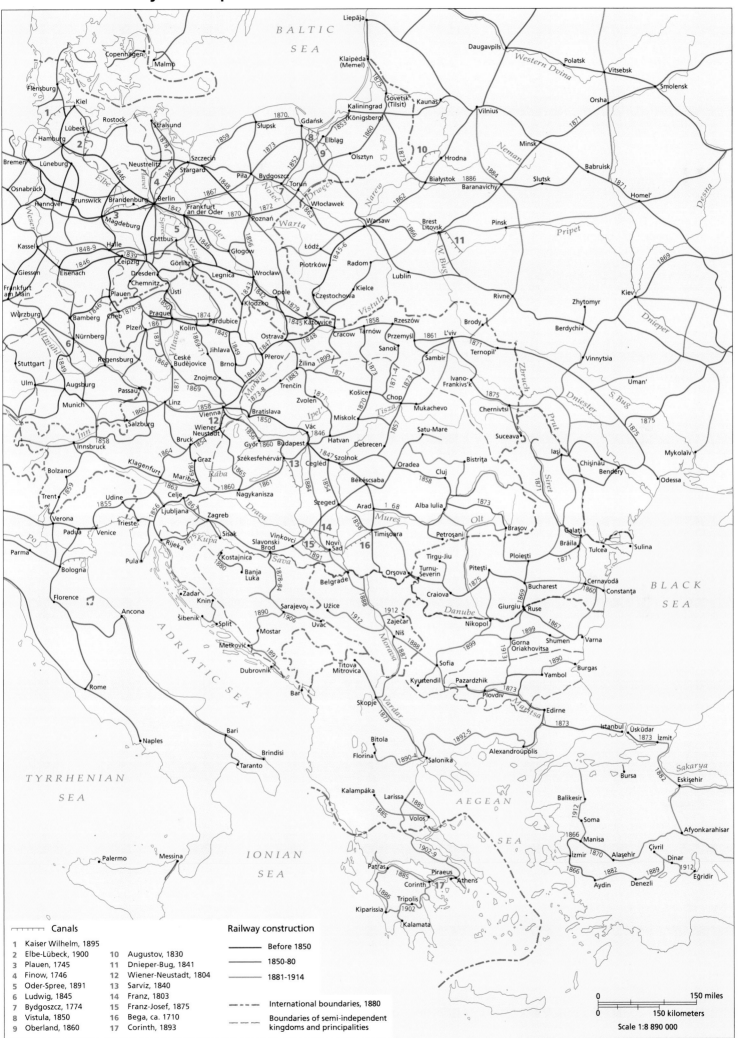

Canals

1 Kaiser Wilhelm, 1895
2 Elbe-Lübeck, 1900
3 Plauen, 1745
4 Finow, 1746
5 Oder-Spree, 1891
6 Ludwig, 1845
7 Bydgoszcz, 1774
8 Vistula, 1850
9 Oberland, 1860
10 Augustov, 1830
11 Dnieper-Bug, 1841
12 Wiener-Neustadt, 1804
13 Sarvíz, 1840
14 Franz, 1803
15 Franz-Josef, 1875
16 Bega, ca. 1710
17 Corinth, 1893

Railway construction

— Before 1850
— 1850-80
— 1881-1914

—·—·— International boundaries, 1880

—·—·· Boundaries of semi-independent
kingdoms and principalities

0 ————— 150 miles
0 ————— 150 kilometers
Scale 1:8 890 000

Historical Atlas of East Central Europe

Copyright © by Paul Robert Magocsi

have direct rail service from Istanbul to Vienna and points west. This was achieved by the Oriental Railway Company, whose Paris to Istanbul run became subsequently famous as the Orient Express. When it first began service in the 1870s, the Orient Express went from Vienna via Budapest, Szeged, Timişoara, Orşova, Bucharest, and Ruse to Varna on the Black Sea coast, where passengers transferred to steamers that took them on the last leg of the journey via ship to Istanbul. Later, when the Hungarian state railway completed a new line from Budapest via Novi Sad to Belgrade (1884), and when the Serbian state railway completed a line from Belgrade to Niš (1888) and from Niš to Sofia (1888) or to Skopje (1887), Istanbul and Salonika finally achieved direct daily railroad connections with Vienna, and therefore with the rest of Europe.

Nonetheless, despite the presence of the Orient Express beginning in the 1870s, large parts of the Balkans had very few railways until as late as 1914. This was particularly true in the southwest, where Albania had none at all and the Greek system, begun in earnest during the 1880s, remained unconnected with the Ottoman lines in Macedonia, and therefore separated from the rest of Europe.

Undoubtedly the improved transportation system brought about by railways had an impact on economic developments. That impact, however, was uneven. On the one hand, railways facilitated movement of products and people in areas near existing lines, enabling such regions to distribute local products to wider markets. At the same time, these regions became more accessible to outside producers who might compete with or even undermine local industries. Generally, it seems that for East Central Europe the coming of the railroad favored regions already endowed with raw materials and labor or entrepreneurial skills that could be exported to more industrially advanced areas. Thus in many ways the railroads simply perpetuated the distinctions between the rural areas producing agricultural products and raw materials and the industrial areas manufacturing finished products that might be sold back to the less developed regions.

29 Population, 1870–1910

The four decades preceding the outbreak of World War I were marked by enormous changes in the population of East Central Europe. Three characteristics are especially notable for this period: (1) a significant increase in the total number of inhabitants; (2) internal migration from the countryside to towns and cities; and (3) out-migration to other parts of Europe and, most especially, to the United States.

The table below reveals that between 1870 and 1910 the population of East Central Europe rose from 98 to 143 million persons, or an increase of nearly 50 percent.

Population density and spatial patterns are indicated on accompanying Maps 29a and 29b. In 1870 there were only four small areas in East Central Europe where the population density exceeded 200 persons per square kilometer. These included far-western Kingdom of Saxony and three greater metropolitan areas surrounding the cities of Berlin, Vienna, and Istanbul. Beyond that, the only other densely populated areas (100 to 200 persons per square kilometer) included the rest of the Kingdom of Saxony; parts of neighboring Silesia, Bohemia, and Moravia roughly bounded by the cities of Leipzig, Wrocław, Prague, and Brno; and northern Italy. Throughout the rest of East Central Europe there were fewer than 50 inhabitants per square kilometer, with the least numbers of people in the Balkans, where large blocks of territory had fewer than 20 inhabitants per square kilometer.

During the next four decades, until about 1910, there was a general increase in the total number of people throughout East Central Europe. While the Balkan region (Bulgaria, Walachia-Moldavia/Romania, Serbia) experienced a 3 to 4 percent greater increase than the northern two-thirds of the region (Austria-Hungary, Germany, and Russia), it nonetheless remained the least inhabited part of East Central Europe. Marked growth took place in the Kingdom of

Saxony, which increased the extent of its over-200-inhabitants category; while central Prussia, parts of central Poland, more of Bohemia, Lower Austria, eastern Moravia, southern Silesia, a central strip of Galicia, central Hungary, and regions of Gdańsk/Danzig and Athens increased their densities to 100–200 inhabitants per square kilometer.

Associated with overall demographic growth was internal movement from the countryside to urban areas. This resulted in the rapid growth of towns and cities. If we exclude Italy and include only those parts of the German Empire that were within Bavaria and the area that later became East Germany and Poland, the accompanying list shows that in 1870 there were 21 cities in East Central Europe—Berlin, Vienna, Istanbul, Budapest, Warsaw, Wrocław, Prague, Bucharest, Munich, Leipzig, Dresden, Odessa, İzmir, Kiev, Kaliningrad, Magdeburg, Trieste, Üsküdar, Edirne, L'viv, Chişinău—that had more than 100,000 inhabitants. Of these, only three had over 500,000 inhabitants—Vienna, Berlin, and Istanbul. By 1910, the number of cities in the area delineated above having more than 100,000 inhabitants had nearly doubled to 38, of which two (Berlin and Vienna) had more than 2 million inhabitants and eight (Budapest, Istanbul, Warsaw, Munich, Leipzig, Dresden, Odessa, and Wrocław) had more than 500,000.

Despite such urban growth, a glance at the symbols for city size on Map 29b reveals that most of the settlements in the "city" category in East Central Europe were in the 50,000 to 100,000 range, while an even greater number remained small rural-like towns or oversized villages of less than 50,000 inhabitants. This restraint in urban growth simply confirms that the population of East Central Europe in 1910 remained overwhelmingly rural and agricultural.

The absolute growth of population in East Central Europe between 1870 and 1910 was tempered somewhat by emigration, most especially to the industrial regions of the northeastern United States. In the choice between economic problems at home and the difficulties of emigration, the outlook for emigration was enhanced by the marked decline in the time (and cost) it took to make the transatlantic voyage (from 44 days in 1850, to 9.7 days in 1875, to only 4.5 days in 1914), and by the growth of railroads (see Map 28), which made access to ports like Hamburg, Bremen, and Rijeka/Fiume quicker and cheaper. An estimated 7 million persons emigrated from East Central Europe to the United States between 1870 and 1914.

It should be remembered, however, that there was also a large degree of return migration. The largest percentages of these returnees or "sojourners" came from Balkan countries like Bulgaria, Serbia, and Montenegro, where as many as two-thirds of the emigrants returned home before 1914. Comparable percentages were 50 percent returnees to Austria, 33 percent to Hungary, and 20 percent to Germany.

Population change, 1870–1910

	Ca. 1870	Ca. 1910	Percentage of change
Germany[1]	23,472,000	34,281,000	+46
Russia[1]	21,945,000	38,568,000	+76
Austria-Hungary	35,904,000	48,500,000	+35
Serbia	1,377,000	2,800,000	+103
Walachia-Moldavia/ Romania	5,180,000	6,700,000	+29
Bulgaria	—	4,200,000	
Montenegro	200,000	282,000	+41
Greece	1,485,000	2,632,000	+77
Ottoman Empire in Europe	8,200,000	5,475,000	−33
	97,763,000	143,438,000	+47

1. This includes only certain parts of these countries covered on the accompanying maps. For the specific parts, see notes 1 and 3 on the table accompanying Map 30.

People per square km

More than 200

100-200

50-99

20-49

Less than 20

International boundaries, 1870

Boundaries of semi-independent
kingdoms and principalities, 1870

Population of major cities

⊡ 500 000-1 000 000

□ 250 000-500 000

◉ 100 000-250 000

○ 50 000-100 000

0 _____ 150 miles

0 _____ 150 kilometers

Scale 1:8 890 000

Historical Atlas of East Central Europe

Copyright © by Paul Robert Magocsi

People per square km

- More than 200
- 100-200
- 50-99
- 20-49
- Less than 20

Population of major cities

- ■ More than 2 000 000
- ▣ 1 000 000-2 000 000
- ▣ 500 000-1 000 000
- □ 250 000-500 000
- ◉ 100 000-250 000
- ○ 50 000-100 000

— ·· — International boundaries, 1910

— — — Boundaries of semi-independent kingdoms and principalities, 1910

0 — 150 miles
0 — 150 kilometers

Scale 1:8 890 000

Copyright © by Paul Robert Magocsi

Largest cities in East Central Europe, ca. 1870 and 1910[1]

	Ca. 1870	Ca. 1910	Percentage of increase
1. Berlin	826,000	2,071,000	151
2. Vienna	834,000	2,031,000	143
3. Budapest	320,000	880,000	175
4. Istanbul	531,000	782,000	47
5. Warsaw	308,000	771,000	150
6. Prague	252,000	640,000	154
7. Munich	212,000	595,000	180
8. Leipzig	209,000	588,000	181
9. Dresden	197,000	547,000	178
10. Odessa	185,000	520,000	181
11. Wrocław/Breslau	239,000	512,000	114
12. Łódź	39,000	352,000	803
13. Nürnberg	95,000	333,000	250
14. Kiev	127,000	323,000	154
15. Bucharest	222,000	300,000	35
16. Chemnitz	85,000	287,000	238
17. Magdeburg	123,000	280,000	128
18. İzmir	192,000	250,000	30
19. Charlottenburg	20,000	240,000	1,100
20. Kaliningrad/ Königsberg	123,000	246,000	100
21. Szczecin/Stettin	81,000	236,000	191
22. Trieste	119,000	230,000	93
23. L'viv/Lemberg	103,000	207,000	101
24. Salonika/Selānik	80,000	174,000	117
25. Gdańsk/Danzig	98,000	170,000	73
26. Athens	45,000	168,000	273
27. Vilnius/Vil'na	64,000	168,000	166
28. Poznań/Posen	66,000	157,000	139
29. Graz	81,000	152,000	88
30. Cracow	50,000	150,000	200
31. Chişinău/Kishinev	102,000	129,000	26
32. Brno/Brünn	73,000	126,000	73
33. Plauen	29,000	121,000	317
34. Üsküdar	110,000	112,000	2
35. Edirne	110,000	110,000	0
36. Sofia	20,000	103,000	415
37. Szeged	70,000	103,000	47
38. Minsk	36,000	100,000	178

1. Arranged according to order of largest cities in 1910. The 1870 figures are based on Elisée Reclus, *Nouvelle Géographie universelle*, vols. 1, 3, 5, 9 (Paris, 1876–84); the 1910 figures are from *The Library Atlas of the World*, vol. 2 (Chicago and New York, 1913).

In the nineteenth century, the population of East Central Europe contained peoples from the three major ethnolinguistic groups of Europe—the Germanic, Romance, and Slavic—as well as from the smaller Baltic, Finno-Ugric (Magyars), Turko-Tataric, Albanian, and Greek groups. By far the largest in numbers and geographical distribution was the Slavic group, which in turn was subdivided into East, West, and South Slavic ethnolinguistic groups.

On the accompanying map, ethnolinguistic groups are categorized by certain distinguishing criteria. For some, language is the primary distinguishing characteristic: Germans, Lithuanians, Latvians, Belorussians, Russians, Ukrainians, Czechs, Lusatian Sorbs, Poles, Slovaks, Bulgarians, Slovenes, Friulians, Italians, Magyars, Albanians, Greeks, Turks, Tatars. For others, religious orientation has distinguished groups that are otherwise related linguistically: Serbo-Croatian-speaking Muslim Bosnians (Bošnjaks) and Roman Catholic Croats from Orthodox Serbs; Bulgarian-speaking Muslim Pomaks from Orthodox Bulgarians; and Turkic-speaking Orthodox Gagauz from Muslim Turks. For still others, regional and/or historical factors have distinguished groups that are otherwise related by language and/or religion: Croats and Montenegrins (each group being aware of its distinct history of statehood) from Serbs; Orthodox Macedonians from linguistically related Bulgarians and Serbs; Romanian-speaking Vlachs (also known as Kutzo-Vlachs or Arumanians) from Romanians; and, in Transylvania, German-speaking Saxons (Transylvanian Germans) from other Austro-Hungarian Germans, and Magyar-speaking Székelys from the Magyars.

Finally, some groups, because of their geographic location, had the potential to develop into distinct entities. By the twentieth century, some or most members of these groups had been absorbed into the ethnolinguistic group with whom they were most closely related—Wends becoming Slovenes, Kashubes becoming Poles, Carpatho-Rusyns becoming Ukrainians—although in the case of the Kashubes and most especially the Carpatho-Rusyns, since the Revolution of 1989 there has been a revival promoting the idea of a distinct national identity.

At least three other groups are widespread throughout East Central Europe but not indicated on the accompanying map: Gypsies, Jews, and Armenians. Gypsies were generally scattered throughout the countryside, usually inhabiting the outskirts of rural villages; Jews and Armenians (see Map 33) inhabited for the most part cities and towns.

The accompanying map also does not reveal a basic characteristic of East Central Europe. For most of the nineteenth century, cities and even towns were, in ethnolinguistic terms, alien from their surrounding countrysides. Thus north of the Carpathians the cities and towns were mainly German, Polish, and Jewish-inhabited enclaves surrounded by a Polish countryside; or Polish, Russian,

and Jewish enclaves surrounded by a Lithuanian, Belorussian, or Ukrainian countryside. In the Danubian basin the cities were largely German and Jewish, Magyar and Jewish, or, along the Adriatic Sea, Italian. In the Balkans it was the Greek and, in certain areas, Turkic populations that dominated the cities.

The urban demographic picture gradually changed during the second half of the nineteenth century. Peasants from the surrounding countryside were drawn for economic reasons to settle in towns and cities, making them in some instances more ethnolinguistically similar to the surrounding areas in which they were located.

Ethnolinguistic groups in East Central Europe, ca. 1900

Germans		42,304,000
Germany[1]	29,228,000 (1900)	
Austria	9,171,000 (1900)	
Hungary	1,902,000 (1900)	
Hungary—Transylvanian Saxons	233,000 (1900)	
Russia[2]	1,719,000 (1897)	
Italy	43,000 (1901)	
Romania	8,000 (1899)	
Poles		15,352,000
Austria	4,259,000 (1900)	
Germany (with Masurians)	3,228,000 (1900)	
Russia	7,865,000 (1897)	
Ukrainians		13,573,000
Galicia and Bukovina	3,376,000 (1900)	
Russia[3]	10,197,000 (1897)	
Romanians		9,810,000
Romania	5,489,000 (1899)	
Austria	231,000 (1900)	
Hungary	2,799,000 (1900)	
Croatia-Slavonia	3,000 (1890)	
Serbia	90,000 (1900)	
Bulgaria	71,000 (1900)	
Russia	1,127,000 (1897)	
Magyars		8,252,000
Austria	9,000 (1900)	
Hungary	8,152,000 (1900)	
Croatia-Slavonia	91,000 (1900)	
Jews		7,468,000
Germany[4]	465,000 (1900)	
Austria (plus Bosnia)	1,233,000 (1900)	
Hungary	846,000 (1900)	
Russia (excluding Poland)[3]	3,167,000 (1897)	
Poland	1,316,000 (1897)	
Romania	267,000 (1899)	
Bulgaria	37,000 (1901)	
Serbia	6,000 (1900)	
Greece	10,000 (1900)	
Ottoman Empire	121,000 (1897)	

Czechs		6,087,000
Austria	5,955,000 (1900)	
Germany (with Moravians)	107,000 (1900)	
Russia	25,000 (1897)	
Belorussians (1897)		5,853,000
Serbs		4,698,000
Austria (Orthodox "Serbo-Croats")	93,000 (1900)	
Hungary	438,000 (1900)	
Croatia-Slavonia	611,000 (1900)	
Bosnia (Orthodox)	825,000 (1910)	
Serbia	2,331,000 (1900)	
Ottoman Empire	400,000 (1900)	
Greeks		4,278,000
Greece	2,218,000 (1896)	
Crete	249,000 (1894)	
Ottoman Empire	1,637,000 (1897)	
Russia[2]	87,000 (1897)	
Bulgaria	67,000 (1901)	
Romania	20,000 (1899)	
Bulgarians		3,283,000
Bulgaria	2,888,000 (1901)	
Ottoman Empire	132,000 (1897)	
Romania	90,000 (1899)	
Russia (including Gagauz)	173,000 (1897)	
Croats		2,731,000
Austria (Catholic "Serbo-Croats")	615,000 (1900)	
Hungary	191,000 (1900)	
Croatia-Slavonia	1,491,000 (1900)	
Bosnia (Catholics)	434,000 (1910)	
Turks in Europe		2,424,000
Ottoman Empire	1,812,000 (1897)	
Bulgaria	531,000 (1901)	
Romania	23,000 (1899)	
Crete	33,000 (1900)	
Greece	25,000 (1901)	
Slovaks (1900)		2,002,000
Lithuanians		1,756,000
Russia	1,650,000 (1897)	
Germany	106,000 (1900)	
Slovenes		1,254,000
Austria	1,193,000 (1900)	
Italy	40,000 (1900)	
Croatia-Slavonia	21,000 (1890)	
Albanians		853,000
Ottoman Empire	733,000 (1897)	
Greece	120,000 (1896)	
Gypsies/Rom		820,000
Austria (plus Bosnia)	34,000 (1893)	
Hungary	275,000 (1893)	
Russia[2] (excluding Poland)	58,000 (ca. 1905)	
Poland	15,000 (ca. 1905)	

Romania	225,000 (1895)	
Serbia	47,000 (1900)	
Bulgaria	90,000 (1901)	
Greece	10,000 (ca. 1905)	
Ottoman Empire in Europe	66,000 (1903)	
Italians—outside Italy		742,000
Austria	727,000 (1900)	
Croatia-Slavonia	4,000 (1890)	
Greece	11,000 (1896)	
Macedonians (1897)[5]		693,000
Bosnian Muslims (1910)		612,000
Carpatho-Rusyns		540,000
Hungary	425,000 (1900)	
Croatia-Slavonia	15,000 (1900)	
Austria (Galicia)—Lemkos	100,000 (1900)	
Székelys (1910)		500,000
Friulians		402,000
Lombardy-Venetia	352,000 (1851)	
Austria	50,000 (1851)	
Montenegrins		294,000
Orthodox in Montenegro		
Armenians		249,000
Ottoman Empire	178,000 (1897)	
Romania	50,000 (1900)	
Bulgaria	15,000 (1901)	
Austria	3,000 (1910)	
Hungary	3,000 (1890)	
Pomaks (1888)		200,000
Vlachs/Kutzo-Vlachs/Arumanians		156,000
Greece	60,000 (1901)	
Serbia	10,000 (1895)	
Ottoman Empire	86,000 (1907)	
Kashubes		100,000
Lusatian Sorbs		93,000
Wends (1910)		67,000
Gagauz (1879)		56,000
Ladins (1910)		28,000

1. Included are Germans only in Mecklenburg-Schwerin and Mecklenburg-Strelitz; Saxony; Brunswick; Bavaria; the various duchies and principalities of Anhalt, Saxe, Schwarzburg, and Reuss; and Prussia (only the provinces of East and West Prussia, Berlin, Brandenburg, Pomerania, Silesia, Posen, and Saxony).

2. European Russia.

3. Only provinces west of the Dnieper River: Vil'na, Vitebsk, Grodno, Kovno, Minsk, Mogilev, Volhynia, Kiev, Podolia, Bessarabia, Kherson, and those in the former Congress Kingdom of Poland (Warsaw, Kalisz, Kielce, Łomża, Lublin, Piotrków, Płock, Radom, Suwałki, Siedlce).

4. Included here are Jews in the areas indicated above (note 1) as well as those throughout all of Prussia.

5. Refers to "Bulgarians" in Ottoman statistics from the districts of Monastir, Kosova, and Selānik.

ETHNOLINGUISTIC GROUPS

Germanic
1. Danes   2. Frisians
3. Germans   4. Swedes
5. Transylvanian Saxons

Baltic
6. Latvians   7. Lithuanians

East Slavic
8. Belorussians
9. Carpatho-Rusyns
10. Russians   11. Ukrainians

West Slavic
12. Czechs   13. Kashubes
14. Lusatian Sorbs
16. Slovaks   15. Poles

South Slavic
17. Bosnian Muslims
18. Bulgarians   19. Croats
20. Macedonians
21. Montenegrins   22. Pomaks
23. Serbs   24. Slovenes
25. Wends

Finno-Ugric
26. Magyars   27. Szekelys

Romance
28. Friulians   29. Italians
30. Ladins   31. Romanians
32. Romansch   33. Vlachs

Albanians(34)

Greeks(35)

Turco-Tataric
36. Tatars   37. Turks

Copyright © by Paul Robert Magocsi

31 Cultural and educational institutions before 1914

During the nineteenth century, most of the ethnolinguistic groups in East Central Europe went through periods of national awakening or revival that for some led to greater cultural, administrative, and political autonomy, and for others even independence. Educational, scholarly, and cultural organizations were of enormous importance in promoting the activity of the national revivals, and virtually all groups had at least one or more of these organizations.

Among the earliest of such organizations, uniquely among the Slavs, were the so-called maticas, or cultural foundations, established to promote the publication and distribution of books and related cultural activities in the vernacular language. Most Slavic groups founded maticas—Serbs (Pest, 1826, moved to Novi Sad in 1864); Czechs (Prague, 1831, and Brno, 1853); Croats (Zagreb, 1842); Lusatian Sorbs (Bautzen/Budyšin, 1847); Ukrainians (L'viv, 1849); Slovaks (Martin, 1862–75); Slovenes (Ljubljana, 1863); and Poles (L'viv, 1882). There were also other organizations similar to the maticas, especially with regard to publication and distribution of inexpensive books and journals for the masses. The following are among the more prominent organizations for each group:

Bulgarians
  Karastojanov publishing house (Gabrovo, 1847)
Carpatho-Rusyns
  Prešov Literary Institute (Prešov/Priashiv, 1850)
  Saint Basil the Great Society (Uzhhorod, 1865)
Croats
  Saint Jerome Society (Zagreb, 1868)
Czechs
  Jan Nepomuk Society (Prague, 1829)
Jews
  Society of Friends of the Hebrew Language (Kaliningrad/Königsberg, 1783)
  Society for the Promotion of Culture Among the Jews of Russia (Odessa, 1867, and Kiev, 1908)
Lithuanians
  Saint Casimir Society (Kaunas, 1906)
Romanians
  Association for Romanian Literature and Culture in Transylvania (Sibiu, 1861)
  Society for Romanian Literature and Culture in Bukovina (Chernivtsi/Cernăuţi, 1865)
  Petru Maior (Pest, 1862)
  League for Cultural Unity of all Romanians (Bucharest, 1891)
Slovaks
  Slavic Literary Society (Trnava, 1793)
  Slovak Literary Society (Bratislava, 1801)
  Tatrín (Liptovský Mikuláš, 1844)
  Saint Adalbert Society (Trnava, 1879)
Slovenes
  Saint Mohor Society (Klagenfurt/Celovec, 1852)
Ukrainians
  Prosvita Society (L'viv, 1868)
  Ruthenian Besida Club (Chernivtsi, 1869)
  Kachkovs'kyi Society (Kolomyia, later L'viv, 1874).

Also of importance to several groups were national museums, theaters, and academies of science. The significance of these organizations lay not only in their cultural activity but also in their symbolic presence, which often took the form of large buildings in urban centers—frequently constructed after fund-raising drives among the people. The museums preserved archaeological and geographic artifacts, and they often had archival and publishing programs. The Poles had museum-like institutions that were national in character in each of the three empires where they lived: the Czartoryski Museum, which dated from the late eighteenth century (first in Puławy, transferred to Paris in 1831, then to Cracow after 1876); the Ossolineum in L'viv (1817); and the Kórnik in Poznań (1817, transferred to Kórnik in 1829). Some groups, such as the Slovenes, used the facilities of a regional museum, as in Germanic Graz (Johanneum, 1811). Others transformed regional museums into national institutions, such as the Magyar National Museum in Pest (1802) and the Czech Museum in Prague (1820). Still others, like the Croats (Zagreb, 1841), Serbs (Belgrade, 1844/1869), and Romanians (Bucharest, 1891), founded from the outset national or historical museums.

National theaters were also important in terms of their function as well as their architectural presence in the center of large cities. The often opulent and pompous style of the architecture of these theaters was intended to enhance the prestige of lesser-known cultures through the performance of plays in native languages and, most especially, of operas that were often based on patriotic themes. Although many ethnolinguistic groups had theatrical troupes dating from the late eighteenth and early nineteenth centuries, only a few were able to support permanent companies. Among the national theaters housed in permanent homes before World War I were those for the following groups (a second date refers to reconstruction of the building):

Bulgarians	Montenegrins
Ruse (1891)	Cetinje (1896)
Sofia (1907)	**Romanians**
Croats	Bucharest (1834/1852)
Zagreb (1895)	Iaşi (1836/1846)
Czechs	**Serbs**
Prague (1786/1868)	Novi Sad (1861)
Brno (1825)	Belgrade (1868)
Italians	**Slovenes**
Trieste	Ljubljana (1892)
Magyars	**Ukrainians**
Cluj/Kolozsvár (1792/1821)	L'viv (1864)
Pest (1837/1875)	Kiev (1907)
Bratislava/Pozsony (1886)	
Timişoara/Temesvár (1869–70)	

The Poles had a national theater dating back to pre-partition times (1765); its first building was located in Warsaw (1770),

SWEDEN

DENMARK

BALTIC SEA

Copenhagen · Malmö

Kiel

HOLSTEIN

Lübeck

Rostock

Greifswald

RÜGEN

Bremen

POMERANIA

MECKLENBURG

Szczecin (Stettin)

Gdańsk (Danzig)

PRUSSIA

Telšiai (Tel'she)

Panévežys (Ponevezh)

LITHUANIA

Kaunas (Kovno)

Slobodka

Vilnius (Vil'na)

Veiveriai

Vitsebsk (Vitebsk)

Liubavichi

Smolensk

Western Dvina

Hannover

Berlin

BRANDENBURG

Magdeburg

Warta

Poznań (Posen)

Kórnik

Toruń (Thorn)

Płock

Vistula

Suwałki

Radun

Valozhyn (Volozhin)

Minsk

Navahrudak (Novogrudok)

Mir

Mahilioŭ (Mogilev)

B E L A R U S

Slutsk

Neman

Hrodna (Grodno)

Łomża

Białystok (Belostok)

Baranavichy (Baranovichi)

Chernihiv (Chernigov)

Desna

Wolfenbüttel

Göttingen

Kassel

Dessau

Halle

SAXONY

Leipzig

Dresden

Cottbus

Bautzen

LUSATIA

Oder

Neisse

SILESIA

Kalisz

Łódź

Warsaw

Siedlce

Brest-Litovsk

RUSSIA

Pinsk

Pripet

POLAND

Elbe

Marburg an der Lahn

Giessen

Jena

THURINGIA

Frankfurt am Main

Würzburg

Erlangen

Nürnberg

Stuttgart

Litoměřice

Jičín

Prague

Plzeň

Klatovy

BOHEMIA

Kolín

Hradec Králové

Kutná Hora

Tábor

Golčův Jeníkov

Třebíč

MORAVIA

Opava

Olomouc

Cieszyn

Cracow

Warta

Piotrków

Radom

Puławy

Lublin

Western Bug

G A L I C I A

L'viv (Lemberg)

Przemyśl

Brody

Kremianets'

Ternopil'

V O L H Y N I A

Zhytomyr (Zhitomir)

Berdychiv (Berdichev)

Vinnytsia (Vinnitsa)

Kiev

U K R A I N E

Dnieper

Lipnik nad Bečvou

Prostějov

Přerov

Morava

Ivano-Frankivs'k

Kolomyia

Kamianets'-Podil'skyi

Uman'

P O D O L I A

S. Bug

Munich

BAVARIA

Danube

Linz

České Budějovice

Jindřichův Hradec

Mikulov (Nikolsburg)

Brno (Brünn)

Banská Bystrica

Kežmarok (Késmark)

Levoča

Prešov

Košice (Kassa)

S L O V A K I A

CARPATHIAN RUS'

Uzhhorod

Mukachevo (Munkács)

Khust

Chernivtsi (Czernowitz)

B U K O V I N A

Dniester

Siret

B E S S A R A B I A

Chişinău (Kishinev)

Odessa

AUSTRIA-HUNGARY

Salzburg

SALZBURG

AUSTRIA

Vienna

Bratislava (Pozsony)

Trnava

Nitra

Banská Štiavnica

Rožňava

Lučenec (Losonc)

Miskolc

Mukachevo

Sárospatak

Sighetul

Satu-Mare (Szatmárnémeti)

Bistriţa (Beszterce)

Iaşi

M O L D A V I A

Innsbruck

SWITZ.

TYROL

CARINTHIA

Klagenfurt

St. Veit

Graz

STYRIA

Eisenstadt

Sopron

Szombathely

Győr

Buda

Pest

Kecskemét

Debrecen

Mád

Trent

Idrija

Ljubljana

CARNIOLA

Celje

Varaždin (Varsad)

Zagreb

Pécs

Sombor

H U N G A R Y

Timişoara (Temesvár)

BANAT

Beiuş

Aiud

Cluj (Kolozsvár)

Tirgu-Mureş (Marosvásárhely)

Odorheiu

T R A N S Y L V A N I A

Brad

Blaj

Mediaş

Sighişoara

Sibiu (Nagyszeben)

Braşov

Olt

Galaţi

Brăila

ROMANIA

Padua

Venice

VENETIA

Trieste

ISTRIA

Pula

DALMATIA

Rijeka

Senj

Sisak

S L A V O N I A

Osijek

Novi Sad

Vinkovci

Sremski Karlovci

BAČKA

Drava

Sava

Tisza

W A L A C H I A

Bucharest

Danube

Constanţa

BLACK SEA

Bologna

SAN MARINO

Florence

Zadar (Zara)

Gospić

BOSNIA

Travnik

Livno

Split

HERZEGOVINA

Sarajevo

Požega

Kragujevac

SERBIA

Niš

Morava

Belgrade

Ruse

Svishtov

Razgrad

Pleven

Veliko Tŭrnovo

Gabrovo

Varna

Burgas

DOBRUJA

Rome

I T A L Y

A D R I A T I C   S E A

Dubrovnik (Ragusa)

Kotor (Cattaro)

MONTENEGRO

Cetinje

Shkodër (Işkodra)

Skopje (Üsküb)

Veles

Stara Zagora

E A S T   R U M E L I A

Plovdiv

B U L G A R I A

Sofia

Maritsa

Edirne

Vardar

Naples

Durrës (Diraç)

Elbasan

Bitola (Monastir)

Korçë

M A C E D O N I A

T H R A C E

Istanbul

İzmit

Bursa

ANATOLIA

Sakarya

T Y R R H E N I A N   S E A

E P I R U S

Ioannina (Yanya)

THESSALY

LEMNOS

AEGEAN SEA

LESBOS

Ayvalık

İzmir

OTTOMAN EMPIRE

CORFU

GREECE

IONIAN SEA

CEPHALONIA

Patras

Corinth

Athens

CHIOS

SAMOS

ZANTE

PELOPONNESE

CERIGO

CYCLADES

RHODES

KARPATHOS

Candia (Iráklion)

Canea

CRETE

Legend

- ▬ ▪ ▬ International boundaries, 1900
- ▬ ▬ Boundaries of Hungary and Bulgaria
- ▪ Universities
- ▫ Secondary schools of national importance
- ● Academies of arts and sciences
- ○ Maticas, national museums and other cultural organizations
- ⋈ National theaters

0   150 miles

0   150 kilometers

Scale 1:8 890 000

followed later by a grand new structure (1833). Poles also had theaters in each of the empires where they lived: Cracow (1799/1843/1893), Ľviv/Lwów (1809, with buildings in 1842 and 1900), Poznań (1875), Łódź (1878), Lublin (1886), Kalisz (1900), and a second in Warsaw (1913).

The other cultural institutions that became widespread were the academies of science, art, and learning. Such academies, under a variety of names, came into being among the following peoples:

Bulgarians	Cracow (1856/1872)
Brăila (1869), later	Poznań (1857)
Sofia (1911)	Toruń (1875)
Croats	Ľviv/Lwów (1901)
Zagreb (1868)	Vilnius/Wilno (1907)
Czechs	Warsaw (1907)
Prague (1784)	**Romanians**
Lithuanians	Iaşi (1864)
Vilnius (1907)	Bucharest (1866/1879)
Magyars	**Serbs**
Pest (1825)	Belgrade (1864)
Poles	**Ukrainians**
Warsaw (1800-48)	Ľviv (1873)

Perhaps of greatest significance in preserving the future existence of ethnolinguistic groups was the educational system. Several new universities were founded in East Central Europe in the nineteenth century (compare Map 17). Some functioned as national universities from the outset, while others were later transformed into national institutions. Still others included a few departments (chairs/ *katedra*) or faculties (often theology) with instruction intended for a specific ethnolinguistic group.

In East Central Europe's Germanic lands, several older universities (Frankfurt an der Oder, Erfurt, Bamberg, Altdorf, Ingolstadt, Landshut, Linz, Salzburg) were closed, a few others reorganized (Wrocław/Breslau, 1811; Olomouc/ Olmütz, 1827–55; Innsbruck, 1826) or opened anew (Berlin, 1809; Munich, 1826). Among the Poles in the Russian Empire, older establishments in Warsaw (1816–69) and Vilnius/Wilno (1803–30) functioned for a while as Polish universities, while in Warsaw a new one was opened in 1906. In Austria, the older institutions at Ľviv/Lwów and the Jagiellonian University in Cracow became polonized respectively in 1873 and 1879. Other new or renewed universities which became or were from the outset national institutions were established for the following groups:

Bulgarians	Cluj/Kolozsvár (1872)
Sofia (1909)	Debrecen (1912)
Croats	Bratislava/Pozsony (1912)
Zagreb (1874)	**Romanians**
Greeks	Iaşi (1860)
Athens (1837)	Bucharest (1864)
Magyars	**Serbs**
Buda (1777, later moved	Belgrade (1905)
to Pest, 1784)	

The Austrian government opened a new German university in Chernivtsi/Czernowitz (1875), which also had separate Ukrainian and Romanian departments, whereas in Prague it allowed East Central Europe's oldest institution of higher learning, Charles University, to become separate Czech and German institutions in 1882. Farther east, new Russian universities were opened in Kiev (1834)—to replace the Polish university in Vilnius—and in Odessa (1864).

Perhaps even more important than universities were secondary schools (*gymnasia, lycées*), which promoted a national consciousness among even larger numbers of young people from ethnolinguistic groups who did not have their own states or who lived as minorities in other states. The following were among the prominent secondary schools where the language and culture of minority groups were taught:

Albanians	Trieste
Elbasan	Zadar/Zara
Korçë	**Lithuanians**
Shkodër	Veiveriai (1866)
Bosnian Muslims	**Poles**
Sarajevo (1864)	Białystok
Bulgarians	Cieszyn
Gabrovo (1835)	Cracow
Pleven	Hrodna/Grodno
Plovdiv	Kalisz
Razgrad	Kiev/Kijów
Ruse	Kremianets'/Krzemieniec
Sofia	Ľviv/Lwów
Stara Zagora	Łódź
Svishtov	Łomża
Veles	Lublin
Veliko Tŭrnovo	Minsk
Croats	Piotrków
Dubrovnik	Płock
Gospić	Poznań
Kotor	Przemyśl
Livno	Puławy
Osijek	Radom
Sarajevo	Siedlce
Senj	Suwałki
Sisak	Ternopil'/Tarnopol
Travnik	Vilnius/Wilno
Varaždin	Vinnytsia/Winnica
Vinkovci	Warsaw
Zagreb (1607/1850)	**Romanians**
Czechs	Beiuş
Brno	Blaj
Jičín	Brad
Jindřichův Hradec	Braşov
Litoměřice	Bucharest
Olomouc	Chernivtsi/Cernăuţi
Plzeň	Iaşi
Prague	**Serbs**
Greeks	Belgrade
Ayvalik/Aivali	Kragujevac
Ioannina	Novi Sad
Istanbul	Požega
İzmir/Smyrna	Sarajevo
Odessa	Sombor
Italians	Sremski Karlovci (1728)
Dubrovnik/Ragusa	**Slovaks**
Pula/Pola	Banská Bystrica
Rijeka/Fiume	Bratislava
Split/Spalato	Levoča
Trent/Trento	Martin

Slovenes
- Celje
- Idrija
- Ljubljana (1418/1788)
- St. Veit/St. Vid

Transylvanian Saxons
- Bistritz/Bistriţa
- Braşov/Kronstadt
- Mediaş/Mediasch
- Sibiu/Hermannstadt
- Sighişoara/Schässburg

Ukrainians
- Chernivtsi
- Ivano-Frankivs'k/Stanyslaviv
- Kolomyia
- L'viv
- Przemyśl/Peremyshl'
- Ternopil'

Vlachs
- Bitola (1886)

Secondary schools were also of great importance to state nationalities like the Hungarians. The Hungarian government used secondary schools as instruments for maintaining a national identity among the Magyar population in the kingdom (Debrecen, Győr, Kecskemét, Miskolc, Odorheiu/Székelyudvarhely, Pécs, Pest, Sárospatak, Sopron, Szombathely, Tîrgu-Mureş/Marosvásárhely), as well as for encouraging cultural adaptation and national assimilation —Magyarization—in areas inhabited largely by non-Magyar minority populations (Aiud/Nagyenyed, Banská Štiavnica/Selmecbánya, Bratislava/Pozsony, Cluj/Kolozsvár, Kežmarok/Késmárk, Košice/Kassa, Levoča/Lőcse, Lučenec/Losonc, Novi Sad/Újvidék, Rijeka/Fiume, Rožňava/Rozsnyó, Satu-Mare/Szatmárnémeti, Sibiu/Nagyszeben, Sighetul/Máramarossziget, Timişoara/Temesvár, Trnava/Nagyszombat, Zagreb/Zágráb).

One other group, the Jews, developed as well a broad network of educational institutions. Unlike East Central Europe's other ethnolinguistic groups, who used cultural and educational institutions to promote national self-awareness and ideas of territorial autonomy or independence, the Jews were primarily concerned with preserving their religious traditions in an otherwise alien Christian or Moslem world. One of the earliest formal means of doing this was through the creation of the yeshivah, an academy of learning which later came to be associated with any traditionalist-oriented secondary school.

The "golden age" of yeshivahs in East Central Europe was in the sixteenth and first half of the seventeenth centuries; thereafter, they witnessed a decline that lasted throughout the eighteenth century. A revival began in the early nineteenth century with the opening of yeshivahs at Valozhyn in Belarus (1803–92) and at Bratislava/Pressburg in the Hungarian Kingdom (1807). For the rest of the nineteenth century, at least down to the outbreak of World War I in 1914, the most important yeshivahs were to be found in the western regions of the Russian Empire, especially in Lithuania (Slobodka/Vilyempole, Telšiai, Panėvežys/Ponevizh, Vilnius/Vilne) and Belarus (Liubavichi, Radun, Hrodna/Grodne, Minsk, Navahrudak, Mir, Baranavichy, Slutsk, Pinsk, Brest Litovsk/Brisk-de-Lite), and in the northern regions of the Hungarian Kingdom (Nitra, Vrbové, Eisenstadt, Mukachevo/Munkatsh, Khust, Mád). Bohemia and Moravia also had several noted yeshivahs (Prague, Mikulov, Kolín, Golčův Jeníkov, Lipník nad Bečvou, Třebíč), although these functioned at best only until the first third of the nineteenth century, when Jewish assimilation in those Austrian provinces resulted in the closing of these traditional centers of learning.

Alongside the religious-oriented yeshivahs were Jewish schools and seminaries associated with the Haskalah, or enlightenment, which began in Germany in the 1780s and then moved rapidly eastward in the early nineteenth century. The emphasis of the Haskalah was on providing a modern secular-oriented education in a Jewish religious context through the use of the official languages of the day (German, Italian, Hungarian, Russian) as well as Modern Hebrew, but not Yiddish. The earliest Haskalah centers, each with a modern secondary school, were in Germany (Berlin, Kaliningrad/Königsberg, Wrocław/Breslau, Dessau, Wolfenbüttel), Hungary (Buda, Bratislava/Pozsony), and in the Austrian port city of Trieste. At the beginning of the nineteenth century, the movement spread eastward, first to the Germanic and Czech lands of the Austrian Empire (Vienna, Prague, Prostějov/Prossnitz), and then to Austria's eastern province of Galicia (Ternopil'/Tarnopol, Brody, L'viv/Lemberg) and the western regions of the Russian Empire (Odessa, Uman', Chişinău/Kishinev).

The Haskalah also benefited from its cooperation with the tsarist authorities, which, beginning in 1847, established a broad network of Jewish state-sponsored secondary schools (Warsaw, Vilnius/Vil'na, Minsk, Kamianets'-Podil's'kyi/Kamenets-Podol'sk, Berdychiv/Berdichev, Chişiňau/Kishinev, Vitsebsk, Mahilioŭ/Mogilev, Odessa, Zhytomyr/Zhitomir) and rabbinical seminaries in Warsaw (1826), Vilnius (1847), and Zhytomyr (1847). And during the second half of the century, the Haskalah took root in Romania with secondary schools in Bucharest and Galaţi. Also of importance for the secular-oriented Jewish enlightenment was the establishment of rabbinical seminaries at Padua (1829), Wrocław (1854), Berlin (1873), Budapest (1877), Rome (1887), and Vienna (1893), and of teaching seminaries at Kassel (1810), Dessau (1825), Hannover (1848), Berlin (1857), Pest (1857), and Zhytomyr (1873).

32 Germans in East Central Europe, ca. 1900

At the outset of the twentieth century, there were over 42 million Germans in East Central Europe alone, making them by far the largest ethnolinguistic group in the region. They lived exclusively in the northern two-thirds of East Central Europe, where their settlement pattern was basically of two kinds: (1) contiguous German-inhabited territory, and (2) colonies surrounded by or intermixed with settlements containing other groups. The largest number of Germans lived in the German Empire (29,228,000), followed by those in the Austro-Hungarian Empire (11,306,000), the Russian Empire (1,719,000), Italy (43,000), and Romania (8,000). Germans living beyond contiguous German ethnolinguistic territory were often referred to by regional names: Baltic, Polish, Volhynian, Black Sea, and Bessarabian Germans in the Russian Empire; Gottschee, Galician, and Bukovinian Germans in the Austrian half of the Habsburg Empire; Zipser Germans, Sathmar Germans, Transylvanian Saxons, and Danube Swabians in the Hungarian Kingdom; and the Dobruja Germans in Romania.

Other groupings were also frequently used in descriptions of Germans, especially in the Austro-Hungarian Empire. Thus those in the provinces of Upper and Lower Austria, Salzburg, Tyrol, Vorarlberg, Styria, Carinthia, and Carniola as well as in Bohemia, Moravia, and Silesia were referred to as Austro-Germans. On the other hand, those in the eastern half of Austria-Hungary might be distinguished by geographic criteria: the Carpathian Germans (Karpatendeutsche) lived in the mountains and adjacent foothills of Slovakia, Carpathian Rus', Galicia, Bukovina, and Transylvania; the lowland Swabians (Schwaben), or Danube Swabians (Donauschwaben) as they came to be known after World War I, lived in the plains along the Danube (as well as Tisza and Drava) rivers.

After World War I, and especially under the impact of Nazi ideology, all Germans in East Central Europe who lived beyond contiguous ethnolinguistic territory came to be known as Volksdeutsche. It was also during the interwar period that the Germans of Bohemia, Moravia, and Silesia, while living within contiguous ethnolinguistic territory, began to be called Sudeten Germans. This became a generic term for all Germans in the three western provinces of Czechoslovakia, whether or not they actually lived in the Sudeten Mountains.

The evolution of German settlement in East Central Europe goes back to early medieval times. Until the year 700, German settlement barely reached as far east as the Elbe River, the middle Danube no farther than Linz, and in the south the foothills of the Alps just beyond present-day Munich and Salzburg as well as the valley of the Inn River. From that time, German settlement moved gradually eastward, whether through military conquest, peaceful expansion into previously unsettled and sparsely settled lands, or a combination of both. This process, which began in earnest during the twelfth century with the defeat of the

Slavic Obodrites, Polabians, and Veletians along the lower Elbe (see Maps 4 and 5), continued down to the nineteenth century.

In this regard, it is useful to note that not all peoples in East Central Europe who later spoke German owed their heritage to German settlers. Many were descendants of Germanized Slavs and in some cases Magyars whose ancestors had intermarried with neighbors of Germanic origin. Thus assimilation at the family level was a long and gradual process, which by the nineteenth century was assisted in certain areas by a state-sponsored program of assimilation, such as in the western Polish lands under German imperial rule. Whatever form it took—military conquest, peaceful colonization, natural or forcible assimilation of surrounding peoples—the centuries-long process of the German advance into East Central Europe came to be known as the colonization of the East (*Ostkolonisation*), or, by those who considered it a threat, as the drive to the East (*Drang nach Osten*).

Their technical skills also made Germans attractive to rulers in medieval Poland, Bohemia-Moravia, and Hungary-Croatia, who invited them to settle in agricultural areas, to initiate mining operations, and to develop new or previously existing cities (see Map 12f). These same skills were highly valued by rulers of states in the more modern era, including the Habsburgs in formerly Ottoman-controlled Hungary and the Russians in their newly acquired lands along the Black Sea. Thus there are two distinct phases in the German colonization of East Central Europe: the medieval, which lasted from about 1200 to 1400, and the modern, from 1500 to 1900.

Among the earliest German colonies in East Central Europe were those begun in the late twelfth century in Transylvania (with settlers primarily from Luxembourg and the Mosel region) and in the mountainous area of Spiš/Zips/Szepes county in northern Hungary near the towns of Levoča/Leutschau and Kežmarok/Käsmark.

The next major advances occurred in the thirteenth century. Far to the southeast, the Transylvanian and Spiš enclaves were expanded through special privileges granted in 1224 and 1271. It was at this time that the "Saxons" (actually Germans not from Saxony but from the Rhineland, Flanders, and Mosel area) came in large numbers, creating a solid demographic basis for what became known as the Transylvanian Saxon community. It was north of the Carpathians, however, where the Germans made the greatest permanent advances, displacing Slavs throughout the whole Oder valley as far as upper Silesia, forcibly liquidating the Baltic Prussians in the lower Vistula valley, and settling upon the invitation of Czech rulers the mountainous (Sudeten) ring around Bohemia and Moravia. From these areas, German settlement gradually expanded in subsequent centuries.

During the modern era, a German presence came into

The evolution of German settlement

32b

International boundaries, 1900

Boundaries of semi-independent kingdoms

Provincial boundaries

Contiguous German settlement

Mixed settlement of Germans and others

Scale 1:8 890 000

Scale 1:15 000 000

International boundaries

German-inhabited area, 700

Extent of settlement

By 1100

By 1400

By 1200

By 1700

By 1300

By 1900

Copyright © by Paul Robert Magocsi

being in territories where it had not existed before. This had to do largely with the loss by the Ottoman Empire of lands it had held since the sixteenth century in the Danubian basin and along the Black Sea. The Habsburg program of resettling former Ottoman Hungary in the eighteenth century both revitalized the older Transylvanian Saxon area, which had decreased in size during the Ottoman era, and brought in new German colonists. These came to be known as Danube Swabians, only a small portion of whom actually came from Swabia (most came from other south German states and Austria's Germanic provinces). They arrived in three phases (1718–37, 1744–72, 1782–87), settling in the Bakony Forest area north of Lake Balaton as far as Buda and farther south in the former frontier areas of Banat, Bačka, and Slavonia (see also Map 20d).

Russian interest in German colonists dates from the reign of Catherine II and her famous invitation (with numerous privileges) of 1763. Most of the earliest German colonists went farther east to the lower Volga region, and it was not until the outset of the nineteenth century that significant numbers of agricultural colonists (to whom various kinds of incentives were offered) began to settle in what was then known as New Russia—the lands recently conquered from the Ottoman Empire north of the Black Sea which later became the provinces of Kherson and Bessarabia. The last wave of Germans arrived in the Russian Empire during the 1860s, specifically in Volhynia, where they bought up land formerly belonging to Polish landowners who were having difficulty adjusting to the economic changes of Russia's reform era.

33 Jews and Armenians in East Central Europe, ca. 1900

Jews and Armenians in East Central Europe have several characteristics in common: (1) both have been there as long or even longer than some of the area's "indigenous" peoples; (2) neither has ever had its "own" territory in the region; (3) for the most part their members have resided in towns and cities where they have been associated with urban professions; and (4) both have played a significant role in the economic, cultural, and, to a degree, political life of the countries where they have resided.

The Jewish presence, at least in certain parts of East Central Europe, dates from classical times, when Jews appeared in Greek cities along the Adriatic, Aegean, and Black Sea coasts. However, by the nineteenth century, the vast majority of Jews in East Central Europe were not descendants from those earlier times but the descendants of immigrants who came to the region in the Middle Ages and who comprised two distinct groups—the Ashkenazim and Sephardim. It is also interesting to note the sheer size of these groups, in particular the Ashkenazim. In 1900, of the estimated 10,600,000 Jews throughout the world, over 70 percent were Ashkenazim living in East Central Europe. (For the statistical distribution of Jews according to country, see the chart accompanying Map 30.)

The Ashkenazim are Jews from Germanic Central Europe who are distinguished from Sephardim by certain matters of ritual, dress, and speech—an older form of German (influenced by Slavic and Hebrew borrowings) that is called Yiddish. When discrimination and persecution of Jews was on the rise in the Holy Roman Empire during the twelfth century, they began to move eastward, in particular to the Kingdom of Poland, which encouraged and welcomed them. The migration into Poland continued during the thirteenth and fourteenth centuries. Then, in the fifteenth and sixteenth centuries, when Poland expanded eastward and was transformed into the Polish-Lithuanian Commonwealth, Jews were encouraged to settle in the eastern parts of the country (Lithuania, Belarus, Ukraine). This trend was halted during the Zaporozhian Cossack revolt of 1648, in which thousands of Jews were killed or fled from Ukraine. Within the next half century, however, the community there was restored and it even expanded in numbers, at least in Ukrainian territories west of the Dnieper River under Polish rule.

At the end of the eighteenth century, when Poland was partitioned by its neighbors and eventually ceased to exist (1772, 1793, 1795, see Map 22a), most of the heaviest areas of Jewish settlement in the old Polish-Lithuanian Commonwealth came under Russian rule. Almost immediately, the imperial authorities placed restrictions on the movement of Jews to other parts of tsarist Russia. Thus they were, with few exceptions, forced to remain in the western part of the Russian Empire—those lands that had once been part of historic Poland. With reference to Jews, these lands came to be known as the Pale of Settlement, or simply the Pale.

The Pale encompassed all the Russian imperial provinces shown on the accompanying map, minus Courland, Pskov, and Smolensk in the north, but including all of Chernigov, Poltava, and Kherson, as well as Ekaterinoslav and Taurida (with the Crimea) east and south of the Dnieper River. The only other heavily Jewish-inhabited area that had once been part of historic Poland was Galicia, which in 1772 was incorporated into the Austrian Empire.

It was the Pale together with Galicia and Moldavia that became the heartland of Ashkenazic Jewry. And it is from this part of the Ashkenazic world that some of the most important developments in modern Jewish history arose—Hassidism, Zionism, and, of course, Yiddish literature and scholarship.

It was also in the Pale and Galicia where by far the greatest number of Jews in East Central Europe lived. Of the estimated 7,468,000 Jews living in East Central Europe in 1900, as high as 70 percent lived in the Pale and Galicia. Moreover, of the fifty-eight largest "Jewish" cities in the region, twenty-six were in either the Pale or Galicia (see the accompanying list). The only other areas of significant Jewish population were: (1) Romania's Moldavia together with the neighboring Russian province of Bessarabia, and Austria's Bukovina (both of which were part of Moldavia before 1774); (2) northeastern Hungary (eastern Slovakia and Carpathian Rus'); and (3) Budapest and Vienna, the second and third largest "Jewish" cities. All three areas experienced an influx of Jews from either the Pale or Galicia, with Vienna and Budapest receiving Jews directly from Galicia or via northeastern Hungary.

Jewish migrations to these three areas from the Pale and Galicia were motivated by economic and sometimes political reasons. Migration began in the century between 1750 and 1850 as newcomers arrived in Moldavia, Bukovina, and northeastern Hungary (Carpathian Rus' and northern Transylvania). From the latter regions some began to move on to Budapest as well. Later, with the outbreak of pogroms in the Russian Empire, especially in the 1880s and early 1900s, Jews from the Pale sought refuge in neighboring Austrian Galicia and Bukovina, and in Romanian Moldavia. In turn, poverty-stricken Galician Jews sought to improve their economic status by migrating to northeastern Hungary (and from there to Budapest) or directly to the imperial capital of Vienna. It should also be mentioned that these same decades (1880–1914) witnessed a massive emigration of East Central Europe's Jews to western Europe (350,000) and most especially to the urban northeast of the United States (2,400,000). For instance, as high as 52 percent of the immigrants from the Russian Empire residing in the United States in 1910 were Jews.

In contrast to the Ashkenazic Jews of Russia, Austria-

Density of Jewish population
- More than 15%
- 10-14%
- 5-9%
- 1-4%

Percent of Jews in towns and cities
- ■ More than 50%
- □ 30-50%
- ◉ 10-29%
- ○ 5-9%
- 5.1 Percent of Jews in Austrian and Russian provinces
- Sarajevo Other important Jewish communities
- Plovdiv Historically important Armenian communities

International boundaries, 1900
Boundaries of kingdoms
Provincial boundaries

0   150 miles
0   150 kilometers
Scale 1:8 890 000

Hungary, Romania, and Germany were the Jews in the Balkans. For the most part, these were descendants of the Spanish or Sephardic Jews, who were expelled from Spain in 1492, after which as many as 250,000 emigrated to North Africa, Italy, and in particular to the Ottoman Empire, where they were welcomed. The Sephardic Jews had their own language called Ladino, a form of archaic Spanish heavily influenced by Hebrew and Aramaic. Like the Yiddish of the Ashkenazim, the Sephardim developed Ladino into a standard language (first in Hebrew and later Latin letters) with its own literature.

The Sephardic Jews were numerically much smaller than the Ashkenazim. For the most part they comprised those Jewish communities in the Balkans that for the longest time were under direct Ottoman rule—Bosnia-Herzegovina, Serbia, Bulgaria, Greece, and lands still under Ottoman rule in the late nineteenth century. This means that in 1900, when there were an estimated 193,000 Sephardic Jews in East Central Europe, the vast majority (140,000) lived in the European portion of the Ottoman Empire.

Like the Ashkenazim, the Sephardim also experienced migration within the region. This was particularly the case with the Sephardic Jews of Greece, which, after gaining its independence and progressively expanding its boundaries northward, persecuted Jews who were suspected—often with justification—of having supported the Ottoman state. The Greek Jews sought refuge in the remaining Ottoman territory, in particular Salonika, the major Sephardic center, as well as in Sarajevo, Edirne, and the imperial capital of Istanbul. It should also be remembered that after the Sephardim came from Spain to the Balkans, some went farther north (Budapest, Vienna, Cracow, Zamość), where their small communities continued to function in the nineteenth century.

Whereas there were marked similarities between the Jews and Armenians in East Central Europe, there was a substantial difference in their relative population sizes. By 1900 there were only 246,000 Armenians throughout all of East Central Europe, the vast majority of whom (178,000) lived in the European part of the Ottoman Empire, in particular Istanbul. Moreover, in the rest of East Central Europe (again in contrast to the Jews, whose numbers increased in the course of the eighteenth and nineteenth centuries), the number of Armenians continued to decline.

Largest "Jewish" cities in East Central Europe, ca. 1900 (Yiddish or Ladino names follow the slash)

	Jews	Percentage of Total Population			Jews	Percentage of Total Population
1. Warsaw/Varshe	219,000	32.5		35. Prague/Prag, Prog	19,000	9.4
2. Budapest	166,000	23.6		36. Bila Tserkva/Sadeh Lavan	19,000	52.9
3. Vienna/Vin	147,000	8.7		37. Uman'	18,000	59.0
4. Odessa/Odes	139,000	34.4		38. Kolomyia/Kolomea, Kolomey	17,000	49.3
5. Łódź/Lodzh	99,000	31.8		39. Kamianets'-Podil's'kyi/		
6. Berlin	92,000	4.6		Kumenets-Podolsk	16,000	40.0
7. Vilnius/Vilne	64,000	41.0		40. Edirne/Adrianopel	15,000	18.5
8. Salonika/Saloniki	60,000	57.1		41. Łomża/Lomzhe	14,000	53.8
9. Chişinău/Keshenev	50,000	46.0		42. Rivne/Rovne	14,000	56.0
10. Istanbul/Kushta	48,000	4.4		43. Ivano-Frankivs'k/		
11. Minsk	48,000	52.3		Stanislav, Stanisle	14,000	46.1
12. Iaşi/Yas	45,000	57.7		44. Balta/Balte	13,000	57.0
13. L'viv/Lvuv, Lemberik	44,000	27.7		45. Przemyśl/Premishle	13,000	28.1
14. Białystok	42,000	63.4		46. Ternopil'/Tarnopol	13,000	44.2
15. Berdychiv/Barditshev	42,000	78.0		47. Tarnów/Tarnuv, Torne	12,000	41.2
16. Bucharest	40,000	14.1		48. Brody/Brod	12,000	72.1
17. Vitsebsk/Vitebsk	34,000	52.4		49. Polatsk/Polotsk	12,000	61.0
18. Daugavpils/Dvinsk	32,000	46.0		50. Mohyliv-Podil's'kyi/		
19. Kiev	32,000	12.8		Molev-Podolsk	12,000	55.3
20. Brest/Brisk	31,000	65.8		51. Oradea/Groysvardayn,		
21. Zhytomyr/Zhitomir	31,000	46.6		Nagy Varad	12,000	25.8
22. Poznań/Pozna, Pozen, Poyzn	30,000	22.2		52. Częstochowa/Tshenstokhov	12,000	26.7
23. Kaunas/Kovne	28,000	37.1		53. Galaţi/Galats	12,000	19.2
24. Cracow/Kroke, Kruke	26,000	28.1		54. Vinnytsia/Vinitse	12,000	38.3
25. İzmir/Smirna	25,000	12.4		55. Słonim	11,000	78.0
26. Lublin	24,000	47.0		56. Khmel'nyts'kyi/Proskurov	11,000	49.9
27. Hrodna/Grodne, Horodna	23,000	49.0		57. Radom/Rodem, Rudem	11,000	37.7
28. Pinsk	22,000	77.3		58. Siedlce/Shedlets	11,000	31.8
29. Chernivtsi/Tshernovits	22,000	31.9				
30. Mahilioŭ/Molev	22,000	50.0				
31. Babruisk/Bobroysk, Bobruysk	21,000	60.0				
32. Homel'/Homel, Homlye	20,000	56.4				
33. Mykolaïv/Nikolayev-Nayshtetl	20,000	21.9				
34. Wrocław/Bresloy, Bresle	20,000	5.0				

SOURCES: Alfred Nossig, ed., *Jüdische Statistik* (Berlin, 1903); *Jüdisches Lexikon*, vol. 4/2 (Berlin, 1930), pp. 630–701; *Encyclopedia Judaica*, 16 vols. (Jerusalem, 1972); Adam Wandruszka and Peter Urbanitsch, eds., *Die Habsburgermonarchie, 1848–1918*, vol. 3: *Die Völker des Reiches*, pt. 2 (Vienna, 1980).

This was, in part, due to the relatively easier possibility for assimilation, at least with fellow Christians.

The Armenian presence in East Central Europe dates from the Byzantine era, specifically during the late sixth-century rule of Emperor Maurice (r. 582–602), himself of Armenian origin. Many Armenians left their homeland in what was then Byzantine-controlled eastern Anatolia and settled in northern Thrace, in particular the Plovdiv region. This became the foundation for Bulgaria's Armenian communities that lasted throughout the two Bulgarian empires and the Ottoman period. In the early nineteenth century, there were 140,000 Armenians in Bulgaria living in twenty towns, the most important of which were Plovdiv, Ruse, Sofia, Shumen, Varna, and Burgas. By 1900, however, the Armenian community in Bulgaria numbered only about 15,000.

Much larger was the Armenian community in Romania, which in 1900 was estimated at 50,000. The oldest Armenian communities there were in Moldavia and dated from the thirteenth and fourteenth centuries. It was from this same period that neighboring Podolia also had an important Armenian colony at Kamianets'-Podil's'kyi and two smaller communities in Galicia at L'viv and Iazlovets'. The Galician and Podolian Armenian settlements were to flourish during the sixteenth and seventeenth centuries, and even though new ones were founded in Podolia in the eighteenth century, by 1900 assimilation with Poles or Ukrainians had reduced the number of Armenians in both Austrian Galicia and Russian Podolia to a few thousand. Thus, if in 1857 Austria-Hungary had an estimated 13,000 Armenians, by 1910 they numbered under 3,000.

The largest percentage of Armenians remained in lands under Ottoman rule, where their number in the European part of the empire reached 178,000 (1897). Small communities were found in towns in Macedonia and Thrace, with a sizable group in Edirne. But by far the vast majority (158,000) resided in the largest "Armenian" city anywhere—the imperial capital of Istanbul.

34 The Catholic Church, 1900

At the outset of the twentieth century, Catholics—of both the Latin (Roman) rite and Greek (Eastern) rite —numbered 56,502,000, thus amounting to more than two-fifths of the population of East Central Europe. They were not, however, distributed evenly throughout the region but were concentrated north of the Danube and Sava rivers. In Austria-Hungary, the most Catholic of countries in the region, they represented as high as 91 percent of the inhabitants in the Austrian lands (ecclesiastical provinces of Prague, Olomouc, Vienna, Salzburg, Gorizia, and Sarajevo) and 61 percent in Hungary (ecclesiastical provinces of Esztergom, Eger, Kalocsa, Zagreb, and Zadar). Four other areas of high Catholic concentration were in lands immediately adjacent to Austria-Hungary: Bavaria (ecclesiastical provinces of Bamberg and Munich-Freising); Silesia (diocese of Wrocław); the Polish-inhabited areas of Germany (ecclesiastical province of Gniezno-Poznań) and Russia (ecclesiastical province of Warsaw); and the adjacent Lithuanian and Polish-inhabited Russian provinces of Kovno, Vil'na, and Grodno (dioceses of Samogitia and Vilnius).

The basic administrative structure of the Catholic Church consisted of ecclesiastical provinces, which generally were subdivided into an archdiocese and one or more dioceses. One exception was the office of the Latin-rite patriarchate, which remained largely an honorary title. The pope, as bishop of Rome, was also theoretically patriarch of all the West. Another patriarchate was at Venice, where the patriarch functioned basically as an archbishop; while the patriarchate of Aquileia (since 1348 with its seat in Udine) was abolished in 1751, its territory divided between the archdioceses of Udine and Gorizia.

An ecclesiastical province was headed by an archbishop, whose residence was the seat of the archdiocese. Although the archbishop was nominally the superior of all hierarchs within a given ecclesiastical province, in practice the bishops

who headed dioceses had complete control over their respective jurisdictions.

In the course of the nineteenth century, the diocesan structure was stabilized in East Central Europe. For the most part, ecclesiastical provinces formed parts of existing countries, and with only a few exceptions (such as the diocese of Wrocław in southern Silesia) did they cross international frontiers. On the other hand, there was little coincidence between diocesan and secular provincial boundaries within countries, except for the Polish lands in the western Russian Empire, where secular province and diocesan boundaries did largely coincide.

In those places where the Catholic Church had relatively few adherents, there was not an independent ecclesiastical structure. Thus in northern Germany, where the Catholic Church had once been strong, many archdioceses and dioceses ceased to exist after the Reformation (compare Maps 13 and 16). By the nineteenth century they had been replaced by dioceses (Wrocław with the apostolic delegation of Brandenburg; Ermland), apostolic vicariates (North Germany; Anhalt; Saxony), and apostolic prefectures (Lusatia), all under the direct jurisdiction of the Holy See in Rome.

Similarly, in the southern Balkans, where the Orthodox and Muslim presence predominated, large territories, even those with their own Latin-rite archdiocesan and diocesan structures, such as in Albania (Shkodër, Durrës), were under the direct jurisdiction of the Holy See. An exception was made for Greece and the Aegean islands, where the Catholics had retained a strong ecclesiastical presence dating back to the fall of Constantinople (1204) and the establishment of the Latin kingdoms. In an effort to preserve the memory and symbolic presence of that era (which lasted less than a century), the Catholic Church maintained three ecclesiastical provinces with nine archepiscopal or diocesan sees despite their very small numbers (35,000 throughout all of Greece and Crete) and the opposition of the Orthodox-oriented Greek government.

The situation in the Russian Empire was somewhat different. There, the Catholic presence was significant, most especially in the Polish ecclesiastical province of Warsaw and in the immediately adjacent dioceses of Samogitia and Vilnius, inhabited largely by Lithuanians and Poles. Sheer numbers—over 10 million Catholics in this part of the Russian Empire—justified an extensive ecclesiastical structure, but this was permitted by the Orthodox-oriented tsarist Russian government only in the westernmost areas of the empire that had once been part of the Congress Kingdom of Poland (see Map 24).

In contrast, the Lithuanian, Belarus, and Ukrainian lands, where the Catholic presence had expanded when these territories were part of the Polish-Lithuanian Commonwealth, experienced a marked decline in Catholic

Catholic population in East Central Europe, ca. 1900

Austria-Hungary (1900)	35,571,000
Austria 23,797,000 (66.9%)	
Hungary 11,774,000 (33.1%)	
Russia (1897)[1]	10,791,000
Poland 6,987,000 (65%)	
Germany (1900)[2]	9,871,000
Romania (1899)	150,000
Bulgaria (1900)	41,000
Greece and Crete (1900)	35,000
Ottoman Empire Europe (1897)	19,000
Montenegro (1897)	13,000
Serbia (1895)	11,000

1. European Russia west of the Dnieper River.
2. Includes only Bavaria and lands in the former German Empire in what is now eastern Germany and western Poland.

The Catholic Church, 1900

BALTIC SEA

Varniai
(Medininkai)
SAMOGITIA
POLATSK
Smolensk

SCHLESWIG-
HOLSTEIN

Kaunas
Vilnius
MAHILIOŬ

NORTH
GERMANY

Kołobrzeg
Kamień
Pelplin
Frombork
Malbork
Kwidzyń
ERMLAND
Wygry
Sejny
Minsk

HAMBURG
BREMEN

Osnabrück
Hildesheim

BRANDENBURG

Chelmno
CHEŁMNO
Włocławek
Płock
GNIEZNO
POZNAŃ
AUGUSTÓW
ZHYROVYCHY

Paderborn

Brandenburg
Lebus
ANHALT

MAGDEBURG

Merseburg

WŁOCŁAWEK
WARSAW
Janów
Podlaski
Brest
Pinsk
Chernihiv

Fulda
Erfurt
Meissen
LUSATIA
Dresden
SAXONY
Litoměřice

Wrocław
Kalisz

Kielce
Sandomierz
Lublin
Chełm
Volodymyr
Luts'k
**LUBLIN-
PODLACHIA**
KIEV

Würzburg

BAMBERG
PRAGUE
Hradec
Králové
PRAGUE

Cracow
Tarnów
Przemyśl
L'VIV
Zhytomyr

Eichstätt
Regensburg
České
Budějovice
Brno
OLOMOUC
Spišská
Kapitula
Kamianets'-
Podil's'kyi

Rottenburg

Augsburg
Freising
Passau
Linz
Nitra
Rožňava
Košice
Satu-Mare
Suceava
TIRASPOL

**MUNICH-
FREISING**
St. Pölten
VIENNA
Banská
Bystrica

St. Gallen
Chur
SALZBURG
Leoben
ESZTERGOM
Győr
Vác
EGER
Oradea
Iaşi
Tiraspol

Bressanone
SEKKAU
Graz
GURK Gurk
Klagenfurt
Szombathely
Veszprém
Székesfehérvár
TRANSYLVANIA

Trent
Belluno
LAVANT
Maribor
Celje
Pécs
KALOCSA
Cenad
Alba Iulia

Bergamo
Vicenza
Treviso
Céneda
Concordia
UDINE
Ljubljana
GORIZIA
Trieste
Koper
ZAGREB
Timişoara

Brescia
Verona
Padua
AQUILEIA
VENICE
Poreč
BAČ
Cenad

Mantua
Parma
Adria
Chioggia
Pula
Krk
Senj
Modruš
Dakovo
**SREMSKA
MITROVICA**
BUCHAREST
**BLACK
SEA**

MODENA
FERRARA
Banja
Luka

BOLOGNA
RAVENNA
ZADAR

LUCCA
FLORENCE
URBINO
ANCONA
Šibenik
SPLIT
SARAJEVO
**SERBIA
(TO BAR)**
Ruse

SIENA
CAMERINO
Duvno
Mostar
Nikopol

PERUGIA
FERMO
Hvar
Makarska
NICOPOLIS
SOFIA-PLOVDIV
Plovdiv

SPOLETO
AQUILA
Trebinje
DUBROVNIK
Kotor
Pult
SHKODËR
Sapë
Orosh
(Mirditë)
SKOPJE
Edirne

CHIETI
LANCIANO
BAR
Lesh
Kobrin
Plovdiv

ROME
GAETA
MANFREDONIA
**TRANI-
BARLETTA**
DURRËS
ISTANBUL

CAPUA
BENEVENTO
CONZA
BARI
Salonika

NAPLES
SALERNO
ACERENZA
BRINDISI

AMALFI
TARANTO
**TYRRHENIAN
SEA**

OTRANTO

ROSSANO
CORFU
IZMIR

COSENZA
Chios
Andros
ATHENS
Tinos
Syros
Mykonos
Leros
Kalymnos
**IONIAN
SEA**
Zante
Melos
NAXOS
Thira

**CANDIA
(TO IZMIR)**
Canea
Kárpathos
RHODES

Boundaries of ecclesiastical
provinces

Archdiocesan and diocesan
boundaries

Under the direct jurisdiction
of the Holy See

Latin-rite patriarchal seat

Latin-rite archbishop's seat

Latin-rite bishop's seat

Seat of Latin-rite apostolic
vicariate or prefecture

ERMLAND Diocesan name other than episcopal seat

Extinct or transferred Latin-rite patriarchal,
archdiocesan, or diocesan seats

Seat of Greek-rite apostolic vicariate
or administrator

Extinct or transferred Greek-rite
metropolitan or eparchial seats

Seat of Armenian-rite Catholic patriarch

Scale 1:8 890 000

0   150 miles
0   150 kilometers

Copyright © by Paul Robert Magocsi

ecclesiastical structures beginning in the late eighteenth century. Hence, several Catholic dioceses were abolished (Zhytomyr, 1778, and Smolensk, 1798), then restored (Zhytomyr and Kiev, 1798) or reorganized (Kiev transferred to Zhytomyr, 1798). A definitive church organization was established in 1798, at which time all lands east of the Warsaw ecclesiastical province came under the ecclesiastical province of Mahilioŭ. These included the archdiocese of Mahilioŭ and the dioceses of Samogitia (seat at Kaunas), Vilnius, Minsk, Kamianets'-Podil's'kyi and Luts'k-Zhytomyr (seat at Zhytomyr). Subsequently, Kamianets'-Podil's'kyi was joined to Luts'k-Zhytomyr (1815) and then abolished entirely in 1866, the same year Minsk ceased to function as a distinct diocese. On the other hand, a new diocese called Tiraspol or Kherson (with its seat farther east at Saratov on the lower Volga River) was established in 1847, primarily for German colonists.

Whereas some ecclesiastical jurisdictions may have been suppressed, Latin-rite Catholics could at least still function in the Russian Empire. This was not the case for the Uniates or Byzantine-rite Greek Catholics of Belarus and Ukraine. In the course of the nineteenth century, the fate of the Uniates varied greatly on territories that came under the rule of the Russian Empire. The Uniate metropolitanate of Kiev (with eparchies in Chełm, Luts'k, Volodymyr-Brest, Pinsk, Polatsk, and Smolensk) was abolished in 1796. Subsequently, two eparchies (Volodymyr-Brest and Luts'k) were restored in 1798, and the church was fully restored in 1806 as the Uniate metropolitanate of Russia (with its seat in Polatsk). Again the church was reorganized in 1828, with metropolitanates for Belarus (seat in Polatsk) and Lithuania (seat in Zhyrovychy). Less than a decade later, however, these two metropolitanates were abolished (1839), leaving Chełm as the last Uniate eparchy until it, too, was finally suppressed in 1875. All Uniates/Greek Catholics in the Russian Empire were forced to become Orthodox or Roman Catholics after the jurisdictional closures in 1839 and 1875.

With the suppression of Greek Catholicism in the Russian Empire, that faith was able to survive for the most part only in Austria-Hungary. It was also there that in 1774 an imperial decree was passed replacing the older name Uniate (by then perceived to be a derogatory term) with a new name, Greek Catholic, emphasizing thereby that the church was Catholic but of the Byzantine or Greek rite. The Greek Catholics of Austria-Hungary were made legally equal with Latin-rite or Roman Catholics, and many of the hierarchs and clergy soon became outstanding defenders of the national groups they represented. This was particularly the case among the Romanian and Ukrainian Greek Catholics.

Of the estimated 5 million Greek Catholics in East Central Europe at the outset of the twentieth century, virtually all of them (99.8 percent) lived within the Austro-Hungarian Empire. There they were divided into four ecclesiastical provinces. Two (L'viv and Alba Iulia–Făgăraş) had their own suffragans in the person of a resident archbishop or metropolitan, the others (Mukachevo and Križevci) had only dioceses (eparchies) subordinate to a Latin-rite archbishop (see Map 35a).

In terms of faithful, the largest of the Greek Catholic ecclesiastical provinces was L'viv in Galicia, with 3,134,000 members. The vast majority were Ukrainians (92.8 percent) with a small number of Poles (6.9 percent). Next largest was the ecclesiastical province of Alba Iulia–Făgăraş in Transylvania and eastern Hungary, with its metropolitan residence in Blaj. Most of its 1,267,000 members were Romanians (81.8 percent) with a smaller number of Magyars (18.2 percent).

Unlike L'viv and Alba Iulia–Făgăraş, which were independent, the two smaller Greek Catholic ecclesiastical provinces in Hungary were subordinate to Latin-rite archbishops. The Greek Catholic eparchies of Mukachevo (its seat in Uzhhorod) and Prešov—together with about 562,000 members divided between Carpatho-Rusyns (73.1 percent), Slovaks (18.1 percent), and Magyars (8.8 percent)—were under the jurisdiction of the archbishop of Esztergom, the Roman Catholic primate of Hungary. The eparchy of Križevci, with only 25,000 members (mostly Croats and Carpatho-Rusyns), was under the jurisdiction of the Latin-rite archbishop of Zagreb.

There were also smaller numbers of Greek Catholics who derived from an aborted movement for church union in Bulgaria during the 1860s. By 1900, most of the 13,000 Bulgarian Greek Catholics lived in the Ottoman Empire, where they had apostolic vicariates in Thrace (with a seat at Edirne) and Macedonia (with a seat at Salonika)—see Map 34.

Finally, Catholics of the Armenian rite numbered about 15,000 in East Central Europe. Nearly two-thirds of these lived in the Ottoman Empire, where they were under the leadership of a patriarch resident in Istanbul. The remaining 5,000 were in Austria-Hungary (2,100 in Galicia and Bukovina; 2,900 in Transylvania), where they were under the jurisdiction of an Armenian-rite archbishop in L'viv with an administrator in Suceava in Bukovina (see Map 34). The Armenian Catholics also had a small community of Mechitarist (Benedictine) monks in Vienna, whose headquarters became a major center of Armenian cultural activity.

35 The Orthodox Church, 1900

At the outset of the twentieth century, the number of Orthodox adherents in East Central Europe was 44,382,000, about one-third the total population of the region. The Orthodox were concentrated primarily in the Russian Empire (in particular those lands east and south of the Polish and Lithuanian-inhabited provinces); in Romania; and in all countries south of the Danube-Sava rivers. The only other significant Orthodox presence was in the southern and far-eastern lands of Austria-Hungary. In the rest of that empire as well as in the German Empire, the Orthodox were virtually nonexistent.

Within the framework of the four ancient patriarchates of the Orthodox Eastern Christian Church—Alexandria, Antioch, Jerusalem, Constantinople—East Central Europe came under the jurisdiction of the so-called Great Church, or Patriarchate of Constantinople (the New Rome). The head of that Church, the ecumenical patriarch, resided in Istanbul (Constantinople), more specifically after the onset of Ottoman rule in 1453 in the Greek or Phanar quarter of the city.

After the fall of Constantinople in the mid-fifteenth century, the ecumenical patriarchate of Constantinople experienced both the immediate loss of sociopolitical influence in the new Ottoman Muslim world in which it found itself and the gradual decline of control over Orthodox communities in East Central Europe. This occurred when independent or autocephalous national churches were established in different countries throughout the region. In almost every case, the ecumenical patriarch initially opposed the establishment of newly formed independent Orthodox churches. While it is true that most were eventually recognized and accepted back into the fold of the larger eastern patriarchal Orthodox community, the ecumenical patriarch's authority over the autocephalous churches was reduced to a mere symbolic function.

Orthodox population in East Central Europe, ca. 1900

Russia (1897)[1]	24,535,000
Romania (1899)	5,452,000
Austria-Hungary (1900)	3,556,000
Austria 607,000	
Hungary 2,199,000	
Bosnia-Herzegovina ca. 750,000	
Bulgaria (1900)	3,019,000
Ottoman Empire (1897)[2]	2,490,000
Serbia (1900)	2,461,000
Greece (1896)	2,400,000
Montenegro (1900)	294,000
Crete (1894)	175,000

1. Only provinces west of the Dnieper River, listed in note 3 in the table accompanying Map 30.
2. Greeks, Bulgarians, and Vlachs in the European part of the Ottoman Empire.

The first of the national churches to act in an independent manner was that of Muscovy, whose independence (autocephaly) as the Russian Orthodox Church began in 1448, but was not finally recognized by Constantinople until 1589 (see Map 13). Subsequently, the growth of the Russian Orthodox Church with its patriarch in Moscow followed the expansion of the tsarist Russian state. When in the seventeenth and eighteenth centuries Russia expanded into East Central Europe, annexing lands formerly part of Poland-Lithuania (see Map 22a), some Orthodox eparchies dating from Kievan Rus' times were restored while others were created anew. By the outset of the twentieth century, most of the Russian Orthodox eparchies west of the Dnieper River, as elsewhere in the empire, coincided with provincial boundaries (Volhynia, Kiev, Podolia, Kherson, and Chişinău in Bessarabia). The only exceptions were the eparchy of Lithuania (with an eparchial seat at Vilnius); the eparchy of Minsk, abolished 1869 and made part of Mahilioŭ; and the archeparchy of Warsaw (whose boundaries coincided with the former Congress Kingdom of Poland less the eparchy of Lublin, which was set up in 1905).

The most intensive drive toward establishing independent Orthodox churches in East Central Europe was to take place between the late eighteenth and late nineteenth centuries. This process, moreover, was directly related to the decline of the Ottoman Empire and the rise of new nation-states in the Balkans, each of which hoped to enhance its political prestige by having its own "national" Orthodox church independent of the ecumenical patriarch in Istanbul. Closely linked to these desires was a rejection of the dominance of Greek language and culture that was associated with the ecumenical patriarchate, whose liturgical and educational practices frequently reflected a sense of superiority for things Greek as well as scorn for the languages and cultures of the Slavs, Romanians, and other Balkan peoples.

The first of the new autocephalous Orthodox churches arose among the Serbs. Already in the fourteenth century the Serbs had an autocephalous church with their own patriarch at Peć/Ipek (see also Map 13). When independent Serbia fell to the Ottoman Empire in the fifteenth century, the Sultan ordered in 1459 that the Serbian church be placed under the jurisdiction of the archbishop of Ohrid, who in turn was subordinate to the ecumenical patriarch in Constantinople. However, in 1557, the Serbian patriarchate at Peć was restored and given jurisdiction over the Orthodox faithful in an extensive territory that included —besides Serbia—Montenegro, northern Macedonia, Bosnia-Herzegovina, Slavonia, and Hungary. The ecumenical patriarch remained opposed to this development and continually urged the Ottoman government to dissolve the Serbian patriarchate of Peć. This finally happened in 1766. As a result, the Serbs under Ottoman rule would henceforth be within the jurisdiction of the ecumenical patriarch.

35a The Greek Catholic Church, 1900

- ———— Boundaries of ecclesiastical provinces
- - - - - Archeparchial (Metropolitanate) and eparchial boundaries
- ‡ Greek-rite metropolitan archbishop's seat
- ⊙ Greek-rite bishop's seat
- † Latin-rite archbishop's seat
- MUKACHEVO Eparchial name other than eparchial seat
- ⚲ Extinct or transferred archeparchial or eparchial seat

Inset map labels: Przemyśl (Peremyshl'), L'VIV, Prešov, Vienna, Ivano-Frankivs'k, Uzhhorod, Mukachevo, MUKACHEVO, STANYSLAVIV, ESZTERGOM, Budapest, ARMENOPOLIS, Gherla, Oradea, Križevci, ZAGREB, ALBA IULIA-FĂGĂRAS, BLAJ, Alba Iulia, FĂGĂRAŞ, Lugoj, Bucharest

Scale 1:14 140 000

Main map labels: RIGA, PSKOV, BALTIC SEA, LITHUANIA, Polatsk (Polotsk), Smolensk, GERMANY, Vilnius (Vil'na), Mahilioŭ (Mogilev), Minsk, Hrodna (Grodno), R U S S I A, Chernihiv (Chernigov), WARSAW, Chełm (Kholm), VOLHYNIA, Volodymyr (Vladimir-Volynski), Zhytomyr (Zhitomir), KIEV, POLTAVA, Ostrih (Ostrog), Pereiaslav, L'viv, Kamianets'-Podil's'kyi (Kamenets-Podol'sk), PODOLIA, CHERNIVTSI, AUSTRIA-HUNGARY, BUKOVINA, Rădăuţi, IAŞI, Chişinău (Kishinev), KHERSON, Szentendre, Buda, HUNGARY, Roman, Huşi, MOLDAVIA, SWITZ., Odessa, Arad, TRANSYLVANIA, Timişoara, SIBIU, Braşov, Galaţi, Karlovac, CROATIA-SLAVONIA, Pakrac, Novi Sad, Caransebeş, Curtea de Argeş, Buzău, Plaški, SREMSKI KARLOVCI, Vršac, Rîmnicu Vîlcea, ROMANIA, Banja Luka, Tuzla, Šabac, BELGRADE, TIMOK, BUCHAREST, BLACK SEA, Venice, Zadar, DALMATIA, BOSNIA-HERZEGOVINA, SARAJEVO, SERBIA, Negotin, WALACHIA, Užice, Čačak, Vidin, Silistra, Mostar, Niš, Pirot, Vratsa, Lovech, Veliko Tŭrnovo, Ruse, Varna, ITALY, ADRIATIC SEA, MONTENEGRO, Ostrih (Ostrog), PEĆ (IPEK), Sofia, BULGARIA, Sliven, CETINJE, Kotor, Prizren, Samokov, Plovdiv, Rome, Skopje, Veles, Melnik, Gotse Delchev (Nevrokop), Edirne (Adrianopolis), Silivri, Kadiköy (Chalcedon), Durrës, ALBANIA, MACEDONIA, Debar, Kruševo, Strumica, Komotinē, Keşan, ISTANBUL, İzmit (Nicomedia), Elbasan, OHRID, Bitola, Kilkis, Serrai, Büyükada (Prinkipo), İznik (Nicaea), Berat, Korçë, Edessa, Verroia, Salonika, Alexandroúpolis, Marmara, Cyzicus, Caesaria, Bursa (Prusa), Kastoria, Siátista, Servia, Kitros, Imroz (Imbros), Gelibolu (Gallipoli), Gjirokastër, Grevená, Pétra, Kassándra, Mírina, OTTOMAN, Ioannina, Elasson, ANATOLIA, Yalvaç (Pisidia), Corfu (Kérkyra), Paramithiá, Deskáti, Larissa, Trikkala, AEGEAN, Kalloni, EMPIRE, Preveza, Arta, Karpenision, Mytilene (Mitilini), Leukas, Amphissa, Chálcis, Chios, İzmir (Smyrna), Alaşehir (Philadelphia), Návpaktos, Lebadéa (Levádhia), SEA, Ephesus, Argostolion, Patras, Aígion, Corinth, ATHENS, GREECE, Samos, Zante (Zákinthos), Pyrgos, Nauplia (Návplion), Hydra (Ídhra), Hermoupolis, Naxos, Megalópolis, Kiparissia, Kalymnos, Kos, Kalamata (Kalámai), Sparta, Yíthion, Monemvasía, Thíra, Rhodes (Rodos), Cerigo (Kíthira), Kárpathos, Canea (Khaniá), CANDIA (IRÁKLION), Kastéllion, Rethymnon, Neápolis, CRETE, Spíli, Moires, Hierápetra, TYRRHENIAN SEA, Naples, IONIAN SEA

- ══════ International boundaries, 1900
- —————— Boundaries of kingdoms and principalities
- —————— Boundaries of Orthodox jurisdictions
- - - - - Boundaries of Orthodox eparchies
- —————— Boundary of the Bulgarian Exarchate, 1870
- - - - - Lands added to the Bulgarian Exarchate after 1870
- ● Seat of ecumenical patriarch
- ‡ Seats of archbishops (metropolitans)
- ▲ Seats of bishops (eparchs)
- KHERSON Eparchial name other than seat of bishop
- ⊗ Extinct or transferred patriarchal, metropolitan or eparchial seat
- ▲ Seats of bishops (eparchs) of the Bulgarian Exarchate
- ▽ Extinct or transferred eparchial seats of the Bulgarian Exarchate

0 ———— 150 miles
0 ———— 150 kilometers
Scale 1:8 890 000

However, Serbs outside the Ottoman Empire were not under such pressure, and in 1737 those living in the Austrian Empire (southern Hungary) established an Orthodox metropolitan province at Sremski Karlovci which was recognized by the Serbian patriarch at Peć. Then, in 1766, when the Ottomans abolished Peć, the Karlovci province became an independent body, eventually with six suffragan bishops (Novi Sad, Timişoara, Vršac, Buda, Pakrac, and Karlovac), known as the Serbian Orthodox Slav Oriental Church.

Similarly, the Orthodox Church of Montenegro became independent. In that country, from 1516 to 1852 the ruling princes had been Orthodox bishops (vladikas) subordinate to the Serbian patriarchate of Peć, until the latter's dissolution in 1766.

A third independent Serbian Orthodox church that considered itself a descendent of the Peć patriarchate was in Serbia proper. In 1830, when Serbia was still an autonomous principality of the Ottoman Empire, the local ruler, Prince Miloš Obrenović, set up an independent metropolitan province based in Belgrade with three suffragan bishops (Šabac, Užice, Timok at Negotin). Initially, the ecumenical patriarch in Istanbul reserved for himself the right to confirm the election of new metropolitans, but after 1879, when Serbia expanded its borders and became fully independent, its Orthodox Church became autocephalous as well.

Even before the creation of a fully autocephalous Serbian Church in 1879, two other distinct Orthodox bodies came into being in the Balkans. As early as 1822, while Greece was still in the midst of its struggle for independence, the country's fledgling national assembly declared Orthodoxy the state religion—without, moreover, any reference to the ecumenical patriarch in the Ottoman capital. Then, in 1833, three years after the country had won its independence, the Greek parliament proclaimed its Orthodox national church to be autocephalous. Initially, the new Orthodox Church of Hellas, as the Greek church was called, was not recognized by the ecumenical patriarch, although the latter finally relented in 1850.

But the 1850 decision (Tomos) did not end friction between the ecumenical patriarch and the Greek Orthodox Church, because as Greece expanded its borders—the Ionian Islands (1866) and Thessaly (1881)—the parishes and eparchies in those lands that had until then been under the jurisdiction of the ecumenical patriarch were simply coopted by the autocephalous Greek Orthodox Church. By 1900, the church within Greece had thirty-two eparchial sees (whose bishops carried the title metropolitan) under the leadership of the metropolitan archbishop of Athens.

The efforts throughout the Balkans to promote the national cause and to coordinate political and ecclesiastical expansion led to conflicting claims over certain areas, the most serious of which focused on Macedonia and Thrace. By 1900, those regions were still part of the Ottoman Empire; therefore, the Orthodox parishes and bishops there were theoretically still under the jurisdiction of the ecumenical patriarch. But the situation had become even more complex in 1870, when the so-called Bulgarian Exarchate came into being.

The tradition of a distinct church in Bulgaria dates from the tenth century, when an autocephalous Bulgarian Orthodox Church was established (see Map 13). After an interrupted existence, which was directly related to the political fortunes of Bulgaria's two medieval empires, the tradition of Bulgarian Orthodox autocephaly was maintained by a patriarch at Ohrid in Macedonia until 1767, when as at the nearby Serbian patriarchate of Peć, the ecumenical patriarch succeeded in convincing the Ottoman government to abolish the last remnants of Bulgarian ecclesiastical independence.

In the course of the nineteenth century, the question of a Bulgarian Orthodox church became intimately tied to the national revival. Under pressure from the Bulgarian movement's greatest ally, tsarist Russia, the Ottoman government in 1870 recognized the Orthodox Bulgarians as a distinct community (millet) with the right to its own church organization. The result was the creation of a new church headed by a prelate, known as an exarch, who resided in Istanbul. The Bulgarian Exarchate included eparchies that were both within and beyond what subsequently (1878–85) became the autonomous state of Bulgaria.

It is not surprising that the ecumenical patriarch refused to accept what he perceived as a challenge to his own ecclesiastical authority—as well as the loss of eparchies and parishes within and beyond the Ottoman-decreed boundaries of the Bulgarian Exarchate (see the accompanying map). Hence he promptly (in 1872) excommunicated the Bulgarian exarch and all those subordinate to him. For its part, the Bulgarian Exarchate continued to function with exclusive control over the Orthodox community within the autonomous principality of Bulgaria as well as beyond its borders. While the Bulgarian Exarchate lost the eparchies of Niš and Pirot when Serbia was awarded that territory in 1878, the Ottoman government allowed for an expansion of its jurisdiction into central Macedonia (Skopje, Strumica, Debar, Ohrid, Bitola eparchies) and permitted the establishment of vicariates in southern Macedonia and Thrace, often in the same places that were subordinate to the ecumenical patriarch (Kastoria, Verroia, Salonika, Alexandroúpolis, and others).

As a result, throughout Macedonia and Thrace there were two rival Orthodox churches, each with its own bishops and parishes owing jurisdictional allegiance either to the ecumenical patriarch (the Patriarchists) or to the Bulgarian Exarchate (the Exarchists). Generally, the supporters of each were divided along nationality lines: the Greeks, most Vlachs, Albanians, and those Bulgarians frightened by the 1872 excommunication decree supported the ecumenical patriarchate; nearly all the Bulgarians and some Vlachs supported the Exarchate. By the outset of the twentieth century, the Vlachs were becoming a force to reckon with in their own right, and they demanded that the Ottoman government give them their own Orthodox church (neither Patriarchist nor Exarchist), as it had previously done for the Bulgarians in 1870. In 1905 the Vlachs obtained their own bishop at Bitola/Monastir under the jurisdiction of the Romanian Autocephalous Orthodox Church.

Somewhat less problematic were four other independent Orthodox churches that came into being during the second half of the nineteenth century. In 1864, the Romanians of Transylvania, discontented with the Serbian-dominated church of Sremski Karlovci of which they were a part, received permission from the Austrian government to establish a separate autonomous church with its metropolitan seat in Sibiu and two suffragan bishops at Arad and Caransebeş. Similarly, in Bukovina, where the metropolitan of Rădăuti (since 1781 resident in Chernivtsi) was subordinate to the Serbian Church of Sremski Karlovci, a new church was established in 1873. This happened because the Habsburgs wished to have ecclesiastical lines coincide with the greater political distinctions brought about in 1868 between Hungary and the Austrian provinces. Thus the Orthodox in the "Austrian half" of the empire were placed into one Orthodox Church of Chernivtsi, even though this meant joining Romanian- and Ukrainian-inhabited Bukovina with the Orthodox Serbs living on the other side of the empire in Austria's Adriatic province of Dalmatia (with eparchial seats at Zadar and Kotor).

Another distinct Orthodox church within the Austro-Hungarian polity was that of Bosnia-Herzegovina. Since the province was from 1878 to 1908 still theoretically part of the Ottoman Empire, its church remained nominally under the authority of the ecumenical patriarch. However, after 1908, when Austria-Hungary annexed the province outright, the Church of Bosnia-Herzegovina became fully autocephalous with a metropolitan at Sarajevo and three suffragan bishops (Mostar, Tuzla, Banja Luka).

As for the church in Romania, soon after Walachia and Moldavia were united into an autonomous state (1858–62), the new government proclaimed its Orthodox church independent of the ecumenical patriarchate. The church authorities comprised the metropolitan of Walachia resident in Bucharest (the primate of the whole church), the metropolitan of Moldavia resident in Iaşi, and seven suffragan bishops. Even though the ecumenical patriarch finally recognized the Romanian church in 1885, friction between the two continued over the degree of Romanian autocephaly, the problem of indemnification for government confiscation of patriarchal monastic property, and eventually the conflict in Macedonia, where Romania supported Vlach demands for their own Orthodox Church.

Despite the complaints of the ecumenical patriarch about the Romanian and other national churches in the Balkans, there was little he could do to stop what became the dominant trend: the creation of independent states in the Balkans, each of which was to coopt former churches of the ecumenical patriarchate into its own independent or autocephalous national church. As a result of the Balkan Wars (see Map 26b), the ecumenical patriarch's influence receded even further as Greece and Bulgaria expanded their boundaries (along with their ecclesiastical jurisdictions) and the new state of Albania came into being with eventually its own autocephalous Orthodox Church as well.

On the eve of World War I, the administrative structure of East Central Europe—in particular those lands within the German, Russian, and Austro-Hungarian empires—had remained relatively stable since about 1870. South of Austria-Hungary, however, political changes were still occurring as the Ottoman Empire receded and was replaced by several independent states. By about 1900, each of these states had administrative subdivisions which remained more or less unchanged until the Balkan Wars of 1912–13 (see Map 27b).

The German Empire in East Central Europe consisted of parts or all of four kingdoms (Prussia, Bavaria, Saxony, Württemberg); two grand duchies (Mecklenburg-Schwerin, Mecklenburg-Strelitz); two duchies (Brunswick, Anhalt); and, within Thuringia, several minuscule entities —one grand duchy (Saxe-Weimar), three duchies (Saxe-Meiningen, Saxe-Altenburg, Saxe-Coburg-Gotha), and four principalities. Most of these states already had a long historical tradition, although their constellation shown on the accompanying map took form in 1871 with the creation of a confederation known as the German Empire.

Each of the states mentioned above (as well as the free towns of Lübeck, Bremen, and Hamburg) had its own representative assembly located in its capital. The largest of the German states in East Central Europe was Prussia (indicated in dark purple on the accompanying map), which in turn was divided into several provinces (East and West Prussia, Pomerania, Posen, Brandenburg, Silesia, and Saxony—the latter Prussian province not to be confused with the Kingdom of Saxony).

Immediately to the east, the structure of the Russian Empire remained basically the same throughout the nineteenth century. Tsarist Russia gradually divided the empire into provinces in response to administrative reforms of 1802, with each province (guberniia) ruled by a tsarist-appointed governor residing in the provinciál capital. Initially, the only exception to this pattern was the Congress Kingdom of Poland, which functioned as a semi-autonomous unit until 1861, when it too was brought into administrative line with the rest of the empire and subdivided into ten provinces—Suwałki, Łomża, Płock, Warsaw, Kalisz, Piotrków, Kielce, Radom, Lublin, and Siedlce (compare Map 24). In 1912, a slice of eastern Lublin and Siedlce provinces inhabited by a mixed Polish-Ukrainian population was detached to form a new province of Kholm.

Administrative stability also marked the Austro-Hungarian Empire, especially from the 1870s to World War I. The basic division of the "Austrian half" of the empire into seventeen provinces and the Hungarian Kingdom into seventy-one counties, including those in semi-autonomous Croatia-Slavonia, remained unchanged. From its incorporation into the empire in 1908, Bosnia-Herzegovina remained under the joint rule of both Austria and Hungary (compare Map 25b).

The rest of the smaller and newer states in the southern third of East Central Europe set up new administrative structures in the lands that came under their authority. The Kingdom of Romania, which became fully independent in 1878, retained the historic provinces of Moldavia (with its capital at Iaşi), Walachia (with its capital at Bucharest), and added the newly acquired Dobruja. By the end of the century, local government was based in thirty-two departments throughout the country, each headed by a prefect appointed by the state and resident in the departmental center.

Similarly, neighboring Serbia was divided into seventeen departments, each ruled by a prefect (načalnik) resident in the departmental center. As for Bulgaria, between 1878, when it became an autonomous principality, and 1908, when it became an independent kingdom, there were three changes in the administrative subdivision of the country (1880, 1887, 1901). By the outset of the twentieth century, Bulgaria was divided into twelve departments, each department (okrug) administered by a prefect (upravitel) resident in the departmental center.

Farther south, Greece, which had been divided into sixteen departments, or nomarchies (nomoí), was in 1899 redivided into twenty-six. Each department was headed by a prefect, or nomarch, appointed by the central government in Athens. When, in 1908, Greece established its authority over Crete, it left in place the five departments that had functioned as sanjaks when the Ottomans ruled the island.

By the first decade of the twentieth century, the territory of the Ottoman Empire in East Central Europe was substantially reduced, so that there were only eight districts (vilayets) left, including the city and district of Istanbul (compare Map 26a).

International boundaries

Boundaries of semi-independent kingdoms, duchies, principalities, and free cities

Provincial boundaries

Boundaries of counties, districts, and departments

⊙ State capitals

◉ Capitals of kingdoms, duchies, and principalities

• Provincial capitals

○ Departmental centers

KOSOVA Names of provinces other than capitals

0   150 miles
0   150 kilometers
Scale 1:8 890 000

Copyright © by Paul Robert Magocsi

Departments and counties, 1900 (Seat indicated in parentheses if different from district/county name)

Hungary
(If two county seats are given, the second is the Hungarian name)

1. Trencsén (Trenčín/Trencsén)
2. Árva (Dolný Kubín/Alsókubin)
3. Turóc (Martin/Turócszentmárton)
4. Liptó (Liptovský Mikuláš/Liptószentmiklós)
5. Szepes (Levoča/Lőcse)
6. Sáros (Prešov/Eperjes)
7. Pozsony (Bratislava/Pozsony)
8. Nyitra (Nitra/Nyitra)
9. Bars (Zlaté Moravce/Aranyosmarot)
10. Hont (Šahy/Ipolyság)
11. Zólyom (Banská Bystrica/Beszterczebánya)
12. Nógrád (Balassagyarmat)
13. Gömör és Kishont (Rimavská Sobota/Rimaszombat)
14. Borsod (Miskolc)
15. Abaúj-Torna (Košice/Kassa)
16. Zemplén (Sátoraljaújhely)
17. Szabolcs (Nyíregyháza)
18. Ung (Uzhhorod/Ungvár)
19. Bereg (Berehovo/Beregszász)
20. Ugocsa (Vynohradiv/Nagyszőllős)
21. Szatmár (Carie/Nagykároly)
22. Máramaros (Sighetul Marmaţiei/Máramossziget)
23. Sopron
24. Moson (Magyaróvár)
25. Győr
26. Komárom
27. Esztergom
28. Heves (Eger)
29. Hajdú (Debrecen)
30. Vas (Szombathely)
31. Veszprém
32. Fejér (Székesfehérvár)
33. Pest-Pilis-Solt-Kiskun (Budapest)
34. Jász-Nagy-Kun-Szolnok (Szolnok)
35. Békés (Gyula)
36. Bihar (Oradea/Nagyvárad)
37. Szilágy (Zalău/Zilah)
38. Kolozs (Cluj/Kolozsvár)
39. Szolnok-Doboka (Dej/Dés)
40. Beszterce-Naszód (Bistriţa/Beszterce)
41. Zala (Zalaegerszeg)
42. Somogy (Kaposvár)
43. Tolna (Szekszárd)
44. Csongrád (Szentes)
45. Csanád (Makó)
46. Arad
47. Torda-Aranyos (Turda/Torda)
48. Maros-Torda (Tîrgu-Mureş/Marosvásárhely)
49. Csík (Miercurea-Cius/Csíkszereda)
50. Varasd (Varaždin/Varasd)
51. Belovár-Körös (Bjelovar/Belovár)
52. Baranya (Pécs)
53. Bács-Bodrog (Sombor/Zombor)
54. Torontál (Bečej/Nagybecskerek)
55. Temes (Timişoara/Temesvár)
56. Krassó-Szörény (Lugoj/Lugos)
57. Hunyad (Deva)
58. Alsó-Fehér (Aiud/Nagyenyed)
59. Kis-Küküllő (Tîrnăveni/Dicsőszentmárton)
60. Udvarhely (Odorhei/Székelyudvarhely)
61. Nagy-Küküllő (Sighişoara/Segesvár)
62. Szeben (Sibiu/Nagyszeben)
63. Fogaras (Făgăraş/Fogaras)
64. Brassó (Braşov/Brassó)
65. Háromszék (Sfîntu-Gheorghe/Sepsiszentgyörgy)
66. Lika-Krbava (Gospić)
67. Modrus-Fiume (Ogulin)
68. Zágráb (Zagreb/Zágráb)
69. Pozsega (Slavonska Požega)
70. Verőce (Osijek/Eszek)
71. Szerém (Vukovar)

Romania

1. Dorohoi
2. Botoşani
3. Suceava (Fălticeni)
4. Iaşi
5. Neamţ (Piatra)
6. Roman
7. Vaslui
8. Fălciu (Huşi)
9. Bacău
10. Tecuci
11. Tutova (Bîrlad)
12. Putna (Focşani)
13. Covurlui (Galaţi)
14. Mehedinţi (Turnu-Severin)
15. Gorj (Tîrgu Jiu)
16. Dolj (Craiova)
17. Vîlcea (Rîmnicu Vîlcea)
18. Romanaţi (Caracal)
19. Argeş (Piteşti)
20. Muscel (Cîmpulung)
21. Olt (Slatina)
22. Teleorman (Turnu Măgurele)
23. Dîmboviţa (Tirgovişte)
24. Vlaşca (Giurgiu)
25. Prahova (Ploieşti)
26. Ilfov (Bucharest)
27. Buzău
28. Rîmnicu Sărat
29. Brăila
30. Ialomiţa (Călăraşi)
31. Constanţa
32. Tulcea

Serbia

1. Podrinje (Šabac)
2. Valjevo
3. Belgrade
4. Smederevo
5. Požarevac
6. Krajina (Negotin)
7. Užice
8. Gornji Milanovac
9. Kragujevac
10. Morava (Ćuprija)
11. Timok (Zaječar)
12. Rudnik (Čačak)
13. Kruševac
14. Niš
15. Toplica (Prokuplje)
16. Vranje
17. Pirot

Greece

1. Corfu
2. Leukas
3. Cephalonia (Argostolion)
4. Zante
5. Arta
6. Trikkala
7. Karditsa
8. Larissa
9. Magnesia (Volos)
10. Eurytania (Karpenision)
11. Phthiotis (Lamia)
12. Acamania (Mesolóngion)
13. Phocis (Amphissa)
14. Euboea (Chalcis)
15. Boeotia (Lebadea)
16. Attica (Athens)
17. Elis (Pyrgos)
18. Achaea (Patras)
19. Corinth
20. Arcadia (Tripolis)
21. Argolis (Nauplia)
22. Triphylia (Kiparissia)
23. Messenia (Kalamata)
24. Lacedaemon (Sparta)
25. Laconia
26. Cyclades (Hermoupolis)
27. Canea
28. Sfakion
29. Rethýmnē (Rethymnon)
30. Hērákleion (Candia)
31. Lasithion (Hagios Nikólaos)

37 World War I, 1914–1918

In the summer of 1914, Europe's great powers declared war on each other and entered into a conflict that was to last over four years. When it was over, the costs were enormous—65 million men mobilized, 8.5 million military dead, 21 million wounded, and 6.6 million civilians dead. The causes of World War I were complex and are still being debated by historians. The event that precipitated the immediate actions leading to war took place in East Central Europe.

On June 28, 1914, a Serbian revolutionary conspirator (with the approval of Serbian military intelligence but not the Serbian government) shot and killed Archduke Franz Ferdinand (1864–1914), the heir to the Habsburg throne, during an official visit to Sarajevo, the administrative center of Bosnia-Herzegovina. The Austro-Hungarian military blamed Serbia for the assassination and urged the government to declare war on its small south Slav neighbor. Backed by Germany, Austria-Hungary declared war on Serbia on July 28 and the following day bombarded Belgrade. In turn, tsarist Russia came to the aid of its Balkan ally, mobilizing its troops against Austria-Hungary.

These moves set in motion a series of declarations and counterdeclarations of war beginning on August 1, 1914, and effectively continuing until the summer of 1917, when the last of East Central Europe's states, Greece, entered the war. With regard to East Central Europe, the declarations of war occurred in the following order:

1914
July 28	Austria on Serbia
August 1	Germany on Russia
August 5	Montenegro on Austria
August 6	Austria on Russia
	Serbia on Germany
August 8	Montenegro on Germany
November 4	Russia on Turkey
	Serbia on Turkey

1915
May 24	Italy on Austria
August 21	Italy on Turkey
October 14	Bulgaria on Serbia
October 15	Montenegro on Bulgaria
October 19	Russia on Bulgaria
	Italy on Bulgaria

1916
August 27	Romania on Austria
August 28	Italy on Germany
	Germany on Romania
August 30	Turkey on Romania
September 1	Bulgaria on Romania

1917
June 27	Greece on Austria, Bulgaria, Germany, and Turkey

The other major declarations were those of Germany against France, and Great Britain against Germany, both of which took place in the first week of August 1914. This meant that already by that fateful month, two alliances were pitted against each other: the Entente (France, Britain, Russia) versus the Central Powers (Germany and Austria-Hungary). By the end of 1914, Turkey had joined the Central Powers, while the following year Italy joined the Entente and Bulgaria the Central Powers. Romania and Greece were the last to enter the conflict, both on the side of the Entente respectively in 1916 and 1917. Finally, the United States joined the Entente in 1917, and America's presence had an immediate impact on military developments along the western front. By early 1918, American influence was also to be felt in the political sphere, most especially in East Central Europe, where the pronouncement of President Woodrow Wilson about the principle of self-determination of nations was to have a great impact on local national leaders.

The two major fronts in Europe during World War I were the western (basically northeastern France and Belgium) and the eastern. The eastern front ran through the heart of East Central Europe and included at least four military theaters: the long Russian and Austro-German front from the Baltic Sea to the Carpathian Mountains; the fronts surrounding Serbia; the Romanian-Austrian front; the Austro-Italian front.

The first of the military theaters to see action was that of Serbia. After bombarding Belgrade (July 29, 1914), the Austro-Hungarians invaded northern Serbia (August 13), but were defeated at the battle of Cer Mountain (August 15–20). The Serbians not only drove the Austrian army out of the country but they themselves crossed the Drina River into eastern Bosnia. The Austrians counterattacked, defeating the Serbians in the drawn out battle of the Drina (September 8–17) and then capturing Belgrade (December 2). The Serbs retaliated with a victory at the battle of Kolubara (December 3–6), so that by the end of 1914 the Austrians were once again driven out of Serbian territory.

Along the German-Austrian frontier with Russia the first major engagements came in the north, when a massive Russian invasion of East Prussia turned back the German army at Gusev/Gumbinnen (August 20) until it was repulsed by German victories at the battles of Tannenberg near Stębark (August 26–31) and the Masurian Lakes near Lec/Lötzen (September 6–15). Farther south the Russians were more successful against the Austro-Hungarian army. Following an initial advance into Russian territory and an Austro-Hungarian victory at the battle of Zamość-Komarów (August 26–September 2), the Russians drove back their adversary with a victory at the battle of Rava Rus'ka (September 3–11), the capture of L'viv/Lemberg (September 8–12), and a siege at the Austrian fortress of Przemyśl

International boundaries, 1914
Boundary of the Hungarian Kingdom, 1914
Boundary of the Polish Kingdom, 1916
States created in 1918

Central powers, 1915

Entente powers, 1917

Neutral powers

Front line, December 1914
Front line, December 1915
Front line, August-September 1916
Armistice line, December 1917
✳ Major fortresses
✕ Major battles

0 ————————— 150 miles
0 ————————— 150 kilometers
Scale 1:8 890 000

Copyright © by Paul Robert Magocsi

(September 16), which did not finally capitulate until half a year later (March 22).

Following their victories in East Prussia, the Germans sent an army to relieve their Austro-Hungarian allies in Galicia, fighting indecisive battles along the way at Warsaw and Dęblin/Ivangorod (October 9–20). Nonetheless, despite a German victory at Łódź (November 11–25), they were unable to reach their Austrian allies, who, following the battles of Cracow (November 16–December 2) and Limanowa (December 5–17), were forced back beyond the crest of the Carpathians. In effect, by the end of 1914 the eastern front had yielded small parts of East Prussia to Russia and west Poland to Germany. Farther south, however, the Russians held virtually all of Galicia and Bukovina, as well as the northeastern part of Slovakia and Carpathian Rus' in Hungary. The tsarist government was particularly pleased with its acquisition of Galicia, which it considered an age-old "Russian land." It immediately set up a civil administration to govern what was expected to be a permanent territorial acquisition.

The Russian presence in Austria-Hungary was to give way, however, in the spring of 1915, following a combined German-Austrian counteroffensive. The counteroffensive began at first on the northern flank in East Prussia, where the Germans were victorious at the second battle of the Masurian Lakes near Lec/Lötzen (February 7–12, 1915), pushing back the Russians to the forest near Augustów, where they surrendered (February 21). In the south, the Austro-Hungarian advance against the Russians was slower (Chernivtsi was retaken on February 17), until they were joined by the Germans in a combined assault that led to victories at Gorlice (May 2), the San River (May 15–23), and the retaking of Przemyśl (June 3) and L'viv (June 22). By the end of June 1915, all of Bukovina and Galicia (with the exception of a small strip of land east of Ternopil') was returned to Austrian rule.

Farther north, a second offensive saw the Austrians take Lublin, Chełm (July 31), Dęblin (August 4), Luts'k (August 31), and Dubno (September 8), and the Germans Warsaw (August 4–7), Kaunas (August 18), Modlin (August 20), Brest Litovsk (August 25), Hrodna (September 2), and Vilnius (September 19). Thus, by the fall of 1915, all of Russia's Courland, Lithuania, Poland, and western Ukraine (Galicia, Bukovina, and western Volhynia) were in Austro-German hands.

The year 1915 also witnessed Italy's entry into the war. In May, following the secret Treaty of London with the Entente (signed on April 26 with generous guarantees of territorial concessions), Italy renounced the prewar Triple Alliance which had united it with Germany and Austria-Hungary. Before the end of May, Italy declared war on Austria-Hungary, thereby mobilizing its forces in the north as well as occupying in the east the port of Vlorë in Albania, whose neutrality was about to be completely violated by its neighbors.

The Italo-Austrian conflict began on May 24, 1915, and for the next two years until September 12 it was to be concentrated along the Isonzo River, where as many as twelve exceedingly costly but inconclusive battles were fought to the north and south of Gorizia. The only change in this theater came in the fall of 1917, when a combined Austrian-German offensive at the battle of Kobarid/Caporetto (twelfth battle of the Isonzo, October 24–November 12) pushed the Italians westward to the Piave River.

Bulgaria also entered the war in 1915 (October 15) as an ally of the central Powers, and this was to contribute to a radical change of forces in the Balkans. Whereas Serbia had held its own against the Austro-Hungarians in 1914, it now faced a combined Austro-German attack from the north and a Bulgarian attack from the east. Throughout October and November 1915, one by one Serbia's cities fell to either the Austrians and Germans (Belgrade, October 9) or the Bulgarians (Skopje, October 22; Pirot, October 28; Niš, November 5; Prizren, November 29; Bitola, December 2). By December 1915 virtually all of Serbia was in the hands of the Central Powers, while in January 1916 Montenegro and Albania fell to the Austrians. The remnants of the Serbian army retreated under French and Italian protection to the island of Corfu.

Even before Italy and Bulgaria entered the war, the Entente powers had begun a military campaign against the Ottoman Empire in Europe. The British and French landed on the Greek island of Lemnos (February 23, 1915) in the northern Aegean Sea and from there launched the Gallipoli campaign in an attempt to gain control of the strategic Dardanelles waterway. The campaign began in February and March 1915 with several naval engagements and the bombardment of Ottoman forts along the Dardanelles. In April, troops from Britain, Australia, New Zealand, and France began to land at several places on the Gallipoli peninsula, and for the next several months there were fierce battles on Cape Helles, Kirte, and along the Bay of Suvla (Anafarta) and the nearby Anzac Cove. By the end of the year, the expeditionary forces had to evacuate their lines at both Suvla-Anzac (December 18–19, 1915) and Cape Helles (January 8–9, 1916), bringing the Gallipoli campaign to an unsuccessful end for the British, French, and their allies.

The year 1916 witnessed costly efforts to change the status of the three fronts in East Central Europe which had been fixed in the previous year. The Russians launched an offensive under General Brusilov, and following battles at Baranavichy (July 2–9) and Kovel' (July 28–August 17) they recaptured Austrian Bukovina and a strip of eastern Galicia and western Volhynia. However, one year later in the summer of 1917, the Germans and Austro-Hungarians drove the Russians back and even beyond where they had been at the end of 1915.

In the Balkans, the Entente launched an offensive in 1916 by landing in Salonika the Serbian army that had been reconstituted at Corfu together with Russian troops from France and an Italian contingent. Not only was this force defeated by the Bulgarians and Germans at Doiran (August 2–21) and Florina (August 17–19) in Macedonia, but parts of northeastern Greece now came under the control of the Central Powers. The Entente pressured and eventually convinced the Greek government to allow a new British and French force to land on its territory, in order to undertake an offensive in Macedonia. After several inconclusive battles (Bitola, November 19, 1916; Lake Presba, March 11–19, 1917; Doiran, May 5–19), the front in Macedonia remained basically unchanged until the end of the war.

A new theater of operations was opened in 1916, when Romania, after receiving assurances of territorial gains at the expense of the Central Powers (treaty of August 17, 1916), entered the war August 27 on the side of the Entente by declaring war on Austria-Hungary. The next day the Romanians invaded Transylvania, but within two months a German army turned them back with victories in battles at Sibiu/Nagyszeber (September 27–29) and Brașov/Brassó (October 7–9). The Germans then crossed the Carpathians into Walachia, defeating the Romanians at Tîrgu-Jiu (October 15–16) and the Argeș River (December 1–5) and capturing the country's capital of Bucharest (December 6). Meanwhile, from the south a combined Bulgarian-German force moved into the Dobruja, taking Silistra (September 10), Constanța (October 22), and Cernavodă (October 25). This meant that by the outset of 1917, Romanian territory was reduced to a small strip of land in eastern Moldavia, where its government reestablished itself at Iași.

The most important event to affect East Central Europe in 1917 was of a political, not military, nature. The first Russian revolution of 1917, which broke out on March 8 (o.s. February 23), overthrew the tsar. In early November (the October Revolution) the post-tsarist Russian Provisional Government was replaced by a Bolshevik regime which set out to transform the Russian Empire into the world's first socialist state. On December 3, 1917, the new Bolshevik government fulfilled its promise to drop out of the war, signing an armistice and entering into peace negotiations with Germany and Austria at Brest Litovsk. Also, throughout 1917, Russian territories in East Central Europe were experiencing national revolutions.

On November 5, 1916, the Germans and Austrians, who had occupied Poland for nearly a year, announced their intention to establish a fully independent Polish state, which largely coincided (minus eastern Lublin and Suwalki provinces) with the early nineteenth-century Congress Kingdom of Poland (compare Map 24). Although a provisional state council was formed, this new Polish kingdom was in effect a puppet of Germany. Then after the two revolutions in Russia during 1917 and the resultant inability of the new Bolshevik government to enforce its authority throughout the former empire, the Romanians in Bessarabia (December 23, 1917), followed by the Ukrainians (January 22, 1918) and Lithuanians (February 16, 1918), proclaimed the formation of independent states. When a peace treaty between the Central Powers and Soviet Russia was finally signed on February 9, 1918, all parties agreed to recognize an independent Ukraine and an independent Lithuania (as of February 18), although both these states would in effect, like the Polish Kingdom, become satellites of Germany. The Moldavian Republic in Bessarabia proclaimed its union with Romania (April 9, 1918), which in turn signed the Treaty of Bucharest (May 7) with the Central Powers, whereby the country regained Walachia but lost Dobruja and the mouths of the Danube to the Central Powers, and was forced to give up control of the Carpathian passes to Austria (see Map 40b).

The war was to continue throughout most of 1918. The first of the fronts to break was in the Balkans. A major offensive under French direction against German-Bulgarian forces culminated in an Entente victory at the battle of the Vardar River which took place at Dobro Polje, Bitola, and Doiran (September 15–24). The Bulgarians surrendered, signing an armistice on September 30. On the other hand, the Austrians maintained their positions along the Piave River in northern Italy, holding off an Italian counteroffensive that began in July. While the Austrians were still able to score a victory at the battle of Monte Grappa (October 23), French reinforcement of the Italian army finally led to an Entente victory at Vittorio Veneto (October 24–November 4). As a result, the Austrians were finally pushed back to the Isonzo River, which became part of the armistice line decided upon on November 3. One week later, on November 11, Germany signed an armistice and the Great War was over.

The end of World War I resulted in profound changes in the political boundaries of East Central Europe. Because of the extent of these changes and the new military conflicts that broke out in many parts of the region, it was to take at least half a decade before new boundaries were finally stabilized.

The political transformation of East Central Europe was prompted by the disintegration of the German and Austro-Hungarian empires during the last months of 1918 and the unsettled western borders of the former Russian Empire, which was still going through a period of revolution and civil war. Most of the boundary changes in East Central Europe were the result of decisions reached by the victorious Allied and Associated Powers (the Entente) at the Paris Peace Conference that began in early 1919. Eventually the Paris Peace Conference resulted in five treaties, named after the palaces outside Paris where they were signed: Versailles (June 28, 1919), Saint Germain-en-Laye (September 10, 1919), Neuilly (November 27, 1919), Trianon (June 4, 1920), and Sèvres (August 10, 1920). Each of these treaties dealt in part, and in certain cases entirely, with countries in East Central Europe.

The Paris Peace Conference also brought into being an international organization of states, the League of Nations (January 1920), while the foreign ministers of the four leading western allies (France, Great Britain, United States, and Italy) constituted the so-called Council of Four, or Council of Ambassadors, who were to meet periodically even after the five peace treaties were completed, in order to decide on several territorial questions pertaining to still-unsettled boundary disputes.

As a result of the post–World War I political changes in East Central Europe, four new countries came into being —Lithuania, Poland, Czechoslovakia, and Yugoslavia; four countries expanded their boundaries—Italy, Romania, Albania, and Greece; and three countries lost' territories —Germany, Bulgaria, and Turkey. Finally, two countries —Serbia and Montenegro—ceased to exist, being amalgamated into the new state of Yugoslavia; while two others —Austria-Hungary and Russia—were transformed entirely from what they had been previously, giving up most of the lands they had once held in East Central Europe.

Lithuania declared itself independent of Russia in early 1918 (February 16) and was recognized by both Germany and Russia in the weeks following the Treaty of Brest Litovsk (March 3). Lithuania's initial boundaries (see Map 37) were challenged by Poland, in particular along its eastern border, so that throughout 1919–20 the city of Vilnius/Wilno and the surrounding area known as Central Lithuania changed hands several times. By October 1920 the Poles had seized Vilnius and the rest of Central Lithuania, which was to remain, despite Lithuanian objections, within Poland for the rest of the interwar period. At the opposite

end of the country along the Baltic coast near Klaipėda/Memel, in January 1923 the Lithuanians occupied the Memel region, formerly German territory that had been administered by Allied troops since the Treaty of Versailles. By an agreement with the League of Nations Council of Ambassadors signed in May 1924, Memel was recognized as an autonomous region of Lithuania.

Poland's boundaries were determined by the Paris Peace Conference, whether through decisions of the Council of Ambassadors or plebiscites held under Allied direction, and by the outcome of the war with Soviet Russia in the east. Added to the former Polish Kingdom (proclaimed by Germany and Austria in November 1916 on Polish lands within the Russian Empire) were the former German provinces of Posen and part of West Prussia. Part of West Prussia had been within the Polish-Lithuanian Commonwealth before its first partition (see Map 22a); now in its new form it became known as the Polish corridor separating East Prussia from the rest of Germany and giving Poland access to the Baltic Sea at its new port of Gdynia. These decisions were part of the Treaty of Versailles, which also granted the older Baltic port of Gdańsk/Danzig and its surrounding area the status of an independent city-state.

The Versailles agreement also called for plebiscites in East Prussia and in upper Silesia. In East Prussia, two plebiscites were held between May 28 and June 17, 1920, in the area surrounding Kwidzyn/Marienwerder and Olsztyn/Allenstein, both of which declared overwhelmingly for Germany. In upper Silesia the situation was more complex. With the exception of a small area around Hlučín/Hultschin assigned to Czechoslovakia, the rest of upper Silesia east of Opole held a plebiscite on March 20, 1921. The results were inconclusive, however, so that a final decision to divide the area between Poland and Germany (over the latter's protest) was made by the Allied Council of Ambassadors (October 19, 1921).

In neighboring Cieszyn/Těšín/Teschen, which had been the easternmost part of the former Austrian province of Silesia, the Allies rejected the idea of a plebiscite and simply divided the area and its main city between Poland and Czechoslovakia. At the same time (July 28, 1920), the Council of Ambassadors assigned to Poland small fragments of the former Hungarian counties of Orava/Árva and Spiš/Szepes in the Tatra region of north-central Slovakia.

As for Poland's eastern boundary, its final settlement was much more complex. The first problem arose over Galicia, where Poles clashed with Ukrainians over the largely Ukrainian-inhabited part of the province east of the San River. The very day that Habsburg rule collapsed in the area (November 1, 1918), local Ukrainian leaders proclaimed the existence of the West Ukrainian People's Republic. This new republic (which claimed Galicia east of the San River as well as northern Bukovina and Carpathian

Legend:

- ——— International boundaries, 1914
- ———— Hungarian Kingdom, 1914
- —··—··— International boundaries, 1923
- ———— Soviet republic boundaries, 1923
- ········· Temporary boundaries, 1918–23
- ⊏⊐ Curzon line
- ▥ Plebiscite area
- ▨ Demilitarized 'Zone of the Straits'

- ▲▲▲ Allied-Hungarian demarcation line, November 1918
- ▬▬ Farthest advance of Hungarian communist troops, June 1919
- ▬▬ Farthest advance of Polish troops, June 1920
- ▬▬ Farthest advance of Soviet troops, August 1920
- ▬▬ Internationalized rivers

0   150 miles
0   150 kilometers
Scale 1:8 890 000

Copyright © by Paul Robert Magocsi

Rus') was immediately challenged by local Poles who wanted all of Galicia united with Poland. The result was a Polish-Ukrainian war that lasted until the summer of 1919, when the Galician-Ukrainian forces were driven out of the province. The Allied powers, which were concerned with the threat of Bolshevik revolution from the east, granted Poland the right to occupy East Galicia temporarily. The Treaty of Saint Germain (September 1919) gave only Galicia west of the San River to Poland, leaving the problem of East Galicia unresolved. In December 1919, the British statesman, Lord Curzon, suggested two possible boundaries through Galicia, one of which would serve as the southern extension of what he proposed should be Poland's eastern frontier (the so-called Curzon Line). Should East Galicia become an independent Ukrainian republic, then the Curzon variant (A) would be accepted; but should such a republic not be recognized, then the variant (B), which was farther east and included L'viv/Lwów, would serve as Poland's border. In fact, neither of these variants nor any subsequent proposals were accepted by Poland, whose annexation of all of East Galicia was, in March 1923, recognized by the Council of Ambassadors.

With regard to the rest of Poland's eastern boundary, in March 1920 the government in Warsaw demanded that Bolshevik Russia renounce its claim to all territories that had before 1772 belonged to the Polish-Lithuanian Commonwealth (see Map 22). Poland promised to hold a plebiscite in these territories so that the local populations could determine their fate. When the Bolsheviks refused, Polish forces moved eastward in April 1920, and a full-scale Russian-Polish war ensued. Within a month, the Poles under General Józef Piłsudski (1867–1935), in cooperation with non-Bolshevik Ukrainian forces, captured Kiev (May 7), while in the north they reached the Western Dvina River. The Polish victory was to be short-lived, however, because in mid-May the Bolsheviks began a counteroffensive that drove back the Poles. By August the Bolsheviks were already in control of most of Poland east of the Vistula and Western Bug rivers and were at the outskirts of Warsaw. French military assistance helped to push the Bolsheviks back again following a major Polish victory at the battle of Warsaw in mid-August and subsequent victories at several smaller battles in the area of Hrodna and the upper Neman River during the last weeks of September. A truce (October 12) and then treaty (March 18, 1921), both signed at Riga, fixed Poland's eastern boundary with Soviet Russia and with the closely allied Bolshevik-ruled states of Soviet Belorussia (proclaimed January 1919) and Soviet Ukraine (proclaimed December 1917). In December 1922, Soviet Belorussia and Soviet Ukraine became fully subordinate to a new federation, based in Moscow, called the Union of Soviet Socialist Republics—the Soviet Union.

Czechoslovakia was proclaimed an independent state on October 28, 1918, and its borders were subsequently recognized by the Paris Peace Conference treaties of Saint Germain (September 10, 1919) and Trianon (June 4, 1920). To the historic Austrian provinces of Bohemia, Moravia, and Silesia (including the Hlučín area in former German Silesia) were added Slovakia and Carpathian Rus', both of which had been part of the prewar Hungarian Kingdom.

The delineation of the Czechoslovak boundary in its new eastern regions was particularly difficult because of the challenge of both Hungary and Romania. Hungarian troops were not driven out of what became Czechoslovak territory until June 1919; the Romanians not before March 1920. Also in 1920 (July) the Council of Ambassadors made a few small border rectifications: the Cieszyn area of former Austrian Silesia was divided between Czechoslovakia and Poland; and northern Orava and Spiš counties in central Slovakia were given to Poland.

It was in part Czechoslovakia's concern with its landlocked status that prompted demands for a Slovak border along the Danube River, providing thereby access to this international waterway. Czechoslovakia was also guaranteed free harbors in the German ports of Hamburg and Szczecin (Stettin), which it could reach via the internationalized Elbe and Oder rivers.

Hungary's new and sharply reduced borders were determined by its status as a defeated wartime power and by the radical turn of its political life in the postwar era. Following the collapse of the Habsburg monarchy, a Hungarian republic was proclaimed in November 1918. With its new government, Hungary hoped somehow to maintain most if not all of the lands that had until then belonged to the historic kingdom. In November, the Hungarians asked and received from the Allied military commander a separate armistice and demarcation line which assigned much of the north (Slovakia), east (Transylvania), and south (Croatia, Slavonia, Bačka, Banat) of the country to Hungary's new neighbors. Immediately, Romanian and Serbian troops occupied the east and south, and by the end of December 1918 the Czechs were in Slovakia.

In March 1919, the Allied powers announced at the Paris Peace Conference that Transylvania would go to Romania, and to protect this acquisition Romanian troops pushed farther west beyond the demarcation line into the Hungarian lowland. Meanwhile, a new communist government came to power in Hungary (March 21), which under the leadership of Béla Kun (1886–1939) proceeded to fight the Romanians in the east and attempt to regain Slovakia, where it briefly set up a pro-Hungarian Soviet republic at Prešov/Eperjes in June 1919. At the same time, a noncommunist counterrevolutionary movement had begun, and this, combined with the ongoing war against Czechoslovakia and Romania (whose troops reached as far as Budapest, remaining there from August to November), led to the downfall of Hungary's communist government on August 1. In November 1919, the Allies pressured the Romanians to leave Hungary, whose boundaries were subsequently finalized by the Treaty of Trianon (June 4, 1920).

The Trianon treaty assigned as much as two-thirds of the former Hungarian Kingdom to neighboring states: Slovakia and Carpathian Rus' to Czechoslovakia; Transylvania, the Hungarian Plain east of Oradea, and the eastern Banat to Romania; and Croatia, Slavonia, the Bačka, and the western Banat to Yugoslavia.

The Treaty of Trianon also confirmed the cession of the Burgenland to Austria, which had already appeared as a clause in the earlier Treaty of Saint Germain. Austria had originally asked the Paris peacemakers to conduct a plebiscite in the area, but Czechoslovakia argued that the Burgenland should be divided between itself and Yugoslavia, and therefore serve as a corridor between the two new "Slavic" states. Czechoslovakia's request was rejected, however, and in the face of communist rule in Hungary the peacemakers simply assigned the Burgenland to Austria. The only exception was Sopron/Ödenburg, where local Hungarians attacked Austrian troops when they entered the city. Under the direction of the Allied powers, a plebiscite was held in Sopron and the immediately surrounding areas (December 14–15, 1921). As a result, this small part of the Burgenland remained with Hungary.

As for Austria, it had actually come into existence on October 30, 1918, when the republic of German-Austria (Deutschösterreich) was proclaimed in Vienna. From the outset, its intention was to become part of a new German republic based in Berlin. But the Allies forbade such a union. This left the rump state of Austria, which consisted of the pre-1526 Habsburg Germanic hereditary lands (Erbländer) minus the southern Tyrol (which was ceded to Italy), as well as southern Styria, southern Carinthia, and Carniola (which were ceded to Yugoslavia).

Of the states that existed in East Central Europe before World War I, Romania gained the most territory in the years after 1918. The Moldavian republic in Bessarabia, which declared its independence from Russia at the end of 1917, joined Romania in April 1918. The Dobruja, which Romania was forced to cede to Bulgaria after its military defeat (Treaty of Bucharest, May 7, 1918), was regained in early 1919. Farther north, a Romanian popular assembly meeting in former Austrian Bukovina called for union with Romania on October 28, 1918. One week later, Romanian troops entered the province. Romania's acquisitions of the Dobruja and Bukovina as well as Transylvania and other former Austro-Hungarian territories were confirmed at the Paris Peace Conference by the treaties of Saint Germain, Neuilly, and Trianon.

Yugoslavia came into being on December 1, 1918, when the Kingdom of Serbs, Croats, and Slovenes was formally proclaimed under the leadership of the Serbian dynasty. The previous week (November 26), the Serbian government had chosen its own representatives from independent Montenegro who proclaimed that country's unification (over the opposition of its king) with Serbia. Even earlier, on October 29, 1918, Croatian leaders had severed their ties with both Austria and Hungary, a decision that was subsequently confirmed by the Treaty of Saint Germain (September 1919), which awarded to Yugoslavia the former Habsburg provinces of Carniola, Bosnia-Herzegovina, part of Styria, and most of Dalmatia. Besides these areas, Serbian troops had occupied the city of Klagenfurt and the surrounding basin of the Drava River, where a plebiscite was held on October 10, 1920, as a result of which this area was awarded to Austria (see Map 41b—inset). Also added to the former Kingdom of Serbia (according to its boundaries of 1913) were four small areas along the Bulgarian border.

While the Treaty of Trianon awarded the former Hungarian territories of Croatia-Slavonia and the Bačka to Yugoslavia, it was not until 1922 that the Hungarian-Yugoslav border was finally confirmed by the Allied ambassadors. Besides the above-mentioned territories, Yugoslavia was awarded the southern Baranya and two other small pieces of former Hungarian territory north of the Drava (Medjumurje/Muraköz) and Mur (Prekomurje) rivers (see Map 41a).

Serious conflicts arose for Yugoslavia in fixing its border with Romania and Italy. Two-thirds of the Banat went to Romania, although the final boundary with Yugoslavia was not fixed until 1922. With regard to Yugoslavia's northwestern border, the former Austrian province of Gorizia-Gradisca and the city of Trieste were awarded to Italy by the Treaty of Saint Germain (September 10, 1919). Istria, western Carniola, and northern Dalmatia (in particular the former Hungarian port of Rijeka/Fiume) remained contested between Italy and Yugoslavia until the Treaty of Rapallo (November 12, 1920). According to this bilateral agreement: (1) Istria, southwestern Carniola, a few islands off the Dalmatian coast (Cres/Cherso, Lošinj/Lusino, Lastovo/Lagosta), and the city of Zadar/Zara were awarded to Italy; (2) most of Dalmatia was awarded to Yugoslavia; and (3) Rijeka/Fiume was declared an independent city-state. However, Rijeka's independent status was ended by an Italian fascist coup against the city in March 1922. Rijeka's incorporation into Italy was eventually accepted by Yugoslavia at the Treaty of Rome (1924). Rijeka's suburb, Sušak, remained in Yugoslavia, and henceforth it became that country's most important port along the northern Adriatic.

Farther south in the Balkans, Bulgaria was forced by the Treaty of Neuilly (November 1919) to make several territorial concessions: (1) four small border areas to Yugoslavia; (2) southern Dobruja (which it had acquired during World War I) to Romania; and (3) western Thrace, including its access to the Aegean Sea at the port of Alexandroúpolis, to the Allied powers (later to be transferred to Greece).

In Albania, the end of the war saw its territory still occupied by foreign powers. Parts of the north were in the hands of the Montenegrins and Serbs; the far south was under French military protection, where an autonomous Albanian republic was proclaimed at Korçë; the vast majority of the rest of the country was in the hands of Italy. The secret wartime Treaty of London (1915) had accepted the dismemberment of Albania, and in July 1919 Italy and Greece (which had claims to the Korçë-Gjirokastër area that it called northern Epirus) reached an agreement to divide the country between themselves. In response, the Albanians from their new capital at Tiranë again proclaimed their independence (February 1920); and in return for its gains in the negotiations over Rijeka/Fiume and northern Dalmatia, Italy conceded the restoration of Albania according to its 1913 boundaries. Although reluctant to do so, the Italians finally left their coveted stronghold at Vlorë/Valona (September 1920), while Greek claims to northern Epirus were rejected by the Council of Ambassadors, which in November 1921 fixed Albania's boundaries with some slight increase from the 1913 border.

Greece had much grander territorial desires. Aside from northern Epirus, Greece's major political goal remained one that harked back to its early nineteenth-century nationalist movement. This was the fulfillment of the Great Idea, which included the "reconquest" of Thrace, the imperial "Greek" capital of Konstantinoúpolis (Istanbul), and the Greek-inhabited coastal areas of western Anatolia. As for the Ottoman state, the sultan's government decided that resistance to the demands of the victorious Allies was impossible. In December 1918, Allied troops had already set up a military administration in Istanbul.

Among the Allied demands were those decided upon in secret treaties reached during the war years. Besides Greek interests, these demands included a postwar Italian presence in western Anatolia. The Italians had already landed a force at Antalya/Adalia (April 1919), and to forestall Italian advances the Greeks, encouraged by Britain, landed in İzmir/Smyrna (May 1919). Greece and Italy soon reached agreement on how to press the Paris Peace Conference to divide between them the Aegean region and Albania. According to the first of these agreements, the Treaty of Neuilly with Bulgaria (November 1919), Greece received western Thrace. Subsequently, the Treaty of Sèvres with the Ottoman Empire, announced in May 1920, gave Greece the rest of Thrace to a line just before Istanbul, and it permitted the Greeks to administer a large section of western Anatolia for a period of five years, after which a plebiscite was to be held.

The Greeks feared that the proposed Treaty of Sèvres might be ratified, so even before it was submitted to the sultan's government on June 19, 1920, they occupied eastern Thrace and advanced into Anatolia beyond the territory assigned to them. This unilateral action prompted resistance by the Turkish nationalist Mustafa Kemal (Atatürk, 1881–1938), resulting in a Greek-Turkish war. Despite the eventual acceptance of the Treaty of Sèvres by the sultan's government (August 10, 1920), the war continued. In 1921 the Greeks reached as far as Eskişehir (March) and the outskirts of Ankara in central Anatolia (August-September). Meanwhile, the Turkish leader Kemal rejected the Ottoman sultan's submission to the Allies and set up a revolutionary government in Ankara (April 1920), which in early 1921 declared the new state to be called Turkey. In March 1921, Italy agreed to withdraw from the Antalya region along the Mediterranean, and in the summer of 1922 Kemal launched a counteroffensive that drove the Greeks back until they were forced entirely out of Anatolia and their last stronghold of İzmir/Smyrna (September 9–11).

With the Greek-Turkish war over and the last Ottoman sultan deposed (November 1922), the Allies were finally able to reach a new settlement with Kemal's Turkey. The Treaty of Sèvres was scrapped and replaced by the Treaty of Lausanne (July 24, 1923). According to this new agreement, eastern Thrace, western Anatolia, and the islands of Imbros/İmroz and tiny Bozcaada/Tenedos (just off the Anatolian coast that had been ceded in the Sèvres treaty were all restored to Turkey. The Dodecanese Islands, however, were despite Greek protests to remain with Italy. The internationally important straits connecting the Aegean and Black seas were to be open to all nations in peacetime, and a broad swath of territory on both banks of the Sea of Marmara, the Dardanelles, and the Bosphorus was to remain demilitarized.

39 Poland, Danzig, and Czechoslovakia in the 20th century

Poland

Of all postwar alterations to countries in East Central Europe, the boundaries of Poland were to undergo the most radical changes. The territorial unit that most closely coincided with Polish ethnolinguistic boundaries was the Kingdom of Poland proposed jointly by the Central Powers —Germany and Austria-Hungary—in November 1916, when they were occupying the region. These were roughly the same boundaries of the Polish republic when it was declared independent on November 11, 1918, the day the German garrison was disarmed in Warsaw and Józef Piłsudski (1867–1935) seized power.

It was from this base that Polish troops under the direction of Marshal Piłsudski expanded the Polish sphere of influence in all directions. Proposals for Poland's boundaries were then put forth at the Paris Peace Conference in early 1919 by another important political leader of the time, Roman Dmowski (1864–1939).

Dmowski's line, as it came to be known, included the former German provinces of West Prussia, much of East Prussia, Posen, and parts of northern and eastern Silesia. These were territories in which there was a significant—and in some areas a majority—German population. In the east, the Dmowski line did not go as far as the pre-partition 1772 boundary (see Map 22a), but it nonetheless encompassed all of Lithuania (that is, Samogitia/Żmudź, and so-called Central Lithuania), most of Belarus, western Volhynia, western Podolia, and all of Galicia. These were lands inhabited for the most part by Lithuanians, Belorussians, and Ukrainians.

When the boundaries of the new Polish state were fixed between 1920 and 1923, they differed significantly from the Dmowski line. Lithuania had become an independent state; East Prussia was made a part of Germany; Danzig was declared a free city-state; and upper Silesia was split between Germany, Poland, and Czechoslovakia. In the east, however, Poland got most of what Dmowski had originally proposed, except for the far-eastern part of Belarus and Podolia east of the Zbruch River. Poland's boundaries remained unchanged until 1938, when following the Munich crisis in September, Poland annexed from Czechoslovakia the rest of the Cieszyn region and a small piece of land in north-central Slovakia.

With the German and then Soviet invasion in September 1939, Poland's entire territory was divided and annexed by Germany and the Soviet Union. Then, with Hitler's invasion of the Soviet Union in June 1941, the former eastern Polish lands were either annexed to Germany or placed under German administration (see Map 45).

At the close of World War II in 1945, Poland was restored, although the whole country, according to decisions reached by the victorious Allies, was shifted westward. The Soviet republics of Lithuania, Belorussia, and Ukraine received Poland's pre-1939 eastern borderlands (the so-called Kresy). As "compensation," Poland received in the north and west the former free city-state of Danzig, and the former German territories of southern East Prussia as well as eastern Pomerania and all of Silesia as far as the Oder and Neisse rivers (see Map 47). The German population east of the Oder-Neisse line—in what was now referred to as Poland's "Recovered Lands" (Ziemie Odzyskane)—had either disappeared as a result of the war or were in the immediate postwar period deported westward to what remained of Germany (see Map 48).

The goals of Poland's World War I leaders were directed toward expanding its boundaries as far as possible eastward—in an effort to approximate, if possible, the boundaries of the pre-partition Polish-Lithuanian Commonwealth. The result was that nearly one-third of the inhabitants of interwar Poland comprised national minorities (mainly Ukrainians, Jews, Belorussians, and Germans). With the physical destruction of large segments of the population (notably Jews) during World War II and the radical changes in Poland's boundaries, as well as forced expulsion and population exchanges with neighboring countries (affecting primarily Ukrainians, Belorussians, and Germans) during the immediate postwar years, the ethnolinguistic composition of Poland changed significantly in the second half of the twentieth century. Between 1931 and 1985 the proportion of Poles within Poland increased from 68.9 to 97.7 percent, while minorities decreased from 31.1 to a mere 2 percent.

Danzig

The free city-state of Danzig was brought into being through a special treaty signed in Paris on November 9, 1920. This self-governing state was placed under the protection of the League of Nations. Danzig consisted not only of its main port of Gdańsk/Danzig but also a hinterland territory on both banks of the lower Vistula (map 39b—inset). Its interwar territory was larger than either the free city of Danzig, which with 30 villages under its authority was part of Poland from 1454 to 1793, or the short-lived republic of Danzig set up under Napoleon's protection, lasting from 1807 to 1814 (see Map 23).

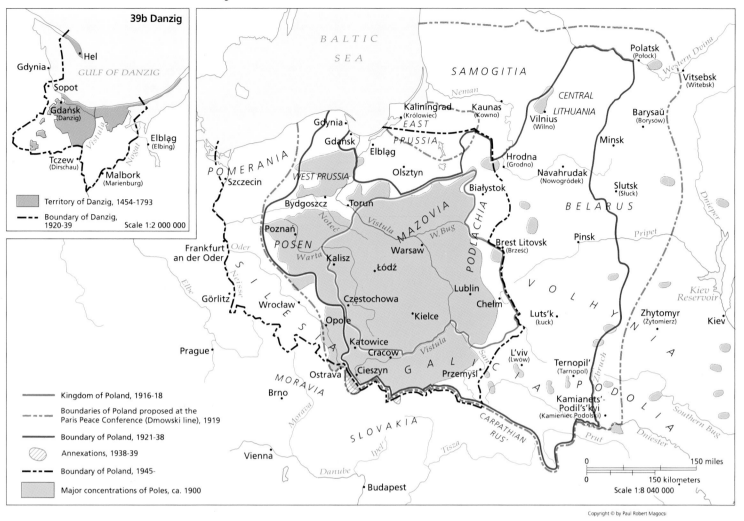

Ethnolinguistic-national composition of Poland

	1931		1991	
	Number	Percentage	Number	Percentage
Poles	21,993,000	68.9	[36,194,000]	[97.2]
Ukrainians	4,442,000	13.9	[220,000]	[0.6]
Ukrainians (3,222,000)				
Rusyns (1,220,000)				
Lemkos	—	—	[60,000]	[0.2]
Jews	2,733,000	8.6	[15,000]	[0.0]
Yiddish 2,489,000				
Hebrew 244,000				
Belorussians	1,697,000	5.3	[230,000]	[0.6]
Belorussians 990,000				
Locals 707,000				
Germans	741,000	2.3	[400,000]	[1.0]
Russians	139,000	0.4	[16,000]	[0.0]
Lithuanians	83,000	0.3	[20,000]	[0.0]
Czechs	38,000	0.1	[3,000]	[0.0]
Slovaks	—	—	[20,000]	[0.0]
Gypsies	—	—	[25,000]	[0.0]
Macedonians	—	—	[3,000]	[0.0]
Greeks	—	—	[3,000]	[0.0]
Others	50,000	0.2	[10,000]	[0.0]
TOTAL	31,916,000		37,219,000	

SOURCES: Joseph Rothschild, *East Central Europe between the Two World Wars* (Seattle, 1974), p. 36; Marek Hołuszko, *Sytuacja mniejszości narodowych w Polsce* (Warsaw, 1993), p. 6. Figures in brackets are estimates; others are drawn from governmental statistics.

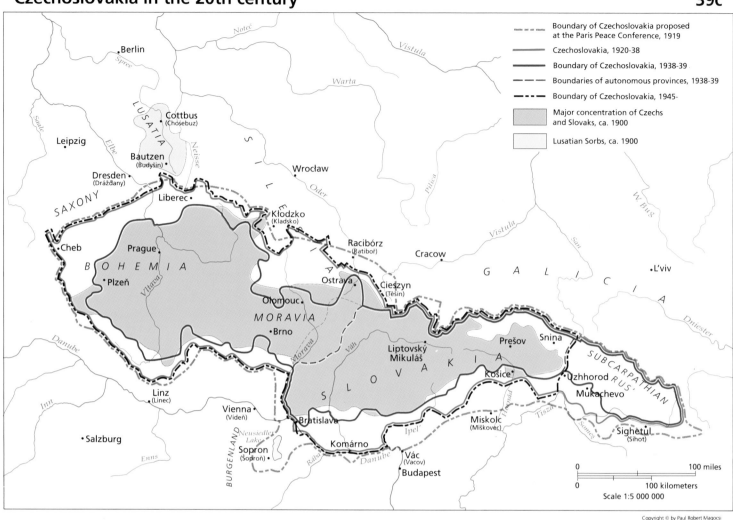

Legend:
- Boundary of Czechoslovakia proposed at the Paris Peace Conference, 1919
- Czechoslovakia, 1920-38
- Boundary of Czechoslovakia, 1938-39
- Boundaries of autonomous provinces, 1938-39
- Boundary of Czechoslovakia, 1945-
- Major concentration of Czechs and Slovaks, ca. 1900
- Lusatian Sorbs, ca. 1900

Scale 1:5 000 000

Copyright © by Paul Robert Magocsi

Czechoslovakia

An independent Czechoslovakia was declared on October 28, 1918. Even before that time, Czech and Slovak leaders had been lobbying for recognition from the Entente, which by September 1918 recognized the yet-to-be-formed Czechoslovak republic as a de facto belligerent power. The question of the new republic's boundaries was put forth in early 1919 at the Paris Peace Conference by Czech and Slovak delegates in a series of eleven memoranda.

The Czechoslovak delegation demanded all of the formerly Austrian provinces of Bohemia, Moravia, and Silesia. Aside from a few slight boundary modifications in northern, western, and southern Bohemia (for the most part to the advantage of Czechoslovakia), the three former Austrian provinces together with the region south of Kłodzko in former German Silesia were expected to become part of Czechoslovakia. Also, former Austrian Silesia's boundaries were to be expanded northward to include Racibórz, while south of Moravia Czechoslovakia demanded a strip of land west of the Morava River and a salient extending southward beyond Sopron/Šoproň. The latter territorial demand was to provide a common border with Czechoslovakia's ally Yugoslavia, since it was hoped that the two countries would divide a corridor of land along the old Austro-Hungarian border in the Burgenland.

In eastern (former Hungarian) territory, the Czechoslovak delegation demanded Slovakia as far south as the Danube River and the outskirts of the city of Miskolc/ Miškovec. Finally, following up on a decision reached in November 1918 by Carpatho-Rusyn immigrants in the United States, who had the backing of the American government, Czechoslovakia requested that "all Rusyns south of the Carpathians" be joined with guarantees of autonomy to the new republic. The Czechoslovak delegation also submitted a memorandum on behalf of the "Sorbs of Lusatia," demanding independence for their ethnolinguistic territory. A Lusatian Sorb state, should it come into existence, would be closely allied to Czechoslovakia.

As a result of the Treaty of Saint Germain (September 10, 1919) and the subsequent decisions made by the Council of Ambassadors (July 1920), Czechoslovakia was granted many but not all of its demands. The historic boundaries of Bohemia and Moravia remained unchanged, as did those of former Austrian Silesia, with the small exceptions of Hlučín, which went to Czechoslovakia, and lands east of Cieszyn/ Těšín, which went to Poland (see Map 38). Czechoslovakia was not granted the bridgehead south of the Danube into the Burgenland, and the anticipated corridor link with Yugoslavia never came about. All that was obtained was a small piece of land (the village of Petržalka/Pozsonyliget-falu) on the south side of the Danube immediately opposite

Bratislava. Nor did the Lusatian Sorbs attain independence; their homeland (with no specific international guarantees) was simply left within Germany.

On the other hand, Czechoslovakia did receive most of what it claimed as Slovak and Carpatho-Rusyn lands with only some slight rectification in favor of Hungary and Romania. Yet despite such changes, the new border with Hungary and Romania did not follow ethnolinguistic lines (the original principle given to the Peace Conference for these territories), so that significant Magyar minorities remained in both Slovakia and Subcarpathian Rus' (Czech: Podkarpatská Rus).

Czechoslovakia's territory remained unchanged until the Munich Pact of September 29, 1938, which at the insistence of Hitler's Germany was organized specifically to revise its eastern neighbor's boundaries. The result was the annexation by Germany of large parts of Bohemia, Moravia, and all of Silesia (regions which in popular parlance were referred to as the Sudetenland), and by Poland of a small strip of territory west of Cieszyn. One month later a negotiated settlement (the Vienna Award, November 2, 1938) gave Hungary most of the Magyar-inhabited lands in southern Slovakia and Subcarpathian Rus', including the cities of Komárno, Košice, Uzhhorod, and Mukachevo. The remaining "rump state," known as the second Czecho-Slovak republic, was a short-lived federal entity in which Slovakia and Subcarpathian Rus' (renamed Carpatho-Ukraine) each received its autonomy. However, on March 15, 1939, Hitler decided to liquidate what remained of Czechoslovakia: Bohemia and Moravia were incorporated into Germany; Slovakia—with a slight loss of territory to Hungary east of Snina (March 31)—became an independent state closely allied to Germany; Subcarpathian Rus'/Carpatho-Ukraine was forcibly annexed to Hungary.

The restoration of Czechoslovakia according to its pre-Munich boundaries was one of the war aims of the Allied powers during World War II. When the country was restored in 1945, however, its former eastern province of Subcarpathian Rus' (with only slight changes around Uzhhorod) was ceded in June to the Soviet Union as the Transcarpathian oblast of the Ukrainian S.S.R. The rest of Czechoslovakia followed the boundaries that had existed before 1918, with the exception of a small extension of the bridgehead on the south side of the Danube opposite Bratislava.

The ethnolinguistic-national composition of Czechoslovakia has changed in the period before and after World War II largely because of the forced expulsion of over three million Germans in 1945. Other marked changes include: (1) the virtual disappearance of Jews due to their annihilation during World War II; (2) a substantial decrease in the number of Rusyns (also known as Ukrainians and Russians) following the cession of the province of Subcarpathian Rus' to the Soviet Union in 1945 and the assimilatory trends since then among the Rusyn minority in eastern Slovakia; and (3) a sharp increase in the number of Gypsies, which reflects both a substantial immigration from Romania in the years just after World War II and their subsequent rapid demographic increase due to a high birthrate.

Consequently, if during the interwar years the "state nationalities"—Czechs and Slovaks who were known at the time officially as "Czechoslovaks"—made up only 66.9 percent of the population (1930), by the last decade of the twentieth century these state nationalities (including Moravians and Silesians as well as Czechs and Slovaks) amounted to 94.1 percent (1991) of the country's inhabitants.

Ethnolinguistic-national composition of Czechoslovakia

	1930		1991	
	Number	Percentage	Number	Percentage
Czechs	7,406,000	51.1	8,426,000	54.1
Moravians	—	—	1,360,000	8.7
Silesians	—	—	45,000	0.3
Germans	3,232,000	22.3	53,000	0.2
Slovaks	2,282,000	15.8	4,820,000	31.0
Magyars	692,000	4.8	587,000	3.8
Rusyns (also Russians and Ukrainians in 1930)	549,000	3.8	19,000	0.1
Russians	—	—	6,000	0.0
Ukrainians	—	—	21,000	0.1
Jews (Hebrew and Yiddish)	187,000	1.3	[12,000]	—
Poles	82,000	0.6	62,000	0.4
Gypsies	32,000	0.2	114,000	0.7
Romanians	13,000	0.1	1,000	0.0
Serbo-Croats	3,000	0.0	—	—
Bulgarians	—	—	4,000	0.0
Greeks	—	—	3,000	0.0
Others/Unknown	2,000	0.0	47,000	0.1
TOTAL	14,480,000		15,568,000	

SOURCES: *Statistická ročenka Republiky československé 1934* (Prague, 1934), p. 11; *Czech and Slovak Federal Republic: Preliminary Results of the Population and Housing Census, March 3, 1991* (Prague, 1991), pp. 30–31.

40 Hungary and Romania in the 20th century

Hungary

In the course of the twentieth century, the boundaries of Hungary changed radically. Until 1918, Hungary still comprised the historic lands of the crown of Saint Stephen, which had been reincorporated into the kingdom under the direction of the Habsburgs in the early eighteenth century (see Map 20b). This changed in November 1918, with the end of World War I, the breakup of Austria-Hungary, the abdication of the Habsburgs, and the transformation of Hungary into a republic.

Both the new republic, which came into being on November 16, 1918, under the leadership of Count Mihály Károlyi (1875–1955), as well as the Soviet Hungarian regime which followed it on March 21, 1919, under the leadership of Béla Kun (1886–1939), attempted to maintain the Hungarian Kingdom's historic boundaries. Those efforts were foiled, however, by the claims of neighboring states and by the peacemakers in Paris. According to the Treaty of Trianon (June 4, 1920), Hungary lost as much as two-thirds of its former territory to Czechoslovakia (Slovakia, Carpathian Rus'), Romania (Transylvania, Banat), Yugoslavia (Croatia, Slavonia, Syrmia, Bačka, Banat), and Austria (Burgenland).

Following the collapse of the Hungarian republic and the Soviet regime that followed it, in the summer of 1919 the Hungarian Kingdom was restored under the leadership of a former Austro-Hungarian naval commander, Miklós Horthy (1868–1957), who served as a regent in the absence of a ruling monarch. As a defeated power, Hungary was forced to accept the Allied peace proposals and the boundaries of what became known as Trianon Hungary. Nonetheless, interwar Hungarian political circles were virtually unanimous in calling for a revision of the boundaries set by the Treaty of Trianon.

Border revision finally became a practical reality on the eve of World War II. In cooperation with Hitler and with the backing of Mussolini, Hungary received the so-called Vienna Award (November 2, 1938), which was a strip of what the Hungarians called their Felvidék, or Highlands, including southern Slovakia and southern Carpathian Rus' together with the cities of Komárno/Komárom, Rožňava/Rozsnyó, Košice/Kassa, Uzhhorod/Ungvár, and Mukachevo/Munkács. Then, in March 1939, Hungarian troops invaded the rest of Carpathian Rus', annexing it and a small strip of far-eastern Slovakia.

One year later, in June 1940, when Germany's ally, the Soviet Union, annexed the eastern region of Romania (Bessarabia), Hungary pressed Hitler for satisfaction of its own territorial claims against that country. Consequently, a Second Vienna Award was concluded in August 1940, whereby Hungary acquired from Romania northern and eastern Transylvania as well as a connecting strip of land including the cities of Oradea/Nagyvarad and Satu-Mare/Szatmár Németi. Finally, in April 1941, when the Axis powers led by Germany invaded and liquidated Yugoslavia, Hungary was given the Bačka, southern Baranya, and two small territories north of the Drava (the Medjumurje/Muraköz region) and the Mur (Prekomurje region) rivers. With these acquisitions, Hungary regained about two-fifths of what it had lost through the Treaty of Trianon.

With the end of World War II in 1945, Hungary was again on the losing side. Therefore, the Allies stripped the country of all its post-Munich (1938) acquisitions and, in 1945, returned the country to its Trianon boundaries. This meant that once again there were significant Magyar minorities living in Czechoslovakia, Romania, and Yugoslavia.

Of all the countries in East Central Europe, Hungary has in the twentieth century come closest to becoming an ethnolinguistically homogeneous state. This occurred, of course, at the expense of leaving large Magyar minorities outside the borders of the country. In the six decades between 1930 and 1990, the percentage of Magyars in Hungary has actually increased (from 92.1 to 99.5 percent). This is in large part the result of the decimation of Hungary's Jews during World War II and to an increased level of assimilation among the remaining minorities, in particular Germans (Swabians) and Slovaks, during the postwar decades.

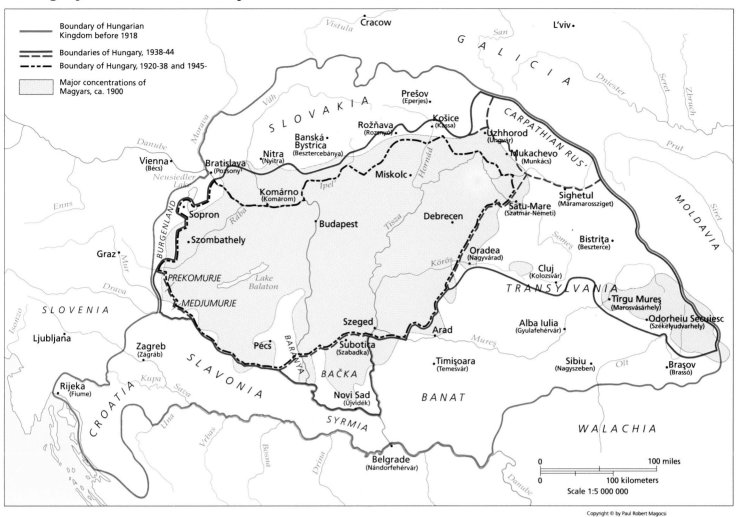

Boundary of Hungarian Kingdom before 1918

Boundaries of Hungary, 1938-44

Boundary of Hungary, 1920-38 and 1945-

Major concentrations of Magyars, ca. 1900

Copyright © by Paul Robert Magocsi

Ethnolinguistic-national composition of Hungary

	1930		1990	
	Number	Percentage	Number	Percentage
Magyars	8,001,000	92.1	10,326,000	99.5
Germans	478,000	5.5	22,000	0.2
			[220,000]	
Jews	[445,000]		[100,000]	
Slovaks	105,000	1.2	7,000	0.0
			[110,000]	
Croats, Serbs,				
Slovenes	—	—	15,000	0.1
Croats	28,000	0.3	[80,000]	
Bunyevci, Šokci	21,000	0.2	—	—
Serbs	7,000	0.1	[5,000]	
Slovenes	—	—	[5,000]	
Romanians	16,000	0.2	5,000	0.0
			[25,000]	
Gypsies	—	—	[500,000]	
Poles	—	—	[13,000]	
Greeks	—	—	[6,000]	
Armenians	—	—	[3,000]	
Bulgarians	—	—	[3,000]	
Others	32,000	0.4	—	—
TOTAL	8,688,000		10,375,000	

SOURCES: *Annuaire statistique hongrois 1931*, nouveau cours, vol. 39 (Budapest, 1933), p. 10; *National and Ethnic Minorities in Hungary*, Ministry of Foreign Affairs Fact Sheets on Hungary, no. 9 (Budapest, 1991).

NOTE: Figures for both censuses relate to mother tongue of the respondent, except those figures for Jews, which relate to religious affiliation. Figures in brackets are informed estimates; others are drawn from governmental statistics.

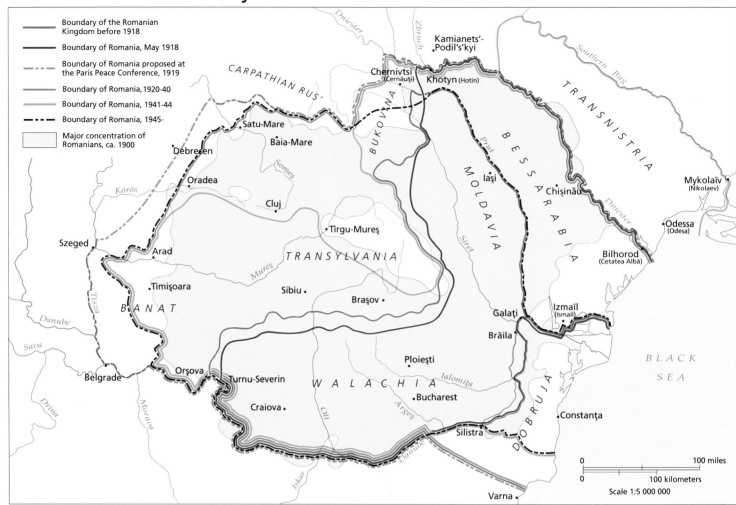

Boundary of the Romanian Kingdom before 1918

Boundary of Romania, May 1918

Boundary of Romania proposed at the Paris Peace Conference, 1919

Boundary of Romania, 1920-40

Boundary of Romania, 1941-44

Boundary of Romania, 1945-

Major concentration of Romanians, ca. 1900

Romania

Walachia and Moldavia have in modern times formed the core provinces of Romania. In the course of the twentieth century, those provinces remained for the most part intact, while the rest of the country's boundaries beyond the core have fluctuated westward and eastward depending on the fortunes of Romania and its neighbors.

The first change in the territorial status of the Kingdom of Romania (Walachia, Moldavia, Dobruja) came after its defeat by the Central Powers in late 1916. According to the Treaty of Bucharest (May 7, 1918), Romania was forced to cede: (1) all of its Carpathian passes to Austria-Hungary; and (2) the Dobruja—the area north from Constanța including all three mouths of the Danube to be ruled as a German-Austrian-Bulgarian mandate, and the rest farther south to be ruled by Bulgaria. In compensation, the Central Powers authorized the Romanians to occupy Bessarabia (historic eastern Moldavia), which had become a separate Soviet republic (December 1917) and then an independent Moldavian republic (March 1918). The Romanians entered Bessarabia in April 1918, and before the end of the year (December 10) the local Romanian national council at Chișinău declared its union with Romania.

By that time, the war had ended and the Romanians put forth the following demands before the Paris Peace Conference in early 1919: the return of the entire Dobruja and mouths of the Danube; all of Bukovina, the Banat, and Transylvania; and a strip of the Hungarian Plain running from Szeged northward past Debrecen. According to the treaties of Saint Germain (September 1919) and Trianon (June 1920), Romania was granted all these demands, with the minor exception of the western Banat, which went to Yugoslavia, and the narrow strip east of the Szeged-Debrecen line, which went to Hungary.

Romania's expanded boundaries were to remain unchanged until World War II. Initially, Romania tried to remain neutral, but this did not stop Germany's allies from achieving their territorial designs. In June 1940, the Soviet Union annexed Bessarabia and northern Bukovina (up to the present-day boundary); in August, Hungary was awarded (through the Second Vienna Award brokered by Germany and Italy) northern Transylvania; and in September, Bulgaria was given southern Dobruja. In part to avoid further incursions on its territory, Romania became, in November 1940, an ally of Germany. As Hitler's ally, Romania joined the German war effort and its invasion of the Soviet Union in June 1941. As a reward, Romania received back northern Bukovina and Bessarabia, and it was given a large block of territory between the Dniester and Southern Bug rivers in the southwestern part of the Ukrainian S.S.R. This territory, which included the major port of Odessa, was called Transnistria (the land beyond the Dniester River).

According to the peace treaties that formally ended World War II (Paris, February 1947), the Soviet Union got back Transnistria as well as Bessarabia (which became the basis for the Moldavian S.S.R.) and northern Bukovina, which it had first annexed in the summer of 1940. Southern Dobruja, including the Danubian port of Silistra, remained with Bulgaria. The rest of Romania's boundaries remained the same as they had been during the interwar years.

The decrease in Romania's territory along its eastern frontier as a result of World War II decidedly altered the ethnolinguistic composition of the country. The loss of northern Bukovina and Bessarabia to the Soviet Union reduced substantially the size of the Ukrainian and Russian minorities, while the loss of southern Dobruja to Bulgaria reduced the over half million Bulgarians and Turks to a total of no more than 33,000. These territorial losses, together with the decimation of Romania's Jews during World War II and substantial assimilation among several smaller national groups, have helped to increase the percentage of Romanians in the country from 71.9 percent (1930) to 88.1 percent (1977).

Ethnolinguistic-national composition of Romania

	1930		1977	
	Number	Percentage	Number	Percentage
Romanians	12,981,000	71.9	18,997,000	88.1
Magyars	1,426,000	7.9	1,713,000	7.9
Székelys	—	—	1,000	0.0
Germans	745,000	4.1	349,000	1.6
Saxons	—	—	6,000	0.0
Swabians	—	—	4,000	0.0
Jews	728,000	4.0	25,000	0.1
Rusyns, Ukrainians	582,000	3.2	54,000	0.3
Hutsuls	12,000	0.0	—	—
Rusyns	—	—	1,000	0.0
Russians	409,000	2.3	21,000	0.1
Lipovans	—	—	11,000	0.0
Bulgarians	366,000	2.0	10,000	0.0
Gypsies	263,000	1.5	227,000	1.1
			[2,000,000]	
Turks	155,000	0.9	23,000	0.1
Tatars	22,000	0.1	23,000	0.1
Gagauz	106,000	0.6	—	—
Czechs, Slovaks	52,000	0.3	—	—
Czechs	—	—	8,000	0.0
Slovaks	—	—	21,000	0.1
Serbs, Croats, Slovenes	51,000	0.3	—	—
Serbs	—	—	34,000	0.2
Croats	—	—	8,000	0.0
Slovenes	—	—	1,000	0.0
Poles	48,000	0.3	5,000	0.0
Greeks	26,000	0.1	6,000	0.0
Armenians	16,000	0.0	2,000	0.0
Vlachs (Macedo-Romanians)	—	—	2,000	0.0
Others	69,000	0.4	7,000	0.0
TOTAL	18,057,000		21,559,000	

SOURCES: *Recensământul general al populaţiei României din 19 decemvrie 1930*, vol. 2 (Bucharest, 1938), p. xxiv; *Anuarul statistic al României 1990* (Bucharest, 1990), p. 64.

NOTE: Figures in brackets are informed estimates; all others are drawn from governmental statistics.

41 Yugoslavia in the 20th century

Yugoslavia to 1941

On December 1, 1918, Yugoslavia—the land of the South Slavs, or more precisely the Kingdom of Serbs, Croats, and Slovenes—was declared an independent state. Whether within the boundaries its leaders proposed or those that were finally accepted by international treaty, the lands that made up the new country of Yugoslavia were undoubtedly the most complex in all East Central Europe. Those lands included five of the South Slavic peoples (ca. 10 million inhabitants) as well as numerous minority peoples from virtually every ethnolinguistic group in the Balkans (ca. 2 million inhabitants). Moreover, because Yugoslav territory had been ruled by four different countries before 1918, there were at least four different currencies, railway networks, and banking systems. Finally, at the time of the country's declaration of independence it even had two governments—the National Council (Narodno Vijeće) in Zagreb and the royal Serbian government in Belgrade.

During the first two decades of the twentieth century, Yugoslav territory was basically divided between (1) the independent South Slavic countries of Serbia and Montenegro (each of which increased its territory in 1913—see Map 27b), and (2) the Habsburg Empire, which in turn was subdivided on Yugoslav territory into several Austrian provinces (Carniola, Styria, Dalmatia), the Hungarian Kingdom (Croatia, Slavonia, Bačka, Banat), and the jointly administered Austro-Hungarian land of Bosnia-Herzegovina.

By the time World War I was in its last months, the idea of Yugoslav unity was propounded by three distinct bodies: (1) the Yugoslav Committee, formed in November 1914 by a group of Croat, Serb, and Slovene political exiles from the Habsburg Empire; (2) the National Council, formed in Zagreb on October 29, 1918, at which time it declared the independence of all South Slavic lands in the Austro-Hungarian Empire; and (3) the government of Serbia, which as an ally of the Entente finally regained full control of its own territory in November 1918. As for Montenegro, exile leaders had their own wartime committee in Paris and favored joining Serbia, although this did not happen until the Montenegrin king—who opposed the union—was deposed on November 24, 1918, by the Montenegrin assembly. The last of the South Slavic groups, the Macedonians, were represented by no one and were simply treated as Serbs within a Serbia according to its 1913 boundaries. By December 1, 1918, all these disparate groups were brought together in the Kingdom of Serbs, Croats, and Slovenes under the leadership of the Serbian Karadjordjević dynasty.

With regard to the new country's borders, Yugoslavia's delegation at the Paris Peace Conference assumed that besides formerly independent Serbia (expanded along its eastern and northern boundaries) and Montenegro (expanded along its southern boundary), the new country would include all former Austro-Hungarian territory south of the Drava and Danube rivers as well as several territories (Klagenfurt region, Prekomurje, Medjumurje, Bačka, half of the Banat) north of that line.

The greatest challenge to Yugoslav territorial claims came from another Entente power, Italy, which itself was interested in acquiring large parts of the eastern Adriatic. The final boundary between the two countries was agreed to at the Treaty of Rapallo on November 12, 1920, by which Italy acquired Austria's former coastal provinces (Gorizia-Gradisca, Trieste, Istria), a few eastern Adriatic islands (Cres, Lošinj, Lastovo), and the city of Zadar (see also Maps 38 and 42a).

Yugoslavia's other boundaries were settled at the Paris Peace Conference and its diplomatic aftermath. Yugoslavia's claims on Bulgarian territory were fulfilled only with slight gains in four places (Strumica, Bosilegrad, Dimitrovgrad/Caribrod, and east of the Timok River in the north), as decreed in the Treaty of Neuilly (November 27, 1919). Its claims over northern and eastern Albania (including the city of Shkodër) were rejected by the Allied Council of Ambassadors in November 1921, at which time Yugoslav troops were forced to leave the area (see also Map 42b). On the other hand, the Paris peacemakers in the Treaty of Trianon (June 4, 1920) upheld most of Yugoslavia's demands for territory that previously had been part of the Hungarian Kingdom, including all of Croatia, Slavonia, and Syrmia as well as the Prekomurje (excluding Szentgotthárd), the Baranya (south of and excluding Mohács), the Bačka (south of and including Subotica), and the far-western Banat.

In only one of the postwar Yugoslav border disputes was a plebiscite held. This was called for by the Treaty of Saint Germain (September 10, 1919) in the so-called Klagenfurt/Celovec area—that is, the valley of the Drava River between Villach/Beljak and Lavamund/Labot located north of the crest of the Karawanken range of the Dinaric Alps (see Map 41b—inset). The inhabitants there, most especially between the Drava River and the Karawanken crest, were primarily Slovene-speaking, although they called themselves Winds (in German: Windisch) and generally refused to associate with Slovenians, favoring instead Austria.

The plan was to divide the area into two zones, with a plebiscite to be held first in primarily Slovene-speaking Zone A. Should the result be a majority in favor of Austria, a plebiscite in primarily German-speaking Zone B would not be necessary. On October 10, 1920, the plebiscite took place in Zone A in the presence of Yugoslav troops, who had been present in the area since the armistice.

The result, with 96 percent of the population participating, was 59 percent in favor of Austria. Therefore, a second

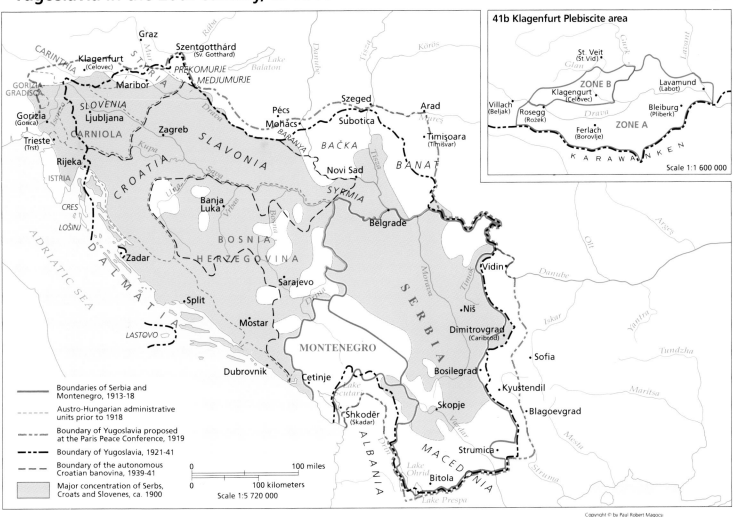

41b Klagenfurt Plebiscite area

Boundaries of Serbia and Montenegro, 1913-18

Austro-Hungarian administrative units prior to 1918

Boundary of Yugoslavia proposed at the Paris Peace Conference, 1919

Boundary of Yugoslavia, 1921-41

Boundary of the autonomous Croatian banovina, 1939-41

Major concentration of Serbs, Croats and Slovenes, ca. 1900

0   100 miles
0   100 kilometers
Scale 1:5 720 000

plebiscite in Zone B, including Klagenfurt/Celovec itself, was never held. Yugoslavia protested that the plebiscite was fixed, but under pressure of the Allied powers it was forced to withdraw its troops from the area, which became part of Austria.

By the end of 1921, Yugoslavia's international boundary was settled and was to remain unchanged for the next two decades. Internally, the boundaries of pre-1918 Serbia and Montenegro as well as those of the various Austro-Hungarian divisions initially remained intact. In January 1929, however, the country was formally renamed Yugoslavia, it was administratively centralized, and it was redivided into nine districts (banovinas). The new districts had little relationship to any historic boundaries (see Map 44). With one exception, the 1929 administrative reorganization remained in place until Yugoslavia was drawn into World War II (1941). That exception was Croatia.

Throughout the interwar years, Yugoslavia had increasingly become a Serbian-dominated state. This caused friction among the other nationalities, most especially the Croats. In order to assuage Croatian complaints, a separate autonomous unit known as the Banovina of Croatia, with its own parliament in Zagreb, was established on August 20, 1939. Its boundaries encompassed the historic Croatian provinces of Croatia-Slavonia and Dalmatia, as well as the south-central and northeastern regions of former Bosnia-Herzegovina where Croats lived. Thus, on the eve of World War II, the Croats were the only national group in Serbian-dominated Yugoslavia to have their own distinct administrative and governmental unit.

Yugoslavia, 1941–1989

After the outbreak of World War II on September 1, 1939, the royal Yugoslav government hoped it might stay out of the war until there was a suitable opportunity to join the Allies. The country was virtually surrounded (except for the border with Greece) by the Axis powers and their allies. Finally, in April 1941, Hitler's Germany and his Italian, Bulgarian, and Hungarian allies invaded from all sides. Before the end of the month Yugoslavia ceased to exist. Parts of the country were annexed outright by Germany, Italy, Hungary, and Bulgaria (see Map 45); the remainder was divided into three states—Croatia, Serbia, and Montenegro—each of which was in varying degrees subordinate to the Axis powers.

The largest of these wartime entities was the Independent State of Croatia (Nezavisna Država Hrvatska). Croatia was theoretically a kingdom under Tomislav II, a member of the Italian House of Savoy whose new Croatian name was adopted as a symbol of the continuity the wartime state

claimed from the tenth-century kingdom of Tomislav I. In fact, however, Croatia was headed by the Ustaša leader Ante Pavelić (1889–1959), whose government became subordinate to German military policy. The new state's boundaries largely coincided with the 1939 Croatian autonomous banovina to which the rest of Bosnia-Herzegovina was added. After the fall of Italy in September 1943, this "Greater Croatia" increased its size with the addition of Italy's wartime acquisitions in Dalmatia (compare Maps 45 and 46).

The other two wartime states were Serbia, which had a Serbian civil administration that was completely subordinate to the occupying German military, and Montenegro, which was occupied by the Italians. Italy restored the Montenegrin kingdom (abolished by Belgrade in November 1918), and although a pro-Italian national assembly was convened, the local royalists were unable to persuade anyone from the old Montenegrin royal line to rule under the new conditions of subordination to Italy. After Italy fell and its troops left in the fall of 1943, the German army entered Montenegro and set up a puppet administration loyal to the Third Reich.

Before the end of 1941, large parts of former Yugoslav territory (especially Serbia and Bosnia-Herzegovina) had become a field for guerilla operations led by two groups: the Četniks under General Draža Mihailović (1893–1946),

and the Partisans under Josef Broz Tito (1892–1980). By the end of the war, the Partisans under Tito had become the dominant force and were recognized by the Allies (see also Map 44). When at the war's end Yugoslavia was restored, the political vision of its wartime hero and Communist leader, Marshal Tito, was implemented: in November 1945 the country was transformed into a federal republic. Since Yugoslavia was a partner of the victorious Allies, there was no question that the country's boundaries would be restored according to its pre-1941 frontiers with Hungary, Romania, Bulgaria, and Albania. The Yugoslavs also expected favorable territorial rectifications along its border with defeated Italy and Austria, whose interwar boundaries had included Croatian and Slovenian minority populations.

At the peace conference in Paris (July–October 1946), the Yugoslav government demanded from Italy its eastern Adriatic territories as far west as a line that reached the outskirts of Udine. Similarly, it demanded the whole Klagenfurt plebiscite area north of the mountain crests in the Drava valley. The Treaty of Paris (February 10, 1947) gave Yugoslavia all its demands vis-à-vis Italy except for a small strip of land (including the towns of Tarvisio and Gorizia) west of the Isonzo River. Trieste, with its surrounding area, was transformed into a Free Territory until 1954, when it was divided between Yugoslavia and Italy (see Map 42a). On the other hand, Yugoslavia's demands for the Klagenfurt area were, after several proposals and counterproposals, finally rejected by the peace conference in June 1949.

As for the postwar internal composition of Yugoslavia, the former prewar Serbian-dominated kingdom was replaced by a federation of six equal republics and two autonomous regions. In a sense, there was a return to many of the pre–World War I borders within those Yugoslav territories that had been part of Austria-Hungary. Slovenia comprised all of Carniola, part of Gorizia-Gradisca, and southern Styria, including the Prekomurje. Croatia was basically identical with the formerly Hungarian-ruled Croatia, Slavonia, and Austrian Dalmatia, with the addition of southern Istria and southern Baranya, but not including the far-eastern part of Slavonia (known as Syrmia/Srem). Bosnia-Herzegovina was restored according to its Austro-Hungarian boundaries. Montenegro, too, was restored according to its pre–1918 borders, with the addition of the coastal area around Kotor.

Serbia, on the other hand, changed substantially. The southern part of the old 1913 kingdom became the republic of Macedonia—in recognition that the local Slavic population there was a distinct nationality. In contrast to its pre–World War I boundaries, the Serbian republic was now extended north of the Drava and Danube rivers into historic Syrmia, Bačka, and the western Banat. These three ethnically diverse territories became the autonomous region of the Vojvodina within the Serbian republic. At the far southern end of Serbia, a second autonomous region called Kosovo, inhabited primarily by Albanians, also came into being. The country's federal structure was to remain in place until 1991–92, when Yugoslavia as a unified state ceased to exist (see Map 50).

The enormous ethnolinguistic complexity of Yugoslavia's population remained more or less constant during the half century between 1931 and 1981, although the manner of classifying the country's national groups changed. The state nationalities—Serbs, Croats, Bosnian Muslims, Macedonians, Montenegrins, Slovenes—together with the "Yugoslavs" retained the same proportion of the total population: 85.1 percent in 1931 and 85.8 percent in 1981. Otherwise, the only significant changes came in the more than twofold increase in the number of Albanians (due to immigration from Albania at the close of World War II and a high birthrate since then) and the virtual disappearance of the German minority (as a result of wartime flight and subsequent expulsion).

Ethnolinguistic-national composition of Yugoslavia

	1931		1981	
	Number	Percentage	Number	Percentage
Serbo-Croatians	10,731,000	77.0	—	—
Serbs			8,140,000	36.3
Croats			4,428,000	19.7
Bosnian Muslims			2,000,000	8.0
Macedonians			1,340,000	6.0
Montenegrins			579,000	2.6
Slovenes	1,135,000	8.1	1,754,000	7.8
Albanians	505,000	3.6	1,730,000	7.7
Germans	500,000	3.6	9,000	0.0
Magyars	468,000	3.3	427,000	1.9
Romanians, Vlachs	138,000	1.0	—	—
Romanians	—	—	55,000	0.2
Vlachs	—	—	32,000	0.2
Turks	133,000	0.9	101,000	0.5
Slovaks	76,000	0.5	80,000	0.4
Gypsies	70,000	0.5	168,000	0.7
Czechs	53,000	0.4	20,000	0.1
Russians	36,000	0.3	4,000	0.0
Ukrainians	28,000	0.2	13,000	0.1
Jews	18,000	0.1	1,000	0.0
Italians	9,000	0.1	15,000	0.1
Bulgarians	—	—	36,000	0.2
Rusyns	—	—	23,000	0.1
Russians	—	—	4,000	0.0
Poles	—	—	3,000	0.0
Yugoslavs	—	—	1,219,000	5.4
Others/Unknown	34,000	0.3	90,000	0.4
TOTAL	13,934,000		22,425,000	

SOURCES: Ivan Bertić, *Veliki geografski atlas Jugoslavije* (Zagreb, 1987), p. 198; *Statistički godišnjak Jugoslavije 1990* (Belgrade, 1990), p. 129.

42   Trieste, Istria, and Albania in the 20th century

Trieste and Istria

The Istrian peninsula with the city of Trieste as well as the borderlands farther north between Friuli (historic Venetia) and Slovenia (historic Carniola) had for centuries changed hands between the two leading powers in the northern Adriatic—Venetia and Austria. For most of the nineteenth century, Venetia was a province of the Austrian Empire (see Map 25a), but in 1866 it was awarded to Italy. Subsequently, the area along the Isonzo River became a fierce battleground between Austria and Italy throughout World War I (see Map 37).

When Italy abandoned its alliance with the Central Powers after the war had begun, its new agreement with the Entente included the secret Treaty of London (April 26, 1915). Among the territories promised Italy in that document were all of Istria and western Slovenia (Carniola) more or less along what later became the Italian-Yugoslav boundary of 1920–41. While the Paris Peace Conference refused to recognize the concessions made in wartime secret treaties, Italy nonetheless received—at least in the northern Adriatic region—even more than it had been secretly promised. The new boundary as outlined in the Treaty of Rapallo, reached with Yugoslavia on November 12, 1920, awarded to Italy all of former Austrian Gorizia-Gradisca, Istria, western Carniola (Slovenia), and a few Dalmatian islands (see Maps 38 and 41a).

The city of Rijeka—or, as the Italians called it, Fiume—posed special problems. Until 1918, it was part of the Hungarian Kingdom. Together with Budapest, Rijeka was the only self-governing city outside Hungary's county administration. Even before the Treaty of Rapallo was signed, Rijeka and the immediate hinterland was occupied (September 1919) by independent Italian troops led by the nationalist poet Gabriele D'Annunzio (1863–1938). An Italian regency under D'Annunzio's leadership functioned in Rijeka until it was forced out in December 1920 by the Italian government, which the previous month had accepted the Rapallo treaty provision that made Rijeka, or Fiume, a free city. Despite the Rapallo treaty, however, Fiume's independent status was short-lived. In March 1922 an Italian fascist coup overthrew the city-state's government and annexed it to Italy.

The next boundary change in the area did not come until after World War II. At the war's end in 1945, Yugoslavia's Partisan forces under Marshal Tito held all of Istria and Trieste. Much like those who faced the boundary decisions after World War I, the new peacemakers proposed a whole series of variant Italian-Yugoslav boundaries in this area. According to the final peace treaty signed with Italy at Paris (February 10, 1947), the so-called Free Territory of Trieste was created. This, in turn, was divided into Zone A (including the city of Trieste) administered by Anglo-American forces, and Zone B administered by Yugoslav forces. As for the rest of Istria, it became part of Yugoslavia. North of Trieste the Yugoslav boundary was pushed west of the Isonzo River except for the city of Gorizia, which remained in Italy.

The last territorial change occurred in 1954. In that year, the Free Territory of Trieste was abolished. Zone A was given to Italy; Zone B, with only a slight boundary change, to Yugoslavia. This decision reached at London by the Western powers was done over the objection of Italy, which had hoped through a plebiscite to receive the whole Free Territory of Trieste.

Albania

Albania was declared an independent state on November 28, 1912, and the following month it was recognized by the great powers at a conference in London. In the course of 1913 (at London in March and at Florence in December), the great powers fixed the boundaries of the new country. Nonetheless, Greece refused until March 1914 to leave the southern part of Albania (including Korçë and Vlorë), which it claimed to be part of "Greek" northern Epirus. Albanian control over its own territory proved to be short-lived, because just after the outbreak of World War I its neighbors occupied various parts of the country (see Map 37). The secret Treaty of London of 1915 called for the dismemberment of Albania.

When the war was over, the Peace Conference in Paris was unable to resolve the question of a renewed Albanian state, proposing that it might become an Italian mandate. U.S. President Wilson in particular opposed this option as part of his general opposition to "secret" treaties. Meanwhile, the Albanians themselves met at Lushnjë in early 1920; they declared their independence a second time (February 11); and they accepted as their boundaries not those of 1913, but rather those proposed in 1919 by a provisional Albanian government to the Paris Peace Conference. These boundaries included parts of Montenegro, much of Kosovo, far-western Macedonia, and the coastal region of Epirus known as Çamëria—all territories that included substantial Albanian populations.

Albanian territorial demands were blocked, however, especially by Greece in the south and by Yugoslavia in the north and east. Yugoslavia even set up under its military occupation a short-lived "republic" in the Mirditë region (1921) between the town of Prizren and the Drin River. Finally, the Allied Council of Ambassadors, accepting the principle of Albanian independence, met in November 1921. The council declared that Albania's boundaries should be those of 1913 with some small changes: the "republic" in the Mirditë region was divided between Albania and

Trieste and Istria in the 20th century

42a

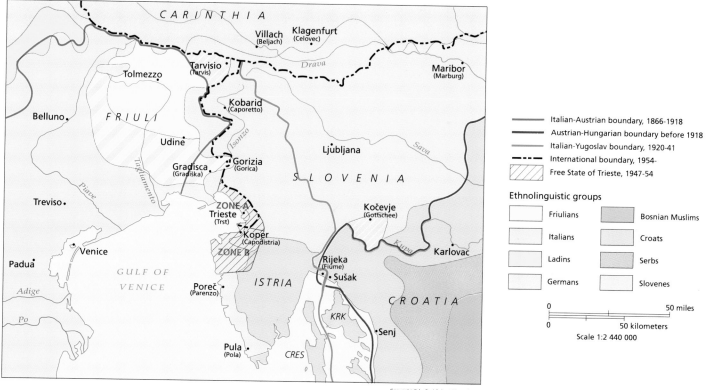

Legend

- Italian-Austrian boundary, 1866-1918
- Austrian-Hungarian boundary before 1918
- Italian-Yugoslav boundary, 1920-41
- International boundary, 1954-
- Free State of Trieste, 1947-54

Ethnolinguistic groups

- Friulians
- Italians
- Ladins
- Germans
- Bosnian Muslims
- Croats
- Serbs
- Slovenes

0 — 50 miles
0 — 50 kilometers
Scale 1:2 440 000

Map labels (42a)

CARINTHIA, Villach (Beljach), Klagenfurt (Celovec), Drava, Maribor (Marburg), Tarvisio (Tarvis), Tolmezzo, Kobarid (Caporetto), FRIULI, Belluno, Udine, Ljubljana, Sava, Gorizia (Gorica), Gradisca (Gradiška), Isonzo, SLOVENIA, Kočevje (Gottschee), Treviso, Piave, Tagliamento, ZONE A, Trieste (Trst), Koper (Capodistria), ZONE B, Karlovac, Venice, Padua, GULF OF VENICE, Adige, Po, Poreč (Parenzo), ISTRIA, Rijeka (Fiume), Sušak, Kupa, CROATIA, KRK, Senj, Pula (Pola), CRES

Copyright © by Paul Robert Magocsi

Albania in the 20th century

42b

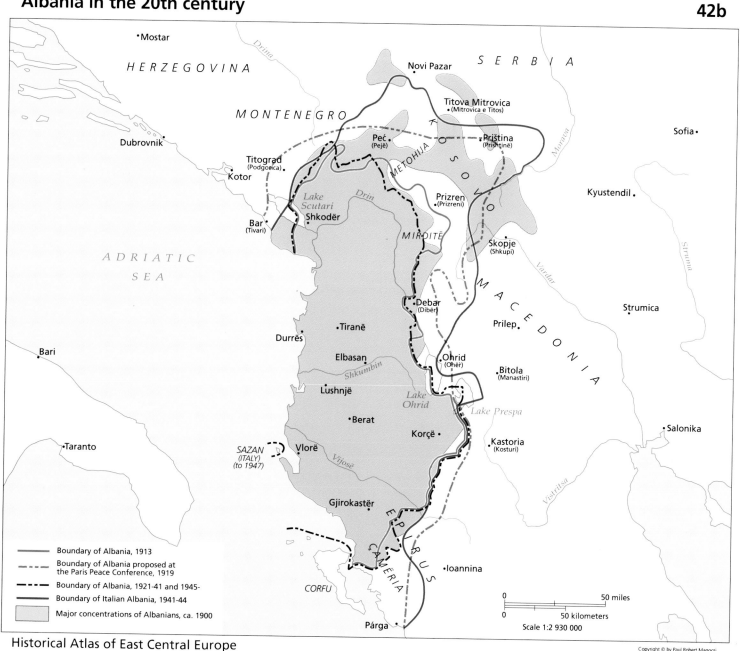

Legend

- Boundary of Albania, 1913
- Boundary of Albania proposed at the Paris Peace Conference, 1919
- Boundary of Albania, 1921-41 and 1945-
- Boundary of Italian Albania, 1941-44
- Major concentrations of Albanians, ca. 1900

Map labels (42b)

Mostar, Drina, SERBIA, Novi Pazar, HERZEGOVINA, MONTENEGRO, Titova Mitrovica (Mitrovica e Titos), Pristina (Prishtinë), Sofia, Dubrovnik, Peć (Pejë), Morava, Titograd (Podgorica), METOHIJA, Kotor, KOSOVO, Kyustendil, Lake Scutari, Drin, Prizren (Prizreni), Bar (Tivari), Shkodër, MIRDITË, Skopje (Shkupi), ADRIATIC SEA, Debar (Dibër), MACEDONIA, Tiranë, Prilep, Durrës, Vardar, Strumica, Elbasan, Ohrid (Ohër), Shkumbin, Bitola (Manastiri), Bari, Lushnjë, Lake Ohrid, Lake Prespa, Berat, Struma, Korçë, Kastoria (Kosturi), Salonika, Taranto, SAZAN (ITALY) (to 1947), Vlorë, Vijosë, Gjirokastër, EPIRUS, Ioannina, Vistritsa, CAMÉRIA, CORFU, Párga

0 — 50 miles
0 — 50 kilometers
Scale 1:2 930 000

Copyright © by Paul Robert Magocsi

Historical Atlas of East Central Europe

Yugoslavia; and in northern Epirus, Albania received a bit more territory along the boundary with Greece.

Albania's boundaries remained unchanged until World War II. Even before the outbreak of the war, Albania ceased to exist as an independent country. In April 1939, Italy invaded Albania, and its national assembly (abolished in 1928) was recalled to declare the personal union of the country with Italy. In effect, Albania became a province of Italy. Two years later, in April 1941, when Hitler's Germany decided to dismember Yugoslavia, fascist Italy added to its province of Albania most of Kosovo, western Macedonia, and—from Greece—the coastal region of Çamëria as far south as Párga. With the end of World War II in 1945, Albanian independence was restored with its boundaries returned to what they had been during the interwar years.

Like Hungary, Albania has been, since its establishment in 1912, one of the most nationally homogeneous countries in East Central Europe. On the other hand, two-thirds as many Albanians live outside the country—1,800,000 alone in the Kosovo region of Yugoslavia. Whereas the total number of inhabitants from the ethnolinguistic minorities in Albania has remained more or less the same in the six decades between 1930 and 1989, the number of Albanians has tripled.

Ethnolinguistic-national composition of Albania

	1930		1989	
	Number	Percentage	Number	Percentage
Albanians	983,000	92.4	[2,865,000]	[96.7]
Greeks	50,000	4.7	[55,000]	[1.8]
Vlachs	10,000	0.9	[15,000]	[0.5]
Macedonians	10,000	0.9	[10,000]	[0.3]
Gypsies	10,000	0.9	[5,000]	[0.1]
Montenegrins	7,000	0.6	[5,000]	[0.1]
Others	—	—	[7,000]	[0.1]
TOTAL	1,070,000		3,182,000	

SOURCES: Marvin R. Jackson, "Changes in Ethnic Populations of Southeastern Europe," in Roland Schönfeld, ed., *Nationalitätenprobleme in Südosteuropa* (Munich, 1987), p. 75; Iurii V. Bromlei, *Narody mira: istoriko-ètnograficheskii spravochnik* (Moscow, 1988), p. 545.

NOTE: Figures in brackets are informed estimates; all others are drawn from governmental statistics.

43 Bulgaria and Greece in the 20th century

Bulgaria

Although Bulgaria was restored as a distinct principality in 1878, it was not until the outset of the twentieth century, in 1908, that the country gained full sovereignty following its unilateral declaration of independence from the Ottoman Empire. Most of the country's subsequent history during the first half of the twentieth century was concerned with restoring the boundaries of "historic Bulgaria," which were drawn up at the short-lived Treaty of San Stefano in 1878 (see Map 26b). Bulgaria was most anxious to "reacquire" Macedonia and Thrace, and did so for a short period in 1912–13 during the First and Second Balkan Wars (see Map 27b).

Bulgaria's frustration at losing the Second Balkan War was compensated during World War I. On the eve of its entry into the war, Bulgaria received from its future ally, the Ottoman Empire, a small strip of land east of the Maritsa River, including the port of Enez/Enos near its mouth (September 6, 1915). But the biggest prize was Macedonia, which was offered Bulgaria should it join the Central Powers. Bulgaria did join the Central Powers in October 1915, and following a joint Austro-German and Bulgarian offensive that same month, it administered (although it did not annex) until the end of the war Macedonian territory more or less according to the San Stefano boundaries. Another territorial promise by the Central Powers was not fulfilled until the last year of the war, when Romania surrendered and Bulgaria was awarded the southern Dobruja by the Treaty of Bucharest (May 7, 1918). The treaty also stipulated Bulgarian, German, and Austrian joint control over the rest of Dobruja, including the three mouths of the Danube. Within a few months, however, Bulgarian forces surrendered as the Central Powers went down to defeat.

As a defeated power, Bulgaria was at the mercy of the Allies meeting to draw new boundaries in Paris. Bulgaria realized that "in the present circumstances" any of its claims to Macedonia would be impossible to fulfill, although its diplomats did request that a Macedonian state "within its historical boundaries" be established under Allied protection. In the end, not only was no such state created, but according to the Treaty of Neuilly (November 27, 1919), Bulgaria was forced to give up western Thrace with its Aegean port of Alexandroúpolis/Dedeagach to Greece;

small chunks of territory near Negotin, Dimitrovgrad/Tsaribrod, Bosilegrad, and Strumica to Yugoslavia; and the recently acquired southern Dobruja to Romania.

Bulgaria's new reduced boundaries remained unchanged until World War II, during which it hoped to restore the 1878 boundaries of San Stefano. At the encouragement of Germany, Romania was forced, on September 7, 1940, to cede to Bulgaria southern Dobruja (including the region around Tolbukhin/Dobrich and the Danube port of Silistra), thereby restoring to the Bulgarians what they had lost in the Second Balkan War (1913). In March 1941, Bulgaria joined the Axis and one month later participated with Germany, Italy, and Hungary in the dismemberment of Yugoslavia. In July, Bulgaria annexed a strip of southeastern Serbia (including the cities of Pirot and Vranje), and it also acquired the long-coveted territory of Yugoslav Macedonia. Although Bulgaria gained only the town of Florina in Greek Macedonia, it did gain from Greece all of western Thrace between the Maritsa and Struma rivers, including the Aegean ports of Kavalla and Alexandroúpolis as well as the islands of Thasos and Samothrace.

When World War II came to a close, Bulgaria was again on the losing side. Despite the backing its new Communist government received from the Soviet Union at the peace negotiations in 1946 (Bulgaria hoped to retain western Thrace according to its 1913 boundaries), Bulgaria was stripped of all its wartime acquisitions and returned to its interwar boundaries with the exception of the southern Dobruja, which it obtained from Romania in 1940. With this acquisition, approved by the Treaty of Paris (1947), Bulgaria was unique among the defeated powers in that it actually increased (however slightly) its postwar boundaries beyond what they had been during the interwar years.

In the absence of official statistics it is difficult to compare the ethnolinguistic evolution of Bulgaria before and after World War II. It seems that the percentage of Bulgarians declined (or perhaps they were overcounted in 1926) from 81.3 to 69.7 percent of the country's population. As for the minorities, the percentages of Turks, Gypsies, Macedonians, and Vlachs have by the 1980s probably risen (or have been corrected from undercounting in 1926), while the numbers of Romanians and Jews have been reduced substantially due to death and population exchange during World War II.

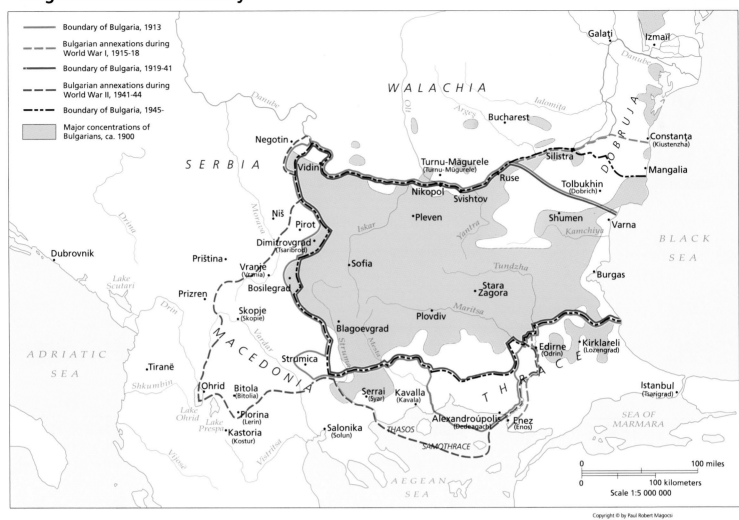

Ethnolinguistic-national composition of Bulgaria

	1926		1985	
	Number	Percentage	Number	Percentage
Bulgarians	4,455,000	81.3	[6,219,000]	[69.7]
Pomaks	102,000	1.9	[269,000]	[3.0]
Turks	578,000	10.5	[1,338,000]	[15.0]
Gypsies	135,000	2.5	[577,000]	[6.5]
Macedonians	—	—	[250,000]	[2.8]
Romanians	69,000	1.3	[1,000]	[0.0]
Jews	47,000	0.9	[5,000]	[0.0]
Armenians	27,000	0.5	[20,000]	[0.2]
Russians	20,000	0.4	[10,000]	[0.1]
Greeks	11,000	0.2	[8,000]	[0.0]
Tatars	6,000	0.1	[5,000]	[0.0]
Gagauz	4,000	0.1	—	—
Germans	4,000	0.1	[1,000]	[0.0]
Vlachs (Karaka-chani, Tsintsari)	1,500	0.0	[200,000]	[2.2]
Albanians	—	—	[10,000]	[0.1]
Others	19,000	0.4	[4,000]	[0.0]
TOTAL	5,479,500		8,950,000	

SOURCES: *Statisticheski godishnik na Tsarstvo Bulgariia*, vol. 26 (Sofia, 1934), p. 25; *Statisticheski godishnik na Narodna Republika Bulgariia 1989* (Sofia, 1989), p. 33; Hugh Poulton, *The Balkans: Minorities and States in Conflict* (London, 1991), pp. 105–18.

NOTE: Figure in brackets are informed estimates; all others are drawn from governmental statistics.

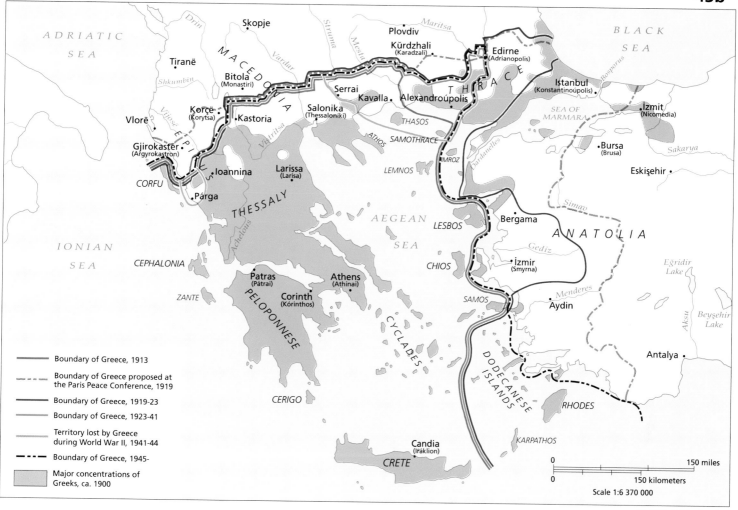

Boundary of Greece, 1913

Boundary of Greece proposed at the Paris Peace Conference, 1919

Boundary of Greece, 1919-23

Boundary of Greece, 1923-41

Territory lost by Greece during World War II, 1941-44

Boundary of Greece, 1945-

Major concentrations of Greeks, ca. 1900

Scale 1:6 370 000

Copyright © by Paul Robert Magocsi

Greece

The outset of the twentieth century saw Greece expand its boundaries in the south and north. In 1908 it gained formal control over the island of Crete, which until then was under the protection of the great powers; and in 1913, following the First Balkan War, it acquired southern Epirus, southern Macedonia, and western Thrace as far as the Mesta/Nestos River (see Map 27b). Greece was on the side of the Entente during World War I, and when that conflict was over its diplomats put forth extensive demands at the Paris Peace Conference in 1919.

The basic object was to fulfill Greece's nineteenth-century Great Idea (Megali Idea)—control of both shores of the Aegean Sea. Among the Greek demands put forth at Paris were northern Epirus, eastern Thrace (including Istanbul/Konstantinoúpolis and the peninsula east of the Bosporus), western Anatolia, and the Dodecanese Islands. All these areas had a significant Greek population, especially along the coastal regions.

Although Greece was not accorded all its demands, the Treaty of Neuilly (November 27, 1919) did give the Greeks Thrace as far east as the Maritsa River. The following year, the Treaty of Sèvres (August 10, 1920) awarded them the rest of Thrace, as far as the Black Sea, although excluding Istanbul and an internationalized zone along the Sea of

Marmara and the Dardanelles (see Map 38). Sèvres did, however, recognize Greek rule over part of western Anatolia, including the cities of İzmir/Smyrna and Bergama. Western Anatolia was theoretically assigned to Greece by the Allied powers for a period of five years, after which a plebiscite would be held to decide its fate permanently.

But even before the Sèvres treaty was signed by the Ottoman government, the Greeks initiated a war that pushed their boundary farther east into Anatolia. A Turkish counterattack resulted in a defeat for the Greeks in 1923. Consequently, a new treaty signed at Lausanne (July 24, 1923) restored all of western Anatolia to what by then had become the republic of Turkey, which also gained eastern Thrace as far as the Maritsa River, including the city of Edirne/Adrianopolis. That same year Greece was also obliged to leave northern Epirus, which it had claimed at the Paris Peace Conference and occupied since the end of the war but which the Allies had assigned to Albania.

The boundaries of Greece remained stable until World War II. By 1941, Greece found itself threatened by the Axis powers and their allies. In that year, Greece was forced to cede to Bulgaria all of its part of Thrace as far as the Struma River as well as the offshore islands of Thasos and Samothrace, and to Italy's province of Albania a small part of coastal Epirus north of and including the port of Párga.

Since Greece fought on the side of the Allies, when

World War II was over the restoration of its prewar boundaries was considered a minimum demand. In the north, Greece's prewar boundaries were indeed restored, but its demands put forth at the peace negotiations in Paris (1946) for territories claimed ever since 1919—Albanian northern Epirus and the so-called Pomak country south of the Bulgarian town of Kŭrdzhali/Karadzali—were turned down. On the other hand, Greek control since 1945 of the formerly Italian-ruled Dodecanese Islands was recognized, so that Greece finally controlled almost all the islands in the Aegean Sea.

While for most of the twentieth century the boundaries of Greece remained relatively the same, the ethnolinguistic composition of the country underwent a steady transformation. The general trend has been an increase in the absolute and relative number of Greeks and a decrease in the percentage of minorities in the country. This process was effected primarily through population exchanges that began even before the period covered on the accompanying statistical charts. Thus, as a result of the Treaty of Lausanne signed in 1923, the next four years witnessed an influx of 1,250,000 Greeks from Turkey (mostly western Anatolia and eastern Thrace) and from Bulgaria, coupled with the simultaneous exodus from Greece of 370,000 Turks to Turkey and 200,000 "Slavophones" (Macedonians and Bulgarians) to Bulgaria. Since the prewar years, Greece has provided no data on the linguistic or national composition of its population. The informed estimates for the late 1980s indicate the same percentage (7.2) of minorities as existed during the interwar years, although it would be misleading to accept these comparisons at face value. Indeed, the number of Jews (Ladinos) did decline drastically because of their virtual elimination during the German occupation of World War II, and the number of Turks was reduced at least in half because of emigration since the war. On the other hand, the estimated high numbers of Macedonians, Vlachs, and Gypsies in the 1980s do not reflect a particularly high demographic gain, but rather that they were undercounted in the official 1928 statistics.

Ethnolinguistic-national composition of Greece

	1928		1985	
	Number	Percentage	Number	Percentage
Greeks	5,760,000	92.8	[9,510,000]	92.8
Turks	191,000	3.0	[100,000]	1.0
Macedonian Slavs	82,000	1.3	[200,000]	2.0
Jews	63,000	1.0	[6,000]	0.0
Armenians	34,000	0.5	[14,000]	0.1
Vlachs	20,000	0.3	[150,000]	1.5
Albanians	19,000	0.3	[95,000]	0.9
Bulgarians, Pomaks	17,000	0.2	[30,000]	0.3
Gypsies	5,000	0.0	[140,000]	1.4
Others	13,000	0.2	—	—
TOTAL	6,204,000		9,950,000	

SOURCES: *Annuaire statistique de la Grèce 1930* (Athens, 1931), p. 98; Hugh Poulton, *The Balkans: Minorities and States in Conflict* (London, 1991), pp. 173–92.

NOTE: Figures in brackets are informed estimates; all others are drawn from governmental statistics.

The international order that came into being in the years immediately following World War I created new states and changed the territorial extent of old ones. Initially, several postwar states in East Central Europe retained the administrative subdivisions of the prewar political entities from which they derived. By 1930, however, most states had either replaced entirely the old administrative subdivisions or had altered substantively their functions as part of a general trend throughout the region toward centralization of political authority.

Germany's lands in East Central Europe, which experienced no basic changes, were somewhat of an exception. The historic divisions into kingdoms, grand duchies, duchies, principalities, and free cities remained for the most part the same in Germany's interwar Weimar Republic as they had been in the pre–World War I empire (compare Map 36). The only alterations came in the consolidation of smaller units: in 1920, one grand duchy, two duchies, and four principalities were formally united as Thuringia, which at the same time ceded Coburg to Bavaria; and in 1934, the formerly separate grand duchies of Mecklenburg-Schwerin and Mecklenburg-Strelitz were united into a single grand duchy of Mecklenburg. In the eastern part of the country, those remnants of the Prussian province of Posen and West Prussia which were not incorporated into Poland remained in existence, while the disputed eastern part of the province of Silesia that was awarded to Germany in 1921 by the Allied powers became the separate Prussian province of Upper Silesia (Oberschlesien).

Poland was reconstructed entirely anew and divided into sixteen palatinates (województwa). These, however, had no relation either to the boundaries of the prewar German, Russian, and Austrian provinces on Polish territory or to the administrative divisions—also known as palatinates—of eighteenth-century pre-partition Poland. Unlike the pre-partition palatinates with their own dietines and self-governing institutions, the interwar palatinates were subordinate to the central government in Warsaw. The only exception was the tiny palatinate of Śląsk/Silesia, which had its own diet (Sejm) and statute (Statut Organiczny) that provided it with a degree of autonomy.

Farther to the north and east, in lands that had once belonged to historic Poland and later the Russian Empire, were Lithuania, Belarus, and Ukraine. Lithuania was a unitary state with only the Memel region—acquired from Germany with the acquiescence of the League of Nations in 1924—having a separate autonomous status. Belarus and Ukraine were Soviet socialist republics that came into being in 1920 and which joined in late 1922 with the Russian S.F.S.R. to form the Union of Soviet Socialist Republics —the Soviet Union. The Ukrainian S.S.R. was, in turn, subdivided into districts (oblasts), and also included the Moldavian Autonomous Soviet Socialist Republic after it was created in 1924.

Czechoslovakia initially retained the administrative subdivisions that had existed previous to its establishment in 1918–19. These included the three Austrian provinces of Bohemia, Moravia, and Silesia and the several Hungarian counties (župy) in Slovakia and Subcarpathian Rus' (see Map 36). In 1927 the former Hungarian counties were abolished; the temporary border between Slovakia and Subcarpathian Rus' was made definite; Silesia was united with Moravia; and Bohemia's borders remained unchanged. Each of Czechoslovakia's four provinces —Bohemia, Moravia-Silesia, Slovakia, Subcarpathian Rus'—had its own assembly responsible for certain self-governing functions.

In Austria, the prewar Habsburg provinces (Länder) continued to exist, and in the federal structure of the new interwar state they retained a substantive number of self-governing functions. In the case of Tyrol, Carinthia, and Styria, however, their territory was reduced through losses to neighboring states. On the other hand, a new province called the Burgenland was created from lands formerly belonging to the Hungarian Kingdom that were ceded to Austria at the Paris Peace Conference.

Interwar or post-Trianon Hungary retained those historic counties (megye) that still fell within its new boundaries. Since those boundaries were now much smaller than the prewar kingdom, the number of Hungarian counties was reduced from seventy-one to twenty-five. From the latter, only ten remained territorially intact; the others were reduced in size or, as along the border with Slovakia, consolidated from small parts of several prewar counties (Győr-Moson-Pozsony, Komárom-Esztergom, Nógrád-Hont, Borsod-Gömör-Kishont, Szabolcs-Ung, Szatmár-Bereg-Ugocsa).

Those areas of Austria-Hungary that became part of Italy were made to coincide with the rest of the Italian administrative subdivisions. Whereas Italy's late nineteenth-century provinces (compartimenti) continued to exist, more important were the smaller districts (provincie). In 1926, twenty new districts were created and some came into being on lands in the northern part of the country. Venetia-Tridentina (former Austrian southern Tyrol) was in that year divided into the Bolzano and Trent districts; the following year Venetia-Giulia (formerly Austrian Gorizia-Gradisca, Trieste, Istria, southwestern Carniola, and northern Dalmatia) was divided into the districts of Gorizia, Trieste, Rijeka/Fiume, and Pula/Pola.

In Yugoslavia, the historic divisions that had existed before World War I—independent Serbia and Montenegro as well as the former Austro-Hungarian lands of Slovenia (Carniola, southern Styria, and Prekomurje); Croatia-Slavonia; Vojvodina (Bačka and Banat); Dalmatia; and Bosnia-Herzegovina—remained intact during the first decade of the new country's existence. However, in 1929, the Yugoslav king suspended the constitution and transformed

East Central Europe, ca. 1930

1 LIPPE
2 BRUNSWICK
3 ANHALT
4 THURINGIA

International boundaries, 1930

Boundaries of kingdoms, duchies,
principalities, free cities and Soviet republics

Boundaries of provinces and
autonomous republics

Boundaries of districts and counties

⊙ State capitals

◉ Capitals of kingdoms, duchies,
principalities, and socialist republics

• Provincial capitals

○ District or county centers

ZETA Names of provinces and administrative subdivisions
other than their capitals or centers

0 ———————— 150 miles

0 ———————— 150 kilometers

Scale 1:8 890 000

Copyright © by Paul Robert Magocsi

the Kingdom of Serbs, Croats, and Slovenes into a centralized kingdom. To emphasize the centralizing tendencies of the new governmental structure, the historic lands were abolished and replaced by nine districts (banovinas) named in most cases after the rivers that in part or wholly ran through them.

Romania, Bulgaria, and Greece retained the administrative units they had before World War I, but in all three cases the boundaries of those units changed and their number expanded because of increased territorial acquisitions after World War I. Romanian territory expanded most noticeably as did the number of its districts (judeţe)—from thirty-two in 1910 to seventy-one in 1930. In Bulgaria between those same decades, the number of districts (okrugs) increased from twelve to sixteen. Greece was divided into ten regions (dhiamérisma), although as before World War I it was the smaller district subdivisions called nomes (nomoí) that were the most important administrative units. Of the thirty-eight nomes in Greece in 1930, only one had a special status, the self-governing monastic community of Mount Athos, represented by a civil governor resident in Karyés (see Map 13a). As for Albania, when its boundaries were finally stabilized in 1923, the country was divided into ten prefectures (prefekturats).

Districts and counties, ca. 1930 (Seat indicated in parentheses if different from district or county name)

Hungary

1. Sopron
2. Győr, Moson, and Pozsony (Győr)
3. Komárom and Esztergom (Esztergom)
4. Nógrád and Hont (Balassagyarmat)
5. Heves (Eger)
6. Borsod, Gömör, and Kishont (Miskolc)
7. Abaúj-Torna (Szikszo)
8. Zemplén (Sátoraljaújhely)
9. Szabolcs and Ung (Nyíregyháza)
10. Szatmár, Bereg, and Ugocsa (Máteszalka)
11. Vas (Szombathely)
12. Veszprém
13. Fejér (Székesfehérvár)
14. Pest-Pilis-Solt-Kiskun (Budapest)
15. Jász-Nagy-Kun-Szolnok (Szolnok)
16. Hajdú (Debrecen)
17. Bihar (Berettyóújfalu)
18. Zala (Zalaegerszeg)
19. Somogy (Kaposvár)
20. Tolna (Szekszárd)
21. Baranya (Pécs)
22. Bács-Bodrog (Baja)
23. Csongrád (Szentes)
24. Békés (Gyula)
25. Csanád, Arad, and Torontál (Makó)

Romania

1. Satu-Mare
2. Maramureş (Sighet)
3. Rădăuţi
4. Storojineţ
5. Cernăuţi (Chernivtsi)
6. Hotin (Khotyn)
7. Soroca
8. Sălaj (Zalău)
9. Someş (Dej)
10. Năsăud (Bistriţa)
11. Cîmpulung (Cîmpulung Moldovenesc)
12. Suceava
13. Dorohoi
14. Botoşani
15. Bălţi
16. Orhei
17. Bihor (Oradea)
18. Cluj
19. Mureş (Tîrgu Mureş)
20. Neamţ (Piatra Neamţ)
21. Fălticeni
22. Roman
23. Iaşi
24. Vaslui
25. Fălciu (Huşi)
26. Lăpuşna (Chişinău)
27. Tighina (Bendery/Tighina)
28. Arad
29. Turda
30. Alba (Alba Iulia)
31. Tîrnava Mica (Blaj)
32. Tîrnava Mare (Sighişoara)
33. Odorhei
34. Ciuc (Miercurea Ciuc)
35. Trei Scaune (St. Gheorghe)
36. Putna (Focşani)
37. Bacău
38. Tecuci
39. Tutova (Bîrlad)
40. Covurlui (Galaţi)
41. Cahul
42. Ismail (Izmaïl)
43. Cetatea Albă (Bilhorod)
44. Timiş-Torontal (Timişoara)
45. Caraş (Oraviţa)
46. Severin (Lugoj)
47. Hunedoara (Deva)
48. Sibiu
49. Făgăraş
50. Braşov
51. Mehedinţi (Turnu-Severin)
52. Gorj (Tîrgu Jiu)
53. Vîlcea (Rîmnicu Vîlcea)
54. Argeş (Piteşti)
55. Muscel (Cîmpulung)
56. Dîmboviţa (Tîrgovişte)
57. Prahova (Ploieşti)
58. Buzău
59. Rîmnicu Sărat
60. Brăila
61. Tulcea
62. Dolj (Craiova)
63. Romanaţi (Caracal)
64. Olt (Slatina)
65. Teleorman (Turnu Măgurele)
66. Vlaşca (Giurgiu)
67. Ilfov (Bucharest)
68. Ialomiţa (Călăraşi)
69. Durostor (Silistra)
70. Constanţa
71. Caliacra (Balchik)

Bulgaria

1. Vidin
2. Vratsa
3. Pleven
4. Tŭrnovo
5. Ruse
6. Shumen
7. Varna
8. Kyustendil
9. Sofia
10. Plovdiv
11. Stara Zagora (Nova Zagora)
12. Burgas
13. Petrich
14. Pashmakli (Smolian)
15. Khaskovo
16. Mustanli (Momchilgrad)

Albania

1. Shkodër
2. Kosovë (Kukës)
3. Dibër (Peshkopi)
4. Durrës
5. Tiranë
6. Elbasan
7. Berat
8. Korçë
9. Vlorë
10. Gjirokastër

Greece

1. Florina
2. Pella
3. Kilkís
4. Serrai
5. Drama
6. Kavalla
7. Rhodope (Komotiní)
8. Évros (Alexandroúpolis)
9. Kozáne
10. Thessalonike (Salonika)
11. Chalcidice (Polygyros)
12. Mount Athos (Karyai)
13. Corfu/Kérkira
14. Ioannina
15. Trikkala
16. Larissa
17. Lesbos (Mytilene)
18. Préveza
19. Arta
20. Aetolia and Acarnania (Mesolóngion)
21. Phthiotis and Phocis (Amphissa)
22. Euboea/Évvoia (Chalcis)
23. Cephalonia/Kefallinía (Argostolion)
24. Zante/Zákinthos
25. Elis (Pyrgos)
26. Achaea (Patras)
27. Corinth/Kórinthos and Argolis (Corinth)
28. Attica and Boeotia (Athens)
29. Chios/Khíos
30. Arcadia (Tripolis)
31. Messenia/Messiní (Kalamata)
32. Laconia/Lakonikós (Sparta)
33. Cyclades/Kikládhes (Hermoupolis)
34. Samos (Vathy)
35. Canea/Khaniá
36. Rethýmne (Rethymnon)
37. Hērákleion (Candia)
38. Lasithion (Hagios Nikólaos)

45 World War II, 1939–1942

The outbreak of World War II on September 1, 1939, like the outbreak of World War I a quarter century earlier, began in East Central Europe. The newest world conflict, Europe's second great "civil war" in the twentieth century, was directly related to the rise of Germany's Third Reich and to the desire of its leader (Führer) Adolf Hitler (1889–1945) to expand his country's boundaries, most particularly into East Central Europe. Hitler's territorial advances had begun in 1938 even before military conflict broke out. These were complemented on a somewhat smaller scale in the Balkans by Germany's ally, fascist Italy. In effect, by the end of 1942—a little over three years after the outbreak of World War II—the entire area of East Central Europe, with the exception of European Turkey, was either directly controlled by Germany and Italy or in the hands of states cooperating with them: Slovakia, Hungary, Romania, Croatia, and Bulgaria.

Hitler's advance into East Central Europe began in March 1938 with the annexation (Anschluss) of Austria. This was followed in September by the Munich Pact, according to which Germany and Italy together with France and Great Britain pressured Czechoslovakia to cede to the Third Reich the predominantly German-inhabited areas around the peripheries of its provinces of Bohemia and Moravia—the so-called Sudetenland. The Munich solution proved to be only temporary, however, and on March 15, 1939, one year after Hitler had annexed Austria, he destroyed what remained of Czechoslovakia. The rest of Bohemia and Moravia (renamed the protectorate of Bohemia-Moravia) was incorporated into the Third Reich, and Slovakia was recognized as a separate state closely allied to Germany.

Germany's final moves against Czechoslovakia convinced France and Great Britain that appeasement-like negotiations with Hitler were futile. Hitler's actions also enraged his ally, Italy's Benito Mussolini (1883–1945), who felt he should have been consulted in advance regarding the destruction of Czechoslovakia. Consequently, Mussolini felt the time had come for his country to begin expanding into what it considered its traditional sphere of interest, the eastern shore of the Adriatic Sea. The first step was Italy's invasion on April 7, 1939, of Albania, which was transformed into an Italian-ruled province on the model of Italian fascism.

Hitler's next moves began in earnest during the summer of 1939 and were directed at Poland, in particular the Polish corridor that separated the "historically German" city-state of Danzig and the province of East Prussia from the rest of the Third Reich. The Danzig issue served as a convenient excuse to eliminate entirely the Polish state. In order to achieve this, Hitler reached an agreement with Stalin (the Molotov-Ribbentrop Nonaggression Treaty of August 23, 1939), whose secret protocol provided for the division of Poland between Germany and the Soviet Union in the event of war. That eventuality came within a few days, when on September 1, 1939, Germany invaded Poland along a broad front that stretched from the Baltic Sea to Slovakia. World War II had begun. Two days later, Poland's allies, Great Britain and France, declared war on Germany. It was to take nearly two more years before the remaining countries of East Central Europe were drawn into the conflict, whether as allies of Germany (Hungary, Slovakia, Romania, Bulgaria) or as the object of invasion by Hitler and his allies (Yugoslavia and Greece).

As foreseen in the Molotov-Ribbentrop Pact, on September 17, 1939, the Soviet Union's Red Army invaded Poland from the east, helping to force the surrender of the last resisting Polish forces on October 6. East of the Soviet-German demarcation line, which was to form part of the Soviet Union's new western boundary, former Polish territory (inhabited primarily by Belorussians and Ukrainians) was in November 1939 formally annexed to the Belorussian S.S.R. (including the district around Białystok) and the Ukrainian S.S.R. (including western Volhynia and Galicia). By agreement with the Soviets (October 10, 1939), Lithuania annexed formerly Polish-held territory around Vilnius (claimed by the Lithuanians in the post–World War I period as Central Lithuania; see Map 38). Finally, in June 1940, the Soviet Union expanded its sphere of influence by entering Lithuania, Latvia, and neighboring Estonia. Two months later, all three Baltic states were annexed and each was transformed into a Soviet socialist republic.

Farther south, both Germany and Italy urged Romania to accede to the Soviet Union's demands (June 28, 1940) for northern Bukovina and Bessarabia. Consequently, northern Bukovina was added to the Ukrainian S.S.R., as was the coastal region of Bessarabia; the remaining and largest part of Bessarabia was added to Soviet Moldavia, which was promoted in status from an autonomous to a Soviet socialist republic with its new capital at Chişinău. The changes along the Soviet Union's western frontier that occurred in 1939–40 were, as we shall see, soon to be undone by German military activity. Nonetheless, the otherwise brief Soviet presence in the Baltic states, western Belarus, western Ukraine, and Moldavia in the years 1939–41 provided a model and served as the international justification for the return of those areas to Soviet rule after World War II.

Of the other states cooperating with Germany and Italy, Hungary was the first to expand its boundaries. In the immediate post-Munich period in the fall of 1938, a German-Italian sponsored conference at Vienna (November 2) awarded southern Slovakia and southern Subcarpathian Rus' (Carpatho-Ukraine) to Hungary (see Map 39b). Then, during the final dismemberment of Czechoslovakia on March 14–15, 1939, Hungary forcibly annexed the

World War II, 1939-1942

1 LIPPE
2 BRUNSWICK
3 ANHALT
4 THURINGIA

Legend:

- International boundaries, January 1938
- International boundaries, November 1942
- Boundaries of German administrative units and of other subject territories, 1942
- German district boundaries, 1942
- Western boundary of Soviet Union before June 1941
- Boundaries of Soviet Socialist Republics before June 1941
- German-Italian military demarcation line
- Greater Germany, 1942
- Territories subject to German civil administration, 1942
- Territories subject to German military occupation, 1942
- Italy, 1942
- Territories subject to Italian administration, 1942
- States co-operating with the Axis Powers
- States occupied by German and Italian forces
- Unoccupied Soviet territory
- Neutral States
- ⊙ Country capitals
- ◉ Administrative centers of subject territories
- □ German land, province, and Gau centers
- ○ District centers
- • Other towns and cities
- STYRIA Land, Gau, and district names other than their centers
- ◆ Concentration or slave-labor camp
- ☠ Death camp

Scale 1:8 890 000

0 — 150 miles
0 — 150 kilometers

Historical Atlas of East Central Europe

Copyright © by Paul Robert Magocsi

rest of Carpatho-Ukraine, which it renamed Carpathia/Kárpátalja. The following summer, Hungary turned to Germany and Italy for help in securing territory from Romania. Since Romania, still a neutral state, was at the very same time being pressured by the Soviet Union to give up northern Bukovina and Bessarabia, the government in Bucharest requested that a German military mission enter the country to help protect its eastern and northern frontier. Hitler refused until the territorial demands of Romania's neighbors were met. Consequently, Romania was compelled to cede to Bulgaria the southern Dobruja (September 7, 1940), thereby restoring the pre–World War I border in that area. Negotiations with Hungary proved more difficult until Hitler intervened, arranging the Second Vienna Award (August 30, 1940), which gave north-central Transylvania and the other Romanian territory north of Oradea to the Hungarians. These territorial losses provoked an internal political crisis in Romania (September 14, 1940), whose new government repudiated its neutral and often western-leaning orientation for an open alignment with Germany. Hitler now guaranteed what remained of Romanian territory, and by mid-October German troops began to be stationed in the country in order, as was said, "to protect the Ploiești oil fields."

The next major territorial changes in East Central Europe came in Yugoslavia and were related to the ongoing rivalry between Germany and Italy in the Balkans. Mussolini felt that Italian territorial ambitions were consistently being thwarted by Hitler. When the Italian leader learned of the German military presence in Romania, he promptly launched an invasion of Greece from Italian bases in Albania (October 28, 1940), hoping to transform Greece into an Italian dependency. The Greek army decisively defeated the Italians, however, drove them out of Greece, and then crossed into Albania, one-third of which was in Greek hands before the end of 1940. The Greek victory was a great morale booster to the anti-Axis struggle, and Britain dispatched troops to Greece in support of its ally.

In order to make up for the Italian failure and drive the British out of Greece, Hitler realized that Yugoslavia, Greece's ally, had to be eliminated first. On the diplomatic front, the Axis or Tripartite Pact was signed on September 27, 1940, by Germany, Italy, and Japan to coordinate their military and political action. Germany's eastern neighbors wanted to join as well, and before the end of the year, Slovakia, Hungary, and Romania, followed in March 1941 by Bulgaria and even Yugoslavia, had all formally become Axis states. A few days before Yugoslavia finally joined the Axis, Yugoslav military officers staged a coup (March 27, 1941) which was essentially anti-Nazi in character. In an attempt to appease Hitler, however, the new government accepted membership in the Axis. Simultaneously with the Yugoslav coup, the British had defeated Italian naval forces at the battle of Cape Matapan, assuring their continued presence in Greece. These events forced Hitler to conclude that the battle for Greece could be won only if Yugoslavia was eliminated as well, regardless of its new government's pro-Axis position.

On April 6, 1941, German forces invaded Yugoslavia and Greece, while the Italians entered Yugoslav Dalmatia and Greece's Ionian Islands. Within two weeks Yugoslavia had capitulated and its territory was parceled out by Hitler. Northern Slovenia was annexed directly by the Third Reich as the new Gaus of Upper Carniola and Lower Styria. A territorially reduced Serbia was permitted to have its own government, although the puppet state was in fact ruled by the German military and known officially as the District of the Military Commander of Serbia (Gebiet des Militärbefehlshabers Serbien). The small slice of territory in the western Banat was nominally part of Serbia, but effectively was ruled by the German military in cooperation with local Swabian Germans, who were expected in the future to have their own autonomous region with its capital at Vršac (German: Hennemannstadt).

Italy annexed southwestern Slovenia (including Ljubljana) and Dalmatia (as far as Split), while parts of Montenegro, Kosovo, Metohija, and Macedonia were added to Italian Albania. Montenegro was restored once again as a kingdom (July 1941), but when no descendants of the local royal house (which had been deposed by Serbia in November 1918) could be found to cooperate with the new invaders, the country was administered by Italian military authorities.

Bulgaria's share of Yugoslavia was the larger part of Macedonia, while Hungary obtained the Bačka and small pieces of territory in the Baranya, Medjumurje, and Prekomurje. The largest remaining portion of former Yugoslavia was transformed into the state of Croatia, whose independence was proclaimed on April 10, 1941. Although Croatia was nominally within Italy's sphere of influence, the country had German as well as Italian troops stationed on its territory. Consequently, its government, headed by the Croat fascist leader (poglavnik) Ante Pavelić, recently returned from exile in Italy, fell increasingly under German influence.

The division of spoils in Greece was less formal than in Yugoslavia. A puppet Greek government was established by the Germans in Athens, but it had little authority. Most of the country was divided into German and Italian military zones, and even if Italy was in theory responsible for the largest amount of Greek territory, in practice German forces manned as well all the key strategic positions (including Athens) within the Italian zone. Western Thrace along with a slice of far-eastern Macedonia was recovered by Bulgaria (which had held it before World War I), although that region was never formally annexed by the Bulgarian government. The Bulgarians were also assigned to occupy the town of Florina and surrounding area in southwestern Macedonia. Finally, the coastal region of Epirus, known as Çamëria, was attached to the Italian province of Albania.

With the Balkans secured, Hitler could now turn to his ultimate goal, the overthrow of the Soviet government and the incorporation of at least the European part of the Soviet Union into the German sphere of influence. Disregarding the German-Soviet nonaggression pact of 1939, Hitler launched Operation Barbarossa (150 divisions with about 3 million men) against the Soviet Union on June 22, 1941. Within a few months the Germans controlled virtually all Soviet territory indicated on the accompanying map. As a result, every territorial acquisition the Soviet Union had made since September 1939 was lost to the Germans. Among Hitler's Axis allies who participated in the invasion, only Romania was awarded any territory. By the end of July 1941, the Romanians had regained northern Bukovina and Bessarabia (lost to the Soviets the year before), and in October they annexed a new territory beyond the Dnieper River which they called Transnistria.

Throughout the broad expanse of East Central Europe under the direct control of Germany, there were three categories of territory: (1) lands incorporated directly into the Third Reich or Greater Germany (Grossdeutschland); (2) territories subject to German civil administration but outside Greater Germany; and (3) territories subject to German military occupation.

Within the first and largest of these territorial categories —Greater Germany—there were also at least three different variants of administrative subdivisions. That part of Greater Germany that was within the country's pre-1938 boundaries retained the fifteen historic German states (Länder) that had been in existence when Hitler and the Nazi party came to power in 1933. Within the next two years, however, all self-governing rights of those historic states were abolished as the Third Reich was converted into a centralized state. Those territories of Greater Germany acquired after 1938 from Austria, Czechoslovakia, and Poland were divided into units called Gaus (or Reichsgaus); and like the historic lands, they were headed by an appointee from the central government. Although East Prussia had belonged to Germany before 1938 as part of the historic state of Prussia, it was in 1939 transformed into a Gau with expanded borders, whose head (Gauleiter) was also responsible for the district of Białystok. Finally, within Greater Germany there were two territories that had a particular status as protectorates: Bohemia-Moravia and the General-gouvernement, headed respectively by a Protektor in Prague and a governor general in Cracow appointed by Hitler.

Beyond Greater Germany were the Soviet lands that before September 1939 had been part of Poland, Lithuania, Latvia, Soviet Belorussia, and Soviet Ukraine. On these lands two Reichskommissariats were established (Ostland and Ukraine). Each was headed by a Reich commissar and subdivided into districts; each district was run by a civil administration made up of Germans or, in the case of the former Baltic States, local Lithuanians and Latvians willing to cooperate with the new rulers. Lastly were those areas under the German military, who functioned either as an occupying force (in former Soviet territory) or as the decision-making body behind a puppet government (in Serbia and Greece).

Germany's expansion eastward was part of Hitler's policy to provide *Lebensraum* (living space) for Germans living abroad (see Map 32a). The non-Germanic indigenous populations would be reduced to serving the dominant, or master, German race (*Herrenvolk*). To create the proper conditions for this New Order, certain politically and racially undesirable elements (*Untermenschen*) would have to be eliminated. Thus, beginning in 1933 at Dachau (near Munich) and continuing throughout German-ruled territories, concentration and slave-labor camps were established. By 1941–42 extermination camps were set up as well. The camps were designed to incarcerate or physically annihilate political (socialists, Communists, anti-German representatives of former independent states) and racial (Jews, Gypsies) "undesirables," as well as any persons found or suspected to oppose Germany's New Order. All of Germany's allies in East Central Europe also set up concentration camps to intern political and racial undesirables as well as national minorities (as Croatia did for the Serbs).

46 World War II, 1943–1945

The domination of East Central Europe by Germany and Italy depended on the continued military success of those two countries. The major turning point in Germany's military fortunes came on its eastern front in the Soviet Union, where at the beginning of February 1943, after several months of battle, the German Sixth Army was forced to surrender at Stalingrad along the lower Volga River. Following the battle of Stalingrad, the Soviets began a drive westward. By October 1943 they had pushed back the Germans as far as the Dnieper River and in the north nearly as far as Vitsebsk.

The year 1943 also witnessed a successful Allied invasion against Germany's Axis partner Italy. Anglo-American forces had crossed over from northern Africa in July and captured Sicily. From there, the Americans and British (whose armies also included contingents of Canadians, Australians, New Zealanders, and Poles, among others) pushed into the southern Italian boot, so that by October 1943 the western front was along a line just north of Naples. In the interim, Mussolini was overthrown (July 24–25); a new Italian government signed an armistice with the Allies (September 8); and the following month Italy declared war on Germany. For its part, Germany in October annexed the north Italian regions around Udine, Ljubljana, Istria, and the adjacent Dalmatian islands, which became the Adriatic Littoral (Adriatisches Küstenland) administered by the Gau of Carinthia; and also added South Tyrol, which became the Pre-Alpine Region (Alpenvorland) administered by the Gau of Tyrol-Vorarlberg (see Map 45). Aside from these territorial acquisitions, the rest of northern and central Italy was now in the hands of the German military, against which the western Allies were to be engaged in conflict (joined by Italy as a cobelligerent but not ally) until the end of the war.

The fall of Italy had immediate consequences for its subject territories and dependencies in the Balkans. Italy's wartime acquisitions in Dalmatia were given to what became known as an expanded Greater Croatia. In neighboring Montenegro and Albania, the disarmed Italian troops were replaced by the German military, which set up a puppet "national administration" for the Montenegrins and left the Albanians more or less to govern themselves. Finally, the part of Greece that had been under the nominal control of the Italian military (see Map 45) became, like the rest of the country, dependent on the German military.

On the eastern front, the Soviet war effort was initially most successful along the Red Army's southern flank. By July 1944, most of Germany's Reichskommissariat Ukraine and Romania's Transnistria had been recaptured by the Red Army. A few weeks later the Soviets reached the mouth of the Danube. With the Soviet capture of Iaşi (August 21) and Chişinău (August 24), Germany's erstwhile ally Romania removed its pro-German government,

declared war on the Third Reich (August 26), and subordinated its army to fight under the Soviet command. During the first week of September, the Soviets declared war on Bulgaria. The Red Army entered the country, and on September 9, 1944, a coup in Sofia resulted in the establishment of a pro-Soviet Bulgarian government. From then on Bulgarian troops were, like the Romanians, to fight on the side of the Red Army.

With the loss of Romania and Bulgaria to the Soviets, the Germans began evacuating the southern Balkans in September 1944. Their last troops had left the Greek mainland by the end of October and were replaced by British forces, although German garrisons remained on the island of Crete until the end of the war. By November, the Germans had departed from Albania, where the leftist-oriented National Liberation Movement established its authority. The evacuated armies from Greece and Albania helped for a while to reinforce the German defense against the Soviet advance from Romania and Bulgaria. However, before the end of the month, the Red Army, in cooperation with Tito's Yugoslav Partisans, captured Belgrade (October 20) and eastern Serbia. The Soviets, with their Bulgarian ally, then moved north, concentrating their energies on Hungary and the German forces that had occupied that country since March 1944. By mid-October, the Red Army, joined by the Romanian army, had reached as far as the Tisza River.

In the area north of the Carpathians the Soviets had by the end of August 1944 advanced to the boundaries of East Prussia and the Vistula River as far as the eastern suburbs of Warsaw (known as Praga). Soviet forces also were successful in breaking into Hungary from north of the Carpathians, capturing Uzhhorod on October 27.

Having breached the Carpathians and brought Hungary east of the Tisza River under its control, the Red Army (with a Czechoslovak Army Corps that had been formed on Soviet territory in 1943) concentrated its efforts on entering Slovakia, which because of its vulnerability was being occupied for the first time by German troops in 1944. After fierce German resistance at the battle for the Dukla pass (September–November 1944), eastern Slovakia and Hungary as far west as the bend of the Danube River and Lake Balaton fell to the Red Army. The government of Hungary capitulated to the Soviets on October 15, 1944, but the Hungarian military, backed by openly fascist-oriented Hungarian leaders (the Arrow Cross), continued to fight alongside the German army until its final retreat westward.

After a stalemate during the last months of 1944 along Poland's eastern front, the Red Army launched a massive offensive along the Vistula in January 1945. The Soviets finally reached the heart of the Third Reich—territories that had been part of Germany before the war. East Prussia fell in February-March, and by mid-April the eastern front

Copyright © by Paul Robert Magocsi

north of the Carpathians was stabilized as far west as the Oder-Neisse rivers. Meanwhile, Anglo-American led forces were pushing across Germany from the west, having reached Leipzig and Chemnitz by April 18–19. On April 25, advance units of both the American and Soviet armies met for the first time at Torgau on the Elbe River.

In the Danubian basin, the Red Army drove the Germans and their Slovak and Hungarian allies out of most of Slovakia and western Hungary, reaching Vienna on April 14, 1945. More complex, however, was the military situation in the western Balkans. In the last months of 1944, the Germans evacuated not only Greece but also Macedonia, Albania, and Montenegro, so that by mid-January 1945 they were behind a line that in part followed the Drina River. For its part, the Red Army, following the capture of Belgrade on October 20, 1944, and Stalin's agreement with Tito, moved northward for the offensive in Hungary. They left Tito's Yugoslav Partisan Army to deal with the retreating Germans and their Ustaša allies in the Croatian state. Simultaneous with the German withdrawal from Albania, local partisan forces under the direction of the Communist-dominated National Liberation Movement captured both Tiranë (November 17) and Shkodër (November 29), thereby bringing the entire country under their control. Tito's struggle for the rest of prewar Yugoslavia was to last much longer. Although the Germans were gone by the spring of 1945, there remained the anti-Communist Serbian monarchists (Četniks) and various pro-German elements, whether the Ustaša forces of the Croatian state, Serbian fascists (under Dimitrije Ljotić), or the Slovene Home Guard (under General Rupnik), which was formed by the Germans to fight the Partisans. It was not until the very last days of the war—even after the capitulation of Germany—that Tito succeeded in capturing the Croatian state's capital of Zagreb on May 9, 1945.

The last weeks of April 1945 culminated in the battle for Berlin and the final collapse of Germany. The battle began on April 16 with a Soviet artillery barrage from behind their line along the Oder River, and it lasted until the final capitulation of Berlin on May 2. Meanwhile, farther south, Anglo-American forces had pushed their front farther eastward, capturing Munich (before the end of April), and the western Bohemian cities of Cheb (April 27) and Plzeň (May 6). It is nonetheless ironic that despite the fall of Berlin, most of the lands that had been incorporated into the Third Reich even before the outbreak of World War II, namely Austria and Czechoslovakia's provinces of Bohemia and Moravia, remained in the hands of the German military at the war's end. The conclusion of World War II in Europe was formally proclaimed on May 9, 1945, when the German authorities surrendered in Berlin. Although the Red Army entered Prague that same day, the last German forces did not lay down their arms until May 11.

Besides the military campaigns of the Allied powers in East Central Europe, in particular the Soviet Union's Red Army, there was also considerable activity by partisan groups throughout the region (see Map 46a). The partisan movements, however, were often as concerned with eliminating their political rivals as they were with fighting the forces of Nazi Germany and its Axis supporters. In some

46a Partisan movements during World War II

--- International boundaries, 1943
— Boundaries of subject territories, 1943
▓ Areas held by partisans for significant periods
⠿ Areas of major partisan activity

Scale 1:20 000 000

Copyright © by Paul Robert Magocsi

cases, like Croatia, Serbia, Montenegro, Albania, and Greece, the political infighting was the result of ideological conflict between local leaders who were already preparing to take over the reins of local government once the Axis enemy was driven out. In other cases, the infighting was a result of conflict between those groups that recognized prewar governments-in-exile in the West (generally resident in London) and those that followed the lead of local Communist exiles in Moscow. It should also be noted that the partisan movements were to have great ideological value for the future Communist-dominated governments of East Central Europe. This was especially the case in countries like Czechoslovakia, Romania, and Bulgaria, which during the war were under pro-German regimes. The existence of leftist-oriented partisan groups in those countries was to be hailed as proof of the supposed widespread opposition of the local populations to foreign domination, and in particular to the "anti-populist" and "fascist" indigenous governments whose independence seemingly survived only with German support.

Among the various partisan or resistance movements in Poland was the Home Army (Armia Krajowa), which recognized the Polish government-in-exile in London. Although the Home Army participated with the Red Army in its advance into former eastern Poland (western Belarus and western Volhynia), the Soviets did not support the Home Army when it captured Warsaw from the Germans on August 1, 1944. Two months later, on October 2, the Germans recaptured part of Warsaw (which they razed on

Hitler's orders) and the Home Army effectively ceased to exist. After this debacle, the Polish partisan movement was dominated by (1) the pro-Communist People's Army (Armia Ludowa), which was integrated into the Polish People's Army backed by Moscow, and (2) the ultranationalistic National Armed Forces (Narodowe Siły Zbrojne).

Farther east, in the German Reichskommissariats Ostland and Ukraine, numerous Soviet partisan groups arose, and in 1942 began to harass German supply lines and collaborators with the occupying forces. Among the several non-Soviet partisan groups, the best organized was the Ukrainian Insurgent Army (Ukraïns'ka Povstans'ka Armiia —UPA), founded in 1942, which from its original base in northern Volhynia fought against the Germans and pro-Soviet partisans. As the war ended, the UPA retreated westward toward the Carpathian Mountains, where it fought against nationalist and pro-Communist Polish partisans as well as against the Red Army in an unsuccessful bid to create an independent non-Soviet Ukrainian state.

Among the most celebrated of partisan formations were two operating in the territory of former Yugoslavia. These were known as the Četniks and Partisans. The Četniks were organized by Serbian officers from the disbanded Yugoslav army under the leadership of General Draža Mihailović, who retreated to the rugged and inaccessible mountains of south-central Serbia after the fall of Yugoslavia in April 1941. Made up mostly of Serbs who were both anti-Croat and anti-Communist, the Četniks began resistance to the Germans in the summer of 1941. Mihailović, whose political goal was the reconstitution of a Serbian-dominated kingdom, was recognized by the Yugoslav government-in-exile in London as well as by the western Allies.

Stronger and even more active militarily were the Partisans led by Josip Broz Tito, the general secretary of the Yugoslav Communist party. The Partisans under Tito included former Communist and leftist sympathizers who looked forward to building a socialist state that would guarantee equality of all of Yugoslavia's nationalities. Tito's initial base of operations was the Serbian town of Užice, but before long Partisan military activity and administrative control spread to many other parts of the country, including areas nominally under the authority of the pro-German state of Croatia. In November 1942, at Bihać in the heart of the Croatian state, the Partisans established an Anti-Fascist Council for the National Liberation of Yugoslavia (hereafter: AVNOJ). Exactly one year later, the AVNOJ reconvened at Jajce, also in the Croatian state, where it declared itself the legitimate government of a Yugoslavia that after the war was to be reconstituted on federal principles. Tito was the dominant figure in the AVNOJ, and before long he obtained the support of Britain and the United States as well as the Soviet Union.

There were several attempts to create a common Četnik-Partisan alliance, but these ended after November 1941, when Četnik units cooperated with the German army in its attack against the Partisan base at Užice. By 1943, the Partisans and Četniks were as frequently engaged in combat against each other as they were against the German military and Ustaša forces of its Croatian puppet state. By the war's end, the Četnik leader Mihailović had

been dropped by the western Allies and by the Yugoslav government-in-exile, and he was cooperating with the Axis. On the other hand, Tito was recognized by both the Soviets and the western Allies, and his Partisans were entrusted with driving out all other military and political formations from Yugoslav territory. This did not occur until the week after the war had formally ended (May 9, 1945), when the last battles against the Ustaša forces of Croatia took place in northern Slovenia. About 220,000 pro-German Ustaša and 5,000 Montenegrin Četniks surrendered to the British in southern Austria. Despite promises to the contrary, within a few days the British returned all of them to Yugoslavia except 20,000 Ustaša, who escaped. An estimated 45,000 were summarily shot by Tito's Partisans and the rest were marched off to prison camps, an estimated 100,000 dying along the way. The Četnik leader Mihailović managed to survive in hiding until March 1946, when he was captured by the new Yugoslav government and executed.

Albania had a resistance movement dating back to 1940 that worked for the return of their king, who had been driven out the year before by the Italians. But the most important groups were the Communist-dominated National Liberation Movement established in September 1942 and the antiroyalist republican movement Balli Kombëtar founded in March 1943. By 1944, the National Liberation Movement proved to be the stronger of the two, and when the Germans retreated in November they took over control of the country.

Greece, too, had several resistance groups: the National Popular Liberation Army (ELAS, established 1942), which was dominated by Communists but included other groups, especially republicans and antiroyalists; the non-Communist National Republican Greek League (EDES, established 1941); and the much smaller National and Social Liberation (EKKA, established 1943). All three had carried out sabotage against the Italian and German troops and then participated in the complicated rivalries that marked Greek political life when the British arrived in force on the mainland after the German retreat.

The Czech and Slovak lands were among the last to experience large-scale partisan movements. By 1944, Bohemia and Moravia had several small groupings (R3, ROH, and the Communist underground) that in 1945 coalesced into the Czech National Council. By April 1945, the council coordinated guerrilla-like uprisings against the retreating German troops. The council eventually took control of the uprising in Prague, and after three days of street fighting forced the surrender of the German troops on May 8, 1945—one day before the Red Army arrived in the city. In Slovakia, a national council was formed in late 1943 made up of Communist and non-Communist members, whose goal was to organize an uprising against the pro-German Slovak state. An uprising based in the central Slovak town of Banská Bystrica began on August 29, 1944, but by the end of October—and in the absence of any serious assistance from the Red Army, which by then had already crossed the Dukla Pass into northeastern Slovakia—the resistance was crushed by German troops that had been invited into the country by the Slovak government in Bratislava.

47 East Central Europe after World War II

As a result of World War II and the defeat of Nazi Germany and its allies, the boundaries of every country in East Central Europe (with the exception of Austria and Albania) changed from what they had been during the interwar years. In some cases (Hungary and Bulgaria), those changes were relatively small, while in others, especially in the region north of the Carpathians, they were significant. This was particularly the case for Germany and Poland.

At the first postwar conference of the victors (United States, Great Britain, France, Soviet Union) held near Berlin at Potsdam (July 17–August 2, 1945), it was decided that Germany would not be dismantled but rather divided temporarily into four military zones administered by the military forces of each of the four Allies. Austria, which had been annexed to Germany in March 1938, would be restored as a separate country, but it, too, would be temporarily divided into four Allied military zones.

The division of Germany was simplified and made more permanent in 1949. In September of that year, the Federal Republic of Germany (Bundesrepublik Deutschland—BRD), commonly known as West Germany, was created from the British, American, and French military zones. One month later, the Soviets dissolved their occupation zone, which became the basis for the German Democratic Republic (Deutsche Demokratische Republik—DDR). The Federal Republic of Germany consisted of ten states (Länder), including Schleswig-Holstein, Hamburg, Lower Saxony, Bremen, Hesse, Baden-Württemberg, and Bavaria. The German Democratic Republic initially comprised five states: Mecklenburg, Thuringia, Saxony, Brandenburg, and Saxony-Anhalt (see Map 50). The last two states had previously been provinces of Prussia, which the Allies abolished in 1947, considering it, as the "bearer of militarism and reaction in Germany," to be particularly responsible for the war. In 1952 the East German government in turn abolished its five historic states, replacing them with fifteen smaller districts (Bezirke), including East Berlin as a separate entity.

Like Germany itself, the former capital of Berlin continued to remain divided, with American, British, French, and Soviet troops still in their respective zones. However, the American, British, and French zones were administratively united into an entity known as West Berlin, which was considered part of West Germany. The Soviet sector, or East Berlin, became the capital of East Germany. The artificial division of the city was intensified in 1961, when the East German authorities constructed a wall that divided East from West Berlin.

Neighboring Austria, also divided into four Allied military zones at the close of World War II, evolved differently from Germany. Austria had a provisional government already in 1945, and then in May 1955 it was reconstituted as a sovereign state. Also in contrast to Germany, all

occupying troops left Austria. Vienna, which like Berlin had been divided by the Allied forces, was reunited and restored as the country's capital. The nine provinces (Länder) that had existed during the interwar years were restored as the basis of Austria's administrative structure.

Particularly problematic for the Allies were the future boundaries of Poland. These had been discussed by American, British, and Soviet leaders during their wartime conferences at Teheran (November 28–December 1, 1943) and Yalta (February 4–11, 1945). On both occasions the concept of the Curzon Line—devised by the British statesman Lord Curzon in 1919 (see Map 38)—was accepted as the desirable eastern boundary of restored postwar Poland. This eastern boundary was also accepted by the pro-Soviet Polish Committee of National Liberation (PKWN) established at Chełm in July 1944 and then transformed at Lublin in January 1945 into the Provisional Polish Government.

With regard to Poland's western boundary, the postwar Potsdam Conference agreed to compensate Poland for its

47a Berlin, 1945-1990

Copyright © by Paul Robert Magocsi

47b Vienna, 1945-1955

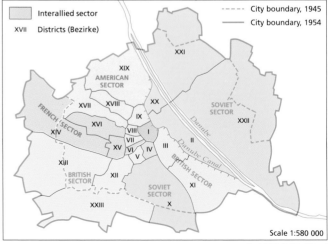

Copyright © by Paul Robert Magocsi

Historical Atlas of East Central Europe

Copyright © by Paul Robert Magocsi

losses to the Soviet Union east of the Curzon Line by separating "provisionally" from Germany all its lands east of the Oder and Neisse rivers. These lands east of the so-called Oder-Neisse Line were to be administered temporarily by Poland until a peace treaty with Germany could be signed (which finally occurred in 1991). Thus all of Silesia, West Prussia, Danzig, most of Pomerania, and east Brandenburg were assigned by the Allies to Poland, which understood these acquisitions to be permanent. By the end of 1945 the Polish government had already established a special commission for what it referred to as the "Recovered Lands" (Ziemie Odzyskane), in order to integrate them fully with the rest of Poland. As for former German East Prussia, it was divided by treaty (August 17, 1949) between Poland and the Soviet Union. The Soviet share of East Prussia, with its administrative center in Königsberg, renamed Kaliningrad, was made part of the Russian S.F.S.R., from which it was otherwise territorially separated.

East of Poland, the territorial situation basically followed what had been achieved by the Soviets after they had cooperated with Nazi Germany in 1939 in the destruction of Poland. Thus, the Belorussian S.S.R. and Ukrainian S.S.R. "reunited" territories they had lost during the German invasion of the Soviet Union in June 1941. Similarly, Estonia, Latvia, and Lithuania (expanded eastward in 1939 to include Vilnius), which had been forcibly transformed into Soviet republics in 1940, were restored to that status once again at the end of the war.

Like Poland, Czechoslovakia had been declared a belligerent state on the side of the Allies, who in 1943 jointly agreed that the country should be restored according to its pre-Munich boundaries (see Map 44). On November 25–26, 1944, however, in the presence of the Red Army, a national council in Czechoslovakia's interwar eastern province of Subcarpathian Rus' met to declare its desire for unity with the "Soviet Ukrainian motherland." This "voluntary" act was confirmed by a bilateral treaty (June 29, 1945) between Czechoslovakia and the Soviet Union, whereby the former Czechoslovak province of Subcarpathian Rus' (with slight border changes near its administrative center of Uzhhorod) became the Transcarpathian region (oblast) of the Ukrainian S.S.R.

As for the rest of East Central Europe south of the Carpathians, the few border changes that took place were decided upon at the Paris Peace Conference (July–October 1946) and confirmed by the Treaty of Paris (February 10–14, 1947). The Paris treaty applied only to those countries that had been Axis partners or at some time had been belligerents against the Allies: namely, Romania, Hungary, Bulgaria, Italy, and—beyond our sphere of concern— Finland. As for Hungary, its claims for Transylvania were rejected and the country was restored to its interwar, or Trianon, boundaries, the only exceptions being a small chunk of land on the southern side of the Danube River near Bratislava.

Romania's prewar western boundary was restored under the protection of the Red Army in late 1944, well before the peace negotiators ever met. The 1947 Paris treaty confirmed those boundaries, which meant that all of Transylvania remained within Romania. The treaty also recognized the Soviet annexation of northern Bukovina and Bessarabia. Both those areas had first come under Soviet control in the summer of 1940 (see Map 45). Now, for the second time, they were being "reunited" with their Soviet motherlands. Northern Bukovina was joined to the Ukrainian S.S.R.; most of Bessarabia, with its capital of Chişinău, became part of the Moldavian S.S.R.; and the southern coastal region of Bessarabia, with the Danubian port of Izmaïl/ Ismail, went to the Ukrainian S.S.R. Romania was also forced to accept the 1940 acquisition of the southern Dobruja, with the Danubian port of Silistra, by Bulgaria.

The Treaty of Paris recognized Yugoslavia's acquisition of all former Italian territory on the eastern side of the Adriatic. This included the Dalmatian city of Zadar/Zara and the islands of Cres/Cherso, Lošinj/Lusino, and Lastovo/ Lagosta, as well as the formerly contentious city of Rijeka/ Fiume (see Map 38) and, farther north, western Slovenia and part of Istria. The fate of Trieste and its immediate hinterland remained undecided. Consequently, it was transformed into a Free Territory administered by Anglo-American forces in the north and by Yugoslav forces in the south (see also Map 42a). Finally, the Paris peace treaty awarded the previously Italian-ruled Dodecanese Islands to Greece, which now ruled virtually all the islands in the Aegean Sea.

As a result of World War II, German and Italian dominance in East Central Europe was replaced by that of the Soviet Union. The Red Army together with its partisan allies in Yugoslavia and Albania was in control of the entire region (with the exception of Greece) at the war's end. The military presence of the Red Army was accompanied by Soviet political influence, so that between 1945 and 1948 all governments in the region with the exception of Greece came to be dominated by Communist parties that transformed their countries into people's republics closely allied, if not completely subordinate, to the Soviet Union.

Although Yugoslavia broke with the Soviet Union in 1948, the remaining Communist-led countries of East Central Europe came to be increasingly under the influence of their powerful neighbor to the east. Consequently, the Soviet bloc, as these states came to be known, grew more and more isolated from the rest of Europe, so much so that in the late 1940s an unbroken frontier of barbed wire, watchtowers, and walls existed along the western boundaries of the Soviet military zone in Germany, Czechoslovakia, and Hungary. In part, this was a concrete realization of the symbolic "iron curtain" that, in 1946, Great Britain's wartime prime minister, Winston Churchill (1874–1965), proclaimed had descended across Europe from "Stettin (Szczecin) on the Baltic to Trieste on the Adriatic." After 1961, the Berlin Wall became the ultimate symbol of the East-West division of Europe and of the worldwide antagonism between the superpowers.

In terms of internal administrative structure, only Yugoslavia and to a very limited degree Romania included within their boundaries territories enjoying some form of local autonomy. In keeping with the promises of Marshal Tito's wartime Partisan movement and the Anti-Fascist Council for National Liberation (AVNOJ), Yugoslavia was transformed into a federal republic whose component parts were intended to coincide in some measure with ethnolinguistic and/or historical boundaries. Six national republics were established: Slovenia, Croatia, Bosnia-Herzegovina, Serbia, Montenegro, and Macedonia. Five of these were to encompass most if not all of the ethnolinguistic group after which the republic was named; the sixth, Bosnia-Herzegovina, was derived from a historic region that included Serbs, Croats, and Bosnian Muslims. For one republic, Serbia, two autonomous regions were created: (1) Kosovo-Metohija, inhabited primarily by Albanians, and (2) the Vojvodina, an ethnolinguistically heterogeneous area that included five official nationalities and several other minorities.

The creation of one autonomous region in Romania came about as a result of external pressure. According to a bilateral treaty of 1947, the Soviets backed Romania's claim for its reacquisition from Hungary of northern Transylvania on condition that it grant autonomy to the part of the region that was inhabited primarily by Magyars and their closely related brethren, the Székelys. An Autonomous Magyar Region was set up in 1952 with its capital at Tîrgu-Mureş/ Marosvásárhely. The Romanians were never satisfied, however, with this externally imposed solution. Hence the Autonomous Magyar Region was reconstituted in 1959, with a reduction of its Magyar- and Székely-inhabited area to the south and an increase in its Romanian-inhabited area on the east and west. While the capital remained Tîrgu-Mureş, the region was renamed in 1960 simply Mureş. Finally, in 1965, it was stripped of its autonomous status, making it no different from any other Romanian province.

48 Population movements, 1944–1948

The end of World War II prompted significant changes in political boundaries, most especially in the northern part of East Central Europe. Even greater, however, was the alteration of the region's ethnolinguistic composition. By the war's end, statesmen had become convinced that the presence of large numbers of ethnolinguistic minorities within the states of East Central Europe was one of the major factors that during the interwar years had created political instability and eventually military conflict. It was thought that this problem could be corrected if political boundaries were altered and people were moved—by force, if necessary—so that ethnolinguistic boundaries would coincide with political boundaries. Thus, in the period from 1944 to 1948, no less than 31 million people in East Central Europe were uprooted and moved from what in most cases had been for decades, even centuries, their homes and the homes of their ancestors.

In fact, the demographic engineering within East Central Europe did not begin with the immediate postwar years. There were two stages in the process during which the following numbers of people were permanently or temporarily resettled: (1) 1939 through 1943—15.1 million people; and (2) 1944 through 1948—31 million people. Added to these were another 16.3 million people who perished during the war because of military, political, or racial policies. This means that a staggering total of 62.4 million people in East Central Europe were either deliberately killed or displaced during the decade following the outbreak of World War II in 1939.

The first period lasted from 1939 through 1943, when Nazi Germany and its Axis partners were still in their ascendancy. The changes in political boundaries which the Axis brought about were accompanied by efforts to eliminate or to resettle whole groups of people. Physical elimination affected, in particular, the Jews and Gypsies, as well as Poles, Ukrainians, Belorussians, and Russians who came under the rule of the Third Reich. Resettlement applied primarily to Germans, although numerous other groups were affected as well.

By 1945 from 4.7 to 5.4 million Jews (out of an estimated 5 to 6 million who perished throughout all of Europe) had been deliberately killed in East Central Europe. This was part of the so-called Final Solution, Nazi Germany's attempt to resolve what it considered the racial problem (the existence of inferior peoples—*Untermenschen*) in territories incorporated into the Third Reich and in those lands that had come under German military control. As a result, by the end of World War II, the centuries-old Jewish civilization that had been an integral part of many areas in East Central Europe (see Map 33) was virtually abolished. The following figures are drawn from studies by Raul Hilberg (Bibliography, Section D) and Evyatar Friesel (Section C).

Estimated deaths of Jews by 1945
(Countries according to boundaries of January 1938)

	Hilberg	Friesel	Percentage[1]
Poland	3,000,000	3,000,000	92
Soviet Union	700,000	1,200,000	42
Romania	270,000	400,000	47
Czechoslovakia	260,000	270,000	85
Hungary	180,000	300,000	75
Lithuania	130,000	135,000	90
Yugoslavia	60,000	55,000	73
Greece	60,000	60,000	80
Austria	50,000	65,000	77
Danzig	1,000	—	—
	4,711,000	5,485,000	

[1] The percentage killed of the 1938 Jewish population in each country is based on Friesel's figures.

Nazi racial policy was also directed against the Gypsies, of whom an estimated 200,000 from East Central Europe perished in German death camps. Added to these were another 9 to 10 million people—mostly Poles, Ukrainians, Belorussians, and Russians—who were killed during the German sweep into East Central Europe or who died after incarceration in prisoner-of-war and slave labor camps where they were sent because of their low standing in the Nazi racial hierarchy.

Also in the category of elimination, although based on political rather than racial policies, was the forced expulsion of peoples who came under Soviet rule in 1939–41. This included the eastward deportation of an estimated 1,500,000 Poles and Ukrainians from former eastern Poland (Volhynia and Galicia) and 60,000 Lithuanians from what became Soviet Lithuania in 1940. Many of these people perished before the end of the war.

With regard to resettlement during World War II, there were two kinds: temporary and permanent. Temporary resettlement affected no less than 13.5 million people. These included an estimated 8 million Poles, Ukrainians, Jews, Belorussians, and Lithuanians who fled eastward following the German invasion of the Soviet Union in June 1941. Then, with the establishment of German rule in this and other parts of East Central Europe, over 5.5 million foreign workers were brought, in most cases forcibly, to Germany. The vast majority of these were Poles, Ukrainians, Czechs, and Russians, although there were also smaller numbers of Slovenes, Serbs, Croats, Romanians, and Bulgarians.

As for permanent resettlement during World War II, this was brought about by several bilateral treaties between those states whose boundaries had changed in the early years of the conflict. Germany, in particular, was concerned with "returning" to the Third Reich those ethnic Germans (Volksdeutsche), who in some cases had for centuries lived

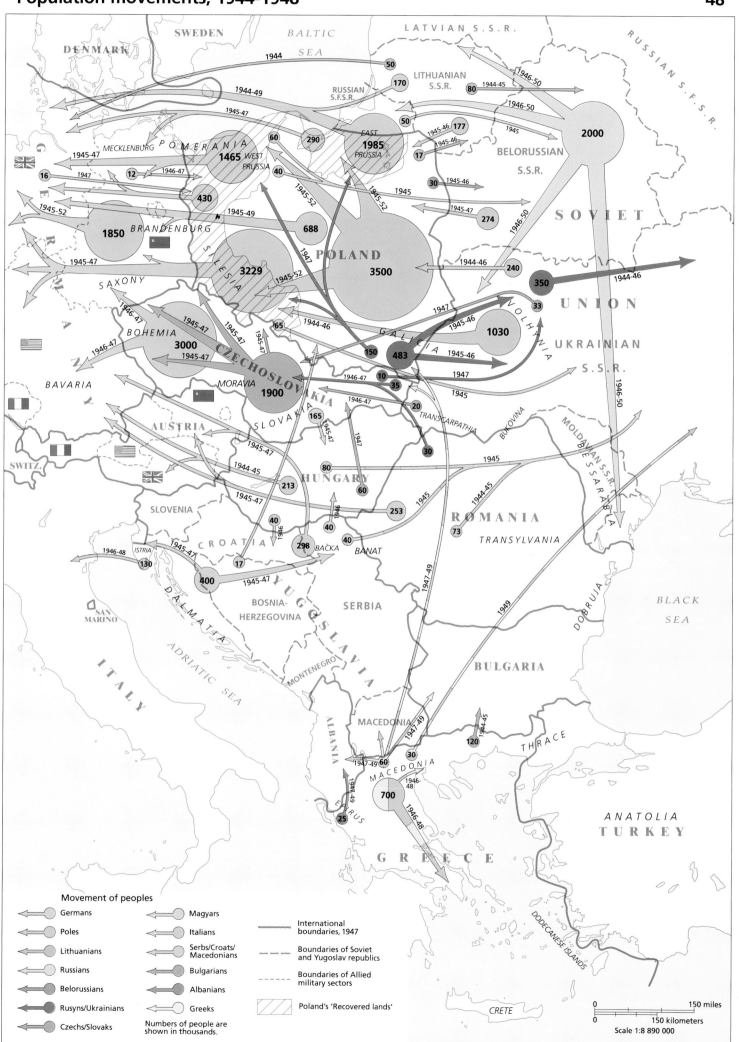

Population movements, 1944-1948

SWEDEN
BALTIC
DENMARK
SEA
LATVIAN S.S.R.
RUSSIAN S.F.S.R.

1944
50
LITHUANIAN S.S.R.
1944-49
170
RUSSIAN S.F.S.R.
1946-50
1945-47
50
80 1944-45
1946-50
MECKLENBURG POMERANIA
60
290
EAST 1985 177
PRUSSIA
1945-46
1945
1465
WEST
40
PRUSSIA
17 1945-46
BELORUSSIAN S.S.R.
2000
16 1947 12 1946-47
430
30 1945-46
1945
SOVIET
1945-52
1850 BRANDENBURG
688
274
1945-49
350
UNION
1945-47
3229 SILESIA
POLAND
240
1944-46
1945-52 3500
1944-46
SAXONY
1945-52
33
VOLHYNIA
BOHEMIA 1946-47
1947
1030
UKRAINIAN
1945-47
65 1944-46 1945-46
3000 1945-47 CZECHOSLOVAKIA
150
483 1945-46
S.S.R.
BAVARIA 1946-47 MORAVIA 1945-47
10
1947
1900
35
1945
SLOVAKIA
20 TRANSCARPATHIA
BUKOVINA
SWITZ. AUSTRIA 165 1946-47
MOLDAVIAN S.S.R. BESSARABIA
1945-47 1945-47
30
1945
1944-45 213 HUNGARY 60
253 ROMANIA
1945-47 80
SLOVENIA 40 40
73 TRANSYLVANIA
CROATIA 298 BAČKA 40
1946-48 ISTRIA 17 BANAT
130 1945-47
400 DALMATIA
DOBRUJA BLACK SEA
SAN MARINO
BOSNIA-HERZEGOVINA YUGOSLAVIA SERBIA
ITALY ADRIATIC SEA
BULGARIA
1947-49
MONTENEGRO
1949
ALBANIA MACEDONIA
1947-49
120 1944-45
THRACE
60 30
1947-49 MACEDONIA 1946-48
700
ANATOLIA
TURKEY
EPIRUS 25 1946-48
G R E E C E
CRETE
DODECANESE ISLANDS

Movement of peoples

Germans	Magyars	
Poles	Italians	
Lithuanians	Serbs/Croats/Macedonians	
Russians	Bulgarians	
Belorussians	Albanians	
Rusyns/Ukrainians	Greeks	
Czechs/Slovaks		

International boundaries, 1947

Boundaries of Soviet and Yugoslav republics

Boundaries of Allied military sectors

Poland's 'Recovered lands'

Numbers of people are shown in thousands.

Scale 1:8 890 000
150 miles
150 kilometers

beyond the boundaries of the German fatherland. The vast majority of these Germans were resettled in the recently acquired areas of the Third Reich (Pomerania, Wartheland, Generalgouvernement) that had been part of prewar Poland (see Map 45).

Transfer of Germans, 1939–1944

Country with whom Germany signed treaty (and date)	Area of residence	Number evacuated
Soviet Union (November 3, 1939)	Volhynia, Galicia, Narev River area	128,000
Soviet Union (September 5, 1940)	Bessarabia, northern Bukovina	93,000 42,000
Romania (October 22, 1940)	Southern Bukovina, northern Dobruja	55,000 14,000
Soviet Union (January 10, 1941)	Lithuania	66,000
Italy (September 1941)	Southern Slovenia (Gottschee)	15,000
Croatia (October 6, 1942)	Bosnia-Herzegovina, northeastern Croatia	19,000
		432,000

Added to the above were another 360,000 Germans transferred from lands that had come under the control of the German military or that were ruled by countries allied to the Third Reich: Soviet Ukraine (190,000), Romanian Transnistria (135,000), Generalgouvernement (30,000), Serbia (2,000), and Bulgaria (2,000). This meant that before the war ended, a total of 784,000 Germans were transferred from their ancestral homelands by the resettlement policy of the Third Reich.

Besides Germans, several other groups were affected by bilateral treaties between countries that hoped their newly drawn political boundaries (see Map 45) might coincide better with ethnolinguistic boundaries.

Besides these were over half a million people displaced in the absence of any formal treaty arrangement: 120,000

Slovenes from German-annexed northern Slovenia, who in 1941 were deported or fled to Serbia, other parts of Germany, or neighboring Italian-held southern Slovenia; 90,000 Greeks from Bulgarian-annexed southeastern Macedonia and western Thrace forced in 1941 to move southward into German-occupied areas of Greece and even to the Third Reich (Austria); 122,000 Bulgarians resettled in 1942–43 into formerly Greek-ruled eastern Macedonia and western Thrace; 120,000 Serbs from Croatia forcibly evacuated after 1941 to German-ruled Serbia; 70,000 Croats from Serbia and the Banat resettled during the same years to Croatia; and the return home of 40,000 Italians from Albania and the Dodecanese Islands after the defeat of Italy in 1943.

In summation, during the first five years of World War II, 15.4 million people were displaced. Of these, nearly 1.9 million were intended to be permanently resettled in an effort to have ethnolinguistic boundaries coincide with political boundaries.

Population transfers, 1939–1943

Temporary resettlement	13,500,000
Permanent resettlement	1,892,000
	15,392,000

This wartime trend at planned demographic change not only continued after hostilities were over but substantially intensified, so that between late 1944 and 1948 an estimated 31 million more people were resettled within and beyond East Central Europe. Some of this resettlement was directly related to the war. As the Soviet military moved farther and farther westward in the course of 1944, military personnel, local functionaries, and other collaborators with Germany and its defeated allies, as well as people who were simply afraid of the approaching Red Army, fled westward to those sectors of Germany and Austria that had come or were about to come under the control of the western Allies (Britain, the United States, and France).

The largest number of those who in 1944–45 fled westward before the Red Army were Germans. No less than 5

Population transfers in the Balkans, 1940–1943

Group	Countries affected (date of treaty)	Original residence and destination	Number transferred
Romanians	Romania-Bulgaria (September 7, 1940)	Southern Dobruja to northern Dobruja	100,000
Bulgarians	Bulgaria-Romania (September 7, 1940)	Northern Dobruja to southern Dobruja	61,000
Romanians	Romania-Hungary (August 30, 1940)	Northern Transylvania to Romania	219,000
Magyars	Hungary-Romania (August 30, 1940)	Southern Transylvania to Hungary	160,000
Croats	Croatia-Germany (August 11, 1943)	Southern Styria to Croatia	6,000
			546,000

million Germans left the collapsing eastern portion of the Third Reich—East Prussia, Danzig, West Prussia, Pomerania, east Brandenburg, and Silesia—as well as another half million who had been resettled during the war in the Generalgouvernement and other eastern lands of the Third Reich (former prewar Poland). Added to these were an estimated 100,000 Germans who fled Romania when its government became an ally of the Soviet Union (August 1944) and an unspecified number of Germans (Danube Swabians) who fled as the Red Army entered Hungary.

Certainly not all who wanted to flee were able to do so. The result was that when the Red Army came to control most of East Central Europe, an estimated 408,000 Germans were in late 1944 and early 1945 forcibly deported to the Soviet Union; specifically 215,000 from the eastern regions of the Third Reich (East Prussia, West Prussia, Pomerania, Silesia); 120,000 together with Magyars from Hungary and Yugoslavia (the Banat); and 73,000 from Romania. Also, from German-held Lithuania, an estimated 50,000 Lithuanians fled westward with the retreating German army in 1944, while among those left behind, approximately 80,000 were deported eastward by the Soviet authorities in 1944–45.

Regarding the eastward flow of population, a special case were former Soviet citizens—that is, persons who lived within the pre-1939 boundaries of the Soviet Union. Of the 8,350,000 Soviet citizens displaced during the war, 5,600,000 survived. Approximately 3 million of the survivors found themselves within the military sphere of the Red Army and were immediately returned to the Soviet Union. As for the remaining 2.6 million, the agreement reached at Yalta (February 1945) obliged the western Allies to repatriate them to the Soviet Union. In 1945–46, about 2 million were repatriated (some forcibly) from the western sectors of Germany and Austria to the Soviet Union. This number (not shown on the accompanying map) included persons who during the war had been deported to Germany as forced laborers and those persons who, for the various reasons elaborated upon above, fled in 1944–45 before the advancing Red Army. The vast majority of the repatriates were Ukrainians (1,250,000), followed by smaller numbers of Belorussians, Russians, and Cossacks. Because the Soviet government was suspicious of the repatriates, especially those returned forcibly, many were deported with other politically unreliable elements (350,000 Ukrainians) to the eastern parts of the Soviet Union.

Numerically more significant, however, were the population transfers carried out in peacetime. The first major postwar conference held by the victorious Allies at Potsdam (July 17–August 2, 1945) agreed to the request of Czechoslovakia and Poland that citizens of German ethnicity living within their respective borders should be transferred to what remained of postwar Germany. Thus, between 1946 and 1947, over 3 million Germans were deported from the Sudetenland of Czechoslovakia (nearly two-thirds to the American zone, the remainder to the Soviet zone); 3,325,000 from the "Recovered Lands" of Poland (57 percent to the British zone, 43 percent to the Soviet zone); and 250,000 from Hungary (mostly to the American zone of Germany and some to the British zone of Austria).

Aside from the German expulsion from Poland, Czechoslovakia, and Hungary, the next largest population transfers resulted from two agreements signed in September 1944 between the Soviet Union and Poland. All persons of Polish and Jewish ethnonational identity who were citizens of Poland before September 17, 1939 (that is, who resided within Poland's prewar boundaries) and who found themselves in the postwar Lithuanian, Belorussian, and Ukrainian Soviet republics could be evacuated to Poland. Correspondingly, Ukrainians, Belorussians, and Lithuanians living within postwar Poland (west of the Curzon Line) could choose Soviet citizenship and move east. In theory, the transfers were to be voluntary, and when they were completed in 1946, a total of 530,000 persons went eastward to their respective Soviet republics—Ukrainians (483,000), Belorussians (30,000), and Lithuanians (17,000). The opposite movement of Poles (and Jews) westward lasted from late 1944 through 1947, during which time 1,481,000 Poles (about 200,000 of whom were Jews) left Soviet territory. At the same time another 256,000 Poles left areas in the Soviet Union beyond the Ukrainian, Belorussian, and Lithuanian republics, whose repatriation was permitted by a third Polish-Soviet agreement reached in July 1945. Besides the over 1.7 million people in the organized transfer, there were another estimated 70,000 demobilized Polish soldiers and 240,000 Polish settlers (mostly from the western Ukraine) who left Soviet territory for Poland. These same years also witnessed the repatriation of 520,000 Poles deported to Germany during the war as forced laborers and the transfer of another 28,000 from Germany (who had been living as colonists especially in Westphalia since the nineteenth century) and 17,000 from Yugoslavia (settled primarily in Bosnia since the 1890s).

There were several other organized population transfers in East Central Europe, but these were much smaller in scale. When Bulgaria surrendered to the Allies in September 1944, it agreed to the repatriation of the 120,000 Bulgarians it had settled after 1941 in that part of Greece (eastern Macedonia and western Thrace) that it had occupied. As part of the June 1945 treaty that ceded Czechoslovakia's former province of Subcarpathian Rus' (Transcarpathia) to the Soviet Union, Czechs and Slovaks living there were given the option to move west to Czechoslovakia, and in 1946–47 about 20,000 did so. Rusyns/Ukrainians living in postwar Czechoslovakia were given the option to move eastward, but few did so. One year later, a second Czechoslovak-Soviet agreement was signed (July 1946) permitting the transfer of 33,000 Czechs from the Soviet Ukraine (they had settled in Volhynia in the 1870s) to Czechoslovakia (primarily Bohemia) in return for about 10,000 Rusyns/Ukrainians from northeastern Slovakia. Czechoslovakia also signed a treaty with Romania, allowing 30,000 Rusyns/Ukrainians into Czechoslovakia.

As with its German population, postwar Czechoslovakia initially hoped to expel most, if not all, of its Magyar minority from southern Slovakia. Between 1945 and 1947, an estimated 165,000 Magyars left for Hungary, which included those (32,000) who had settled in southern Slovakia only after it was annexed by Hungary in November 1938 and who were expelled immediately in 1945; those (60,000) long-time residents of the area who decided to leave between 1945 and 1947; and those (73,000) who in 1947 were exchanged for 60,000 Slovaks from Hungary as part of an agreement on the exchange of populations signed (February 1946) between Czechoslovakia and Hungary.

Yugoslavia reached a bilateral agreement with Hungary in 1946 for the exchange of 40,000 Magyars (mostly from the Bačka) for 40,000 Serbs and Croats. Also with the establishment of Yugoslav rule throughout all of Dalmatia and most of Istria, an estimated 130,000 Italians left for Italy.

Besides the organized transfers of population, there was also large-scale flight in the immediate postwar years. Foremost was the exodus of Germans from the Soviet zone (later East Germany) to what after 1949 became West Germany. Until 1952, while East Germany's western border was not yet sealed, an estimated 985,000 Germans fled westward. Finally, there were the 970,000 Jews in East Central Europe (minus Soviet territory) who either survived the war or were repatriated to their countries of origin. In 1945, the largest Jewish communities were in Romania (430,000), Poland (225,000), and Hungary (200,000), but the trauma of the Holocaust followed by the difficulties and even persecution that some met in the new postwar environment prompted a wave of Jewish emigration that is known in Jewish annals as the Escape (*Briha*). Between 1945 and 1948, a total of 220,000 Jews left Poland (150,000), Romania (40,000), Hungary (25,000), and Czechoslovakia (5,000). Most made their way clandestinely to the American zone in Germany or the British zone in Austria from where they were transferred either to the Mediterranean ports of Italy for the sea voyage to Palestine or to ports in the British zone of Germany for the passage across the Atlantic to North and South America.

Considering the vast number of departures from various parts of East Central Europe, efforts were undertaken to replace the lost population through internal migration. Three and one-half million Poles from central Poland were resettled on the "Recovered Lands" where Germans had once lived. Most of the 1.7 million Poles who came from the Soviet Union were also resettled in the "Recovered Lands," as were the Poles repatriated from the Soviet and British zones of Germany (520,000) and Yugoslavia (17,000), and 150,000 Ukrainians and Rusyns (known locally as Lemkos) forcibly expelled in 1947 from the southeastern corner of Poland during that government's struggle against the Ukrainian anti-Communist underground movement.

In the western regions of the Soviet Union, the departing Poles and Jews were replaced in part by Ukrainians, Lithuanians, and Belorussians who came as part of the population exchange from Poland. However, an even greater portion of the replacements consisted of nearly 2 million people from other parts of the Soviet Union. These included Ukrainians and Belorussians from the eastern (prewar) parts of their republics, as well as Russians who for the first time were to be settled in significant numbers, especially in cities of Soviet Lithuania, western Belorussia, western Ukraine, and Moldavia.

In Czechoslovakia, the departing Germans from the Sudetenland rim of Bohemia and Moravia were replaced by 1,900,000 Czechs, Slovaks, and Carpatho-Rusyns. In Yugoslavia, the departed German, Italian, and Magyar minorities in the north-central and far-western parts of the country were replaced by nearly 400,000 migrants. For the most part these were Serbs from western Croatia and Bosnia-Herzegovina, who with a few thousand Montenegrins moved to the Vojvodina (Bačka and Banat). At the same time, smaller numbers of Croats moved from west-central Croatia to that republic's Istrian peninsula.

Another significant population transfer that took place during the postwar years was the direct result of military conflict—the civil war between Communist and non-Communist forces in Greece. The war and the Communist forces were concentrated primarily in the northern Greek province of Macedonia, and during the conflict (1946–49) nearly 700,000 Greeks and Macedonians were displaced, mostly to Athens and Salonika. Whereas many returned to their villages after the war was over, an estimated 90,000 Greeks (60 percent) and Macedonians (40 percent) were forced to flee to Yugoslavia and other Communist countries (Albania, Bulgaria, Czechoslovakia, Poland, Soviet Union). The refugees included at first children removed for their safety during the civil war, a frightened civilian population, and finally the guerrilla fighters themselves who went mostly to Tashkent in Soviet Central Asia. After 1956, most of the Macedonian refugees (by then with expanded families) settled in Yugoslav Macedonia; during the late 1970s, the Greek refugees were allowed to return to Greece. An Albanian minority (the Çams) numbering about 25,000 were also expelled from their homes along the coastal region of southern Epirus to Albania as a result of the Greek civil war.

In summation, during the last years of World War II and the immediate postwar years, over 31 million were permanently or temporarily moved (sometimes more than once) within East Central Europe.

Population transfers, 1944–1948

Flight before military fronts	5,650,000
Forced deportations to the Soviet Union	488,000
Repatriation to the Soviet Union	5,000,000
Organized postwar transfers	9,937,000
Unorganized postwar resettlement	1,760,000
Internal postwar resettlement (to 1950)	8,300,000
	31,135,000

The unprecedented demographic changes that were set in motion by World War II and accelerated in the immediate postwar years have had two basic results. First, the historic presence of Jews and Germans (with the exception of Transylvania) has been virtually eliminated in East Central Europe. Second, in contrast to the interwar years, countries like Poland, Czechoslovakia, and Hungary (with Bulgaria not far behind) have become more like Albania and Greece in that well over 90 percent of the population in each of these states is represented by a single (or, in the case of Czechoslovakia, dual) state nationality. (See the statistical charts accompanying Chapters 39–43.)

49 Industrial development, 1945–1989

The socioeconomic structure of East Central Europe was profoundly altered as a result of the establishment between 1945 and 1948 of Communist-dominated governments in all countries of the region with the exception of Austria and Greece. The Communists were inspired by Marxism, an ideology concerned with economic evolution. Consequently, each of the new Communist governments set out to create centralized state structures with command economies that would either expand an already existing industrial base or transform agriculturally based economies into industrial ones. The command economy, based largely on the Soviet model, was adopted and was to remain in place until the political changes of the 1980s that culminated in the Revolution of 1989. Since that time, the former Communist-ruled countries of East Central Europe have been trying to adopt market-oriented economies that will be compatible with the rest of Europe. Of the two countries in the region that after World War II were not governed by Marxist ideology, Austria has expanded its historic industrial base while Greece has remained industrially underdeveloped.

With regard to the majority of countries within the former Communist sphere, three trends dominated their socioeconomic development between 1945 and 1989: (1) the steady migration of population from rural to urban areas and the concomitant growth of cities; (2) the establishment of state-run industrial enterprises in agricultural and formerly economically peripheral regions; and (3) the expansion of a network of pipelines from the Soviet Union to supply natural resources (especially oil and natural gas), in particular to Poland, East Germany, Czechoslovakia, Hungary, and Bulgaria. As a result, those countries became economically as well as politically more dependent on their powerful neighbor to the east.

The predominantly agrarian nature that historically had characterized most of East Central Europe (with the exception of the area within the Halle-Łódź-Budapest triangle discussed below) has changed substantially since World War II. Although the definition of "urban" varies greatly from country to country, the general trend seems to suggest a marked increase of urbanization in many of the countries of East Central Europe between the pre– and post–World War II years.

The urbanization process has been especially marked by the growth of large cities. By the late-1980s, East Central Europe (including the western republics of the Soviet Union) had twenty-three cities with more than 500,000 inhabitants, twelve of which had more than a million inhabitants each.

In terms of industrial development, East Central Europe continues to reflect locational patterns established in the past. Ever since the last decades of the nineteenth century, the greatest concentration of industrial enterprises has been around Berlin and Warsaw, and most particularly within an inverse triangle bounded roughly by the cities of Halle (East Germany), Łódź (Poland), and Budapest (Hungary). It was the presence of natural resources within this triangular area—especially coal—that encouraged the three pre–World War I empires to promote industrial growth in the

Population distribution

Country	Population	Percentage of urban population	
	ca. 1990	1930s	1970s
Albania	3,182,000	15.4	33.2
Austria	7,812,000	35.5	44.0
Bulgaria	8,949,000	21.4	46.5
Czechoslovakia	15,568,000	38.9	51.7
East Germany	16,706,000	72.2	73.1
Greece	10,269,000	32.8	56.2
Hungary	10,375,000	33.2	45.0
Poland	37,879,000	30.0	51.2
Romania	23,152,000	21.4	38.2
Yugoslavia	22,424,000	13.2	28.3

Sources: National statistics; Leszek A. Kosiński, "Urbanization in East Central Europe after World War II," *East European Quarterly* 8, 2 (1974): 129–53.

East Central Europe's largest cities

	Ca. 1950	Ca. 1989	Percentage of change
Istanbul	1,179,000	5,843,000	+395
Berlin	3,337,000	3,353,000	+0.5
(West Berlin	2,147,000	2,068,000)	
(East Berlin	1,190,000	1,285,000)	
Kiev	1,104,000	2,587,000	+134
Budapest	1,571,000	2,114,000	+35
Bucharest	886,000	1,990,000	+125
Warsaw	601,000	1,651,000	+175
Vienna	1,616,000	1,488,000	−8
Minsk	509,000	1,589,000	+212
Belgrade	368,000	1,088,000	+196
Prague	922,000	1,214,000	+32
Odessa	667,000	1,115,000	+67
Sofia	435,000	1,137,000	+161
Athens	565,000	886,000	+57
Łódź	593,000	851,000	+44
Zagreb	280,000	650,000	+132
L'viv	411,000	790,000	+92
Cracow	347,000	744,000	+114
Chișinău	236,000	665,000	+182
Wrocław	279,000	637,000	+128
Vilnius	235,000	582,000	+148
Poznań	359,000	586,000	+63
Leipzig	618,000	545,000	−12
Dresden	494,000	518,000	+5

Sources: B. R. Mitchell, *European Historical Statistics, 1750–1970* (London and Basingstoke, 1975), pp. 76–79; *Britannica Book of the Year 1991* (Chicago, 1991).

49b

49a

Legend

Zones of pre-1939 concentration of industry

Natural gas pipeline

'Brotherhood' and 'Alliance' pipelines

Oil pipeline

'Friendship' pipeline

Major gas field

Major oil field

Major coal field (Map 49b only)

Rivers navigable for heavy transport

Canals

- - - International boundaries, 1980

— - — Socialist republic boundaries

Major industrial centers

Existing centers restored and expanded after 1945

Centers newly-established since 1945

```
0                    100 miles
|----|----|----|----|----|
0                    100 kilometers
Scale 1:8 890 000
```

49a Upper Silesia

UPPER SILESIA INDUSTRIAL REGION (GOP)

Kędzierzyn Koźle · Bytom · Zabrze · Dąbrowa Górnicza · Gliwice · Chorzów · Sosnowiec · Katowice · Tychy · Rybnik · Czechowice Dziedzice

POLAND

Opava · Ostrava · Karviná · Frýdek Místek · Kopřivnice · Třinec · Bielsko-Biała

Limit of Coal Field

CZECHOSLOVAKIA

historic regions of Saxony and Silesia (German Empire), western Poland and Upper Silesia (Russian Empire), and Bohemia, Moravia, Lower Austria, and northwestern Hungary (Austro-Hungarian Empire). During the interwar years, Germany, Poland, Czechoslovakia, and Hungary promoted further growth within this triangle, while a few other areas in Poland, Yugoslavia, and Romania also had zones of industrial concentration.

Despite the concerted efforts made since 1945 by the state-run command economies to disperse their industrial sites more evenly throughout their territories, by the mid-1970s as high as 75 percent of industrial output in East Central Europe still came from the Halle-Łódź-Budapest triangle. Within that area, the greatest concentration of heavy industry—in particular steel production, machinery, and chemicals—was found in Upper Silesia. Since 1945, this region has been within the boundaries of Poland and a small section of Czechoslovakia (see the inset Map 49a). The location of large industrial sites in Upper Silesia is directly related to the large bituminous coal field that has traditionally provided power for local factories as well as for export. In order to coordinate industrial production, Poland created within this area a distinct administrative region, the Upper Silesia Industrial Region (Górnośląski Okręg Przemysłowy—GOP), dominated by the city of Katowice. Before World War II, this region was already an important industrial complex with over a million inhabitants; by the mid-1970s, it had grown to over 3 million inhabitants and has remained the largest industrial region throughout all of East Central Europe.

Beyond the Halle-Łódź-Budapest triangle, East Central Europe's Communist governments (excepting Austria and Greece) tried through centralized socialist planning to encourage industrial growth and thereby transfer wealth from advanced to formerly backward agricultural regions. The spread of new industrial enterprises was particularly evident in the northern half of East Germany, northern and eastern Poland, eastern Czechoslovakia (Slovakia), eastern Hungary, Moldavia in Romania, and the upland regions of

Yugoslavia's republics of Bosnia-Herzegovina, Serbia, Montenegro, and Macedonia.

Such geographic dispersion was motivated by economic and political reasons. For instance, the location of industries in the eastern regions of Poland, Czechoslovakia, and Hungary made them nearer to power sources from the neighboring Soviet Union. Dispersion also placed industries closer to local markets and helped to ensure a more even distribution of job possibilities, thus alleviating the formerly chronic underemployment or unemployment as well as poverty in rural areas. Finally, since many of these peripheral regions were inhabited by peoples that before 1945 had been considered national minorities (Slovaks, Bosnian Muslims, Macedonians, etc.), industrial development was expected both to increase living standards and to reduce political tensions.

During the 1950s, each of the East European Communist states promoted industrial diversification which aimed at creating a balanced autarkic economy for each country. By the end of the decade, however, Soviet leaders were calling for regional specialization within these states and for greater economic integration among them and with the Soviet Union. The object was to create a common policy and to coordinate growth so that the "East bloc" nations together with the Soviet Union might eventually form a single economic unit. This was to be achieved through the Council for Mutual Economic Assistance (CMEA), or Comecon, first established in 1949 but not effectively activated until a decade later. Because of political conflicts, Yugoslavia never joined Comecon and Albania played no active part after 1962. On the other hand, beginning in 1964, Yugoslavia participated in certain Comecon activities, especially the hydroelectric power project through the Danube River's "Iron Gates" just west of Turnu-Severin. Thus until 1989, Comecon's program of economic integration in East Central Europe applied to East Germany, Poland, Czechoslovakia, Hungary, Bulgaria, and to a lesser degree Romania.

The most dramatic indication of this integrative trend was the construction of oil and natural gas pipelines from the Soviet Union to its Comecon partners. The "Friendship" (Druzhba) pipeline, originating at Kuibyshev along the middle course of the Volga River basin, reached the Belorussian S.S.R., where it split into southern and northern branches. The southern branch, which supplies Czechoslovakia and Hungary, was completed between 1960 and 1964, with a second expanded parallel pipeline added to Hungary in 1972–74. The northern branch to Poland and East Germany was completed in the early 1980s. In each receiving country a major refinery was built (Płock, Schwedt, Bratislava, Budapest), where the crude oil was transformed into petroleum for local consumption. There was no pipeline to Bulgaria; instead, that country received Soviet oil imports via ship at the Black Sea port of Burgas. Burgas became the site of a refinery with a pipeline supplying the country's southern industrial centers.

Natural gas lines from the Soviet Union to Comecon countries (excepting Romania) were even more widespread. Among the earliest of these was the "Brotherhood" (Bratstvo) pipeline completed in 1967 from gas fields south of L'viv in western Ukraine to Bratislava in

49b Halle-Łódź-Budapest industrial triangle

Czechoslovakia. The further development of major Soviet natural gas fields—the East Ukrainian fields along the middle Dnieper River, the Pechora and Ukhta fields in the Komi A.S.S.R., the Upper Lena fields in central Siberia—prompted the construction of several new lines across Soviet Belorussia and Soviet Ukraine. These all converged in western Ukraine (south and west of L'viv) before entering Poland, Czechoslovakia, Hungary, and from Hungary on to Yugoslavia. Especially important was the "Alliance" (Soiuz) natural gas pipeline completed in 1979. It began at the major field near Orenburg in the southern Urals, and before entering northern Ukraine it had a branch to Bulgaria. The main "Alliance" line passed through Kiev and western Ukraine to a juncture south of L'viv, where it ran parallel to the older "Brotherhood" line in Czechoslovakia with a continuation into East Germany. Aside from branches to Bulgaria, Poland, and Hungary, the "Alliance" line across Czechoslovakia also included branches that provided Soviet natural gas exports to Austria and West Germany, and from those countries to Yugoslavia, Italy, and France as well.

Whereas there were no major exports of Soviet oil to the rest of Europe, a branch of the "Friendship" oil line was extended from Budapest southward to Yugoslavia, supplying until 1989 one-quarter of Yugoslavia's needs. As for the countries that belonged to Comecon, only Romania was to a degree self-sufficient in both oil and gas. On the other hand, by the mid-1970s no less than 94.3 percent of the rest of Comecon's oil consumption came from Soviet imports—Czechoslovakia (100 percent), Poland (97.5 percent), Bulgaria (96.9 percent), Hungary (90.8 percent), and East Germany (86.1 percent).

Aside from Soviet imports, there are a few oil and natural gas fields within East Central Europe itself. The most important of these are the oil fields in Romania west and south of Ploieşti and Piteşti, and the natural gas fields of Transylvania, both of which supply local needs and provide for exports to Hungary. There are also several small oil and/or natural gas fields that provide for local consumption: in southwestern and southeastern Hungary; within the triangle of the Vistula and San rivers in southeastern Poland; near Ostrava in north-central Czechoslovakia; and between Vlorë and Elbasan in Albania.

For more than four decades after the close of World War II, there were no substantive boundary changes in East Central Europe. The only exception was the Free Territory of Trieste. It was abolished in 1954 and divided between Yugoslavia and Italy (see Map 42a). The status quo of the region's international boundaries was not to be challenged until the revolutionary changes that rocked East Central Europe in 1989. In November of that year, the Berlin Wall (see Map 47a)—that ultimate symbol of a divided Europe—was breached and eventually brought down. Within less than one year, the Communist government of East Germany fell, and in October 1990 the whole country ceased to exist. It voluntarily joined (with the approval of the four Allied powers) the Federal Republic of Germany. The five historic states on former East German territory—Mecklenburg, Saxony-Anhalt, Brandenburg, Saxony, and Thuringia—were restored, increasing the total number of states in the new united Germany to fifteen. Berlin was reunited and became once again the capital of Germany.

In contrast to the relative stability of international boundaries during most of the post–World War II period, the internal administrative structures of most East Central European states changed radically. This was directly related to establishment of Communist governments, which favored the principle of centralization. Hence, among Communist-ruled states, all but Yugoslavia adopted more or less uniform internal administrative patterns, which, in order to enhance centralization, tried to minimize any association with historic regions. Beginning in 1945, these pro-Soviet Communist states gradually established new administrative units (in some cases the changes occurred more than once). Despite the political changes that began in the 1980s and that culminated by the end of the decade in the fall or significant transformation of the Communist governments in each country, by 1992 these states still had the same administrative subdivisions that were established by the pre-1989 regimes.

Poland did retain the old provincial name for its basic administrative subdivision—palatinate (województwo)—but already in 1945–46 it had begun to change considerably their number and composition. As of the most recent change (1980), Poland has forty-nine palatinates. Three of these comprise the country's largest cities of Warsaw, Łódź, and Cracow, which have a provincial status distinct from the surrounding area which carries the same name.

In Czechoslovakia, the historic provinces (země/krajina) of Bohemia, Moravia-Silesia, and Slovakia were abolished the same year the Communists came to power (1948). They were replaced by nineteen smaller regions called kraje. In 1960, the kraje were consolidated into ten larger units, which have remained in place until the present. In 1969, the former centralized structure of Czechoslovakia was transformed into a federation of two equal states—the Czech Socialist Republic and the Slovak Socialist Republic. The ten regions remained in place, however, and two more were added encompassing the capitals of the two new republics: Prague and Bratislava. In early 1990, the adjective "socialist" was dropped from the names of the two component parts of what was renamed the Czech and Slovak Federated Republic. For the next two years, the Czech and Slovak republic governments tried to redefine their relationship. When they failed to reach a consensus, both parties agreed to dissolve the unitary state that in January 1993 was replaced by two independent countries: the Czech Republic and Slovakia.

Of all the Communist countries in the Soviet bloc, Hungary's internal administrative structure has been the most stable. The interwar division into counties (megye)—itself a remnant of the pre–World War I historic Hungarian kingdom's administrative divisions—remained in place, although in 1949 the Communist government reduced their number from twenty-seven (in the interwar period) to nineteen. This has remained the structure for Hungary, although the cities of Budapest, Győr, Miskolc, Debrecen, Szeged, and Pécs today have county status.

In contrast, Romania, Bulgaria, and Albania have all changed their administrative structure several times since Communist governments were established. The names of the subdivisions themselves have changed as well. Romania did away with its interwar districts (județe) and replaced them first with regiunes (1950), then raionuls (1960), and finally in 1968 back to județe, thirty-nine of which were established, including the capital of Bucharest as a distinct administrative entity. This is still the situation today. Bulgaria eliminated entirely its former district level (oblast) in 1947, leaving only ninety-five smaller units (okolias). Two years later, another district level (okrug) was established, although since then the number of districts has changed at various times from twelve to twenty-eight. The most recent change, in 1987, has reduced the number of districts to nine, including the city and okrug in the southwest part of the country, both called Sofia. Albania abolished its interwar prefectures, replacing them in 1949 with twenty-six districts (rrethe) plus the capital city of Tiranë as a district distinct from the surrounding area of the same name. Subsequent changes saw the creation of larger regions (1953, revised 1956), although as of 1987 a return to the twenty-seven districts (including the city of Tiranë) has been in force.

While Yugoslavia initially experimented (1949–51) with Soviet style oblasts that were subordinated directly to the central government, the division in 1945 of the federal state into six national republics and two autonomous regions was never abolished, and the power of those republics subsequently increased. Moreover, in 1974 the autonomous status of the provinces of Kosovo and Vojvodina was broadened, and each was given federal status in the new

State capitals

Capitals of socialist republics and German states

Capitals of autonomous regions

Province, district, county, or oblast centers

KOSOVO Names of autonomous regions and other administrative subdivisions other than their capitals or centers

— ·· — International boundaries, 1992

— — — Boundaries of socialist republics and German states

— — — Boundaries of autonomous regions

········· Boundaries of provinces, districts, counties, and oblasts

0   150 miles

0   150 kilometers

Scale 1:8 890 000

presidential council—the highest authority in the republic. In the wake of 1989 revolutionary events, however, the Serbian government revoked the autonomy of Kosovo and Vojvodina, and this contributed to tension with other republics that feared the growth of Serbian power within the Yugoslav federation. This led to an ongoing political crisis that culminated in referenda approving independence for Slovenia (December 23, 1990), Croatia (May 19, 1991), Macedonia (September 8, 1991), and Bosnia-Herzegovina (February 29–March 1, 1992). By 1992, in the midst of a bloody civil war, these new countries (with the exception of Macedonia) were recognized by the European Community and most other European states. What has remained of Yugoslavia are the republics of Serbia (including the formerly autonomous regions of Vojvodina and Kosovo) and Montenegro. Although as of early 1993 the boundaries of the new independent states are in theory the same as when they were republics in the Yugoslav federation, in fact their legitimacy has been challenged, in particular by Serbian minority separatist movements in Croatia and in Bosnia-Herzegovina.

In those areas of East Central Europe that were incorporated into the Soviet Union after 1945, there have also been significant changes. These began in 1985 with the access to leadership in the country by Mikhail S. Gorbachev (b. 1931). The increasing internal political changes initiated by Gorbachev resulted in widespread turmoil that culminated in 1991 with declarations of independence by the Baltic states (Estonia, Latvia, Lithuania) and a short-lived counterrevolutionary coup (in August), which in turn prompted declarations of independence by Ukraine, Belarus, and Moldova.

On January 1, 1992, the Soviet Union ceased to exist. Belarus, Ukraine, and Moldova joined Russia and several other former Soviet republics to form a Commonwealth of Independent States (CIS). At the same time, the independence of each republic was recognized by most countries, and by 1993 it seems that the ties between the former Soviet republics will continue to lessen until the CIS ceases to exist. Despite the enormous change in their status, countries like Belarus and Ukraine still have the same administrative structure as under Soviet rule—division into oblasts. The only exception is Ukraine's oblast of Transcarpathia (formerly Carpathian Rus'/Subcarpathian Rus'), which voted for and was granted self-governing status as a result of the all-union referendum on Ukrainian independence held on December 1, 1991.

In contrast to formerly Soviet and pro-Soviet Communist ruled countries, Greece and Italy have retained basically the same administrative subdivisions they had during the interwar years (see Map 44). Greece is still divided into ten regions (dhiamérisma). All but the capital city of Athens are, in turn, subdivided into nomarchies (nomoí), which have increased in number since the interwar years from thirty-eight to fifty-one. Italy has retained both the interwar smaller districts (provincie) and larger provinces (compartimenti), but it has reversed their order of importance, with more autonomy being given to the provinces. Province boundaries have changed only in the areas bordering on Austria and Yugoslavia. Two new provinces in that area have also been given a special autonomous statute —Trentino-Alto Adige (1948, revised 1972) and Friuli-Venezia Giulia (1963). Although limited in scope, this autonomy is supposed to respond to the needs of the ethnolinguistic minorities living in northern Italy: Germans and Ladins in Trentino-Alto Adige; and Friulians and Slovenes in Friuli-Venezia Giulia.

Districts, counties, regions, and provinces, 1992 (Seat indicated in parentheses if different from district, etc., name)

Poland

1. Szczecin	17. Białystok	33. Radom
2. Koszalin	18. Zielona Góra	34. Lublin
3. Słupsk	19. Poznań	35. Chełm
4. Gdańsk	20. Konin	36. Kamienna Góra
5. Elbląg	21. Skierniewice	37. Opole
6. Olsztyn	22. Warsaw	38. Częstochowa
7. Suwałki	23. Siedlce	39. Kielce
8. Gorzów Wielkopolski	24. Biała Podlaska	40. Tarnobrzeg
	25. Zgorzelec	41. Zamość
9. Piła	26. Legnica	42. Katowice
10. Bydgoszcz	27. Leszno	43. Bielsko-Biała
11. Toruń	28. Wrocław	44. Cracow
12. Włocławek	29. Kalisz	45. Tarnów
13. Płock	30. Zduńska Wola	46. Rzeszów
14. Ciechanów	31. Łódź	47. Przemyśl
15. Ostrołęka	32. Piotrków Trybunalski	48. Nowy Sącz
16. Łomża		49. Krosno

Czechoslovakia

1. North Bohemia (Ústí nad Labem)	5. South Bohemia (České Budějovice)
2. West Bohemia (Plzeň)	6. South Moravia (Brno)
3. Central Bohemia (Prague)	7. North Moravia (Ostrava)
4. East Bohemia (Hradec Králové)	8. West Slovakia (Bratislava)
	9. Central Slovakia (Banská Bystrica)
	10. East Slovakia (Košice)

Austria

1. Upper Austria (Linz)	5. Salzburg
2. Lower Austria (Vienna)	6. Styria (Graz)
3. Vorarlberg (Bregenz)	7. Burgenland (Eisenstadt)
4. Tyrol (Innsbruck)	8. Carinthia (Klagenfurt)

Hungary

1. Győr-Sopron (Győr)	10. Pest (Budapest)
2. Komárom (Tatabánya)	11. Szolnok
3. Nógrád (Sálgótarján)	12. Hajdú-Bihar (Debrecen)
4. Heves (Eger)	13. Zala (Zalaegerszeg)
5. Borsod-Abaúj-Zemplén (Miskolc)	14. Somogy (Kaposvár)
	15. Baranya (Pécs)
6. Szabolcs-Szatmár (Nyíregyháza)	16. Tolna (Szekszárd)
7. Vas (Szombathely)	17. Bács-Kiskun (Kecskemét)
8. Veszprém	18. Csongrád (Szeged)
9. Fejér (Székesfehérvár)	19. Békés (Békéscsaba)

Romania

1. Satu-Mare
2. Maramureş (Baia Mare)
3. Suceava
4. Botoşani
5. Bihor (Oradea)
6. Sălaj (Zalău)
7. Cluj (Cluj-Napoca)
8. Bistriţa-Năsăud (Bistriţa)
9. Mureş (Tîrgu Mureş)
10. Harghita (Miercurea Ciuc)
11. Neamţ (Piatra Neamţ)
12. Iaşi
13. Bacău
14. Vaslui
15. Arad
16. Timiş (Timişoara)
17. Hunedoara (Deva)
18. Alba (Alba Iulia)
19. Sibiu
20. Braşov
21. Covasna (Sfîntu Gheorghe)
22. Vrancea (Focşani)
23. Galaţi
24. Caraş-Severin (Reşiţa)
25. Gorj (Tîrgu Jiu)
26. Vîlcea (Rîmnicu Vîlcea)
27. Argeş (Piteşti)
28. Dîmboviţa (Tirgovişte)
29. Prahova (Ploieşti)
30. Buzău
31. Brăila
32. Tulcea
33. Mehedinţi (Drobeta–Turnu-Severin)
34. Dolj (Craiova)
35. Olt (Slatina)
36. Teleorman (Alexandria)
37. Ilfov (Bucharest)
38. Ialomiţa (Slobozia)
39. Constanţa

Albania

1. Shkodër
2. Tropojë (Bajram Curri)
3. Pukë
4. Kukës
5. Lesh
6. Mirditë (Rrëshen)
7. Krujë
8. Mat (Burrel)
9. Dibër (Peshkopi)
10. Durrës
11. Tiranë
    Tiranë—capital
12. Lushnje
13. Elbasan
14. Librazhd
15. Fier
16. Berat
17. Gramsh
18. Pogradec
19. Skrapar (Çorovodë)
20. Korçë
21. Vlorë
22. Tepelenë
23. Përmet
24. Kolonjë (Erseka)
25. Gjirokastër
26. Sarandë

Map sources

1. East Central Europe: geographic zones
   [A] Darby and Fullard, 64–65; [B] Breu, 121.

1a. Average annual rainfall
   [B] Williams, 59.

1b. Vegetation and land use
   [B] Williams, 59.

2. East Central Europe, ca. 400
   [A] Engel, 1:52; Lendl and Wagner, 30–31, 34; *Westermanns*, 42/43–I, 48–I; Wolski, 26–27; [D] Bartels and Hubner, 3215–16; Carter, 136.

2a. Original homeland of the Slavs
   [A] Purš, 3.

2b. Constantinople, 4th–6th centuries
   [A] Engel, 2:14b; Shepherd, 93.

3. East Central Europe, 7th–8th centuries
   [A] *Atlas po bulgarska istoriia*, 9; Czapliński and Ładogórski, 3; Engel, 2:5a, 14, 51a; Purš, 3a; Wolski, 30–31; [B] *Atlas: Narodna republika Bulgariia*, 12; [D] Klaić, prilog V; Ochmański, 36.

4. East Central Europe, 9th century
   [A] *Atlas po bulgarska istoriia*, 10; Engel, 2:10–11, 14; Purš, 3; Wolski, 34–35; [D] Ochmański, 36.

4a. Cyril and Methodian missions
   [A] Lučić, 17; Purš, 3.

5. Early medieval kingdoms, ca. 1050
   [A] Czapliński and Ładogórski, 4; Engel, 2:18–19, 50b, 51g; Lučić, 14–17, 24; Pitcher, plate VI; Purš, 4, 4a; Shepherd, 64; *Westermanns*, 63; Wolski, 41–43; [B] *Atlas: Narodna republika Bulgariia*, 12; [D] Ochmański, 36.

6. East Central Europe, ca. 1250
   [A] Czapliński and Ładogórski, 7; Engel, 2:34–35; Lučić, 19, 24; Pitcher, plate VI; Shepherd, 72; [B] Kraus, 11; [D] Klaić, prilog IX; Ochmański, 36.

6a. The Mongol invasions
   [A] Lučić, 20, 23; [C] Dobrev, 223.

7a. Poland and Lithuania, 13th–14th centuries
   [A] Czapliński and Ładogórski, 7, 9, 12–13; Engel, 2:64c; [D] Iurginis, 24–25; Žiugžda, 64–65.

7b. Bohemia-Moravia, 13th–15th centuries
   [A] Engel, 2:50a, 66; Purš, 4b and i, 7k.

8. Hungary-Croatia and Venice, 14th–15th centuries
   [A] Darby and Fullard, 158; Engel, 2:48, 50–51, 79, 88; [D] *Révai nagy lexikona*, 13:230–31 and 232–33.

8a. Northern Spiš, 1412–1772
   [A] Purš, 14j.

9. Bulgaria, Serbia, Bosnia, and the Ottoman Empire, 14th–15th centuries
   [A] Darby and Fullard, 158, 164–65; Engel, 2:50, 51g and 3:16; Lučić, 22–27; Pitcher, plates VIII, XI–XVI; Wolski, 53.

9a. Serbia, 14th–15th centuries
   [A] Darby and Fullard, 158, 164–65; Engel, 2:50, 51g and 3:16; Lučić, 22–27; Pitcher, plates VIII, XI–XVI; Wolski, 53.

10. East Central Europe, ca. 1480
   [A] Czapliński and Ładogórski, 16–17; Darby and Fullard, 158; Engel, 2:78–79; Pitcher, plate XIV; Shepherd, 86–87.

11. Economic patterns, ca. 1450
   [A] *Atlas po bulgarska istoriia*, 20; Darby and Fullard, 118–19; Engel, 2:85–86; Lendl and Wagner, 70–71; Pascu (1971), 35; *Westermanns*, 84–85; Wolski, 54, 65; [B] Kraus, 14; [D] Carter (1972), 137, 215, 222; Ochmański, 104–5.

12a. Wrocław/Breslau, ca. 1300
   [A] Czapliński and Ładogórski, 7–II; Engel, 2:82e.

12b. Cracow, ca. 1350
   [A] Czapliński and Ładogórski, 9–II; Engel, 2:82–83k; *Westermanns*, 79–VII.

12c. Vienna, ca. 1300
   [A] Weissensteiner, 85.

12d. Prague, ca. 1350
   [A] Purš, 5j; *Westermanns*, 78–V.

12e. Dubrovnik/Ragusa, ca. 1475
   [D] Carter (1972), 483.

12f. The development of German law cities
   [A] Lendl and Wagner, 54–55; *Westermanns*, 75; [C] Krallert, 6–7.

13. Ecclesiastical jurisdictions, ca. 1450
   [A] Darby and Fullard, 66–67; Engel, 3:4; Lendl and Wagner, 61; *Westermanns*, 88–89; [C] Jedin et al., 46, 71, 81; Matthew, 184–95; [D] Great Britain: *Jugoslavia*, 2:94; Klaić (1976), prilog XV.

13a. Mount Athos
   [C] Jedin et al., 45b.

14. East Central Europe, ca. 1570
   [A] Engel, 3:5; Lučić, 37, 39, 40; Pitcher, plate XXVI; Wolski, 70–71.

15. Protestant Reformation, 16th century
   [A] Engel, 3:8a, 9a; Herrnkind et al., 44ii, 45i; Purš, 8j; [C] Jedin et al., 80.

16. Catholic Counter Reformation, 16th–17th centuries
   [A] Engel, 3:8b, 9b; Purš, 13e; [C] Jedin et al., 78, 80.

17. Education and culture through the 18th century
   [A] Darby and Fullard, 69; Engel, 2:80b and 3:3a-b; Lendl and Wagner, 58; *Westermanns*, 91; [C] de Lange, 121; Jedin et al., 64.

18. East Central Europe, 1648
   [A] Darby and Fullard, 72–73; Manteuffel, 1: map 10; Pitcher, plate XXIV.

19a. Poland-Lithuania, 16th–17th centuries
[A] Czapliński and Ładogórski, 24–27; Wolski, 72.

19b. The Habsburgs, Hungary-Croatia, and Transylvania, 16th–17th centuries
[A] Czapliński and Ładogórski, 20–21; Domokos, 236; Engel, 3:32, 61a; Lučić, 37; *Westermanns*, 115–I; Wolski, 75; [D] *Révai nagy lexikona*, 13:234–35.

20a. The Ottoman Empire, 16th–17th centuries
[A] Domokos, 23b–24a; Engel, 3:16d; Pascu (1983), 38; Pitcher, plate XXIX; Purš, 10; *Westermanns*, 112–I; [D] Eterovich, 1:24.

20b. The Habsburgs, Hungary-Croatia, and Transylvania, 1683–1718
[A] Darby and Fullard, 166–67; Engel, 3:32; Lendl and Wagner, 84–85; *Westermanns*, 112–II.

20c. The Dubrovnik Republic
[A] Lučić, 42a, 51a.

20d. Resettlement of the Danubian basin
[A] *Westermanns*, 112–II.

21. East Central Europe, ca. 1721
[A] Darby and Fullard, 74–75, 132; Engel, 3:32, 33, 38; Lučić, 51a; Wolski, 86–87.

22a. The Partitions of Poland, 1772–1795
[A] Czapliński and Ładogórski, 28–29; Engel, 3:29; [B] *Atlas Belorusskoi SSR*, 135–36.

22b. Austria and the Ottoman Empire, 1718–1792
[A] Engel, 3:32; Lendl and Wagner, 84–85; Lučić, 43, 51b; Pascu (1983), 41; Robertson, 22–23; Wolski, 84.

23. The Napoleonic era, 1795–1814
[A] Czapliński and Ładogórski, 33; Darby and Fullard, 44, 45, 48; Duby, 68; Engel, 3:35, 36a, 40; Lendl and Wagner, 88–89; Lučić, 62; Pascu (1971), 79; *Westermanns*, 124–25; [C] Klíma, 280a.

24. East Central Europe, 1815
[A] Darby and Fullard, 78–79; Engel, 3:46–47; Lučić, 62, 65.

25a. The Austrian Empire, 1815–1866
[A] Darby and Fullard, 102–3; Domokos, 30; Engel, 3:52; Lučić, 55, 61, 62.

25b. The Austro-Hungarian Empire, 1867–1914
[A] Domokos, 34–35; Engel, 3:52.

26a. The Balkan Peninsula, 1817–1877
[A] Darby and Fullard, 168–69; Engel, 3:61b; Lučić, 62, 64; Robertson, 23; [D] Birkin, map 4; *Encyclopedia Britannica*, 11th ed., 3:258–61; Karpat, xvi.

26b. The Balkan Peninsula, 1878–1912
[A] *Atlas po bulgarska istoriia*, 42, 43, 47; *Atlas zur Geschichte*, 1:104; Darby and Fullard, 170a; Engel, 3:61a; Lučić, 62, 64; [D] Sidorova, map 1.

27a. The Balkan Peninsula: ethnolinguistic distribution, ca. 1910
[A] Darby and Fullard, 171a; Engel, 3:53; [C] Cvijić, plate 22; GB War Office: *Ethnographical Maps*; Soteriadis.

27b. Conflicting claims to Macedonia, ca. 1912
[A] *Atlas po bulgarska istoriia*, 34; Darby and Fullard, 172a.

27c. The Balkan Peninsula, 1912–1913
[A] *Atlas po bulgarska istoriia*, 48; Engel, 3:61c; Lučić, 62–64; [C] Klíma, 293A; [D] Rossos, 154.

28. Canal and railway development before 1914
[A] *Atlas po bulgarska istoria*, 48–49; Czapliński and Ładogórski, 39; Darby and Fullard, 86, 87, 89; Engel, 3:58–59; Leisering, 96ii; Lučić, 61; Manteuffel, 3, pt. 1, map 10; Pascu (1983), 49, 58; Purš, 24d, f; Wolski, 111; [C] Imhoff, plate 37; Vogel, plate 10; [D] GB Naval Intelligence: *Greece*, 2:341; GB Naval Intelligence: *Jugoslavia*, 3:416–20; GB Naval Intelligence: *Turkey*, 2:239; Sidorova, map 15.

29a. Population, ca. 1870
[A] Engel, 3:58; [D] Réclus, vols. 1, 3, 5, 9.

29b. Population, ca. 1910
[A] Czapliński and Ładogórski, 39; Darby and Fullard, 91; Engel, 3:59; [B] *Rand McNally Library Atlas*, vol. 2: gazetteer; Romer, map VII; [D] Birkin, map 5.

30. Ethnolinguistic distribution, ca. 1900
[A] Darby and Fullard, 143a, 147; Engel, 3:53; Wolski, 120; [B] Kraus, 30; [C] Bruk and Apachenko, 14–17, 40; Cvijić, plate 22; GB War Office: *Ethnographical Maps*; Held (1887), plate 2; Petermann (1866), plate 16; Phillipson (1890), plate 3; Phillipson (1919), plate 3; Soteridadis; Teleki; [D] Bidlo, map; Carter (1977), 444–49; Réclus, 1:148–49; "Rossiia," *Bol'shaia èntsiklopediia*, 16: 458–59.

31. Cultural and educational institutions before 1914
[A] *Atlas po bulgarska istoriia*, 33; Czapliński and Ładogórski, 42i; Engel, 3:48b; Pascu (1983), 52; Purš, 19j, 28c and j; Wolski, 110; [C] de Lange, 100–102; Friesel (rev. English ed.), 48–49, 56.

32a. Germans in East Central Europe, ca. 1900
[C] Krallert, 18–19.

32b. The evolution of German settlement
[A] Lendl and Wagner, 50–51; *Westermanns*, 74i and ii; [C] Krallert, 3, 5, 11.

33. Jews and Armenians in East Central Europe, ca. 1900
[A] Darby and Fullard, 187; [B] Romer, plate xi; [C] Friesel (rev. English ed.), 32–41, 98–100; [C] Gilbert, 45, 71, 79, 96; [D] *Révai nagy lexikona*, 13:192, plate "Izraelita"; Wandruszka and Urbanitsch, vol. 4, map.

34. The Catholic Church, 1900
[A] Engel, 3:48c; [B] Kraus, 25I; Romer, plate XIV; [C] Langhans (1913), plate 33; [D] Wandruszka and Urbanitsch, 4:72–73; *Catholic Encyclopedia*, 6:514–15; 8:244–45; and 13:264–65.

35. The Orthodox Church, 1900
[A] *Atlas po bulgarska istoriia*, 34; [B] Kraus, 25I; [C] Langhans (1913), plate 33; Mach, plate 8; [D] Wandruszka and Urbanitsch, 4:72–73.

35a. The Greek Catholic Church, 1900
[D] Wandruszka and Urbanitsch, 4:72–73.

36. East Central Europe, 1910
[A] *Atlas po bulgarska istoriia*, 7; Darby and Fullard, 80–82; [D] *Encyclopedia Britannica*, 11th ed., 4:773; 11:808–9; 12:424–25; 23:872–73; 24:686; *Ottův slovník naučný*, 4:904–5.

37. World War I, 1914–1918
[A] *Atlas zur Geschichte*, 1:124; Czapliński and Ładogórski, 43; Darby and Fullard, 52–53; Engel, 3:68; Hubatsch, 21; Leers and Frenzel, 10–11; Lučić, 69; Pascu (1983), 61–62; Wolski, 126–27; [C] Dami, 27–37;

Dobrev, 189; [D] Natkevičius, map 2; Sidorova, maps 10, 11, 12.

38. East Central Europe, 1918–1923
[A] Czapliński and Ładogórski, 44–45; Darby and Fullard, 56–57; Domokos, 39b; Engel, 3:52, 70, 71; Lučić, 61; Wolski, 130, 131, 133; [C] Dami, 30–68; [D] Bowman, 515.

39a. Poland in the 20th century
[A] Czapliński and Ładogórski, 43–44; Darby and Fullard, 179.

39b. Danzig
[A] Darby and Fullard, 176b; Engel, 3:29d.

39c. Czechoslovakia in the 20th century
[A] Purš, 29c and d, 37a and b; Wolski, 135; [C] Dami, 23, 75–80, 92; [D] Bowman, 330, 341; *La Paix de Versailles*, 9, pt. 1: maps; *Ottův slovník naučný*, 23:936–37.

40a. Hungary in the 20th century
[A] Domokos, 38b, 45a; Pascu (1983), 73; [C] Dami, 30, 104.

40b. Romania in the 20th century
[A] Engel, 3:84b; [C] Dami, 16, 21, 104, 111, 120; Langhans (1918), plate 8; [D] *La Paix de Versailles*, 9, pt. 1:383, map 1.

41a. Yugoslavia in the 20th century, to 1941
[A] Darby and Fullard, 169a; Lučić, 74; Wolski, 135iii; [C] Dami, 35, 54, 57, 66, 83, 134–35, 165; [D] *La Paix de Versailles*, 9, pt. 1:392, 403, 415, 421, 458.

41b. Klagenfurt Plebiscite area
[A] *Atlas zur Geschichte*, 74; [C] Dami, 264–65; [D] Bowman, 313.

41c. Yugoslavia in the 20th century, since 1941
[A] Lučić, 77, 82; [C] Dami, 105, 106, 121, 122, 134–37, 164–66.

42a. Trieste and Istria in the 20th century
[A] Engel, 3:53, 85c; Lučić, 67, 82; [C] Dami, 40, 66, 134–36, 164–65; Langhans (1915), plate 32 and plate 54; [D] Bowman, 350–51.

42b. Albania in the 20th century
[C] Dami, 62, 63, 82, 105, 108; [D] Temperley, 338.

43a. Bulgaria in the 20th century
[A] Engel, 3:70–71; [B] *Atlas: Narodna republika Bulgariia*, 15; [C] Dami, 14, 15, 21, 36, 61, 105, 106, 121, 140, 141.

43b. Greece in the 20th century
[A] Darby and Fullard, 169b; Engel, 3:70–71; Wolski, 133; [C] Dami, 140–43; [D] Bowman, 396; *La Paix de Versailles*, 9, pt. 2:60–61.

44. East Central Europe, ca. 1930
[A] Darby and Fullard, 82–83; Domokos, 45a; Engel, 3:72a; Lučić, 74; Pascu (1983), 65; [B] Haack, plates 18/17, 25/19, 26/20, 32/41, 29/55, 30/56; Philip, 61, 62, 77, 78; *Philip's Reader's Reference Atlas*, 15–17, 19, 20, 29; Kraus, 21; [C] Dami, 70, 72; [D] GB Naval Intelligence, *Albania*, 218; GB Naval Intelligence, *Greece*, 1:254.

45. World War II, 1939–1942
[A] *Atlas zur Geschichte*, 2:38–39; Darby and Fullard, 58–59; Engel, 3:82, 89a; Leisering, 68; Lendl and Wagner, 110; Wolski, 146; [B] *Atlas: Narodna republika Bulgariia*, 84; *Atlas Republica Socialistă Rômania*, 50; Kraus, 22; [C] Dami, 77–115; de Lange, 70; Friesel (rev. English ed.), 106–7; [C] USOSS, Greater Germany.

46. World War II, 1943–1945
[A] Czapliński and Ładogórski, 50–52; Engel, 3:83; Lendl and Wagner, 111; Purš, 37f; [C] Klíma, 338–60; Young, 120–31, 210–23, 248–49.

46a. Partisan movements during World War II
[A] *Atlas zur Geschichte*, 2:41, 46.

47. East Central Europe after World War II
[A] Engel, 3:85, 90; Weissensteiner, 86; [C] Dami, 116–46, 183.

47a. Berlin, 1945–1990
[A] Engel, 3:91c.

47b. Vienna, 1945–1955
[A] Lendl and Wagner, 115; Schier, 106.

48. Population movements, 1944–1948
[A] Darby and Fullard, 61; Engel, 3:88–89; Leers and Frenzel, 140–43, 152, 163–67, 170; Leisering, 92–93; [B] *Seydlitz Weltatlas*, 97; [C] Friesel (rev. English ed.), 110; [D] Hillberg, 3:1220.

49. Industrial development since 1945
[A] *Atlas zur Geschichte*, 2:83–85, 109–11; Czapliński and Ładogórski, 53; Domokos, 48; Pascu (1983), 81–82; Purš, 39–40; [B] *Diercke Weltatlas*, 24–25, 100–101, 108–9; Haack, 16–17, 38–39; *Seydlitz Weltatlas*, 8–17, 63, 72–73; Gaebler, 61; *Atlas: Narodna republika Bulgariia*, 152–53; Bertić, 77; Lehmann, plate III; Melis, 111; Radó, 110–11; Ščipak, 34–37; Tochenov, 132–33, 191–94; [C] *Haack Atlas Weltverkehr*, 52–53, 66–67; Mayer, 22–37, 126–131; [D] Hoffman, 180–81.

49a. Upper Silesia
[D] Rugg, 41.

49b. Halle-Łódź-Budapest industrial triangle
[A] *Atlas zur Geschichte*, 2:83–85, 109–11; Czapliński and Ładogórski, 53; Domokos, 48; Pascu (1983), 81–82; Purš, 39–40; [B] *Atlas: Narodna republika Bulgariia*, 152–53; Bertić, 77; *Diercke Weltatlas*, 24–25, 100–101, 108–9; Gaebler, 61; Haack, 16–17, 38–39; Jordan, 3.2-G.2; Lehmann, plate III; Melis, 111; Radó, 110–11; Ščipak, 34–37; *Seydlitz Weltatlas*, 8–17, 63, 72–73; Tochenov, 132–33, 191–94; *Westermann*, 48–49; [C] *Haack Atlas Weltverkehr*, 52–53, 66–67; Mayer, 22–37, 126–31; [D] Hoffman, 180–81.

50. East Central Europe, 1992
[A] Engel, 3:91; [B] Breu, 251; Darkot, 22–23; Darley, 152–63; Melis, 72–73, 84–85, 90–91, 96–97; [D] Hoffman, 36–44.

Bibliography

A. Historical atlases: general (with significant East Central European content) and regionally specific

Adams, Arthur E.; Matley, Ian M.; and McCagg, William O. *An Atlas of Russian and East European History*. New York and Washington, 1966.

Atlas po bulgarska istoriia. Sofia, 1963.

Atlas zur Geschichte. 2 vols. 3d ed. Berlin, 1982.

Baldamus, Alfred; Schwabe, Ernst; Ambrosius, Ernst, eds. *F.W. Putzgers historischer Schulatlas*. 45th rev. ed. Bielefeld and Leipzig, 1924.

Czapliński, Władysław, and Ładogórski, Tadeusz. *The Historical Atlas of Poland*. Warsaw and Wrocław, 1986. Polish edition. Warsaw, 1970. 12th rev. ed. 1993.

Darby, H.C., and Fullard, Harold. *The New Cambridge Modern History*. Vol. 14: *Atlas*. Cambridge, 1978.

Domokos, György, ed. *Történelmi atlasz*. Budapest, 1985.

Duby, Georges, ed. *Atlas historique Larousse*. Paris, 1978.

Dudar, Tibor, ed. *Történelmi világatlasz*. Budapest, 1991.

Engel, Josef, ed. *Grosser historischer Weltatlas*. 3 vols. 3d ed. Munich, 1967.

Herrnkind, Jürgen; Kistler, Helmut; and Raisch, Herbert. *Atlas zur Universalgeschichte*. Munich, 1979.

Hilgemann, Werner. *Atlas zur deutschen Zeitgeschichte, 1918–1968*. Munich and Zurich, 1984.

Hubatsch, Walther, ed. *Deutsche Geschichte: Ereignisse und Probleme—Karten und Stammtafeln zur deutschen Geschichte*. Frankfurt-am-Main, Berlin, and Vienna, 1972.

Leers, Johann von, and Frenzel, Konrad. *Atlas zur deutschen Geschichte der Jahre 1914 bis 1933*. Bielefeld and Leipzig, 1934.

Leisering, Walter. *Putzger historischer Weltatlas*. Bielefeld, 1981.

Lendl, Egon, and Wagner, Wilhelm, eds. *F.W. Putzger historischer Weltatlas zur allgemeinen und österreichischen Geschichte*. Vienna, 1981.

Lučić, Josip. *Povijesni atlas*. Zagreb, 1984.

Magocsi, Paul Robert. *Ukraine: A Historical Atlas*. Toronto, 1985.

Manteuffel, Tadeusz, ed. *Historia Polski*, vol. 1, pt. 3; *Mapy do roku 1764*; vol. 2, pt. 4: 1764–1864; vol. 3, pt. 1: 1864–1900, pt. 2: 1900–1914; vol. 4, pt. 1: 1918–1926. Warsaw, 1958–69.

Mortensen, Hans, et al. *Historisch-geographischer Atlas des Preussenlands*. 10 parts. Wiesbaden, 1968–84.

Motta, Giuseppe, ed. *Atlante storico*. Novara, 1979.

Pascu, Ştefan, ed. *Atlas pentru istoria României*. Bucharest, 1983.

———. *Atlas istoric*. Bucharest, 1971.

Pavlovčič, Roman. *Zgodovinski atlas Slovenije*. Buenos Aires, 1960.

Pitcher, Donald Edgar. *An Historical Geography of the Ottoman Empire*. Leiden, 1972.

Pogonowski, Iwo Cyprian. *Poland: A Historical Atlas*. New York, 1987.

Purš, Jaroslav, ed. *Atlas československých dějín*. Prague, 1965.

Robertson, C. Grant. *An Historical Atlas of Modern Europe from 1789 to 1914*. Oxford, 1915.

Schier, Wilhelm. *Atlas zur allgemeinen und österreichischen Geschichte*. 8th ed. Vienna, 1966.

Shepherd, William R. *Historical Atlas*. 8th ed. New York, 1956.

Shiriaev, E. E. *Belarus', Rus' Belaia, Rus' Chernaia i Litva v kartakh*. Minsk, 1991.

Škalamera, Željko. *Školski istorijski atlas*. 4th ed. Belgrade, 1987.

Spindler, Max. *Bayerischer Geschichtatlas*. Munich, 1969.

Stanojević, Stanoje. *Istoriski atlas*. 3d ed. Belgrade, 1934.

Unat, Faik Reşit. *Tarih atlasi*. Istanbul, 1964.

Weissensteiner, Fritz. *Österreich und die Welt: historischer Atlas*. Vienna, 1976.

Westermanns grosser Atlas zur Weltgeschichte. Braunschweig, 1988.

Wolski, Józef, ed. *Atlas historyczny świata*. 3rd rev. ed. Warsaw, 1991.

Zec, Stevan, ed. *Karte naših podela: politički atlas jugoslovenskih zemalja u 20. veku/Maps of Our Dividings: Political Atlas of Yugoslav Countries in the XX Century*. Belgrade, 1991.

B. Geographic atlases (with significant East Central European content), regional atlases, and national atlases

Atlas Belorusskoi Sovetskoi Sotsialisticheskoi Respubliki. Minsk and Moscow, 1958.

Atlas: Narodna republika Bulgariia. Sofia, 1973.

Atlas Republica Socialistă Rômania. Bucharest, 1974.

Bertić, Ivan, ed. *Veliki geografski atlas Jugoslavije*. Zagreb, 1987.

Breu, Josef, ed. *Atlas der Donauländer*. Vienna, 1971.

Darkot, Besim. *Modern Büyük Atlas*. Istanbul, 1977.

Darley, Richard J. *National Geographic Atlas of the World*. 5th ed. Washington, D.C., 1981.

Diercke Weltatlas. Brunswick, 1988.

Gaebler, V., ed. *Haack Atlas: Sozialistische Staaten Mittel- und Südosteuropas*. Gotha, 1986.

Götz, Antonín, ed. *Atlas Československé Socialistické Republiky*. Prague, 1966.

Haack Atlas für Jedermann. Gotha and Leipzig, 1976.

Haack, Hermann, ed. *Stieler Grand atlas de géographie moderne*. 10th ed. Gotha, 1934–40.

Halász, Albert. *New Central Europe in Economical Maps*. Budapest, 1928.

Jordan, Peter, ed. *Atlas Ost- und Südosteuropa/Atlas of Eastern and Southeastern Europe*. Vienna, 1990.

Kayser, Bernard, and Thompson, Kenneth. *Economic and Social Atlas of Greece*. Athens, 1964.

Kraus, Theodor, ed. *Atlas östliches Mitteleuropa*. Bielefeld, Berlin, and Hannover, 1959.

Kubiiovych, Volodymyr, ed. *Atlias Ukraïny i sumezhnykh kraïv*. L'viv, 1937.

Lehmann, Edgar, ed. *Atlas Deutsche Demokratische Republik*. Gotha and Leipzig, 1976.

Leszczycki, Stanisław, ed. *Narodowy atlas Polski/National Atlas of Poland*. Wrocław, Warsaw, Cracow, and Gdańsk, 1973–78.

Mazúr, Emil, ed. *Atlas Slovenskej socialistickej republiky*. Bratislava, 1980.

Melis, Roberto. *Atlante enciclopedico touring*. Vol. 1: *Italia*; Vol. 2: *Europa*. Milan, 1986–87.

Pantoflíček, Jaroslav, ed. *Atlas republiky československé/Atlas de la république tchécoslovaque*. Prague, 1935.

Philip, George, ed. *Philip's International Atlas*. London, 1931.

———. *Philip's Reader's Reference Atlas of the World*. London, 1935.

Radó, Sándor, ed. *National Atlas of Hungary*. Budapest, 1967.

Rand McNally Library Atlas of the World. Vol. 2. Chicago and New York, 1913.

Romer, Eugeniusz. *Geograficzno-statystyczny atlas Polski/Geographisch-statistischer Atlas von Polen*. Warsaw and Cracow, 1916.

Rónai, Andrew. *Atlas of Central Europe*. Budapest and Balatonfüred, 1945.

Ščipák, Josef, ed. *Atlas ČSSR*. Prague, 1982.

Seydlitz Weltatlas. Berlin, 1984.

Szturm de Sztrem, Edward. *Statistical Atlas of Poland*. Edinburgh and London, 1943.

Tanoğlu, Ali; Erinç, Sirri; Tümertekin, Erol. *Türkiye atlasi/Atlas of Turkey*. Istanbul, 1961.

Tochenov, V. V., ed. *Atlas SSSR*. Moscow, 1984.

Westermann Schulatlas. Braunschweig, 1970.

Williams, Joseph E., ed. *Prentice-Hall World Atlas*. Englewood Cliffs, N.J., 1960.

C. Thematic atlases (with significant East Central European content) and maps

Andree, Richard. "Das Sprachgebiet der Lausitzer Wenden, 1550–1872." *Petermanns Mitteilungen*, 19 (Gotha, 1873), plate 17.

Behm, E. "Karte von Central Europa . . . zur Übersicht der politischen Gestaltung im J. 1867, und der Eisenbahnen und andern Communicationen." *Petermanns Mitteilungen: Ergänzungsband*, 4, no. 19 (Gotha, 1865–67).

Beinart, Hayim. *Atlas Karta le-toledot 'Am Yisrael bi-yemei ha-beinayim*. Jerusalem, 1981.

Brice, William C. *An Historical Atlas of Islam*. Leiden, 1981.

Bruk, S. I., and Apachenko, V. S., eds. *Atlas narodov mira*. Moscow, 1964.

Cambridge Medieval History. Vol. 1: Map supplement. Cambridge, 1911.

Cvijić, J. "Etnographische Karte der Balkanhalbinsel." *Petermanns Mitteilungen*, 59 (Gotha, 1913), pt. 1, plate 22.

Dami, Aldo. *Les frontières européennes de 1900 à 1975: atlas*. Geneva, 1976.

de Lange, Nicholas. *Atlas of the Jewish World*. Oxford, 1984.

Dobrev, Khristo, ed. *Bulgarski voenen atlas*. Sofia, 1979.

Friesel, Evyatar. *Atlas Karta le-toledot 'Am Yisrael ba-zeman he-hadash*. Jerusalem, 1983. Revised and translated edition in English: *Atlas of Modern Jewish History*. New York and Oxford, 1990.

Geisler, Walter. "Karte der Abweichungen zwischen der 'Nationalitätenkarte' von Jakob Spett und der Sprachenkarte der östlichen Provinzen des Deutschen Reichs von Walter Geisler." *Petermanns Mitteilungen: Ergänzungsband*, 47, no. 217 (Gotha, 1933), plate 3.

———. "Sprachenkarte der östlichen Provinzen des Deutschen Reichs im Umfange von 1918 nach den Ergebnissen der amtlichen Volkszählung vom Jahre 1910." *Petermanns Mitteilungen: Ergänzungsband*, 47, no. 217 (Gotha, 1933), plate 2.

Gilbert, Martin. *Jewish History Atlas*. 3d ed. London, 1985.

Gopčević, Spiridion. "Ethnographische Karte von Makedonien und Alt-Serbien." *Petermanns Mitteilungen*, 35 (Gotha, 1889), plate 4.

Great Britain War Office. General Staff, Geographical Section. *Ethnographical Maps of Central and Southeastern Europe and Western Asia*. 5 maps. London, 1919.

Griess, Thomas E., ed. *Atlas for the Second World War: Europe and the Mediterranean*. West Point Military Atlas Series. Wayne, N.J., 1985.

———. *Atlas for Wars of Napoleon*. West Point Military Atlas Series. Wayne, N.J., 1986.

Haack Atlas Weltverkehr. Gotha, 1984.

Hammond, Nicholas G.L. *Atlas of the Greek and Roman World in Antiquity*. Park Ridge, N.J., 1981.

Hátsek, Ignaz. "Ethnographische Karte der Länder der Ungarischen Krone auf Grund der Volkszählung von 1880." *Petermanns Mitteilungen*, 31 (Gotha, 1885), plate 3.

———. "Prozent-Verhältnis der des Lesens und Schreibens kundigen Bevölkerung in Österreich-Ungarn nach den Volkszählungsdaten von 1880/81." *Petermanns Mitteilungen*, 30 (Gotha, 1884), plate 9.

———. "Statistische Karten von Ungarn auf Grund der Volkszählungsdaten von Jahre 1880/81." *Petermanns Mitteilungen*, 28 (Gotha, 1882), plate 19.

Held, F. "Nationalitätenkarte von Mähren und Schlesien." *Petermanns Mitteilungen*, 30 (Gotha, 1884), p. 161.

———. "Sprachen-Karte der westlichen Kronländer von Oesterreich nach dem Zensus von 1880." *Petermanns Mitteilungen*, 33 (Gotha, 1887), plate 2.

Henke, Oskar. "Karte der öffentlichen höheren Unterrichts-Anstalten in Deutschland, 1875." *Petermanns Mitteilungen*, 22 (Gotha, 1876), plate 9.

Hochreiter, E. "Nationalitätenkarte von Böhmen." *Petermanns Mitteilungen*, 29 (Gotha, 1883), p. 321.

Horn, Werner. "Das Ergebnis der Elternbefragung im Memelgebiet (1. April 1921): A. Die Familiensprache der Schüler; B. Die Sprache im Religionsunterricht; C. Die Sprache im Lese- und Schreibunterricht." *Petermanns Mitteilungen*, 80 (Gotha, 1936), plates 12, 13, 14.

Imhoff, D. "Die Eisenbahn-Konzessionen in der Asiatischen Türkei im Jahre 1914." *Petermanns Mitteilungen*, 61 (Gotha, 1915), plate 37.

Ischirkoff, A. "Das Bulgarentum auf der Balkanhalbinsel im Jahre 1912." *Petermanns Mitteilungen*, 61 (Gotha, 1915), plate 44.

Jedin, Hubert; Latourette, Kenneth Scott; and Martin, Jochen. *Atlas zur Kirchengeschichte*. Freiburg, 1970. 2d ed. Freiburg, 1987.

Kassner, C. "Bevölkerungsdichte in Bulgarien, 1887 und 1905." *Petermanns Mitteilungen*, 57 (Gotha, 1911), pt. 2, plate 17.

Klíma, Jan, ed. *Československý vojenský atlas*. Prague, 1965.

Kovalevsky, Pierre. *Atlas historique et culturel de la Russie et du monde slave*. Brussels, 1961. German edition. Munich, Basel, and Vienna, 1964.

Krallert, Wilfried. *Atlas zur Geschichte der deutschen Ostsiedlung*. Bielefeld, Berlin, and Hannover, 1958.

Kutschera, Hugo. "Ost-Rumelien's administrative Eintheilung." *Petermanns Mitteilungen*, 26 (Gotha, 1880), plate 17.

Langhans, Paul. "Deutsche und Tschechen in Nordböhmen." *Petermanns Mitteilungen*, 45 (Gotha, 1899), plate 7.

———. "Die ethnographischen Verhältnisse im Baltland und in Litauen nach der Volkszählung von 1897." *Petermanns Mitteilungen*, 61 (Gotha, 1915), plate 43.

———. "Fremde Volksstämme im Deutschen Reiche." *Petermanns Mitteilungen*, 41 (Gotha, 1895), plate 17.

———. "Gebietsabtretungen Rumäniens an Österreich-Ungarn und Bulgarien nach dem Frieden von Bukarest vom 7. Mai 1918." *Petermanns Mitteilungen*, 64 (Gotha, 1918), plate 8.

———. "Die Grenzen des neuen albanischen Staates nach den verschiedenen Vorschlägen." *Petermanns Mitteilungen*, 59 (Gotha, 1913), pt. 1, plate 33.

———. "Die Herzogtümer Auschwitz und Zator als deutsche Bundesländer bis 1866." *Petermanns Mitteilungen*, 62 (Gotha, 1916), plate 50.

———. "Die italienischen Grenzansprüche in den österreichischen Alpenländern auf ethnographischer Grundlage." *Petermanns Mitteilungen*, 61 (Gotha, 1915), plate 32.

———. "Die Latinität der adriatischen Küste Österreich-Ungarns." *Petermanns Mitteilungen*, 61 (Gotha, 1915), plate 54.

———. "Das litauische Sprachgebiet in Ostpreussen." *Petermanns Mitteilungen*, 67 (Gotha, 1921), plate 2.

———. "Nationalitätenkarte von Galizien nach den Ergebnissen der Volkszählung vom 31. Dezember 1900." *Petermanns Mitteilungen*, 65 (Gotha, 1919), plates 6, 8, 9.

———. "Die neuen Grenzen des Königreichs Serbien nach Angaben des Kgl. Serbischen Generalstabes"/"Die neuen Grenzen des Königreichs Bulgarien . . . nach dem Vertrag von Bukarest von 20. Juli (10 August) 1913." *Petermanns Mitteilungen*, 59 (Gotha, 1913), pt. 2, plate 54.

———. "Die preussischen Provinzen auf polnischem Boden bis 1807." *Petermanns Mitteilungen*, 62 (Gotha, 1916), plate 1.

———. "Die räumliche Entwicklung des Königreichs Montenegro." *Petermanns Mitteilungen*, 56 (Gotha, 1910), pt. 2, plate 20.

———. "Der Rückgang des türkischen Herrschaftsgebietes in Europa." *Petermanns Mitteilungen*, 59 (Gotha, 1913), pt. 1, plate 1.

———. "Der rumänische Anteil an der Bevölkerung Ungarns, der Bukowina und Bessarabiens." *Petermanns Mitteilungen*, 61 (Gotha, 1915), plate 36.

———. "Der rumänische Volksboden und die staatliche Entwicklung des Rumänentums." *Petermanns Mitteilungen*, 61 (Gotha, 1915), plate 35.

———. "Der Schauplatz eines zukünftigen türkisch-griechischen Konfliktes [Macedonia]." *Petermanns Mitteilungen*, 56 (Gotha, 1910), pt. 2, plate 45.

———. "Sprachen und Religionen in Europa und die Grenzen zwischen west- und osteuropäischer Kultur." *Petermanns Mitteilungen*, 63 (Gotha, 1917), plate 1.

———. "Sprachenkarte des Sachsenlandes in Siebenbürgen und seiner geschichtlich-nationalen Entwicklung nach den Ergebnissen der Volkszählung von 31. Dezember 1910." *Petermanns Mitteilungen*, 66 (Gotha, 1920), plates 1, 2, 6.

———. "Sprachenkarte von Russisch-Polen nach der ersten russischen Volkszählung von 1897." *Petermanns Mitteilungen*, 60 (Gotha, 1914), pt. 2, plate 34.

———. "Die Umgangsprache der anwesenden Bevölkerung in der Bukowina." *Petermanns Mitteilungen*, 61 (Gotha, 1915), plate 39.

———. "Verbreitung der Deutschen in den Ländern der Ungarischen Krone . . . auf Grund der Sprachenzählung von 1890." *Petermanns Mitteilungen*, 42 (Gotha, 1896), plate 20.

———. "Verbreitung der Russen, Weissrussen, Tschechen, Litauer, Ruthenen und Deutschen in Polen nach dem 'Atlas Statystyczny' von E. Wunderlich." *Petermanns Mitteilungen*, 78 (Gotha, 1932), plates 9 and 10.

Lejean, G. "Carte ethnographique de la Turquie d'Europe et des états vassaux autonomes." *Petermanns Mitteilungen: Ergänzungsband*, 1 (Gotha, 1860–61), no. 4.

Mach, Richard von. "Karte der Schulsphären der türkischen Balkan-Halbinsel." *Petermanns Mitteilungen*, 45 (Gotha, 1899), plate 8.

Maps Relating to the Ethnical Structure of Slovenian Carinthia. Np., 1943.

Matthew, Donald. *Atlas of Medieval Europe*. Oxford, 1983.

Mayer, Ferdinand. *Petro-Atlas Erdöl und Erdgas*. 3d ed. Brunswick, 1982.

Menke, Theodor. "Die politischen Verhältnisse der Balkan-Halbinsel im 14. Jahrhundert." *Petermanns Mitteilungen*, 24 (Gotha, 1878), plate 8.

Oberhummer, Ernst. "Wirtschaftskarte der Tschecho-Slowakischen Republik." *Petermanns Mitteilungen*, 66 (Gotha, 1920), plate 36.

Olbricht, Konrad. "Die Groszstädte Europas um 1600."

Petermanns Mitteilungen, 85 (Gotha, 1939), plate 33.

Petermann, A. "Die Ausdehnung der Slaven in der Türkei und den angrenzenden Gebieten." *Petermanns Mitteilungen*, 15 (Gotha, 1869), plate 22.

―――. "Deutsche und Romanen in Süd-Tirol und Venetien nach Chr. Schneller." *Petermanns Mitteilungen*, 23 (Gotha, 1877), plate 17.

―――. "Ethnographisch-statistische Karte von Italien." *Petermanns Mitteilungen*, 5 (Gotha, 1859), plate 14.

―――. "Ethnographische Karte von [europäischem] Russland nach A.F. Rittich." *Petermanns Mitteilungen: Ergänzungsband*, 12, no. 54 (Gotha, 1878), plates 1 and 2.

―――. "Etnographische Karte von Kandia oder Kreta." *Petermanns Mitteilungen*, 11 (Gotha, 1866), plate 16.

―――. "Karte des österreichischen Kaiserstaates zur Übersicht der Dichtigkeit der Bevölkerung nach dem Census von 1857." *Petermanns Mitteilungen*, 6 (Gotha, 1860), plate 7.

―――. "Die neueste Eintheilung, die türkischen Gebiete und die Confessionen die europäische Türkei." *Petermanns Mitteilungen*, 22 (Gotha, 1876), plate 13.

―――. "Die politischen Verhältnisse und neuen Staaten-Grenzen von Südost-Europa und Vorder-Asien nach dem Berliner Vertrage 13. Juni-13. Juli 1878." *Petermanns Mitteilungen*, 24 (Gotha, 1878), plate 20.

―――. "Die Staaten der Balkan-Halbinsel nach den Grenzbestimmungen des Friedens von S. Stefano 3. März 1878." *Petermanns Mitteilungen*, 24 (Gotha, 1879), plate 11a.

―――. "Vertheilung der Gross-, Weiss- und Klein-Russen nach A. F. Rittich." *Petermanns Mitteilungen*, 24 (Gotha, 1878), plate 18.

Philippson, A. "Ethnographische Karte des Peloponnes." *Petermanns Mitteilungen*, 36 (Gotha, 1890), plate 3.

―――. "Völkerkarte des westlichen Kleinasien nach eigenen Erkundungen auf Reisen 1900–1904." *Petermanns Mitteilungen*, 65 (Gotha, 1919), plate 3.

Praesent, Hans. "Anteil der Bekenntnisse an der Gemeindebevölkerung des Cholmer Landes." *Petermanns Mitteilungen*, 64 (Gotha, 1918), plate 5.

―――. "Anteil der Bekenntnisse an der Gemeindebevölkerung des Gouvernements Suwalki nach den Erhebungen des Warschauer Statistischen Komitees 1909." *Petermanns Mitteilungen*, 65 (Gotha, 1919), plate 2.

―――. "Anteil der Römisch-Katholischen und der Orthodoxen an der Gemeindebevölkerung des Cholmer Landes." *Petermanns Mitteilungen*, 64 (Gotha, 1918), plate 6.

―――. "Verhältnis von Polen und Litauern im Gouvernement Suwalki nach der Sprachenstatistik 1914." *Petermanns Mitteilungen*, 65 (Gotha, 1919), plate 2.

Rauers, F. "Versuch einer Karte der alten Handelsstrassen in Deutschland." *Petermanns Mitteilungen*, 52 (Gotha, 1906), plate 6.

Schwarz, B. "Dobrudscha zur Übersicht der deutschen Kolonien." *Petermanns Mitteilungen*, 32 (Gotha, 1886), plate 17.

Sellier, André, and Sellier, Jean. *Atlas des peuples d'Europe centrale*. Paris, 1991.

Soteriadis, George. *Hellenism in the Near East: An Ethnological Map*. London, 1919.

Spett, Jacob. "Nationalitätenkarte der östlichen Provinzen des Deutschen Reichs nach den Ergebnissen der amtlichen Volkszählung von Jahre 1910." *Petermanns Mitteilungen: Ergänzungsband*, 47, no. 217 (Gotha, 1933), plate 1.

Staats- und Verwaltungsgrenzen in Ostmitteleuropa. 3 pts: *Baltische Lande, Preussenland, Pommern*. Munich, 1954–55.

Stülpnagel, F. von. "Die russisch-türkische Grenze an den Donau-Mündungen nach . . . Friedens-Congresses von Paris 30. März 1856." *Petermanns Mitteilungen*, 2 (Gotha, 1856), plate 9.

Teleki, Paul. *Ethnographical Map of Hungary Based on Density of Population According to the Census of 1910*. Budapest, n.d.

United States Office of Strategic Services. *Bulgaria: Administrative Divisions*. Washington, D.C., 1943.

―――. *Greater Germany: Administrative Divisions*. Washington, D.C., 1944.

Vogel, C. "Das Deutsche Reich und seine Nachbarländer." *Petermanns Mitteilungen*, 24 (Gotha, 1878), plate 10.

Weise, L. "Die Bevölkerungsverteilung in Europa." *Petermanns Mitteilungen*, 59 (Gotha, 1913), pt. 1, plate 2.

Wittschell, Leo. "Sprachenkarte von Masuren und dem südlichen Ermland auf Grund der Volkszählung von 1910." *Petermanns Mitteilungen*, 71 (Gotha, 1925), plate 22.

Young, Peter, ed. *Atlas of the Second World War*. New York, 1974.

Zaremba, Józef, ed. *Atlas Ziem Odzyskanych/Atlas of the Recovered Territories of Poland*. Warsaw, 1947.

Zimmerman, O. "Das Verbreitungsgebiet der Wenden im Königreich Sachsen 1880 und 1910." *Petermanns Mitteilungen*, 65 (Gotha, 1919), plate 1.

D. Other sources consulted

Attwater, Donald. *The Christian Churches of the East*. 2 vols. 2d rev. ed. Milwaukee, 1947.

Bartels, Klaus, and Huber, Ludwig, eds. *Lexikon der alten Welt*. Zurich and Stuttgart, 1965.

Batowski, Henry K. *Słownik nazw miejscowych Europy Środkowej i Wschodniej XIX i XX wieku*. Warsaw, 1964.

Baum, Wilhelm. *Deutsche Sprachinseln in Friaul*. Klagenfurt, 1980.

Bidlo, Jaroslav et al. *Slovanstvo: obraz jeho minulosti a přítomnosti*. Prague, 1912.

Birken, Andreas. *Die Provinzen des Osmanischen Reiches*. Wiesbaden, 1976.

Bogdanova, I. A. et al., eds. *Teatr v natsional'noi kul'ture stran tsentral'noi i iugovostochnoi Evropy XVIII–XIX vv*. Moscow, 1976.

Bowman, Isaiah. *The New World: Problems in Political Geography*. 4th ed. Yonkers-on-Hudson, N.Y., 1928.

Breu, Josef, and Tomasi, Elisabeth, eds. *Atlas der Donauländer: Register*. Vienna, 1989.

Budiša, Dražen. *Počeci tiskarstva u evropskih naroda*. Zagreb, 1984.

Carter, Francis W. *Dubrovnik (Ragusa): A Classic City-State*. London and New York, 1972.

Carter, Francis W., ed. *An Historical Geography of the Balkans*. London, New York, and San Francisco, 1977.

The Catholic Encyclopedia. 15 vols. New York, 1907–12.

Clair, Colin. *A History of European Printing*. London, New York, and San Francisco, 1976.

Cvijić, Jovan. "The Geographical Distribution of the Balkan Peoples." *The Geographical Review* 5, 5 (1918): 345–61.

Dupuy, R. Ernest and Trevor N. *The Encyclopedia of Military History from 3500 B.C. to the Present*. 2d rev. ed. New York, 1986.

Dvornik, Francis. *The Slavs: Their Early History and Civilization*. Boston, 1956.

Encyclopedia Britannica. 11th ed. 29 vols. Cambridge, 1910–11.

Eterovich, Francis H., ed. *Croatia: Land, People, Culture*. 2 vols. Toronto, 1964–70.

Fortescue, Adrian. *The Orthodox Eastern Church*. New York, 1907.

Fox, Paul. *The Reformation in Poland*. Baltimore, 1924.

Great Britain Naval Intelligence Division: Geographical Handbook Series. *Albania*. Oxford, 1945.

———. *Dodecanese*, 2d ed. Oxford, 1943.

———. *Germany*, 4 vols. Oxford, 1944–45.

———. *Greece*, 3 vols. Oxford, 1944–45.

———. *Italy*, 4 vols. Oxford, 1944–45.

———. *Jugoslavia*, 3 vols. Oxford, 1944–45.

———. *Turkey*, 2 vols. Oxford, 1942–43.

Grigorian, Vartan. *Istoriia armianskikh kolonii Ukrainy i Pol'shi: Armiane v Podolii*. Erevan, 1980.

Grimsted, Patricia Kennedy. *Archives and Manuscript Repositories in the USSR: Estonia, Latvia, Lithuania, and Belorussia*. Princeton, N.J., 1981.

Hilberg, Raul. *The Destruction of the European Jews*. 3 vols. rev. ed. New York and London, 1985, esp. vol. 3.

Hoffman, George W., ed. *Eastern Europe: Essays in Geographical Problems*. London, 1971.

Homán, Bálint, and Szekfü, Gyula. *Magyar történet*. 5 vols. Budapest, 1935–36.

Ischirkoff, A. *La Macédoine et la constitution de l'Exarchat bulgare*. Lausanne, 1918.

Iurginis, Iuozas. *Istoriia Litovskoi SSR*. Kaunas, 1958.

Jackson, Marvin. "Changes in Ethnic Populations of Southeastern Europe: Holocaust, Migration, and Assimilation—1940 to 1970." In Roland Schönfeld, ed., *Nationalitäten-probleme in Südosteuropa*. Munich, 1987, pp. 73–104.

Karpat, Kemal H. *Ottoman Population, 1830–1914: Demographic and Social Characteristics*. Madison, Wis., 1985.

Kimball, Stanley B. *The Austro-Slav Revival: A Study of Nineteenth-Century Literary Foundations*. Philadelphia, 1973.

Klaić, Nada. *Povijest Hrvata u ranom srednjem vijeku*. Zagreb, 1971.

———. *Povijest Hrvata u razvijenom srednjem vijeku*. Zagreb, 1976.

Kłoczowski, Jerzy; Müllerowa, Lidia; Skarbek, Jan. *Zarys dziejów Kościoła katolickiego w Polsce*. Cracow, 1986.

Kornis, Gyula/Julius. *Education in Hungary*. New York, 1922.

———. *A magyar művelődés eszményei, 1777–1848*. 2 vols. Budapest, 1927.

Kosiński, Leszek A. "Changes in the Ethnic Structure in East Central Europe, 1930–1960." *Geographical Review* 59, 3 (1969): 388–402.

———. "Secret German War-Sources for Population Study of East-Central Europe and Soviet Union." *East European Quarterly* 10, 1 (1976): 21–34.

———. "Urbanization in East-Central Europe After World War II." *East European Quarterly* 8, 2 (1974): 129–53.

Kosiński, Leszek A., ed. *Demographic Developments in Eastern Europe*. New York and London, 1977.

Lang, David Marshall. *The Armenians: A People in Exile*. London, 1981.

Marinelli, Olinto. "The Regions of Mixed Populations in Northern Italy." *The Geographical Review* 7, 3 (1919): 129–42.

Mitchell, B. R. *European Historical Statistics, 1750–1970*. London, 1975.

Natkevičius, Ladas. *Aspect politique et juridique du différend polono-lithuanien*. Paris and Kaunas, 1930.

Nossig, Alfred, ed. *Jüdische Statistik*. Berlin, 1903.

Ochmański, Jerzy. *Historia Litwy*. Wrocław, Warsaw, Cracow, Gdańsk, and Łódź, 1982.

Ohiienko, Ivan. *Istoriia ukraïns'koho drukarstva*. Winnipeg, 1983.

Ottův slovník naučný. 28 vols. Prague, 1888–1909. *Nové doby: dodatky*. 6 vols. Prague, 1930–43.

Ovnanian, S. V. *Armiano-bolgarskie istoricheskie sviazi i armianskie kolonii v Bolgarii vo vtoroi polovine XIX v*. Erevan, 1968.

Paikert, G. C. *The Danube Swabians*. The Hague, 1967.

La Paix de Versailles. Vol. 9: *Questions territoriales*. 2 pts. Paris, 1939.

Pičul, Pieri. *Storie dal Popul Furlan*. 2d ed. Udine, 1974.

Pounds, Norman J. G. *Eastern Europe*. Chicago, 1969.

Reclus, Élisée. *Nouvelle géographie universelle*. 19 vols. Paris, 1876–94. Esp. Vols. 1, 3, 5, 9.

Révai nagy lexikona. 21 vols. Budapest, 1911–35.

"Rossiia." In *Bol'shaia èntsiklopediia*. Vol. 16, pp. 436–530. St. Petersburg, 1904.

Rossos, Andrew. *Russia and the Balkans: Inter-Balkan Rivalries and Russian Foreign Policy, 1908–1914*. Toronto, 1981.

Rugg, Dean S. *The Geography of Eastern Europe*. Lincoln, Neb., 1978.

Schechtman, Joseph A. *European Population Transfers, 1939–1945*. New York, 1946.

———. *Postwar Population Transfers in Europe, 1945–1955*. Philadelphia, 1962.

Sebők, László. *Magyar neve? Határokon túli helységnévszótár*. Budapest, 1989.

Senelick, Laurence, ed. *National Theater in Northern and Eastern Europe, 1746–1900*. Cambridge, 1991.

Sidorova, A. L., ed. *Istoriia SSR*. Vol. 2. Moscow, 1965.

Smolitsch, Igor. *Geschichte der russischen Kirche, 1700–1917*. Vol. 1. Leiden, 1964.

Stanislawski, Michael. *Tsar Nicholas I and the Jews*. Philadelphia, 1983.

Supan, Alexander. "Die Bevölkerung der Erde, XIII:

Europa [1900–1907]." *Petermanns Mitteilungen: Ergänzungsband*, 35 (Gotha, 1910), no. 163.

Tamss, Friedrich. "Die Bevölkerung der Erde: Gebietsveränderungen, Flächenberechnungen, Volkszählungen, XIV: Europa ohne Russland." *Petermanns Mitteilungen: Ergänzungsband*, 46 (Gotha, 1933), no. 212.

Temperley, H. W. V., ed. *A History of the Peace Conference of Paris*. Vol. 6. London, 1924.

Váňa, Zdeněk. *The World of the Ancient Slavs*. Detroit, 1983.

Wallis, B.C. "The Peoples of Austria." *The Geographical Review* 6, 1 (1918): 52–65.

———. "The Rumanians in Hungary." *The Geographical Review* 6, 2 (1918): 156–71.

———. "The Slavs of Northern Hungary." *The Geographical Review* 6, 3 (1918): 268–81.

———. "The Slavs of Southern Hungary." *The Geographical Review* 6, 4 (1918): 341–53.

Wandruszka, Adam, and Urbanitsch, Peter, eds. *Die Habsburgermonarchie, 1848–1918*. Vol. 3, 2 pts: *Die Völker des Reiches*. Vienna, 1980. Vol. 4: *Die Konfessionen*. Vienna, 1985.

Weigand, Gustav. *Die Aromunen: etnographisch-philologisch-historische Untersuchungen*. 2 vols. Leipzig, 1895.

Wilkinson, Henry R. *Maps and Politics: A Review of the Ethnographic Cartography of Macedonia*. Liverpool, 1951.

Žiugžda, J., ed. *Lietuvos TSR istorija*. Vilnius, 1958.

Index

This index contains three categories of names. Cities, towns, battles, persons, organizations, and ideologies are in roman typeface; *countries, regions, administrative districts, and ecclesiastical provinces are in italic typeface;* **geographic names and names of peoples are in bold typeface.** Roman-face numbers refer to text pages; *italic numbers refer to maps.* Place names and geographic names are given in their main forms (as explained in the introduction, pp. xi–xii), followed by various linguistic variants. The following abbreviations are used to refer to language variants:

[A]	Albanian	[Lv]	Latvian
[B]	Belorussian	[M]	Macedonian
[Bg]	Bulgarian	[Mg]	Magyar
[C]	Czech	[Ml]	Moldavian
[E]	English	[P]	Polish
[G]	German	[R]	Romanian
[Gr]	Greek	[Ru]	Russian
[Grc]	Classical Greek	[SC]	Serbo-Croatian
[I]	Italian	[Sl]	Slovenian
[L]	Latin	[Sv]	Slovak
[Ld]	Ladino	[T]	Turkish
[LS]	Lusatian Sorbian	[U]	Ukrainian
[Lt]	Lithuanian	[Y]	Yiddish